Soviet Social Problems

The John M. Olin Critical Issues Series

Published in cooperation with
the Harvard University Russian Research Center

Soviet Social Problems, edited by Anthony Jones, Walter D. Connor, and David E. Powell

The Nationalities Factor in Soviet Politics and Society, edited by Lubomyr Hajda and Mark Beissinger

The Soviet Union in the Third World, edited by Carol R. Saivetz

Soviet Social Problems

EDITED BY
Anthony Jones
NORTHEASTERN UNIVERSITY

Walter D. Connor
BOSTON UNIVERSITY

David E. Powell
HARVARD UNIVERSITY

Westview Press
BOULDER • SAN FRANCISCO • OXFORD

The John M. Olin Critical Issues Series

Song on p. 300 by Bulat Okudzhava. Translation by Gerald Stanton Smith. Quoted from Gerald Stanton Smith, *Songs to Seven Strings* (Bloomington: Indiana University Press, 1984), p. 125, reprinted by permission.

All rights reserved. No part of this publication may be reproduced or transmitted in any form or by any means, electronic or mechanical, including photocopy, recording, or any information storage and retrieval system, without permission in writing from the publisher.

Copyright © 1991 by the Harvard University Russian Research Center

Published in 1991 in the United States of America by Westview Press, Inc., 5500 Central Avenue, Boulder, Colorado 80301, and in the United Kingdom by Westview Press, 36 Lonsdale Road, Summertown, Oxford OX2 7EW

Library of Congress Cataloging-in-Publication Data
Soviet social problems / edited by Anthony Jones, Walter D. Connor, David E. Powell.
  p. cm. — (The John M. Olin critical issues series)
Includes index.
ISBN 0-8133-7690-4 (HC) — ISBN 0-8133-0876-3 (PB)
  1. Soviet Union—Social conditions—1970-   . 2. Soviet Union—Politics and government—1985-   . 3. Social problems. I. Jones, Anthony. II. Connor, Walter D. III. Powell, David E. IV. Series.
HN523.5.S665 1991
361'.0947—dc20
                                                                    90-20685
                                                                       CIP

Printed and bound in the United States of America

The paper used in this publication meets the requirements of the American National Standard for Permanence of Paper for Printed Library Materials Z39.48-1984.

10   9   8   7   6   5   4   3   2   1

Contents

Acknowledgments		ix
	Introduction	1
1	Politics and Social Problems, *Paul Hollander*	9
2	Ethnic Differentiation and Political Communication, *Ellen Mickiewicz*	24
3	Pollution in the Soviet Union: The Growth of Environmentalism and Its Consequences, *Marshall I. Goldman*	39
4	Atomic Culture in the USSR: Before and After Chernobyl, *Paul R. Josephson*	57
5	Soviet Health Problems and the Convergence Hypothesis, *Mark G. Field*	78
6	Drug Abuse in the USSR, *John M. Kramer*	94
7	Drinking and Alcohol Abuse in the USSR in the 1980s, *Vladimir G. Treml*	119
8	Equality of Opportunity, *Walter D. Connor*	137
9	*Perestroika* and the Rebirth of Charity, *Mervyn Matthews*	154
10	Aging and the Elderly, *David E. Powell*	172
11	No End of a Problem: *Perestroika* for the Family? *Peter H. Juviler*	194
12	Problems in the Schools, *Anthony Jones*	213

13	Youth Problems in the Soviet Union, *Richard B. Dobson*	227
14	Crime in the Soviet Union, *Louise I. Shelley*	252
15	Prostitution, the Press, and Agenda-Building in the Soviet Policy Process, *Andrea Stevenson Sanjian*	270
16	Adapting to New Technologies, *Loren Graham*	296

About the Contributors — 319
About the Book — 322
Index — 323

Acknowledgments

We wish to thank the John M. Olin Foundation for its generous support of the Olin Lecture Series, at which preliminary versions of the chapters in this book were presented. We would also like to express our appreciation to our friends and colleagues at the Russian Research Center. Adam B. Ulam, the center's director, and Marshall I. Goldman, associate director, have been staunch supporters of all the volumes in this series, including the present one. We are grateful for their encouragement and advice. The contributors to this book deserve our gratitude for their cooperation and good humor during often trying times. Finally, we are especially indebted to Alison Koff of the Russian Research Center and to Susan McEachern, Rebecca Ritke, Jane Raese, and Marian Safran of Westview Press. Without their skills, dedication, and patience, this volume could not have been completed.

Anthony Jones
Walter D. Connor
David E. Powell

Introduction

For most of the Soviet period, the leaders of the USSR have either denied that their society was prone to the same problems that other industrial societies were experiencing or claimed that its problems were a leftover from the past and destined to disappear. This unwillingness to recognize the existence of undesirable phenomena or events extended even to the news coverage of accidents and natural disasters. As a result, Soviet citizens had no way of knowing the true extent of the problems facing their society; they had to rely mainly on personal experience and rumor. This situation has now dramatically changed; consequently, the contributors to this book have been able to describe both the nature and the scope of social problems in the contemporary Soviet Union.

The degree of openness that the policy of *glasnost'* has made possible is so great and so new that we are still trying to sort out and understand all that we are hearing. Whenever a set of issues is opened up to public view for the first time, there are inevitably distortions, exaggerations, and misperceptions that make it difficult for outside observers to evaluate properly what the real situation is. Also, when new problems come under public scrutiny initially, the explanations for their emergence are likely to be distorted. As a result, the analyses in this book should be seen as preliminary, for we shall almost certainly have to revise both the data and our understanding of them as time goes by.

There are virtually no problems that are not now being discussed and investigated in the Soviet Union, including those that were ideologically very sensitive just a few years ago. For example, homelessness was formerly said in the USSR to be a characteristic only of capitalist societies, and as late as October 1986, President Nikolai Ryzhkov still publicly denied that homelessness existed in the Soviet Union. Although there had been occasional references to people without homes during the 1970s, it was not really until *Ogonek* published a story in February 1987 about a journalist who had lived among the homeless while pretending to be one of them that the issue became established as a problem for open discussion.[1]

An astonishing frankness about social problems in the USSR was in evidence at the 19th Party Conference, which took place in Moscow in June 1988. There delegates openly discussed a wide range of issues, including the crisis of the health system, the extent of ecological damage in the Soviet Union, and the difficulties faced by Soviet women. The debate on these and other topics was reported in the Soviet press.[2] Since then, the press has been of crucial importance in alerting the public to the problems the society faces, and both print and electronic media have taken on the role of muckrakers similar to that of media in the West. Indeed, the coverage of prostitution, drug addiction, violence, begging, corruption, and other social ills has become so intense, and often so sensational in its presentation, that there have been many complaints from the public that things have gone too far. Without the contribution of the media, however, it is unlikely that Soviet citizens could have been alerted as quickly and as effectively as they have been to the problems around them. The speed with which these formerly taboo areas have been opened up has its costs, though, since it is painful for people who have for so long been unaware of these issues to confront them all at once. For many, it is a welcome and refreshing change, whereas for others it is unsettling and threatening. As in other societies, therefore, the messenger of these bad tidings has come under much criticism.

It is impossible in a single volume to look at all of the problems currently being discussed in the Soviet Union; thus we have had to be selective in our coverage. Nevertheless, we have tried to present as wide and as representative a sample as possible. As the problems we examine do not exist in isolation, the reader will notice that there is a degree of overlap in some of the chapters. Because social problems are organically interrelated, the overlap has been left (and in some cases encouraged) in order to demonstrate where appropriate that a specific problem is part of a wider set of problems. We have also tried to arrange the chapters so that they build upon one another and give the reader a sense of continuity as well as linkage.

To get us started, in Chapter 1, Paul Hollander examines the politics of social problems. He discusses the political changes that have allowed many social phenomena to be defined as problems and the political consequences of opening up such issues to public scrutiny. As he notes, social problems in the Soviet Union stem from three main factors—the industrialization of the country, which has been occurring since the early part of the century; policies that were pursued for a variety of political and ideological reasons; and attempts to impose a particular moral view on an increasingly diverse society. Responses by the public to these factors have included a wide array of behaviors, including many that are now regarded as problems. The long-term implications of the new willingness to face these issues are set out by Hollander, and he discusses the extent to which Soviet problems are evidence for increasing similarity between the USSR and other industrial societies.

The current degree of public awareness of the problems facing Soviet society could not have been possible without the vigorous activity of the media, especially Soviet television. It is to this issue that Ellen Mickiewicz addresses herself in Chapter 2, in particular to the tension between national and local concerns as reflected in television coverage. As she notes, television functions as a major socializing agent in modern societies. This assumes a special significance in the USSR: The country has a large number of ethnic groups and nationalities, and nationality tensions and conflicts are currently at the center of the stage in Soviet events. The analysis provided by Mickiewicz will help us to understand better the complex role of television in shaping the public's knowledge of, and attitudes toward, social problems in the years to come.

One of the most expensive and frightening problems confronting the new leadership is that of environmental catastrophe, and this is the theme of the next two chapters. Marshall Goldman sets out for us in Chapter 3 the nature of environmental problems in the Soviet Union and the ways in which leaders and officials have responded to them. As in other countries, a real environmental movement has emerged in the USSR, and through a comparison of three environmental problems (the pollution of Lake Baikal, the consequences of trying to reverse the flow of several rivers, and the disaster at Chernobyl), he identifies the factors that make some environmental protests successful and others not. This account provides a valuable background against which to understand the recent proliferation and politicization of environmental-protection groups, including the emergence of the Greens, a political movement similar in its aims to the Greens in Western Europe.

The nuclear accident at Chernobyl has had an effect all over the world on attitudes to nuclear power, and almost five years after the event we are still trying to assess its full consequences.[3] The accident was the culmination of a series of problems in the Soviet nuclear industry, and in Chapter 4, Paul Josephson shows how these problems arose out of the "atomic culture" that has developed in the USSR since the end of World War II. This account helps us to understand not only the events that led up to the accident but also the reactions of the industry and state officials to the accident and to the policies that followed in its wake.

Environmental issues and health are closely linked, and as Mark Field shows in Chapter 5, the health-care system itself has come to be seen as a problem. As he notes, in this area as in so many others, the past habit of blaming individuals for the crisis of health care has given way to a more honest examination of the shortcomings of the system as a whole. The backwardness of Soviet medicine, the lack of basic facilities in the hospitals and clinics, and the inability of the system to deliver adequate health care to people in all social groups and geographic regions have all contributed to difficulties in the rest of society. Infant mortality, high age-specific death rates (especially for males), and the prevalence of incapacitating diseases and conditions have negative consequences for the economy, quite apart from the human suffering. The lack of items as basic as disposable syringes has led to the unnecessary spread of AIDS in the Soviet Union. As Field shows, the cost of dealing with this and other problems in the health-care system will be enormous and will take a considerable amount of time.

Drug abuse is a problem being newly discussed these days, though as John Kramer points out in Chapter 6, it has been around for a long time. As was the case with other social ills, there have been official denials for decades that drugs were a problem in the USSR, and only since 1988 have data been made public on the extent of drug use. In his comprehensive look at this issue, Kramer provides us with a detailed picture of who the drug users are, how usage differs from one part of the country to another, and the factors that have led to increased drug use. The nature and scope of drug abuse, the author concludes, make it likely that for the foreseeable future it will continue to plague the Soviet Union.

Although the drug problem is serious, it is dwarfed by the size of the drinking problem in Soviet society, an issue taken up by Vladimir Treml in Chapter 7. Although the excessive use of alcohol has a long history, during the 1970s overconsumption reached an unprecedented level. This culminated in the ill-fated antidrinking campaign introduced in the spring of 1985, a campaign that was to prove a failure and be ultimately rejected. As Treml shows, the campaign produced a number of worse problems (such as the increased consumption of homemade alcohol and of other more dangerous substances) and even damaged the state of the economy. Both the magnitude and the tenacity of the alcohol problem emerge clearly from the author's detailed account of patterns of drinking.

Some of the changes associated with *perestroika* have raised the question of social justice. Issues of privilege, increasing income inequality, the fortunes being made by many of the private businessmen, and the emergence of private health care and private education have disturbed many people. Walter Connor considers opportunity, success, and fairness in Chapter 8 against the background of economic reform. He shows that there is a complex web linking the economic, educational, and social spheres, and reforms in one area are likely to undermine the effectiveness of reforms in other areas. Because there seems to be no way in which demands for "justice" in all of these spheres can be equally met, definitions of what is and is not just will have to change, a process that is already under way.

For those who have not fared well in the race for equality and justice, much of this debate must seem academic at best. Many people in the Soviet Union live in, or on the margins of, poverty. Others, because of a variety of infirmities, illnesses, and social isolation, live very limited and impoverished lives. In the past, the state was supposed to be responsible for helping them, but now there has been open acknowledgment of a legitimate role to be played by and a desperate need for charity. This relatively new approach to dealing with social problems is analyzed in Chapter 9 by Mervyn Matthews, who describes those parts of the population most in need of help, the extent to which the official policies and agencies aided them in the past, and the new organizations that have sprung up to provide assistance. There are now, as he points out, a growing number of official and unofficial charities in the USSR, and religious organizations of various kinds are becoming increasingly involved in charitable activities. It is also interesting to note the increasing number of charitable "funds" of various kinds, devoted to the needs of children, veterans, Chernobyl victims, and earthquake survivors; there are even funds to help rescue the villages and to help preserve *perestroika* itself. The reemergence of charity is one of the more unexpected developments of recent years and a movement that may well be here to stay.

Many of the elderly are in need of charity, and it is the special status and needs of this group to which Chapter 10, by David Powell, is devoted. The Soviet Union is an aging society (especially in the most industrialized, Western republics), a situation that creates a set of new problems for which the society is unprepared. As in almost every society, the elderly in the USSR are a highly vulnerable part of the population. As Powell shows, the elderly suffer from the shortcomings of the health system and from the faltering economy. Moreover, the lack of sufficient part-time jobs or other ways to supplement their pensions make the elderly especially vulnerable to the current shortages and inflation. Although there are plans to protect the elderly from the full impact of economic restructuring, a significant improvement in their condition will be possible only when the nation's general conditions improve. Moreover, current trends in family life are likely to add to the problems of the elderly.

In a sense, the family has been seen as a problem ever since the Revolution of 1917, and policies regarding the status of the family have changed dramatically from one period to another. As Peter Juviler shows in Chapter 11, an account of the problems facing the Soviet family in the past as well as at the current time, what goes on in the family has important implications for a wide variety of other social issues. With urbanization and industrialization, plus the special characteristics of Soviet development, the family has faced increasing problems, frequently too much for the family to deal with. The number of one-parent families is increasing in the Soviet Union, as it is in other countries, with similar complex effects on society.

The family is a notoriously difficult institution to change through policies, as is the school, which is the topic of Chapter 12, by Anthony Jones. As he shows, at a time when the educational system is being called upon to make major contributions to the program of *perestroika,* the system is facing enormous problems of its own. Not only have recent attempts to reform education been ineffective, having in some ways made the situation worse, but also the schools have been allowed to fall into such a state of disrepair that enormous monetary investments in them will be needed before they can begin to contribute much to the regeneration of Soviet society. In addition, a profound change in the training of teachers, and in the psychology of all those who inhabit the schools, is necessary if the schools are to turn out the kinds of people that an economically, politically, and socially reconstructed USSR will demand. As Jones suggests, however, reforming this inherently conservative and resistant institution is likely to be a long and difficult task.

The problems facing young people are analyzed by Richard Dobson in Chapter 13. As he notes, there are many aspects of youth issues that appear in all industrial societies, and the development of separate youth cultures, a tendency to be drawn toward deviant behavior, and difficulties in making the transition to adulthood are common themes. At the same time, there are a number of problems that are specific to Soviet conditions, and given the nature of the Soviet political system, these have taken on a special significance. It is impossible now to generalize about young people in the Soviet Union, and Dobson provides us with a comprehensive survey of the variety of life-styles, ideologies, and behaviors that characterize youth in the USSR. The fate of *perestroika* in the coming years will depend more and more on the responses of those now entering adulthood, and they are bringing with them a complex and conflict-laden set of desires and attitudes.

The social problem most frightening to many people is crime, the dimensions of which are described by Louise Shelley in Chapter 14. Ironically, public concern about crime is increasing just at the time that judicial and penal reforms are under way and a more humane approach to the treatment of offenders is being introduced. Sociologically, perhaps, this is not surprising, because in times of transition the weakening of old norms frequently increases the incidence of deviance, including criminal deviance. Shelley's analysis provides a valuable survey of how the issue of crime was dealt with before the current reforms and sets the scene for her account of how *glasnost'* has changed the situation. As she notes, a new openness exists about the extent of crime in the USSR, and on the basis of the statistics being published, it is now possible to form some preliminary ideas about that extent. Although honestly facing this issue is necessary if it is to be dealt with, the publicity also fuels people's fears and dissatisfactions, and the rising rate of crime can become a focus for widespread discontent. Efforts are being made to deal with the current spate of crime, but the police seem ill equipped to deal with it, and there are now reports that the KGB is spending most of its time these days investigating crimes.

A noncriminal "crime" getting more attention these days is prostitution, an activity that is dealt with with a degree of frankness that would have been unthinkable just a few years ago. In Chapter 15, Andrea Stevenson Sanjian describes the legal and ideological climate that has surrounded prostitution during the Soviet period and then examines the portrait of prostitutes that emerged from recent Soviet research. As is true of other social problems, prostitution has a Soviet "character" about it, a result of the special conditions within which prostitutes must work. Low wages, high expectations, lack of privacy, and the need to pay many bribes put their special stamp on the way this trade is conducted, and the prudish attitude toward open discussion of sexual matters makes prostitution especially difficult to deal with in a rational way. A recent complication, as Sanjian notes, is the outbreak of AIDS in the USSR, the spread of which has become linked in the public mind (rightly or wrongly) with prostitution. For this and other reasons, there seems to be a move toward the gradual criminalization of prostitution, although it is too early to say just how far this process will go. As the author shows, the role of the press has been of great importance in bringing prostitution to public awareness and in helping to define it as a "problem."

The goal of *perestroika,* and the rationale behind the democratization of the society, are to bring the Soviet Union into the world community of industrial nations and make it a modern, technologically sophisticated nation. It is to this issue that Loren Graham draws our attention in Chapter 16, a probing analysis of the place of technology in Soviet culture since the revolution. In the early Soviet period, there was clearly a cult of the machine, and the utopia that technology was thought able to produce was limited only by the imagination of its acolytes. There seemed no problem that the machine could not solve, no human failing that it could not eliminate. With a degree of industrial maturity, however, and with a recognition of some of the serious repercussions that industrial technology brings in its wake, an inevitable reaction has set in. The result, Graham notes, is a clash between the desire for a return to pastoral innocence and the campaign to move to a high-tech future. The nostalgia for the past comes at an inopportune time, given the extent of the problems and the urgency of finding solutions. Moreover, Graham shows, because of certain characteristics of Soviet society, it is more difficult for the USSR to make the transition to new technologies than it was for most other societies— thus, a change in "ethos" will be necessary in addition to a complete reorganization of systems of management.

As the contributors to this volume show, the Soviet Union is facing a veritable explosion of social problems precisely at the time that a concentration of energies and resources is needed for the transition to a more effective economy, without which the future of the society is very much in doubt. Some of the problems discussed in this volume have been around for a long time, whereas others are relatively new, but in the public mind, unfortunately, they are all linked in some way with *perestroika.* Consequently, changes that are crucial for national survival come to be seen as at best painful and at worst destructive. The effect of this on the national will can be easily imagined, and the possibility that some people will exploit the situation for their own ends is very real. As in any society, there are always those who capitalize on the distress of others.

On a more positive note, the greater honesty with which the society is treating its shortcomings is a necessary step toward finding solutions. It is now a commonplace in the Soviet Union that the decades-long denial that anything was wrong was a recipe for disaster—indeed, the fruits of these years are the disasters that were visited on the society during the second half of the 1980s. It is now clear that problems denied are problems made worse.

It should be remembered while reading the chapters that follow that we have deliberately concentrated on those social problems that are common to industrial societies, in fact, present in some form in every industrial nation, although the extent of the problems differs from society to society. The purpose of this choice was to encourage the reader to see the Soviet Union from a perspective not usually taken. In the past, it was the political differences between the "West" and the "East" that were given most attention, with the result that common features were missed or given little attention. And yet, as we can now see, it was precisely what we had in common, namely, the industrialization and urbanization of the society, that has led to the present state of affairs. As has recently been argued by Moshe Lewin, it was the maturation of an industrial society that made *perestroika* both necessary and possible.[4] This is not to deny (and the chapters in this volume show it very clearly) that the Soviet regime has put its own stamp on the form that these problems have taken, but rather to suggest that the nature of the changes currently taking place cannot be understood unless we see the USSR as a member of the species "industrial society."

Notes

1. Aaron Trehub, "Down and Out in Moscow and Murmansk: Homelessness in the Soviet Union," *Radio Liberty Report,* March 14, 1988.

2. See *Pravda,* June 29, June 30, July 1, and July 2, 1988.

3. See Zhores Medvedev, *The Legacy of Chernobyl* (New York: W. W. Norton Co., 1990), and David Marples, *The Social Impact of the Chernobyl Disaster* (New York: St. Martin's Press, 1988).

4. Moshe Lewin, *The Gorbachev Phenomenon* (Berkeley: University of California Press, 1988).

CHAPTER 1

Politics and Social Problems

Paul Hollander

The Party is engaged in a titanic effort to eliminate phenomena alien to socialism.
—T. I. Zaslavskaia[1]

Western Views of Soviet Social Problems

Western discussions of Soviet social problems and their relationship to Soviet political institutions and trends have been influenced by two conditions. One has been the absence, or limitation, of accurate and comprehensive information. As a Western commentator put it, Soviet authorities "can variously publish no information . . . incomplete information, contradictory information, wrong information . . . or, mischievously correct information."[2] This difficulty has, over the years, considerably diminished: There is now more information and more reliable information available as the authorities have increased their willingness to allow public ventilation of domestic ills. Still, detailed and fully comprehensive statistics on major social pathologies such as homicide, drug addiction, prostitution, or mental illness remain to be made public. At the same time, in the spirit of *glasnost'*, the official monopoly on the definition and discussion of social problems has weakened; in fact, their coverage has become a form of social criticism. (Even begging has become mentionable in the news media.[3])

The second influence on Western views of Soviet social problems has been wishful thinking about the connections between Soviet domestic problems and the nature of the entire political system, including its foreign policies. The long-standing Western disposition has been (even more so since the rise of Gorbachev) to believe that domestic weaknesses and problems are bound to exert a basically benign influence on the Soviet political system: They cry out for alleviation and put pressure on Soviet leaders to reform their institutions and policies. Socioeconomic problems have been seen as significantly limiting the freedom of political action of Soviet leaders; at some point they would be compelled to turn inward, away from "adventures" abroad and regimentation at home in order to make the system more rational, productive, efficient, and satisfactory to its citizens. The leaders have also been seen as bound to respond, sooner or later, to public demands to improve living standards—indeed, the need for the modernization of the economy has emerged (or perhaps reemerged) as the most compelling explanation of why far-reaching reforms can no longer be delayed. Such assessments tend to attribute pragmatism to the Soviet leaders and are permeated with skepticism about the importance of ideology.

For many Western commentators, the discrepancy between a highly authoritarian political system—maintaining a huge bureaucracy, fielding vast armed forces, being active abroad, lavishly subsidizing its internal security and espionage services and propaganda apparatus—and a population suffering a great variety of privations, shortages, mismanagement, and assorted social pathologies has been viewed as irrational. The magnitude of social problems cried out for alleviation, even for thoroughgoing structural changes. Gorbachev has greatly encouraged such beliefs and expectations by dwelling on a variety of social problems with unusual candor.

The idea of "social problems" is distinctly modern because by defining anything as a "problem" we mean not only that it is undesirable but also that it is not an immutable condition, that it can be alleviated. As a past president of the American Social Science Research Council put it, "A renewed determination to ameliorate certain long-standing, as well as recently developed, ills of the society has arisen along with a sense of power and confidence in its ability to do so."[4]

Some recent Soviet discussions echo similar confidence. Whether such optimism is warranted either in the United States or in the Soviet Union is open to question. The fact remains that now, in the second half of the twentieth century, we have more "problems"—both as individuals and societies, in the East and the West—because of our growing intolerance of many deficiencies of social and personal life. For example, poverty used to be a normal condition, whereas today it is a social problem (at any rate in Western societies). Similarly, routinized work, various illnesses, marriages lacking in excitement and intense personal fulfillment, and the underrepresentation of women in various occupational hierarchies used to provide no grounds for public complaint, protest, or scholarly inquiry, but they do so today.

Social problems refer to aspects of social life and group behavior that are perceived as undesirable but remediable. In the Soviet Union they are often called "phenomena alien to socialism." Needless to say, what is defined as undesirable (alien) reflects prevailing social-political norms and standards, which in the Soviet case have been authoritatively determined by the political decisionmakers and guardians of the official values; the link between social problems, political institutions, and values is unusually clear-cut and explicit under such conditions.

To be sure, social problems often are unintended consequences of various social arrangements and attempts at social-economic reorganization, rather than merely matters of political or moral definitions. The chronic food shortages, demographic imbalances, and overall backwardness of the countryside in the Soviet Union have clearly been the unforeseen and unintended results of purposeful institutional change, such as the collectivization of agriculture.

Social problems in the Soviet Union can be separated into at least three distinct groups. In the first group, we find what is often referred to as antisocial behavior. This includes all varieties of crime, delinquency, prostitution, and divorce (antisocial in that it interferes with the upbringing of children, thus with social cohesion). Ethnic and racial discrimination, and its consequences, may also be put into this group.

The second group consists of various types of escapist behavior, including alcoholism, drug addiction, and suicide (the ultimate escape). Escapist behavior, too, has antisocial implications, since it disrupts predictable social interaction, the routines of work and family life.

Third, there are various structural-situational conditions that constitute social problems—particularly relevant to the Soviet case and to the relationship between politics and social problems. Such problems have the most direct connection with the political ordering (or disordering) of society. They include the various scarcities, especially of housing and consumer goods (and the corruption they elicit, which merges into criminal conduct); deficiencies in public health; low birthrates (perhaps, from the authorities' point of view, also a form of antisocial behavior); rural underdevelopment or uneven modernization; bureaucratic mismanagement; environmental problems; lack of work satisfaction; and the excessive mobility of labor. Old age is yet another social problem that falls into this group—it is not antisocial to be old, nor does it represent a form of escapism or violate any social norms. It is a problem created by the combination of improvements in public health and the resulting longevity, the changing family structure and social values (which reduced the respect accorded the old), and lack of resources (required to replace services that used to be provided by the extended family).

Social problems in Soviet society have three major sources, two of which can be defined as political. The first has been the general process of modernization, which always disrupts traditional ways of life, worldviews, modes of production, and stable communities. The second has been the self-conscious application of political-ideological criteria to this process and the associated reorganization of society, creating problems peculiar to Marxist-Leninist one-party systems, such as rural backwardness. Third, some social problems have been created by the application of official conceptions of rectitude and the corresponding (broader) definitions of deviance. The official view of the survival of religious attitudes and behavior provides one example of such a "problem." Insofar as emigration and unregulated internal population movements represent a social problem, it too is a direct result of the imposition of political standards on personal lives and choices. What is socially problematic about emigration in Soviet society is to a considerable degree a result of its prohibition or restriction, which creates pent-up frustrations and discontent and possibly magnifies the attraction of all things foreign, or at any rate, Western. However, allowing people to travel unhindered and to emigrate could create some genuine problems independent of any political label attached to such movements, i.e., the loss of highly skilled citizens, including important scientists, specialists, and artists.

Modernization, in both Soviet and other varieties, is the crucial breeding ground of social problems. It creates high expectations (regarding the various frustrations earlier seen as inevitable or immutable) and the belief that most problems can be solved. Modernization also creates social disruptions more directly as it interferes with stable social relationships and undermines worldviews that used to impart some measure of security to human existence; it makes behavior more uncontrolled and uncontrollable.

Whereas the reluctance to acknowledge publicly the presence of serious social problems—and their connection with modernization—has been predominant for most of Soviet history, since the mid-1980s this attitude has been undergoing substantial change. Until recently, the official article of faith was that socialist modernization was qualitatively different and less traumatic from modernization under capitalism: The community was not being undermined, or if old communities were being destroyed, they were being replaced by new ones, equally sustaining or even more meaningful and vibrant.

Socialist modernization, however, turned out to be as disruptive as the capitalist variety; the disruption was exacerbated by the lavish and arbitrary use of state power, as exemplified by the collectivization of agriculture and the abandon with which large chunks of the population were moved around, in both punitive and nonpunitive ways.

Nevertheless, socialist modernization did not unduly raise expectations, whereas in pluralistic societies rapidly rising expectations underlie many forms of socially problematic behavior. Under conditions of great political violence, high levels of insecurity, and institutionalized scarcities, the type of expectations that elsewhere contribute to social problems (e.g., to many types of crime, juvenile delinquency, divorce, escapism) was absent. As Marshall Goldman has observed, the Soviet Union could simultaneously experience great economic hardships *and* conduct vigorous expansionist policies around the world "because ordinary Soviet citizens seem willing to endure poor conditions at home and . . . allow their leaders to divert so much to defense and heavy industry with a minimum of protest. The Russian people have a higher tolerance for deprivation and suffering than most other peoples of the developed world."[5]

These attitudes were slowly changing in the past two decades, and they have apparently changed quite rapidly since the rise of Gorbachev. Still, over the long haul, the shortages and limits of economic modernization have retarded or circumscribed the development of some social problems: "Consumerism" and associated crimes against personal property, certain types of suicide motivated by endlessly spiraling expectations, neuroses and sexual deviations that are nurtured by an excess of free time and choice— these do not flourish under conditions of serious scarcities, limited expectations and opportunities. (However, petty but widespread pilfering of state property has become virtually institutionalized as a way of gratifying simple, basic needs.) The backwardness of rural life also has meant that certain traditions (and informal group controls) have been easier to preserve in areas subject to little centralized control, whereas in the cities, housing shortages often forced three generations to live together, benefiting the upbringing of children. Thus, Soviet modernization has in some ways been more incomplete, in other ways more sweeping and penetrating than modernization in the West, and this has had an effect on the character of Soviet social problems.

The disruption of community in the Soviet Union was not only an unintended consequence, or by-product, of modernization, it was also a politically motivated process, as was the whole enterprise of Soviet modernization. The connection between the demise of community and particular social problems has been a staple of sociological analysis. The decline of community leads to the loss of informal social controls exercised by people over each other's behavior by virtue of knowing one another and, in some degree, depending on one another. Soviet sociologists have also commented on this phenomenon, noting for example: "People of different cultural and moral levels and of different backgrounds and ways of life mix. They leave behind them traditional forms of control by the family, by the public opinion of the village street, by relatives."[6] The eruption of antisocial behavior is the most direct consequence of the decline of these informal social controls. Formal controls, no matter how enormously strengthened—as they certainly have been in the Soviet Union—cannot replace the informal ones (although they may help, as, for example, does the internal passport system in controlling serious crime).

The Soviet View of Soviet Social Problems

Of late, the Soviet leadership has increasingly acknowledged that Soviet society has not been immune to the problems associated with modernization. At the same time, inadequate, sluggish modernization has itself been defined as a problem, with its perpetuation of technological underdevelopment and a neglected infrastructure, an obsolete system of communications, and a crippling rural backwardness.

Since the mid-1980s there has been a great deal of public discussion and dissection of social problems of a great variety, including hundreds of articles delving with relish into such social pathologies as prostitution, suicide, drug addiction, the neglect of invalids, the unseemly behavior of juveniles, the decay of sexual morality, the hardships of women, and poverty.[7] In contrast to earlier times, today there is less concern with making sure that the social problems singled out for public attention are portrayed as isolated or anomalous phenomena, as alien and unrelated to the major institutions and characteristics of Soviet society.

Gorbachev himself has remarked: "Socialism possesses everything necessary to place present-day science and technology at the service of people.

But it would be wrong to think that the scientific and technological revolution does not pose problems for socialist society as well."[8] As the context suggests, Gorbachev's concerns had more to do with managerial inefficiencies and the difficulties associated with adopting the latest technology than with the more profound dislocations created by modernization. But S. Shatalin, a corresponding member of the Soviet Academy of Sciences, recently acknowledged that socioeconomic problems (especially that of retarded growth) have been virtually systemic.[9] Tatiana Zaslavskaia, a prominent critic of Soviet socioeconomic arrangements and procedures, likewise has repeatedly linked the problems of the economy to the deficiencies of social justice and to "the human factor."[10]

We may be witnessing the beginning of what might be called the "depoliticization" of social problems, that is to say, a new willingness to admit their full range and devastating consequences while also attempting to disassociate them somewhat from the ideological and political foundations of the Soviet system. Undoubtedly, the authorities would like to make the candid analysis of social problems compatible with support for major Soviet institutions and an affirmation of the official values. An effort is being made to convey to the public that no matter how grave and widespread such problems are, they need not delegitimize the Soviet politicial system. For this kind of endeavor to succeed, officials must also convince citizens that the major political institutions and elites of the system need not take credit for either all the failures or all the successes of the system, that the political determination of Soviet life is on the wane and possibly has never been as complete as had earlier been alleged and believed. Still, the uninhibited ventilation of social pathologies is something like opening a Pandora's box, as has been recognized by many in the power elite (for example, Egor Ligachev) who are concerned that such discussions have gone too far and could erode the legitimacy of the system no less effectively than the successive revelations of the misdeeds, errors, incompetence, or corruption of virtually all Soviet leaders who followed Lenin. This is not an unfounded apprehension.

It may well be asked what remains of the distinctiveness, let alone the superiority, of the Soviet social-economic system if it is admitted that its industries pollute the air and earth no less than their capitalist counterparts; if crime has shown no signs of withering away; if it turns out that socialist institutions have no edge in sparing people from personal misery and unhappiness, culminating in heavy drinking, divorce, or suicide; if shortages of essential goods and services continue to cripple daily life; and if caring for the old and sick is no more generous and humane than under capitalism.

There have been over time two conflicting pressures in the Soviet Union exerting influence on the definition, recognition, or denial of social problems. From the standpoint of the ideological legitimation of the Soviet system, serious social problems similar to those in decaying capitalist societies were not supposed to exist and the less said about them the better. The well-known, notorious problems afflicting capitalist, or class, societies—crime, juvenile delinquency, prostitution, alcohol abuse, discrimination against women and ethnic minorities—were supposed to wither away under the more egalitarian, just, and rational social arrangements introduced by the Soviet system; if they did not, they were referred to as if they were some mysterious virus, "survivals" doomed to extinction by the march of history and the relentless improvements in the outlook and consciousness of Soviet people. How indeed could there be such problems in a society that even candid, muckraking Gorbachev described as "a world without oppression and exploitation . . . a society of social solidarity and confidence"?[11]

There has thus been, from its earliest days to the present, a tension between the glorification and ideological legitimation of the Soviet system and the acknowledgment of the existence and gravity of social problems in Soviet society. A Hungarian journal publishing in 1988 under conditions of far greater *glasnost'* than obtained in the USSR recently had this to say about Soviet social problems and their official acknowledgment:

> Institutional assistance for the poor has still not been put on the public agenda in the Soviet Union. After all, the fact that a substantial portion of the citizens live under seriously deprived conditions remains to this day a taboo topic. In a country where until very recently it had not been acknowledged that there were drug addicts and homosexuals, and where it was forbidden to entertain the possibility that anybody could be unhappy, it is hardly surprising that official policy makers were reluctant to take note of poverty.[12]

Modernization under the auspices of, or in the framework of, socialism and inspired by Marxist-Leninist ideology was supposed to be radically and qualitatively different from modernization unleashed by the inhumane forces of capitalism, as both Peter Berger and Adam Ulam have observed. Socialist modernization was expected to spare the participants the deprivations the earlier capitalist variety entailed: both the material deprivations associated with poverty, industrial regimentation, and urban crowding *and* the spiritual losses stemming from the undermining of traditional ways of looking at the social and natural world. The major blow dealt to mental hygiene and emotional well-being was the disruption, or complete loss, of community. The still lingering appeal of socialism has been, in the words of Peter Berger, the "promise [of] all the blessings of modernity and the liquidation of its costs, most importantly, the cost of alienation . . . [by] projecting the redemptive community into the future."[13]

Although insistence on the distinctiveness of socialist modernization and the superiority of the new social institutions predisposed the Soviet authorities to deny the existence of social problems, ideology created its own pressures and requirements for discerning and identifying social problems, for defining situations or forms of behavior as politically unacceptable and hence socially problematic. A political system dedicated to the radical transformation of the human condition and committed to the ceaseless perfection of social institutions and human nature was bound to find more forms of human behavior intolerable and problematic than a social system resigned to human and institutional imperfections. Such intolerance was also enhanced by the Leninist stress on voluntarism and on the political will that increasingly gained influence among the Soviet political elite as it became clear that institutional-environmental changes were failing to eradicate a great variety of human imperfections and as social defects continued to lag behind the sweeping transformations of society. An outlook that was highly politicized and shaped by ideology has further contributed to the perception of social problems by the refusal to regard deficiencies of social existence and institutions as sometimes accidental, if not preordained. When nothing can be attributed to accident or to "the nature of things," problems multiply. Hence, novel (by Western standards) social problems have emerged in Soviet society such as "private property mentality," attachment to religious values, crimes against public property, the "misuse" of free time, and, more recently, low birthrates. Such social problems tend to shade into political problems; given the "overintegrated" character of Soviet society, the distinction between social and political problems (and spheres) has often been difficult to maintain.

Thus, in the Soviet Union ideology has created social problems by providing new, demanding criteria against which to measure social phenomena and human behavior. At the same time, it has generated unease and denial when social problems have persisted, although they should have been relegated to the dustbin of history by the forces of politically ordained social progress.

The conflict between the ideologically imposed restraint on revealing and analyzing social problems and the ideologically inspired soul searching stimulated by increasingly obtrusive deficiencies of the social order has recently tilted decisively toward revelation and public ventilation, as in the famous speech of Gorbachev at the 27th Party Congress:

> While duly assessing what has been achieved, the CPSU leadership considers its duty to honestly and candidly tell the party and the people about our deficiencies in political and practical activity, about unfavorable trends in the economy and in the social and spiritual sphere. . . . For a number of years—not just because of objective factors, but also for reasons that are primarily subjective in nature—the practical actions of party and state agencies lagged behind the demands of the times and life itself. Problems in the country's development grew faster than they were solved. Sluggishness, ossification of the forms and methods of management, decreased dynamism in work, growth of bureaucracy—all these things did considerable damage to the cause. Stagnant phenomena began to show up in the life of society.[14]

The Impact of the Political System on Social Problems

The connection between politics and social problems goes beyond the political definition and determination of what constitutes a "problem" and which of them may publicly be discussed. The political realm can in very tangible ways both stimulate and restrain the growth of social problems. I shall first take note of the restraining effect of the political system.

Generally speaking, numerous social problems are linked to the gap between aspirations and achievements. When people accept material deprivations as normal, there will be relatively few crimes against property; when a degree of monotony or emotional-sexual frustration that often is part of monogamous marriage is accepted and taken for granted, the desire for divorce (or adultery) will be more limited; when people cannot conceive of better ways of life than what is provided by their social environment they will not seek improvement by trying to leave their country; when bleak, deprived living conditions are taken for granted, the pressure for escapist behavior will be more modest. There are many such examples of the connection between expectations and social problems.

During much of its existence, the Soviet political system has been highly successful in containing and stabilizing expectations of much of the population, in the way that traditional societies used to be able to do. Durkheim's words captured the essence of the attitudes that prevail under these conditions: "Each in his sphere vaguely realizes the extreme limits set to his ambitions and aspires to nothing beyond. At least if he respects regulations and is docile to collective authority . . . he feels that it is not well to ask more."[15] In the same spirit Valentin Turchin, the Soviet dissident, has observed: "The basis of the social order is considered by the citizens as absolutely immutable, given once and forever, absolutely unchangeable. . . . They consider it as a given, as Newton's Law. When you fall you don't blame gravity."[16] More recently Natan Sharansky, another leading dissident, made a similar point: "Not only the authorities consider citizens cogs in the wheel of the state, the people so consider themselves too. The Western notion that the government is subject to constraints of law is alien to the Soviet citizen. The government *is* the law. It can grant rights . . . and it can take them away . . . Gorbachev has not changed this principle."[17]

These observations also help to explain why many Soviet citizens are not looking forward to change with joyful anticipation but regard it with foreboding or apprehension. They are inclined to associate the known and stable with at least a minimum of security, whereas change, which has almost invariably been imposed from above, may mean new risks and dangers; hence it reminds them of the limited control they exercise over their lives. Such attitudes explain the mixed reception given to Gorbachev's reform proposals by many groups and strata in Soviet society and also the questioning of the desirability of dwelling on the shortcomings of the Soviet system, including its social problems.

Low expectations have been found to prevail not only in political matters but even in regard to the daily diet. In the early 1980s, a study of Soviet emigrants reflected the modest expectations of Soviet citizens about a wholesome diet. Although the researcher established that by Western standards their diet was extremely poor, "28% of those interviewed termed their diet 'satisfactory'; another 10% had no particular opinion which amounted to the same reaction . . . their answers reflected perennially low expectations or an ignorance of what might be bought under more plentiful conditions."[18] To the extent that expectations have risen recently, at least among certain groups, the proliferation of certain social problems may be expected. More of this below.

Whereas on the one hand, the politically inspired controls over expectations imparted a degree of stability to the life of the citizen and prevented or slowed down the rise of aspirations (which could not have found socially *unproblematic* gratification), many social problems in the Soviet Union can be directly traced, on the other hand, to the political priorities, values, controls, and the resulting politically induced deprivations. These social problems include the whole range of white-collar crimes, crimes against public property, and corruption of many kinds. Thus the politically inspired and determined process of modernization has not been the only link between politics and social problems. The political sphere has created or interacted with social problems in other ways as well. Expectations were not only kept under control by scarcities and major political calamities but were also restrained by regimentation and the control of leisure, social mobility, and, more generally, opportunity.

Resource allocation is the most direct link between politics and a wide range of social problems. Scarcities symbolized by the ever-present necessity to stand in line remain a pervasive part of life and a visible reminder of the consistently low priorities given to consumer needs.[19] Insufficient resources have created or intensified social problems, including (1) poor standards of public health, (2) rural backwardness and migration, (3) insufficient and antiquated housing, (4) the hapless condition of old people, (5) low birthrates (a response to scarcities), (6) threats to the environment, and (7) inadequate treatment and rehabilitation of heavy drinkers and drug addicts (reducing alcohol consumption also conflicts with the need for revenue).

Ultimately it is the politically determined priorities and organizational styles (bureaucratic rigidity, planning, centralization) that underlie the social problems connected with scarcities—problems such as corruption; inequalities, or distributive injustices; as well as waste and mismanagement. Almost all material shortages and deficiencies in services and the provision of consumer goods may be traced to political values and priorities, except for those due to the weather. Even shortages and deficiencies that arise from the Soviet-Russian work ethic can be linked to incentives and thus again to the realm of politics. Above all, these deficiencies are determined by the long-standing, overwhelming bias in resource allocation toward the military-political sector (including state-security and agitprop outreach activities) as opposed to the civilian-social needs.

Sergei Grigoryants, a prominent social critic, has made a connection between social problems associated with technological backwardness and the political realm:

A society deprived of democratic institutions, that is, of the opportunity for growth, improvement and adaptation to changing conditions, proved to be instinctively hostile to the achievement of human genius. . . . Modern technologies are created by people with a different feeling of responsibility toward society, people who utilize the full range of democratic freedoms for that society's improvement. These technologies . . . cannot be employed to their full capacity and without danger in other (in this case, archaic) social structures.[20]

Another area where the connection between social problems and politics is close and clear is that of the nationality question and the ethnic tensions associated with it. These issues are political in origin, since most of the various ethnic groups did not voluntarily join the Soviet nation-state, and once joined by force, they would have preferred greater political and cultural autonomy than was granted. The ethnic problems have two further dimensions: first, the competition between particular ethnic (or nationality) groups and the dominant Russians, and second, the relationship among particular ethnic groups, as for example the Armenians and Azerbaidzhanis. The display of violent hostility between the latter groups in 1990 provided a striking illustration of the connection between rising expectations due to political relaxation and the eruption of certain social problems. In turn the turmoil in the Baltic states has been an obvious example of national-cultural and political self-assertion and of the determination to achieve greater independence of the Soviet Union. Another aspect of the ethnic problem is the gradual numerical decline of the Russian majority, due to differential birthrates among the various ethnic groups.

While, as noted above, some characteristics of the political system directly impinge on the creation of social problems, others continue to exercise a restraining influence. These include administrative measures, such as a system of residence permits used to keep former convicts concentrated in particular areas and to deprive them of mobility; strict controls over the possession of firearms; and the relatively great freedom of the police and the judiciary to prosecute crimes.

The Impact of Social Problems on the Political System

Thus far we have looked at the ways in which the Soviet system, in its capacity as a modern and still modernizing society and as a distinctive political culture, contributes to the rise and persistence of social problems. Next we will examine the obverse: how social problems impinge on the Soviet political system.

Although earlier I questioned some overly sanguine Western assumptions about the inevitable connection between social problems and the liberal-rational reform supposedly necessitated by them, I agree that many if not most of these problems represent at least a drag on the political system: They divert energy, resources, and personnel from other areas and interfere with the political-public agenda. A number of Western observers have, over the years, come to believe that a system so hobbled with socioeconomic problems and deficiencies cannot sustain an aggressive foreign policy, that such a policy requires more ample resources, undivided organizational energies, and unified, supportive public sentiment.

Many social problems undermine economic efficiency and challenge the social order, and the Soviet authorities are well aware of this. Such problems include alcohol abuse and disrespect for public property, undisciplined attitudes toward work, excess mobility of labor, and dissatisfaction with available educational and employment opportunities. Nor does society benefit from the quest for personal happiness that results in divorce and a large number of children who grow up in incomplete families. In turn, low birthrates cut deeply into the supply of manpower for labor and the army and are also deemed to weaken a properly collectivist socialization process; one-child families are often deplored as the cradles of individualism, consumerism, and other evils. Still, the commitment of the authorities to the eradication or significant curtailment of some of these problems conflicts with other priorities; for example, the need for revenue conflicts with cutting back on the production of alcohol (or closing the illegal distilleries, though of late steps were taken to ration sugar required for such operations[21]). Nor are the authorities willing to increase birthrates by prohibiting abortion or other forms of birth control because such measures would greatly increase popular discontent.

It remains an intriguing question whether social problems, or some of them, could, in the not-too-distant future, have a benign effect on matters political, exerting a liberalizing, pluralizing pressure, as had been expected by Western observers for decades. To the extent that several of the social problems mentioned here entail certain individualistic values, as indeed many do—be they oriented toward higher living standards through crimes against public property, or greater personal happiness by discarding unsatisfactory spouses, or reducing family size, or moving into already overcrowded cities in pursuit of better goods and services—such acts and orientations may slowly erode collectivism, respect for authority, and public discipline, thereby weakening the political order. All such aspirations and forms of behavior represent a placing of the "private" above the "public" interest, as such things are defined in the Soviet Union. The growth of these aspirations may portend trends that could reduce the gap between the Soviet Union and Western societies and could bring about a limited pluralization of society and some degree of emancipation from the political determination of the direction pluralization will take.

Unquestionably, many social problems drain the public and political domain. To be sure, this could also lead to a strong reaction, a crackdown, or a renewed program of regimentation, or the reintroduction of social discipline. Nonetheless, as Bialer observed, there is "an incongruity between the harsh and honest judgements about the sorry state of the Soviet society and economy and the relatively feeble remedial actions . . . being taken or proposed."[22]

It is also likely that the relationship between politics and social problems is limited, that, with respect to some problems, the political domain may have only a marginal relevance. This may be a surprising proposition from one who has always regarded matters political as the major driving force in the development (or deformation) of Soviet society. However, I also observed as long ago as the early 1970s, "If, indeed there is any kind of convergence between the U.S. and the Soviet Union, it can be found in the realm of social problems,"[23] suggesting that I saw many problems as largely or partially apolitical phenomena.

Certain social problems have more to do with the human condition and with modernization in general than with any particular political system. Even in the more repressive, more totalitarian, or more highly politicized periods of Soviet history, some forms of human misbehavior and social problems had a measure of autonomy—certain types of suicide, crimes of passion, mental illness, and so forth. At the same time one may also argue that in the more totalitarian phases of Soviet history, it was easier to make the connection between social problems and politics because politics permeated and shaped most aspects of life: Even divorce often had political roots (as during the purges or because of housing shortages and the attendant familial friction, which were in turn determined by political priorities in resource allocation).

In all likelihood social problems will continue to multiply under Gorbachev, rather than merely be given more publicity, for reasons that include the rise of expectations stimulated by his rhetoric and his policies as well as by signs of a somewhat greater political tolerance at the top. Although it is very difficult to tell how widespread the rise of expectations has been since Gorbachev's emergence, it is likely that it has not been confined to the urban intelligentsia. Yet, some reports suggest that although expectations have risen, they are far from explosive, at least not in the industrial hinterlands. Thus for example in Semipalatinsk:

> The residents are not about to revolt, or do much more than complain. They have learned to live with bare store shelves, rationed meat, crowded communal apartments, endless waiting lists for telephones and cars, an absence of cultural institutions and serious air pollution. But Mr. Gorbachev has stirred their expectations without delivering a tangible improvement in their lives, a gap that has the potential to undermine his leadership and throw the wisdom of his programs into doubt.[24]

If the appetites of the Soviet masses continue to grow, literally and figuratively speaking, then social pathologies and a decline of political will and regimentation may turn out to be mutually reinforcing.

In the longer historical perspective, the persistence and proliferation of social problems in the Soviet Union also mean that it is possible for a society to have a limited supply of both "negative" and "positive" freedoms,[25] contrary to earlier hypotheses. The abundance of Soviet social problems demonstrates anew and quite conclusively that a politically motivated campaign of modernization, although bringing about a drastic decline of "negative" (Western) freedoms, is compatible with economic stagnation and a minimal growth of positive freedoms (social and economic rights or entitlements); that is, the modernization can be accompanied by prolonged and oppressive shortages and material deprivations, which were supposed to be eliminated at the expense of personal and group freedoms.

Notes

1. T. I. Zaslavskaia, "The Role of Sociology in Accelerating the Development of Soviet Society," *Soviet Sociology,* Winter 1987–88, p. 7.
2. Cullen Murphy, "Watching the Russians," *Atlantic Monthly,* February 1983, p. 37.
3. I. Rost, "Miloserdie—ne milostinia" [Altruism, not charity], *Literaturnaia gazeta,* February 17, 1988.
4. Henry W. Riecken, "Social Science and Contemporary Social Problems," *Items,* March 1969, p. 1.
5. Marshall I. Goldman, *USSR in Crisis* (New York: Norton, 1983), p. 174.
6. I. Kasyukov and M. Mendeleiev, "Sociologist's Opinion: Must a Family Man Have Talent?" *Nedelia,* transl. in *Current Digest of the Soviet Press* [hereafter *CDSP*], April 19, 1976, p. 25.
7. See, for example, the following articles in *Sotsiologicheskie issledovaniia:* S. I. Kurganov, "Motivy deistvii nesovershennoletnikh pravonarushitelei" [Motives of actions of juvenile lawbreakers], no. 5 (1989), pp. 60–63; "Narkomaniia s tochki zreniia sotsiologa, vracha, pravoveda i zhurnalista" [Addiction from the viewpoint of the sociologist, doctor, lawyer and journalist], no. 2 (1989), pp. 38–51; Ia. I. Gilinskii, "Effektiven li zapret prostitutsii?" [Is the prohibition of prostitution effective?], no. 6 (1988), pp. 68–70; Ia. I. Gilinskii and L. G. Smolinskii, "Sotsiodinamika samoubiistv" [Sociodynamics of suicides], no. 5 (1988), pp. 57–64; T. A. Dobrovol'skaia, N. A. Demidov, and N. B. Shabalina, "Sotsial'nye problemy invalidov" [Social problems of invalids], no. 4 (1988), pp. 79–83; and O. A. Voronina, "Zhenshchina v 'muzhskom obshchestve'" [Woman in a male society], no. 2 (1988), pp. 104–110. See also the articles on deviance and social problems in *Soviet Sociology* 27, no. 4 (1988).
8. Mikhail S. Gorbachev, "27th Congress Speech," *Pravda* and *Izvestiia,* transl. in *CDSP,* March 26, 1986, p. 6.
9. S. Shatalin, "Sotsial'noe razvitie i ekonomicheskii rost" [Social development and economic growth], *Kommunist,* no. 14 (1986).
10. T. I. Zaslavskaia, "Chelovecheskii faktor razvitiia ekonomiki i sotsial'naia spravedlivost'" [Social justice and the human factor in the development of the economy], *Kommunist,* no. 13 (1986).
11. Gorbachev, op. cit., p. 36.
12. Ferenc Szaniszlo, "Szegeny emberek" [Poor people], *Heti Vilag Gazdasag* (Budapest), May 28, 1988.
13. Peter L. Berger, "The Socialist Myth," *Public Interest,* Summer 1976, pp. 8–9; see also Adam Ulam, *The Unfinished Revolution* (Boulder, Colo.: Westview Press, 1979).
14. Gorbachev, op. cit., p. 4.
15. Emile Durkheim, *Suicide* (New York: Free Press, 1951), p. 250.
16. David Shipler, *Russia* (New York: Penguin, 1983), p. 194.

17. Natan Sharansky, "As I See Gorbachev," *Commentary,* March 1988, p. 31.

18. Mervyn Matthews, "Poverty in the Soviet Union," *Wilson Quarterly,* Fall 1985, p. 81.

19. A *Literaturnaia gazeta* article suggested that citizens may spend a total of years waiting in line. L. Velikanova, "Na razny temy" [On various topics], *Literaturnaia gazeta,* April 20, 1988.

20. Sergei Grigoryants, "Three Paradoxes of the Modern World," *Glasnost Information Bulletin,* October 1988, p. 20.

21. Bill Keller, "Soviet Moonshiners Drain Sugar Stocks; Rationing Imposed," *New York Times,* April 26, 1988.

22. Seweryn Bialer, *The Soviet Paradox: External Expansion Internal Decline* (New York: Knopf, 1987), p. 123.

23. Paul Hollander, *Soviet and American Society: A Comparison* (New York: Oxford, 1973), p. 301.

24. Philip Taubman, "Semipalatinsk Journal—If Perestroika Was Steak, Life Would Be Better," *New York Times,* September 22, 1988.

25. Isaiah Berlin, "Two Conceptions of Liberty," in *Four Essays on Freedom* (New York: Oxford, 1969).

CHAPTER 2

Ethnic Differentiation and Political Communication

Ellen Mickiewicz

Television has been excoriated by its critics as the great leveler: destroying high culture, dulling authentic expressions of folk culture, and imposing a political and social/cultural conformity on the masses to whom it communicates. Conversely, television has been lauded as the carrier of the values and techniques of the modern world to those who had been isolated. The isolation may have been the result of geographical obstacles that other mass media have been less successful in overcoming or the result of the stratification system, wherein those on the bottom of the ladder, those with less education, lower social and economic mobility, less-developed cognitive skills, are for the first time in the history of modern societies drawn into the information mainstream.[1]

The debate about the impact of television on social and cultural differences in society is a complex one. In the United States, there are already several generations that may be termed "television generations"—that is, there are new members of society born into a world in which television is already a fixture, in which it is as much a part of everyday life as the wallpaper that surrounds them. This represents a major, indeed revolutionary, change in the way that information is transmitted; by "information" I mean not only the narrowly defined items that are on the news and public affairs programs but also, and perhaps more important, the way that reality is constructed for society. In the past, the ruling myths and principles that explain and load value on the world had been the province of particularly designated individuals: the elders, the priests, the family. Growing up in the culture meant growing up in a particular way of evaluating the world, both micro and macro. The elders and the family as the provider of this evaluative framework may well be retreating into the background; the portrayer of the world, or reality, and the giver of the value loading may now be situated increasingly in that television box that is in view of most people in modern society in much of their waking life.

Television is, for most people in the modern United States, quite simply, an environment. In the majority of households, it is turned on most of the time. Children watch it without adults present to shape or amplify its message. It is both babysitter and teacher, and it consumes more of their time than does schoolwork or time spent with parents. Each new generation will teach us more about this issue, and the issue, itself, has a dynamic. It may be that the very fact of the ordinariness of television dulls its impact; or it may be quite the opposite: that the steady erosion of local culture and local values—generated by the family, the ethnicity, the subculture—is taking place because of television and that there is a substitution of the reality constructed by television for the reality hitherto constructed and transmitted by the carriers of the traditional culture. That television plays a central role in the broad learning process termed *socialization* is undeniable. Researchers in the United States believe that "it [television] contends with some force in competition with such other agents [of socialization] as parents, school, community, siblings, peers, and church."[2]

The socialization process is profoundly affected by television even in those countries where it is relatively new. In the Soviet Union, television has become a mass medium—indeed the country's first truly mass medium—only within the past two decades. Nonetheless, its impact has been striking, especially under the policy of *glasnost'*. Mikhail Gorbachev's first major reform came in the media. *Glasnost'* and all it implied were to reorient the media and mobilize the population for the structural reforms to come. In contradistinction to the media campaigns of the past, under Gorbachev, the media were actually to provide the motor force for thoroughgoing *institutional* change and *structural* reform. To do so effectively, the media had to be credible, a source of authority and trust.

This function creates a dual problematic: As we shall see below, the socialization function of national television tends to erode ethnic particularities over the long term. However, a different vector is also present: Under the new rules of *glasnost'*, genuine concerns of the ethnic minorities have surfaced and have been played out in the media. The media, especially television, have become a central concern for those regional elites seeking to propagate their message. Thus a contrary, centrifugal impulse was released: The particularistic features of the national minorities were actually heightened, as the lid was lifted on their expression and as they entered the mass-media system in their regions. As a consequence, insofar as specifically ethnic issues were or have become salient, the role of *regional* broadcasting was enhanced; insofar as the national networks succeeded in preempting this agenda or setting one of their own relating to other issues, the role of regional broadcasting was reduced.

Television and the Republics

Over 93 percent of the Soviet population watch television; the audience for prime-time national-television programming runs between 150 and 200 million. Although in the past there were significant disparities in the availability of television sets across the republics, those gaps have been markedly reduced. In 1965, for example, differences among the republics as measured by television sets per 100 households were large: In Latvia, there were 35 television sets per 100 families, and in Belorussia, only 14. However, by the beginning of the 1980s, the Russian Republic registered 101 sets per 100 families (multiple-set ownership had arrived), and in Central Asia and Belorussia, there were between 70 and 80 sets per 100 families. Thus even in the less-developed areas, where television sets were least likely to be available, no fewer than three-quarters of the population had them.[3] Moreover, the cost of a television set, although it had affected the probability of saturation in the late 1960s and early 1970s, is no longer a factor affecting ownership. As N. M. Rimashevskaia noted, "The necessity for families to acquire a television set today is so great that it is seen as an object of the first necessity. Its presence can be classified as an inelastic type of utility."[4]

Among all the nationalities, it is television that has claimed first place in the provision of information about "culture," broadly conceived. Arutiunian and Bromlei found that "in all nationalities, in first place in terms of frequency of consumption there is one and the same channel for the assimilation of culture—television. Replicated research carried out in various cities and rural regions of the country show that in the 1970s the growth of preference for television broadcasts over other activities in free time is continuing."[5]

What that means for the nationalities was termed by Arutiunian and Bromlei a "genuine revolution [*perevorot*]."[6] The majority of the non-Russian population can, theoretically, have access to television broadcasting both in Russian and in the people's own ethnic language, some forty of which are used. One might conclude that far from reducing the importance of ethnic identity and culture, republic-level television in the non-Russian republics might serve to reinforce ethnicity, since the most fundamental and important dimension of ethnic identity is, in fact, language.

Arutiunian and Bromlei found that in terms of the preservation and development of differentiated ethnic cultures, television has had a contradictory impact. They argued that television has very substantially broadened the horizons of the "masses." It has introduced people to cultures and habits other than their own; it has internationalized them; it has brought people who would otherwise have been isolated into touch with current events in "the entire world." Without doubt it has aided the process of the "internationalization of the spiritual culture of Soviet people, [and] the formation of a cultural unity of the Soviet people." However, television in the union republics and the autonomous republics helps to diffuse the "achievements of the national culture of the indigenous peoples of these republics. . . . Republic (as well as all-union) television first of all propagandized the achievements of the high professional stratum of national culture, but at the same time to a certain degree assisted the increase of interest in one's own national, folklore culture [and] the perception of it has a national value."[7]

Television, Integration, and Socialization

Transmitting programs from neighboring republics is a relatively straightforward matter in technical terms. A larger and more difficult issue is the general problem of the socialization of a multiethnic state. By what means and utilizing what instruments can national integration be strengthened and tolerance expanded? These are issues that remained critically underanalyzed in the media (and in Soviet public life generally) until the advent of *glasnost'*. It is clear that underlying tensions are durable.

That television can have a powerful role in the socialization and integration of an ethnically differentiated society is apparent from experience both in the United States and in the Soviet Union. Commenting on the U.S. experience, a noted scholar wrote of the socializing effect of television: "Findings also imply an effect for television where experience fails; they also imply that television, because of the limited stereotypic scope of its portrayals, may provide a homogenizing influence—an implication to which the data on ethnic minority children would not by themselves lead."[8] In the Soviet Union, the role of television is considered so central to the function of socialization that the clear failure of previous socialization practices has been, to a large extent, blamed on television. As one Soviet analyst put it, television is the "most powerful and efficacious instrument of influence on public consciousness. Our TV with all self criticism has to take on itself the weight of responsibility for the deficiencies in the internationalist upbringing of the Soviet people."[9]

"Internationalism" is now seen to require greater sensitivity and attention to the ethnic values and ethnic identity. To be sure, some such rhetoric was always advanced in the past, but essentially as a formality. "The thing is that its [television's] multi-nationalism is declaratory, like some given, not demanding comprehension."[10] The new path to national integration, then, must paradoxically go through a terrain of heightened ethnic awareness—or at least a heightened form of expression of an awareness that may have been there in the past as well. First, there must be a reversal of the central broadcasting policy that effectively wiped out autonomous regional broadcasting.

Before the development and deployment of communications satellites, in fact, local studios were considerably more active than subsequently. Precisely because television signals were more difficult to receive, central programming was interrupted for certain localities and Russian-language broadcasts were replaced by programs in the local languages. This practice was viewed negatively by the central authorities, and in 1970, the administrative organization of television broadcasting was reformed. At that time, television was put ahead of radio in the title of the state agency (it became the State Committee for Television and Radio Broadcasting—Gosteleradio).[11] The reorganization abolished the intermediate link between the local studios and the center and resulted in a greater degree of centralization and coordination by the Party. "The party took the entire responsibility for the political, ideological, [and] artistic level of television programs."[12] It is possible to discern two related reasons for this shift: First, with respect to ideology, there was dissatisfaction in Moscow with the political consistency and acceptability of programming emanating from the locales. Second, there was concern in Moscow about the technical and artistic standards employed by the local broadcasters.

The Gorbachev policy attempted to redress the balance. Some sixty-seven new local-television studios were to be created, with less than one-half in the Russian Republic. The rest were to be in oblast centers of the non-Russian republics and in autonomous oblasts and national *okrug*s (areas). Moreover, the national network, Second Program, was to feature special programs from the non-Russian republics. These would be drawn from the best of the republics' telecasts and broadcast either in Russian or in the national language with Russian subtitles.

Even if republic-level television broadcasting becomes more responsive to ethnic demands, it may be no match for Central Television. A study of Azerbaidzhan, where Russians constitute less than 8 percent of the population, found that even though, in terms of hours, programming in Azeri and Russian were equal, the competition was very unequal. The local programs did not, on the whole, match the production standards of the national networks and have been much less popular. The television industry in Armenia came to the same conclusion. As a study there put it: "The research of sociologists and journalists shows that the opportunities for choice of program are reduced as a result of slipshod programming. In other words, the television viewer wants to see the best broadcasts, whether of republic or Central television."[13] It is interesting to note that by far the most popular Kazakh-language programs in Kazakhstan are those devoted to music and humor (similar to preferences in Azerbaidzhan), which draw almost 90 percent of that audience, while the news in Kazakh is watched by only 40 percent.[14] Even Georgian television, the most pioneering in the country (it was first to bring back live telecasts and it sponsored the film *Repentance*), lags far behind Moscow in technical infrastructure and, therefore, in production standards. "Viewers watch, let's say, the Georgian channel and then switch to CTV [Central Television], and—the technical difference is immeasurable."[15] In terms of Soviet-made equipment, the two are, in fact, fully comparable. The supply of foreign equipment makes the difference, and Georgia lacks the foreign currency to purchase on the world market, something that the new self-financing policy may actually alleviate by encouraging direct business ties with foreign companies.

A. N. Dmitriuk, who was in charge of local broadcasting at Gosteleradio headquarters in Moscow, cautioned that locally produced programming could be competitive only in public affairs. He noted that a one-hour documentary film cost 47,000 rubles to make (as compared to 3,000 for a modest studio-television program), while a feature film was a hundred times more costly. In addition to the problem of cost, non–centrally produced programming seemed to have fallen victim to a push toward conformity and homogenization. The national coloration and the national approach, he argued, were being lost, as the national studios made films they saw as competitive for an all-union public.[16]

A policy of more vigorously acquainting the huge Soviet television audience with the lives and cultures of the country's many ethnic groups, though it may be a necessary beginning, is by no means sufficient. Central *Soviet* television is still very heavily *Russian*. As a Soviet observer asked, "Isn't the whole first *all-union* program [network] of television too *Moscow* in its subject matter?" Commentaries on the evening news are mainly about Moscow and its suburbs. After all, he continued, "the overwhelming majority of viewers don't live in the capital."[17]

In fact, in our study of Soviet citizens covered on the nightly news over a three-year period (sampled quarterly from 1987 to 1989), fully 86 percent of all people in the news were Slavs. Moreover, they accounted for 92 percent of all the time in which newsmakers spoke. The ethnic groups accounting for the next largest contribution to the total number of newsmakers were the nationalities of the Caucasus. However, there, the 6.2 percent of the total number of Soviet newsmakers was very significantly dependent on the prominent exposure of Georgia's most powerful national politician: Eduard Shevardnadze. Central Asians, who made up 3.7 percent of the total number of newsmakers, were given only 3.1 percent of the time in which Soviet newsmakers spoke. Their underrepresentation, as compared to their proportion in the population, was severe.

This is a familiar and difficult issue. Television plays an important role in shaping values and attitudes, and the way in which minorities are portrayed (including their absence from or underrepresentation in news and entertainment programming) sends powerful cues about the status, prestige, and opportunities for those groups in society. In the United States

> blacks on television represent three-fourths, and Hispanics one-third of their share of the U.S. population, and a disproportionate number are minor rather than major characters [in entertainment programming]. The point is not that culture should duplicate real-life statistics. It is rather that the direction and thrust of cultural amplification or neglect provide a clue to the treatment of social types, groups, [and] values. . . . For example, the prominent and stable overrepresentation of well-to-do white men in the prime of life dominates prime time and indicates a relatively restrictive view of women's and minorities' opportunities and rights.[18]

Ethnic diversity does not generally appear on Soviet television in the persons of the prestigious political observers or at all among the highly visible anchors and reporters, who present the authoritative nightly news.[19] Igor Kirillov, the senior anchor, regarded his metier in part as the presentation of news, but no less as the preservation and transmission of the Russian language, and in an interview with me remarked that although Gosteleradio holds competitions for reporters, and although minorities have competed, they have not met the rigorous Russian-language standards.

Information Diffusion and Ethnic Disorder in Armenia and Azerbaidzhan

There were serious media issues involved in the Azerbaidzhani/Armenian ethnic conflicts. Those issues were to surface again in the reportage of the suppression of mass protests in Tbilisi and still again in coverage of Lithuanian independence initiatives. In those cases, national television news reporting was faulted for its belated or misleading coverage of critical issues.

The lessons of the Nagorno-Karabakh coverage are several: (1) Because all republics have in their populations several ethnicities, the isolation of some ethnic-minority enclaves from mass communication in their language may be both dangerous and avoidable. (2) The degree of tolerance in general in Soviet society has turned out to be lower than the central officials had imagined, and the mass media must take as one of their primary tasks the legitimation of a multiplicity of cultures and much more vigorous socialization in inter-ethnic relations. (3) The failure of media, local and national, to respond rapidly with complete and timely coverage of ethnic disorders actually exacerbated the situation—something the central officials ought to have learned earlier from the lesson of Chernobyl.

The Demand for Native-Language Broadcasting

The people of Nagorno-Karabakh had been sending large numbers of letters to Central Television officials in Moscow at least two years before the ethnic disorders broke out there. Those letters urged Moscow to make Armenian television programming available to the Armenian enclave in Azerbaidzhan. The official in charge in Moscow admitted that there was no technical obstacle. Almost all the equipment was already in place. Only red tape prevented a solution that in this case, he admitted, "as in many other questions, turned out to have costs of a political character."[20] At the 1988 session of the Presidium of the Supreme Soviet that considered the problems in that area, the head of government of Azerbaidzhan touched first on the question of the extension of Armenian television to Nagorno-Karabakh as evidence of his republic's responsiveness. Naturally, there were many complex issues intertwined in the events that developed into violence and turmoil. What is interesting in terms of political communication is the important role television played as an initial focus of relative deprivation.

The Armenians in Nagorno-Karabakh were not the only ethnic concentration that demanded media messages in its language. In Dzhambul oblast in Kazakhstan, the Uzbeks petitioned Moscow and Alma-Ata to have television programs transmitted from Uzbekistan. In Dmanissky *raion* (district, or borough), in Georgia, the Azerbaidzhani demanded programs in their language. One of them wrote to Central Television headquarters in Moscow: "Our children and old people do not know the Georgian language. . . . In our district they are building a new television station. We ask you to give us help in allocating one channel for broadcasts from Baku." There is, on the part of Moscow officials, a new appreciation of the role that television plays in ethnic issues and that action must be taken "in a timely fashion [*operativno*]" to avoid negative political consequences.[21]

Crisis Coverage

In both Azerbaidzhan and Armenia television has become a vital medium of communication. In Azerbaidzhan a survey found that mass-media consumption was very high and that, for all social classes, the highest percentage of ownership among twenty-nine different consumer durables was for television sets.[22] Alongside this leisure-time pattern, traditional forms of leisure-time use, such as receiving guests and visiting friends and relatives, still frequently practiced by all social classes, have become more characteristic of agricultural workers than of industrial and construction workers, white-collar employees, and the intelligentsia. Activities of a less-traditional sort, such as participation in volunteer civic activities, sports, hobbies, and the arts, attracted relatively few people.[23]

In Armenia, television has developed rapidly as a mass medium. Nearly nine-tenths of the republic watch the television programs of the two republic-wide networks, in addition to the national networks. On the average, republic television broadcasts for a total of 13.5 hours a day. Thus, the two republic networks together produce about as much programming as each of the Moscow-based national networks on a weekday, though less than the weekend average.

When local ethnic issues achieve high salience, television becomes very prominent and, indeed, critical. Analysis of the coverage of the disorders in Azerbaidzhan and Armenia provided additional information about these processes in which the media and national/ethnic concerns intersect. What began as an attempt by the Armenian minority in a province in Azerbaidzhan to dissent (a by-product of *glasnost'*) from the decision of the Soviet government in 1988 against reassigning that territory to Armenia broadened into mass demonstrations in Erevan, capital of Armenia, and then rampaging riots in Azerbaidzhan, which, according to official reports, left more than thirty dead. As in the case of Chernobyl, the original provision of information was sparse. During the Chernobyl events, but after much delay, there was quite ample reporting; following Chernobyl, Central Television and the other media continued the policy of reporting, rather than suppressing, unwelcome news of natural disasters and accidents. The coverage may not have been as full and frank as one would expect from a Western media system, but the change from the pre-Gorbachev era was very clear.[24] In early 1988 in the Caucasus, however, information was again slow to reach the population through the mass media.

The paucity of the provision of information to the affected populations and to the rest of the country had two powerful results, which appear to have convinced the officials in Moscow that much more ample coverage was in the national interest. First, the inadequate coverage severely compromised the credibility of the media and reduced their influence, thus effectively nullifying a powerful instrument of socialization and mobilization. When Moscow did attempt much more large-scale coverage, the government found a population unwilling to cooperate. Correspondents from "Vremya" (the nightly national news program) could not find people who would agree to be interviewed or who would speak on camera. A Soviet observer noted: "As a result, many of the people in Nagorno-Karabakh, in Armenia and Azerbaidzhan, stopped believing the official sources of information. . . . There is the price of the 'figure of silence,' not congruent with *glasnost'*, with the openness of our time."[25]

An equally disturbing consequence of the inadequate coverage of the violent events in the area was the loss of control of the information flow. As the Soviet media officials learned during Chernobyl, the failure to break a story cedes the advantage to those who do. A powerful persuasive advantage is, in fact, enjoyed by the sources presenting the story first, even if those sources are gossip and hearsay. Moreover, messages from these sources may actually exacerbate the situation, foment further strife, and inflame passions. The agenda of these sources will undoubtedly *not* be congruent with that of the Moscow leadership, and it is a grave political error to let those sources gain credibility and attention. Further, it is probable that messages transmitted during a crisis and in an information vacuum will be far from reliable as they pass along the chain of human transmitters.

According to a Soviet publication, the death of a demonstrator on July 5, 1988, at Zvartnots Airport, in Erevan, triggered the decision by Gosteleradio to provide more ample coverage.

> For a long, too long a time, all-union television tried to keep quiet about what was worrying literally all television viewers. The vacuum of objective information gave birth to rumors, heated up conjecture, put weapons into the hands of our ideological adversaries. Not by accident, after the tragic events at the Zvartnots Airport, the program "Vremya" finally began regularly to give videocommunications about the situation in Erevan and Stepanakert.[26]

"Vremya," thus, took roughly four months to offer coverage that met current Soviet standards of *glasnost'*. In fact, it was not "Vremya," but a special program, "Pozitsiia," that provided the first footage from the February 1988 violent clashes in the Azerbaidzhani cities of Sumgait and Stepanakert—some two months after the events. "Pozitsiia," hosted by well-known political observer Genrikh Borovik, was a prime-time program, lasting one-and-a-half hours and airing on April 26, 1988. The first half of the program showed graphic pictures of the riots: burned-out cars, vandalized apartments, masses in the street. There were also highly emotional interviews of Armenians who had fled from Azerbaidzhan and descriptions of the terror inflicted by Azerbaidzhani youth in an atmosphere of pogroms.

The second half was devoted to a more upbeat discussion of what was said to be the rule, not the exception: different ethnic groups living side by side in harmony, sharing a history, intermarrying, and working together. The program included a discussion of the historical context of Nagorno-Karabakh going back to the massacre of Armenians in 1916. Borovik's narration also examined socioeconomic and cultural problems in the disputed area and noted that the policy of Baku resulted in insufficient schools and textbooks for the Armenian population. The Armenian dean of the Stepanakert pedagogical institute remarked that the (predominantly Armenian) students were offered 148 hours of the history of Azerbaidzhan and only 1 hour of Armenian history.

One of the principal themes of this program related to the dual functions of the media: long-term socialization and provision of information for immediate use. The latter is particularly important in times of crisis. Borovik maintained in this program that timely provision of information could have markedly reduced the problems in Sumgait. Instead, "sincere complaints turned into a feeling of nationalism, which created provocations, hooliganism, [and] banditism."[27] After telling the audience about an incident in which a vigilante group went out to avenge an alleged injustice that no one personally had witnessed, Borovik said: "I tell you this as an example. It is easy for a person who is frightened and spreads unconfirmed rumors to be transformed into a provocateur." (Quite the opposite was reported from Latvia, where the prompt and reliable reporting of Latvian television prevented ethnic violence.[28])

The function of this program could be summed up in Borovik's words:

> The press during those February days did not help, did not contain very much about what was going on: nothing about meetings in Erevan or demonstrations in Baku, nothing about the complex situation in Nagorno-Karabakh or Agdam, nothing about the mood of the people, or about the reasons they were provoked. . . . Meanwhile what we read in newspapers and saw on television was mostly many interviews about the friendship between Armenians and Azerbaidzhani. The silence, of course, was motivated by good intentions. It was important to determine what was happening in order to provide correct information. The circumstances were complicated enough that any misstep could cause an explosion of emotion and worsen the situation. That is true. But it is also true that the absence of information did not make things any better, but worse. The idea that "silence is golden" is familiar to us. But in the era of *glasnost'*, other things are golden. This was proved also by the events in Kazakhstan [the Alma-Ata riots], after the explosion at Chernobyl, and in other "extraordinary" situations. The silence of the press [including television] facilitated the freedom of rumors and provocations, while at the time what was needed was honest and full information about the events.[29]

Borovik's was the first attempt to provide that information. It took the events at Zvartnots some two months later to change the position of "Vremya."

National television's failure to cover the events in Tbilisi adequately indicated that the lessons had not been learned. At the first meeting of the Congress of People's Deputies in the spring of 1989, Georgian filmmaker E. N. Shengelya offered to show a documentary record of what really happened in Tbilisi, since, he maintained, "Vremya" had provided only disinformation. There were bitter denunciations in Moscow and in Tbilisi of national print and television coverage of the events, and the military district troop commander, General I. N. Rodionov, and the Tbilisi branch of Gosteleradio traded charges of false reporting. That national television did not, in fact, give the country vital information on the use of poison gas, the number of victims affected, and the brutality of the termination of the demonstration has been confirmed.

In the Baltic republics the rise of the Popular Fronts has had a broad impact on the local media systems. Regional elites there have grasped the importance of media and have also utilized the environment of *glasnost'* to capture "their" media in order to put forward *within* the republic the demands of the indigenous ethnic groups. Coverage of these national movements has been comparatively limited on the national news but extensive inside the republics. Indeed, national television provided sparse and skewed coverage of the events surrounding Lithuania's declaration of independence. The nightly news focused on those who did not wish to break their republic's ties with the Soviet Union; on non-Lithuanian minorities who expressed anxiety about the protection of their rights; on workers who stressed the degree to which their factories were embedded in national production networks; and on parliamentary deputies who faulted Lithuania for its flouting of the newly instituted procedures for secession. Although facts were not withheld from viewers, the purpose of the coverage, both visually and in terms of allotted time, was clearly dissemination of Moscow's strong condemnation of the Lithuanian move and the lesson that the union was to be preserved.

The effectiveness of television as an instrument of national policy depends critically on the degree of trust the public grants it. The examples given above did not enhance that trust with respect to locally important issues. The question remains: How much political caution and control will be traded for long-term effectiveness?

The Effects of Television and Ethnic Issues

Television does present distinct advantages to a leadership that intends its centrally generated messages to reach the country's entire population virtually simultaneously. From the beginning of Gorbachev's tenure in power, an observer of Soviet politics could detect in the use of the media the operation of a key mechanism in effecting major change. *Glasnost'*, the new openness and public discussion, has been a *media* phenomenon. Before any other major reform of the Gorbachev administration was launched—before the economic and political reforms of 1987 and 1988—extensive changes in the system of political communication had been made.

One cannot, however, equate transmission with assimilation. There is no scientific basis for the assumption that a message is received as sent; there is a good deal of research that presents data counterarguing this proposition. This is a matter I have discussed at greater length elsewhere.[30] But neither is it the case that nothing penetrates the viewer. Rather, it is difficult to establish

> external criteria in order to measure what is fundamentally not only an exterior but also a relative process. That is, to the extent that a viewer processes any information, some kind of comprehension occurs. To demonstrate that a viewer understands a television program differently from what is defined as "correct" by a producer or a researcher does not show a lack of comprehension, but that comprehension is an active process dependent as much on the receiver as on the messages.[31]

Some important and, in some cases contradictory, trends are at work here. The national networks, broadcasting in Russian, have a clear advantage. Their programs are more polished and more successful in addressing the demands of the viewers: Their informational resources are greater—they have more foreign bureaus and foreign correspondents, for example. They are, in general, both more entertaining and more informative. To the extent that this advantage continues to be utilized and extended by *glasnost'*, the socializing effect of the national networks will exceed that of the programs of the republics and lower-level administrative units. In particular, this should affect Russian-language acquisition in a positive fashion. But it is a different matter when issues of ethnicity become highly salient.

In the past, the concerns of individuals and groups were relayed to the center in part through the system of agitation. Yet the network of officially structured interpersonal activity does not nearly equal the effect of television on its audience or engage the mind of the viewer on the issues and impressions he or she has assimilated from its programs. O. I. Shkaratan raised this issue with respect to the nationalities. He noted that there were predispositions—cognitive prisms—generated by ethnic differentiation through which the media were received and which, in turn, affected the transmission of information and the shaping of values.[32] The interpersonal dimension of agitation in the past helped to create some sense, on the part of Party officials, that the influence of the ethnic identity could be understood: One-on-one talks or discussions in small groups could elicit that information, attempt to correct the imbalances, and translate national policies into terms and concepts meaningful for the ethnicity. Agitation, then, functioned not only as a source of feedback for transmission back up the line but also as the mediator of national policy for persuasion of the minorities. Although this policy was never wholly realistic and far from adequately implemented, in the television era, agitation has come on hard times: The cadres are still there, of course, but lack immediate responsiveness, information, and flexibility.[33]

The particular concerns and complexities of ethnic life may not be addressed at all by the national television networks. Certainly the Moscow-centric bent of Central Television, as well as its delayed and fragmentary coverage of ethnic disorders and demands, has come under scrutiny and been vigorously criticized. By failing to cover questions of importance to the viewers, television is neither credible nor salient, as the crisis in the Caucasus proved. Although the extension of *glasnost'* and the application of the rapidly changing experience of Central Television to the republics and below are uneven and certainly slower than the authorities would like, the opportunities are there to relate to an audience that has been very largely alienated from local media in general.[34]

Criticism continues to be directed at Central Television for failing to present a balanced view of the continuing Armenian/Azerbaizhani conflicts. The Congress of People's Deputies feared that its debates, and those of the Supreme Soviet, on national issues would exacerbate ethnic sensitivities; deputies argued that such debates should not be shown on national television. "I Serve the Soviet Union," an established Sunday-morning television program for servicemen, was criticized recently for "provocation" when a correspondent interviewing Ukrainian soldiers asked why they spoke Russian, rather than Ukrainian, among themselves.

These examples, as well as those raised earlier in this chapter, suggest that a national television policy regarding credible and salient coverage of ethnic issues has yet to be devised. In fact, the policy that is in place is often articulated in terms of the Hippocratic oath, "do nothing to make the patient worse," or, as Gosteleradio adapts it, do nothing to make the situation worse. The result has been a general inability or unwillingness to engage its multi-ethnic audience with the kind of in-depth interpretive and investigative reporting needed to make the profusion of ethnically based incidents and local policies intelligible to a highly varied and very heterogeneous audience. The most active policy—to create new blocs of republic-produced programming on Second Program—is likely to be a palliative and of very limited impact.

A joint Soviet-American survey[35] in November and December 1989 across seven republics in both urban and rural areas revealed that the non-Slavic nationalities were much more attuned to *their* television programs than to Moscow's. Baltic peoples, Central Asians, and Georgians are far more likely to turn to their own television stations and less attentive to the message from Moscow than are their Slavic counterparts. Multivariate analysis controlling for age, income, education, urban/rural residence, and membership in organizations shows ethnicity as a very powerful factor independently influencing attention to local or national television.

Certainly, such centrifugal pressure would have been found intolerable in the pre-Gorbachev Soviet Union. It may be argued that in the long run, for the republics that do not take the route of secession, the national television networks, with their integrative capacity, will nonetheless be powerful elements in gradually eroding regional differences. Television is an instrument of socialization, not merely a vehicle for entertainment and information; it provides instruction, both overt and latent. In other societies and, apparently, in the Soviet Union, it has a homogenizing effect and tends in the long run to lead to "an increased and wider acceptance of the norms and values on which the [social] hierarchy depends."[36]

In the near term, however, ethnic differences are profound and, especially under conditions of extreme economic deprivation and competition, often conflictual. These differences might be moderated if national television were able to act—as is intended by its mission and role in *perestroika*—as a powerful integrating force, spanning this diverse country with its messages and its Russian language. In the era of television politics, this poses an enormous challenge for what has been one of the key instruments in the Gorbachev reform program, and current programming policy has yet to grapple with its consequences.

Notes

The author wishes to thank the John and Mary R. Markle Foundation for its support of the larger research project of which this is a part.

1. See, for example, the study of Italian peasants and the introduction of television in Lidia de Rita, *I Contadini e la televisione* (Bologna: Il Mulino, 1974). See also Doris A. Graber, *Processing the News: How People Tame the Information Tide,* 2nd ed. (New York: Longman, 1988).

2. George Comstock, Steven Chaffee, Natan Katzman, Maxwell McCombs, and Donald Roberts, *Television and Human Behavior* (New York: Columbia University Press, 1978), p. 285.

3. Iu. V. Arutiunian and Iu. V. Bromlei, *Sotsial'no-kulturny oblik sovetskikh natsii* (Moscow, 1986), p. 191.

4. N. M. Rimashevskaia and S. A. Karapetian (eds.), *Sem'ia i blagosostoianie v razvitom sotsialisticheskom obshchestve* (Moscow, 1985), pp. 204–205. The survey was conducted between 1978 and 1980.

5. Arutiunian and Bromlei, op. cit., p. 221.

6. Ibid., p. 190.

7. Ibid., p. 191.

8. George Comstock and Robin E. Cobbey, "Television and the Children of Ethnic Minorities," *Journal of Communication* 29 (Winter 1979), p. 111.

9. V. Tsvik, "Internatsionalny teleekran," *Televidenie i radioveshchanie,* no. 12 (1988), p. 13.

10. Ibid.

11. V. I. Zadorkin and A. V. Sosnovsky, "Perspektivy kommunikativnykh vozmozhnostei televideniia kak sredstva osveshcheniia kul'turnogo urovnia," *Issledovanie rosta kulturnogo urovnia trudiashchikhsia* (Moscow, 1977), pp. 90–101.

12. V. V. Egorov, *Televidenie i zritel'* (Moscow, 1977), p. 45.

13. S. Eritsian, "Slovo predostavleno zriteliu," *Auditoriia,* no. 1 (1987), p. 79.

14. Communication to the author, Gosteleradio, Alma-Ata, Kazakhstan, November 1989.

15. A. Zagorsky, "TV Gruzii: Den', kak vsegda," *Televidenie i radioveshchanie,* August 1988, p. 34.

16. L. Asoskova, "Kakim byt' oblastomu TV?" *Televidenie i radioveshchanie,* no. 4 (1989), pp. 19-21.

17. Tsvik, op. cit., p. 13.

18. George Gerbner, Larry Gross, Michael Morgan, and Nancy Signorielli, "Living with Television: The Dynamics of the Cultivation Process," in Jennings Bryant and Dolf Zillman (eds.), *Perspectives on Media Effects* (Hillsdale, N.Y.: Erlbaum Assoc., Inc., 1986), pp. 25-26.

19. A study in progress at Emory University examines the roles of ethnic minorities on Soviet television.

20. A. N. Dmitriuk, "Televidenie—mnogonatsional'noi auditorii," *Govorit i pokazyvaet Moskva,* no. 37 (1988), p. 9.

21. Ibid.

22. Ch. A. Mansimov, "Izmeneniia v zhiznennom uklade semei Lenkoranskogo raiona," *Sotsiologicheskie issledovaniia,* no. 3 (1981), pp. 102-105.

23. G. A. Zaikina, "Struktura svobodnogo vremeni naseleniia Lenkorana: Sotsial'no-professional'naia i vozrastnaia differentsiatsiia," *Sotsiologicheskie issledovaniia,* no. 3 (1981), pp. 98-102.

24. For a more detailed examination of these issues, see Ellen Mickiewicz, *Split Signals: Television and Politics in the Soviet Union* (New York: Oxford University Press, 1988).

25. Tsvik, op. cit., p. 14.

26. Ibid.

27. "Pozitsiia," April 26, 1988.

28. Esther Fein, "Latvians Extending a Hand to Outsiders in Their Midst," *New York Times,* October 11, 1988.

29. Ibid.

30. See Mickiewicz, op. cit.

31. Comstock et al., op. cit., p. 271.

32. Mansimov, op. cit.

33. For a discussion of agitation and mass media, see Mickiewicz, op. cit., Chap. 5.

34. On this point, see Ellen Mickiewicz, *Media and the Russian Public* (New York: Praeger, 1981).

35. The survey directors were Professors Ada W. Finifter, George Gerbner, Boris Grushin, Ellen Mickiewicz, and Nikolai Popov. The survey was conducted under the auspices of the National Center for Public Opinion Research in Moscow; the questionnaire was produced by the collaborators.

36. Comstock et al., op. cit., p. 309.

CHAPTER 3

Pollution in the Soviet Union: The Growth of Environmentalism and Its Consequences

Marshall I. Goldman

Economists have long argued that pollution is a negative externality, which is a convoluted way of saying that private polluters are usually able to pass the costs of their pollution on to someone else or to society in general: those who are downwind or downstream. The ability of private individuals to avoid their rightful obligations and costs is considered to be one of the more serious failings of the capitalist economic system. Economists and engineers spend considerable time seeking ways to ensure that the polluters are forced to pay for their transgressions and that social costs are privately shouldered by the perpetrators.

For many years, some critics in the West argued that the only way to ensure that social costs would not be avoided by polluters was to nationalize private property.[1] If there were no private property, then corporate managers would not be under constant pressure to reduce their costs and maximize their profits at the expense of society as a whole. In a socialist society, these critics argued, where the means of production were owned by the state, there would be no such division as "we" and "they." The factory manager would feel as much loyalty to the state as to the factory and would be as concerned about where the pollutants were disbursed as anyone else in the society. Thus, there would be no distinction between private and social costs.

This vision was enhanced by the insistence of many spokespersons in the Soviet Union in the early 1970s that the socialist system adopted there had indeed brought an end to pollution.[2] Pollution was seen as a natural consequence of capitalist greed, and since there was no such thing as private ownership of the means of production in the Soviet Union, there was no such thing as pollution. The way to abolish the private- and social-cost dichotomy was to do away with social costs.

However inspiring and romantic the theoretical analysts may have been, with time the growing evidence of pollution inside the Soviet Union became too blatant to ignore. Ultimately Soviet authorities had to recognize that the Soviet Union and socialism were no more immune to pollution than any other society. The factory managers and industrial ministers might be state employees, but like their capitalist counterparts they faced material imperatives. Although profits might not play as dominant a role in the Soviet Union as elsewhere, the pressures to increase production continued to make the Soviet manager worry more about his own individual output than about the social good. If anything, there seemed to be even fewer restraints on the Soviet factory manager than on his or her counterpart in capitalist countries, because until the past few years the former did not have to worry about stirring up any voluntary environmental-watchdog groups. There were environmental groups in the Soviet Union, such as the Society for the Protection of Nature, but before Mikhail S. Gorbachev and his reforms, these groups, like all such groups in the Soviet Union, were by law official government organizations. Only recently, as part of *glasnost'*, has it become legal to organize independent groups devoted to environmental or other public issues.

Yet the fact that the Society for the Protection of Nature had upwards of 19 million members and was thus the largest environmental group in the world was often portrayed by Soviet authorities as a sign that there has been a strong and effective environmental movement in the country for a long time. What outsiders are usually unaware of is that the head of the society has traditionally been a spokesperson for industry. Thus, for many years the head of the society in the Russian Republic was Nikolai Ovsiannikov, who was also the first-deputy minister of the Ministry of Land Reclamation and Water Management of the Russian Republic.[3] His ministry traditionally has been the country's dam builder and one of the major disrupters of the Soviet environment. His appointment was comparable to appointing the director of the U.S. Corps of Engineers as head of the Sierra Club.

Not all Soviet citizens were pleased with this situation, if for no other reason than that they found themselves belonging to groups that were of no interest to them. Nor were they happy about having their dues for such groups deducted from their salaries without their permission. As one "volunteer" put it, "On payday you get receipts from volunteer societies and your pay is reduced accordingly . . . but I'm not in those societies! It's not a matter of the money. What is offensive is the deception and the arbitrarily inflated membership totals."[4]

Given its origins, it is not surprising that the Society for the Protection of Nature tended to focus more on providing outings for its members than on halting or preventing pollution. In fact, it is hard to find any instance where it sought to prevent, much less succeeded in preventing, any industrial pollution. The society simply did not serve as a gadfly or watchdog the way environmental groups do in the outside world. Nor, until recently, were official organs much help. One must remember that the state has been the sole owner of all the means of production. This is important because the Soviet state views its main function to be that of increasing production. Generally, nothing can be allowed to stand in the way of this, including a shutdown of production because of pollution or emissions. In the late 1980s, there was a somewhat less hard-hearted attitude, but on those occasions when a decision was made to close down a factory, the chief consideration was often that the factory had lost its economic importance. If that is not the case, then there will be resistance to closure despite the fact that orders may have been given to do just such a thing. A good example of this occurred at Togliatti during a visit by General Secretary Gorbachev. The workers in the automobile plant there complained that despite several orders requiring the closing of some chemical companies, they continued to pollute and disrupt the residents' way of life.[5]

Unlike other governments, the government in the Soviet Union until recently has not served as an impartial judge, balancing the needs of the environment with the needs of the economy. In the Soviet Union, the government more often than not has been both the accused and the judge. To the extent that pollution has been controlled, it usually came about because the state was able to allocate new money for pollution control that did not impede ongoing production or because it denied resources for the production of automobiles and other pollution-generating industries. Of course, such decisions are seldom made solely because of environmental reasons. In any event, as the Soviet public begins to speak out about what the people see as environmental-health problems, they find the neglect of the past has created an enormous backlog of problems for the present and future. No wonder pollution is such a serious problem in the Soviet Union.

Given the government's anticonservation tendencies and the absence until recently of an independent environmental watchdog, what explains the fact that the government has sometimes found it necessary to modify or abandon environmentally disruptive projects? In the hope of trying to ascertain why some projects are impeded and why some are not, we shall examine three case studies. We shall look first at the effort to industrialize the area around Lake Baikal. Next we shall examine struggles to reverse the flow of several of the Soviet Union's north-flowing rivers, and then we shall study the explosion at Chernobyl and the impact the environmental movement had on the introduction of nuclear energy to the Soviet Union and on the reaction of Soviet officials to the Chernobyl disaster. Finally, we shall examine how the process of *glasnost'* and the decision to allow the formation of nongovernmental groups has affected the environmental movement.

Polluting Lake Baikal

Lake Baikal, for most Soviet citizens, has been one of the most publicized cases of environmental abuse, and one about which there has been virtually a national consensus. With one or two notable exceptions, almost everyone in the Soviet Union seemed to oppose the introduction of industrial development, even in moderate amounts, to the shores of the lake. Yet industry had its way, and it continues to encroach on the lake despite a spirited effort to oppose all such construction. What is particularly instructive about Lake Baikal is how a national ad hoc group came into existence and attracted attention to its effort, and how, despite that effort, industry has continued to do what it set out to do with just a few financial penalties imposed now and then.

It is both Lake Baikal's bane and blessing that it is such a unique body of water. It is a bane because such a large, pure body of water made industrial officials thirst at the thought of putting all that "cheap" water to use. It is a blessing because once the word started to spread that the lake was to be turned into an industrial raw material, every Soviet citizen understood immediately what a sacrilege that would be and therefore readily agreed that economic exploitation would be a bad thing.

What made the lake so unusual? To begin with, it is probably the oldest lake on the planet. Moreover, it is just over 1.6 kilometers deep, which makes it nearly three times deeper than Crater Lake, the deepest lake in the United States. It is the largest body of fresh water in the world, the present mineral content of the water being 50 to 25 percent lower than most other nonsalt lakes. In other words, the water quality approaches that of distilled water. This is due in part to the nature of the rock in the watershed. The quality of the rock is such that it results in the release of little in the way of dissolved minerals or suspended matter into the inflow to the lake. Similarly, the cold temperatures hold down the evaporation, which in turn holds down the buildup of salts. In this unique environment it is not surprising to discover that the lake contains over 700 living organisms that are unique to it, including the world's only freshwater seals and the *golomyanka*—a transparent fish whose young are born alive.

The uniqueness of the lake, particularly the low mineral content of the water, made the lake a tempting target for the Soviet paper and cellulose industry. A paper (and especially a cellulose) plant requires large quantities of the high-grade water readily available in Lake Baikal but seldom elsewhere. To the extent that Lake Baikal water could be utilized, there would be no need to process it beforehand. That would reduce the direct cost to the factory. In addition, to the extent that the plant could also discharge and dilute its wastes into the vast depths of the lake, it would be spared the direct costs of building a water-treatment plant. The fact that the effluent was of poor quality did not initially deter those who proposed the plant's construction. To the planners, the availability of a cheap, pure source of water, as well as the ability to discharge waste into that water, was what was important. They were not overly concerned that this would impose on society (or at least on nature) the costs that would otherwise have to be carried by what ultimately became the Ministry of Pulp and Paper.

The pressure to avoid what should be individual plant-operating costs by shunting them all onto Soviet society as a whole has not inhibited Gosplan and ministry executives. Although it is hard to explain, these sentiments have been occasionally shared by scientists as well. Thus, P. L. Kapitsa, an academician and one of the Soviet Union's most respected scientists, who was not known for his antienvironmental stance, offered the following rationalization for using Lake Baikal as a recipient of effluent.

> The value of Lake Baikal does not lie simply in the abundance of clean water, but in the fact that it functions as a biological filter of tremendous capacity producing clean water. The water that enters the lake is much dirtier than the water that emerges. This purification is the result of biological processes in Baikal. . . . The industrial significance of Lake Baikal lies in the fact that it represents a huge purifier of water, and our concern should be directed toward preserving that capability. It is therefore wrong to say, "Don't touch Lake Baikal." The lake should be exploited, but so as not to disturb its life processes or interfere with its water-purifying properties. We must therefore know how and to what extent Baikal may be polluted so that it may continue to process dirty water and yield clean water.[6]

The plans of the Ministry of Pulp and Paper were discussed and publicized by limnologists and naturalists working with the lake. At first their warnings in 1960 were directed to residents in the immediate vicinity of the lake, but by 1962 articles had begun to appear in the national press. The uproar that followed was virtually unprecedented. Some of the Soviet Union's leading writers and scholars sent off a barrage of articles and letters, for the most part in uncoordinated fashion, complaining about the avariciousness of the Ministry of Pulp and Paper Industry. Leading Soviet newspapers, such as *Literaturnaia gazeta* and *Komsomol'skaia pravda,* as well as *Pravda* and *Izvestiia,* joined in the debate with articles every few weeks or so. The campaign was partially successful. Ultimately a high-level advisory commission was created to judge charges of malfeasance and a combined session of Gosplan, the Presidium of the Academy of Sciences, and the Committee on Science and Technology was convened to decide upon remedies.[7]

That this effort accomplished anything was most unusual given the preeminence of economic growth and industrial expansion. The Ministry of Pulp and Paper did not agree to cancel construction plans, however, nor did it agree to build what would have been an unusually expensive sewage pipe that would have extended almost 70 kilometers over mountainous terrain, at a cost of at least U.S. $42 million. This was deemed by the experts to be the only treatment method that would have ensured transfer of paper-plant wastes to regions outside the Lake Baikal watershed. Instead the Ministry of Pulp and Paper argued that it would be enough to build an advanced water-treatment facility, despite the fact that the residue from this treatment plant was then discharged into the lake.

I met with N. Chistiakov, the first-deputy minister of the pulp and paper industry, in late 1970, and he exhibited a keen awareness of just how sensitive the matter had become. It was also clear that he was not accustomed to having to defend what normally would have warranted him praise—that is, the increased production of a valuable and a much-needed product. He had readily available the day-to-day reports about the sewage effluent from the plant and even water samples. Unfortunately, although the reports did indicate an impressive level of treatment under normal conditions, when the plant malfunctioned, the effluent went straight into the lake, where it continued to have a deleterious impact.[8]

What has happened since the plant opened? Originally the State Institute for the Designs of the Pulp and Paper Industry Enterprises in Siberia and the Far East had forecast that only a 0.7-square kilometer area would be "stained." In fact, the actual zone of pollution is 60 square kilometers.[9] In the twenty years the plant has been operating, 1 million tons of mineral effluent foreign to the lake have been discharged, and as a consequence, some crustaceans in the region have become endangered.

Unfortunately, encroachment on the lake is no longer limited only to the water emissions of the pulp and paper industry plant. Reports have been published indicating that air pollution from the factory in the Baikal basin has also been causing problems.[10] The emissions of dust and gases have affected an area 2,000 square kilometers in size.[11] This has contributed to the withering of the region's forests.

Potentially even more threatening is that with the opening of the Baikal-Amur Mainline (BAM) Railroad, there was a plan to build the Kholodnaia Lead and Zinc Refinery on the northern shore of the lake.[12] This could have the most destructive impact of all. The prospect of depositing the profits from that ore was very tempting, especially if the refinery could be built in such a way that some of the emissions could be released without full treatment. Once again, the temptation was to avoid some of the private costs by transferring them to the environment at large, particularly since the area is normally so desolate.

As agitation over the fate of the lake continued to grow and, more important, as Mikhail Gorbachev began to encourage open debate about mistakes of the past, pressure to stop the abuse of the lake mounted. Finally, in May 1987, Gosplan announced that no new factories would be built in the area and the Council of Ministers fired and reprimanded several senior officials in the Ministry of Timber, Pulp and Paper and Wood Processing Industry for allowing the pollution to continue. State authorities also agreed to the closing of a yeast factory attached to the pulp operation, a factory that had been particularly hard on the lake. In a more significant move, they decreed that the pulp plant at Baikalsk, on the southern shore of the lake, would be converted into a furniture factory.[13] There was a catch, however: The conversion would take place in 1992. In the interim, the authorities decided, they would build a 65-kilometer-long pipeline in order to divert the effluent from the lake to the Irkut River. The cost would be about $150 million, considerably higher than the original proposal. But as the critics quickly noted, all of this seemed like a strange way to solve a problem. Why spend so much on a pipeline that would be used for such a short period of time (assuming indeed it would even be completed in five years)? Equally strange, even if the planning authorities agreed that the pulp plant was a menace to the lake and to close it down after the pipeline was built, why wait five years? Why not close it down immediately? The questions and lack of sensible answers (by mid-1988, the planners had changed their minds once again and called off the diversion-canal project) suggested that the pollution of Lake Baikal was still a long way from being eliminated.

What are the lessons of Lake Baikal? The first lesson is that the more unusual the target was, the easier it was to mobilize public support even in a country like the Soviet Union, where until very recently the state controlled the public media. But public awareness is not the same as public effectiveness. The fact remains that despite reports to the contrary, the waters of Lake Baikal continue to deteriorate. Moreover, the threat comes not only from what were intended to be cellulose plants (ironically, the plants have been producing ordinary paper and thus could be located near any body of water in the world[14]) but also from the opening up of the northern shore of the lake to industrial development. Conceivably, without all the protests there would be an even greater assault on the lake. But unfortunately a lake like Lake Baikal lends itself to small encroachments, each one a potential battleground. There will probably be more such encroachments in the future.[15] But whatever the future, the fact remains that unless the existing paper plants and the very expensive BAM Railroad are closed down or relocated, it will be industry, not the lake, that has been the winner.

Redirecting the Rivers

From an environmentalist's point of view, the battle to prevent the rerouting of several of the country's major rivers has had a more satisfactory outcome, at least for the near term. But it should be pointed out that the dream of rerouting north-flowing rivers, such as the Vychegda and the Pechora in the northwest of the country and the Ob and the Yenesei in Siberia, is not something unique to the present-day Communist leadership. Ambitious efforts to reroute rivers flowing into the Arctic Ocean were advanced as early as 1784 for the Pechora and 1880 for the Ob and the Yenesei. Reversing the flow of rivers would compensate for nature's oversight. The Arctic Ocean had more than enough water, whereas Central Asia had a longer growing season than more northerly regions but was parched. With more water, Central Asia would be able to increase the irrigation of its fields and thus the size of its harvests. Financially this was attractive. Even though such a project would be very expensive, the extra water would be used for cotton and other valuable crops that the Soviet Union badly needed domestically and for export.

This kind of project, however, would necessitate the construction of massive dams, reservoirs, and canals. In effect, the reservoirs would have to be built high enough so that the water could flow over the Continental

Divide and through tunnels that might have to be drilled through the barriers. In some versions of the plan, there would have to be a canal almost 1,500 kilometers long and a chain of twelve pumping stations. There were at least two variants of the plan to reverse the rivers: One would put more water into the Volga to prevent the Caspian Sea from shrinking further, and the other would lead to water being diverted to the Aral Sea, which was slowly turning into a salt marsh. The Syr Darya and the Amu Darya rivers, the main source of the Aral supply, were being used more and more for irrigation. The same thing was happening to the Volga waters, which in an era of less irrigation, had flowed almost entirely to the Caspian. The existing irrigation was too profitable, at least at the lower (nonexistent) price charged for the river waters. As a result, government authorities in Central Asia kept demanding additional water in order to expand their fields even more. As we have seen in Arizona and southern California, the more you have, particularly if the water appears to be cheap, the more you want.

After the Revolution, there was renewed interest in river reversal in the Soviet Union. The Soviets have been particularly attracted to massive water projects. They tend to see such activities as a way of challenging nature and take pleasure in devoting billions of rubles to such efforts. This includes irrigation and drainage projects as well as river reversal. Numerous variants of river reversal have been offered up from time to time, and periodically segments of the various plans would work their way into one version or another of the Five Year Plans. Occasionally a segment would actually be built, but the overall cost (which some critics estimated to be as high as 20 billion rubles) proved to be a deterrent.

In addition, a growing number of geographers and ecologists began to express concern about the environmental impact of such projects.[16] For example, the flooding of fields that would result from the creation of the large reservoirs became an issue. Admittedly, new fields would be added in the south, but in the process, significant acreage would be lost in the north.[17] This acreage included not only land for agriculture but also land that was located in regions with potential and sometimes actual petroleum deposits. There was also uncertainty about the potential climatic effects of a project of this magnitude. For example, the new large bodies of water that would have been created could affect rain patterns.[18] Similarly, there was concern that the diversion of all that fresh water would increase the salinity of the Arctic Ocean, and more melting and flooding would be the result.[19] Simultaneously, others argued that the draining off of waters to the south from the Arctic would result in a colder Arctic and increase the freezing. No one could agree just what set of changes would prevail, but everyone admitted that it was unlikely that one set of climatic changes would just offset the other.

Those in the north were particularly upset by the prospect that certain very old Russian villages would be flooded. These villages—which had been populated, according to some, since the twelfth century—contained rare examples of old churches and peasant homes.[20] In the end, the destruction of these villages turned out to be a particularly sensitive issue among those Russian nationalist groups, including the right-wing group Pamiat', that have never forgiven Soviet leaders for the past destruction of equally historic buildings. This earlier onslaught was a by-product of the attack on religion and things old, peasant-oriented, and unmodern. Nor were these critics mollified by the thought that the chief beneficiaries of such a reorganization of nature would be the inhabitants of Central Asia, few of whom were Russian, many of whom were Muslim, and most of whom were treated with contempt because they already had an advantage over those in more northern latitudes. There was (and is) deep resentment about the Central Asians, who dominate the peasant markets in the north with their out-of-season, and what always seem to be vastly overpriced, fruits and vegetables. To most Slavic peoples in the north, the southern Uzbeks and their neighbors already had an unfair advantage, so why should they be helped any more?

As might be expected, the Central Asians, particularly the Uzbeks, took a very different view of this matter. As they saw it, the diversion of the waters of the Syr Darya and the Amu Darya for cotton irrigation and the consequent drying out of the Aral Sea were not decisions the Uzbek people would have taken on their own but were actions forced on them from Moscow. Moscow wanted cotton, and the Uzbeks were forced to sacrifice everything else to grow it. As R. N. Nishanov, the first-secretary of the Uzbek Communist party, put it at the 19th Communist Party Conference, the result was a "monoculture policy" that has "had the most serious consequences in the economy and in the environment alike."[21] By this he alluded to the excessive use of pesticides and the salinization of the soil that resulted from excessive cultivation and poor irrigation precedures. No wonder the Uzbeks resent those Russian nationalists who were protesting the diversion of their waters to the south. As Nishanov reminded delegates to the Party conference, "We are clothing the entire country," since 90 percent of the cotton grown in Uzbekistan is sent to the European part of the country or is exported.[22]

The issue seemed to come to a head after the series of poor grain harvests in 1979 and the early 1980s. To make up for the losses, substantial sums of hard currency (as much as $10 billion annually) had to be set aside for food imports. Anything that could increase domestic harvests, whether of grain or cotton (which was exportable), would pay for itself in savings and convertible currency. Those in favor of the river-diversion scheme found themselves with new and powerful allies. In 1984, at a plenum of the Central Committee of the Communist party, a decision was made to begin the first stage of supplementing the Volga River with waters from the central part of the country.[23]

Although not included in the 1984 decision, the Uzbeks continued their efforts to expand the reclamation program to include the Siberian rivers. Sharaf Rashidov, the onetime head of the Uzbek Communist party, lobbied intensively for this. He almost succeeded in 1981 at the 26th Communist Party Congress, where he sought to have preparatory work on the project included in the Eleventh Five Year Plan (1981–1985). He failed, however, and the project was not made part of the plan.

On January 9, 1985, however, an article in the official newspaper of Uzbekistan reported that work on the more than 2,000-kilometer project had finally been approved and was beginning.[24] A work crew from Uzbekistan was sent to the Tumin oblast in the north to begin work on the construction of the support facilities for the work crews that were to be sent to the construction site itself.[25] This initial report was confirmed by an article in *Sovetskaia Kirghiziia,* the official paper of the Kirghiz Republic, and then by an official statement by Nikolai F. Vasilev, the minister of land reclamation and water resources, at a Moscow press conference on June 5, 1985.[26]

But something unexpected happened on the way to the construction site. When the draft guidelines of the Twelfth Five Year Plan were published, there was no mention of any project to divert the Siberian rivers.[27] It was also omitted from a discussion of possible additions to the draft held by a special session of the Supreme Soviet.[28]

The reasons for the omission have not been published. It would seem, however, that the failure of the Central Asians to win support for their project was very much linked to the fate of the project's major proponent, Rashidov. It cannot be mere coincidence that in late 1985 and early 1986, Rashidov, who had died in the interim, was the subject of a scathing attack for his corruption, nepotism, and inept leadership. With the chief patron of the project thoroughly discredited, the nationalist fervor of the Slavs, along with the environmentalists and the Soviet counterpart of the Gramm-Rudman philosophy, prevailed, and the project was scrapped.

That left the plan to supplement the Volga River. That idea did make it into the draft of the Twelfth Five Year Plan and in a short time received the full brunt of the attack of some of the Soviet Union's most popular Russian scientists, writers, and cultural figures. Appropriately enough, their arguments dominated the pages of *Sovetskaia Rossiia,* the official paper of the Russian Republic.[29] All the familiar arguments of cost, cultural genocide, and ecological disruption were paraded once again. As the opponents put it:

> It would be extremely costly—the history of world construction has never seen its equal. . . . The project planners do not know what the effect will be of reducing the flow of fresh water to the Arctic Ocean—the "generator" of weather for not only the northern hemisphere. . . . The project makes no provision whatever for the preservation of historical and cultural monuments in the original part of Russia, where the inspired folk genius has been working for a whole millennium and where world spiritual values have been created.[30]

These emotional published protests were supplemented by public meetings and discussions where, according to one eyewitness, the Russian nationalists in the crowd came close to violence as they protested what they saw as a trampling of their cultural heritage.

Not surprisingly, subsequent drafts of the Five Year Plan omitted reference to any form of river reversal. The decision not to reroute was taken at the party congress in February 1986 and confirmed at a news conference by Leonard Vid, a deputy chairman of Gosplan.[31] Finally, at one of its August 1986 meetings, the Politburo voted to cancel all rerouting plans.

As in the case of Lake Baikal, the campaign against the changes was led by an ad hoc coalition of scientists and nature lovers, especially writers. Unlike the opponents of construction around the shores of Lake Baikal, however, the opponents of river reversal have been successful, at least for now. We can only guess why those opposed to the river project prevailed, while those intent on protecting Lake Baikal were much less successful. In the case of Lake Baikal, the cellulose projects were put forward as important for military purposes. Additionally, the cost of the project was relatively limited and there did seem to be scientific remedies for treating the effluent of the plant. In contrast, the river-reversal project, even if it had worked as promised, would have been enormously expensive. Also, opponents of the river plan were probably able to point to what happened at Lake Baikal as an example of where engineers had been shown to be wrong, with nature being the loser. But probably the most telling factor was that the river project would have imposed enormous costs on the Soviet Union at a time when the new Soviet leadership under Mikhail Gorbachev and Nikolai Ryzhkov had been trying valiantly to marshal its resources for economic reform and reduce the publicly acknowledged budget deficits. A massive drain of this magnitude would have made a difficult task all the more problematic. If costs were not a great enough factor, the appeal to raw nationalism and subtle racism was. Those appeals were all but impossible to ignore, especially when the strongest proponent for the scheme had died and was in national disgrace.

The Nuclear Accident at Chernobyl

The environmental disaster at Chernobyl highlights the inadequacies of the Soviet environmental movement. That is not to suggest that nuclear energy in other countries of the world, including the United States and the Federal Republic of Germany, has always been handled properly. As the accident at Three Mile Island indicated, the construction and operation of nuclear-energy plants in the noncommunist world have also had problems. Moreover, once that accident occurred, it was not handled in an ideal way. Neither the operating personnel at Three Mile Island nor the plant's management were properly prepared for such an emergency.

But as serious as the problems have been in the West, the situation in the Soviet Union has been even more fraught with danger, largely due to the absence of a strong environmental movement. Although the environmentalists in the West often seem hyperactive in their efforts to restrict or ban nuclear energy, their initiatives have nonetheless served to pressure government regulators and the nuclear-power utilities into instituting more controls than they would have chosen on their own. Just as the environmentalists tend to be overcautious and underconfident, so the nuclear industry officials tend to be undercautious and overconfident. The consequence of this pressure and counterpressure is that nuclear energy in the West tends to be more costly but also subject to more safety precautions.

The first nuclear-energy facility in the Soviet Union and in the world was built in Obninsk, in 1954. It was not until the 1970s, however, that Soviet authorities decided to increase their reliance on nuclear power. By then the Soviets had come to appreciate how important their finite supplies of petroleum were, and how much more valuable they could be if set aside for export, rather than used domestically for fuel and electrical-generating plants. Gradually the Soviets adopted a policy that future electrical-generating plants west of the Urals would be fueled with nuclear energy. This reflected not only the need to set aside resources for export but also the fact that some of the best fossil-fuel deposits in the western part of the country had been depleted. If not for nuclear energy, the growing percentage of oil, gas, and coal that would be needed for conventional electrical-generating plants would have to be transported from Siberia, and the fuel used in this process would cut into the amount available for export even more.

The goals for Soviet nuclear energy were ambitious. Whereas nuclear energy accounted for 2 percent of all electrical output in 1975, it was planned to expand that to 14 percent by 1985.[32] In fact, because of production problems at Atommash, a plant designed specifically to mass-produce reactors, the plan was underfulfilled. By the end of 1985, there were forty reactors in operation, producing 170 billion kilowatts of power, which represented 10.8 percent of the Soviet Union's total electrical-generating capacity.[33] At the same time in some parts of the country, the share of nuclear energy was considerably higher. Thus in the Ukraine, nuclear energy accounted for 60 percent of all electricity generated.[34]

For Western observers, the most striking aspect of Soviet nuclear policy was that the obstacle to increased utilization of nuclear energy was the inability to produce more reactors, not environmental protests and bureaucratic red tape that accompany any nuclear proposal in most of the rest of the world. As we have seen, until *glasnost'*, there was no such thing as an independent environmental movement in the Soviet Union. That does not mean that the Soviet people were not concerned about the safety of nuclear energy. There were periodic acknowledgments that some people were worried that nuclear energy could have a serious impact on health. Thus Soviet newspapers published an occasional statement of concern as well as letters from worried readers asking about nuclear energy.[35] For example, on December 19, 1968, the labor newspaper, *Trud,* published the following letter from one of its readers: "I live in Moscow not far from the Institute of Atomic Energy. They say that here there is a high level of radioactivity. This may explain why I am frequently sick. The radiation may be weakening my organisms. Tell me, are we threatened by radiation?"[36] Without hesitation the editors of *Trud* asserted that there was nothing to fear but rumor itself. Although they acknowledged that people who worked and lived nearby were sometimes worried about the hazards of atomic-power plants, they insisted there was no cause for concern. As proof, the newspaper cited the large number of workers of the Institute of Atomic Energy who also lived in the immediate vicinity of the institute. In addition, water wastes from Soviet atomic plants were carefully treated, and tall stacks were used to disperse airborne aerosols.

However, such worries were not eliminated. For instance, sometime in 1963, despite the fact that it was claimed officially that the radioactivity in Moscow did not exceed the maximum permissible norms, there were rumors that radioactivity was causing a health problem in the capital. Reportedly because of lax procedures in handling radioactive materials, there was a serious outbreak of leukemia in various parts of Moscow. In some neighborhoods, the disease was said to have reached near-epidemic proportions.

To the extent that there was debate about nuclear safety, it usually occurred within scientific circles. This was not considered something the general public should concern itself with. This Big Brother attitude was reflected in a fascinating interview with Ivan Y. Yemelyanov, the deputy director of the Institute of Power Engineering. In an interview published in the official Italian Communist newspaper, *L'Unita,* on May 27, 1986, Yemelyanov was asked whether it was "helpful, even necessary to involve people, the public, more in the question of nuclear energy utilization for peaceful purposes." Yemelyanov's answer was "immediate and clear cut": "I am not convinced that scientific progress can be influenced by people's opinions. It is an objective process that proceeds according to its own rules."[37]

Yemelyanov went on to question the value of public debate. "Frankly, I do not know about the effectiveness of certain forms of public discussion that take place in your country. It is not true that there is no debate in our country. It does exist and is conducted in an organized manner—in fact, in a more organized manner than in your country."

Italian Interviewer: "I would not say so. When I visited Borodyanskiy Raion a few days ago, I asked the Chernobyl party First Secretary whether there had been any consultations with local bodies when it was decided to construct the power station. Anatoliy Amelkin replied simply as follows: 'Such matters are decided by Gosplan.'"

Yemelyanov: "Public opinion operates in our country too—increasingly so of late since Gorbachev placed the emphasis on the 'human factor.' There is a great deal of discussion of these matters especially in specialized circles. In my institute there has been an endless series of scientific discussions in which all aspects of safety at power stations have been broached, not to mention the Academy of Sciences meetings, at which differing stances have competed, sometimes very strongly."

Italian Interviewer: "That is exactly what I was saying. It is a discussion among specialists. But is that enough?"

Yemelyanov: "Of course not the entire population takes part, but there is state control—and how!"

Italian Interviewer: "The classic question of the controller controlled."

Yemelyanov: "We do not see it that way. In fact three years ago we formed the State Committee for the Supervision of Safe Working Practices in the Atomic Power Industry. It has very broad powers to take action."[38]

Of course, this arrogant attitude about the views of the general public is not something unique to Soviet authorities and scientists. Specialists in the West frequently tend to respond the same way. However, given the pluralistic nature of Western societies, they find themselves forced to defend themselves in public and in government forums. Until Chernobyl, Soviet officials were generally spared that inconvenience. As a consequence, they tended to be unusually confident about their abilities and the safety of their reactors. Thus, as late as February 1986, Dr. Leonid Il'in, the Soviet chief specialist on the medical effects of nuclear radiation, asserted that concern about radioactivity is "understandable, but unwarranted." In his view, nuclear energy was "minimally dangerous both to nature and people's health."[39] In the same spirit, Soviet authorities concluded that they could safely build nuclear facilities intended for district heating within two to three kilometers from the center of population in Soviet cities.[40]

Such confidence explains why the Soviets decided it was unnecessary to build containment vessels around their reactors. There was no need to. That also explains their smug reaction, at least initially, to what happened at Three Mile Island. Anatoly Alexandrov, then president of the Soviet Academy of Sciences, said that in the Soviet Union, unlike the United States, nuclear-generating facilities "can be built in the middle of residential areas, because they are absolutely safe." Presumably Soviet scientists would not build nuclear-energy plants if they were not safe. In Alexandrov's mind, it was the nuclear protests that were suspect. As he saw it, "the actual reason behind the whole fuss over nuclear construction in the United States has nothing to do with safety. The real reason is that the development of large nuclear power plants could endanger the profits of the fuel-producing monopolies."[41] Amazingly enough, however, that same convoluted thinking reemerged to explain Western publicity about Chernobyl. B. Alekseyev wrote in an article in *Pravda:*

> Those who are opposed to the development of nuclear power at all also have an interest in exaggerating the scale of the Chernobyl Atomic Energy Station accident and its consequences. This means first and foremost, the mighty oil monopolies, which hope that frightened Americans will protest against power stations instead which use oil and gas, and which will enable these monopolies to compensate for their major losses because of the falling oil prices.[42]

What makes this so disturbing is that Soviet workmanship on its nuclear facilities is no better than that in the West, and there is good reason to believe it may frequently be much worse. The Soviets repeatedly complain about poor workmanship.[43] Almost every installation has been criticized at one time or another. The complaints about Balakovo were particularly pointed. "We examined your pipes with ultrasound—complete junk. There are even defects that can be seen with a naked eye."[44] Most embarrassing of all, two articles appeared in the Soviet press in early 1986 complaining about poor workmanship at Chernobyl.[45] Both articles reported that faulty work procedures and supply shortages had plagued construction from the beginning. To make up for the defects of the first reactor built, parts were cannibalized from the construction work on the second reactor. Reactor Two in turn was supplied with parts from Reactor Three and so on to Reactors Five and Six, which were under construction at the time of the explosion. It is arguable that if Soviet authorities had been subject to greater public pressure, they might have been forced to provide better safety controls. It was only after Three Mile Island that the Soviets decided it was necessary to build containment vessels for any nuclear facilities ordered after 1979.

Yet until there is a genuinely independent environmental movement in the Soviet Union, there is still reason to question whether the Soviets have really learned the lessons of Chernobyl. For example, the Soviet news agency, TASS, initially reported that despite the explosion at Chernobyl, the nuclear-energy-construction program in the Soviet Union would proceed as planned. As Aleksei Makukhin, the first-deputy minister for power and electrification of the USSR, put it, "Individual hitches related to mastering the energy of the atom do not mean that we need to renounce the progressive direction of power engineering that people need so much."[46]

However, as the Soviet people became aware of the enormity of what had happened, public pressure increased. Responding to that pressure, state authorities have become more cautious, although it sometimes seems they are doing so against their better judgment. Thus, state energy officials have announced cessation of work on the Krasnodar, Minsk, Odessa, Armenia, Azerbaidzhan, Ignalina, Vitebsk, and Chigirin nuclear-energy plants.[47]

There is strong evidence to indicate, however, that the energy officials have continued to press for the construction of more nuclear-energy facilities. They argued that if the United States could rely on nuclear energy, then there was no reason why the Soviets could not do the same thing.[48] Indeed, the same Soviet officials insisted that the general public was unable to comprehend anything as complicated as nuclear energy, and that because of the need to conserve fossil fuels, the construction of nuclear-energy plants had to continue.[49]

Despite Chernobyl, old attitudes die hard. Moreover, Soviet authorities find themselves beset with pressures that sometimes appear to be more important than the release of radioactivity. For example, defending the failure to notify the world and the Soviet people for almost three full days after the Chernobyl explosion, Ivan Yemelyanov argued that "one of the factors taken into account was the need not to create a tide of panic that could have prompted even more consequences. An option was made for selective information. In the areas near the power station, where there was a specific danger, people were given instructions as soon as possible. But we could not cause terror in Kiev."[50]

Conclusions

What lessons can we draw from these case studies? Environmentalism in the Soviet Union has come a long way from the pre-Gorbachev days, when it was against the law to form any organization that was truly independent of the government. Ad hoc groups coalesced around specific causes such as Lake Baikal, but always with uncertain prospects for success. The chances for success were greatest when the projects being considered endangered some truly historic or revered resource. Equally important, environmentalists had to be able to show that their efforts would not jeopardize the overall economic growth of the country and in fact might actually help it. The latter was generally not done as a formal calculation, but in effect opponents of a project had to demonstrate that costs far outweighed the benefits. The enormous economic cost involved certainly helped to convince Soviet leaders to cancel or at least postpone the rerouting of their rivers. By the same token, Soviet authorities were too heavily dependent on nuclear energy, so that the environmental risks and costs associated with a nuclear-energy project have not always been considered important enough to warrant the automatic closing down of the nuclear reactors, even though they were similar in design to the one that exploded at Chernobyl. It took several months before the Soviets would even acknowledge that it was necessary to make additional safety checks on one-half of those plants.

This hesitancy to act, not to mention the secrecy and distortion about so much that happened at Chernobyl, in some ways has probably done more for the cause of environmentalism in the Soviet Union than has any other single incident. As in the West, it took an environmental catastrophe like Chernobyl to alert the public to just how serious the problem could be and to the fact that their government could not be trusted to tell them the truth. In the case of the Soviet Union, the belated awareness of the deception about the nature of the country's environmental difficulties has helped to fuel the general skepticism about public trust and the extent of secrecy there.

Since environmentalists tend by nature to be more skeptical at an earlier stage than the general public, and since they had begun to organize, even if informally, before the state decided to allow the formal organization of such groups, it was only natural that others turned to these environmental groups when there were issues of concern that went beyond purely environmental problems. This explains why, in almost every one of the non-Russian Soviet republics, environmental groups have gone on to pressure for nationalist and local issues, as in Armenia and the Baltic states.

It would be misleading to suggest that in the aftermath of Chernobyl, Soviet pluralism has become so well established that environmentalists can prevail over Gosplan planners and enterprise managers. As our three case studies showed, that is still not the case, even when it comes to something as revered as Lake Baikal. Yet there is no doubt that there is a new mood in the Soviet Union, one that is more critical and less accepting, one that should strengthen the environmental effort in the future. In the words of one Soviet critic, "The trouble is not that we were lied to. The trouble is that we believed. . . . Because the less people believe—the less they are lied to."[51] Presumably there should be less lying in the future.

Notes

1. Barry Commoner, *The Closing Circle* (New York: Alfred Knopf, 1971), pp. 274-79.
2. I. Petrianov-Sokolov, *Literaturnaia gazeta,* November 24, 1971, p. 13.
3. *Ekonomicheskaia gazeta,* no. 4 (January 1967), p. 38.
4. *Izvestiia,* February 24, 1986, p. 6.
5. *Foreign Broadcast Information Service* [hereafter *FBIS*], April 10, 1986, p. R2 (from Moscow Radio-Television Service, April 6, 1986).
6. Cited in Philip R. Pryde, "The Decade of the Environment in the USSR," *Science* 220, no. 4594 (April 15, 1983), p. 275.
7. Thane Gustafson, "The New Soviet Environmental Program: Do the Soviets Really Mean Business?" *Public Policy* 26, no. 3 (Summer 1978), p. 474.
8. Peter Nijhoff, "Lake Baikal Dangered by Polluters," *Environmental Conservation* 6, no. 2 (Summer 1979), p. 114; see also *Pravda,* January 11, 1986, p. 3.
9. *Izvestiia,* February 17, 1986, p. 3.
10. *Ekonomicheskaia gazeta,* no. 49 (December 1976), p. 13; *Current Digest of the Soviet Press,* September 10, 1980, p. 9.
11. *Izvestiia,* February 17, 1986, p. 3.
12. *Pravda,* January 12, 1986, p. 3.
13. *Moscow News,* no. 25 (1987), p. 8.
14. *Izvestiia,* November 3, 1985, p. 3.
15. Ibid., p. 3; *Pravda,* January 12, 1986, p. 3.
16. *Current Digest of the Soviet Press,* September 26, 1984, p. 8; also March 14, 1984, p. 17.
17. *Literaturnaia gazeta,* October 24, 1984, p. 11.
18. *Izvestiia,* October 20, 1984, p. 2.
19. *Kazakh Edebieti,* January 28, 1983; *Radio Free Europe/Radio Liberty,* RL 196/83 (March 17, 1983).
20. *FBIS,* March 14, 1986, p. R2, from Moscow television, March 13, 1986.
21. *Pravda,* July 11, 1988, p. 9.
22. *Zvezda vostoka,* no. 6 (1987), p. 13-17.
23. *Soviet Panorama,* October 25, 1984.
24. *New York Times,* June 6, 1985, p. A6.
25. *Radio Free Europe/Radio Liberty,* RL 194/85 (June 7, 1985).
26. *Sovetskaia Kirgiziia,* April 5, 1985, p. 2; also *Radio Free Europe/Radio Liberty,* RL 194/85 (June 7, 1985).
27. *Pravda,* November 9, 1985.
28. *Pravda,* November 27, 1985; *Radio Free Europe/Radio Liberty,* RL 420/85 (December 13, 1985).
29. *Sovetskaia Rossiia,* December 20, 1985, and January 3, 1986, p. 3.

30. *Sovetskaia Rossiia,* January 3, 1986, p. 3.
31. *New York Times,* March 5, 1986, p. A13.
32. Office of Technology Assessment, Congress of the United States, *Technology and Soviet Energy Availability* (Washington, D.C.: Government Printing Office, November 1981), pp. 114, 120.
33. *Zaria vostoka,* February 18, 1986, p. 3.
34. *Radio Free Europe/Radio Liberty,* RL 405/85 (December 4, 1985).
35. *Zaria vostoka,* February 18, 1986, p. 3.
36. *Trud,* December 19, 1968, p. 4.
37. *FBIS,* June 5, 1986, p. R4.
38. Ibid., p. R5.
39. *Pravda,* February 20, 1986, p. 3.
40. *Soviet Life,* November 1981, p. 7; also *L'Unita,* May 27, 1986, p. 4.
41. *Soviet News,* May 15, 1979, p. 151.
42. *Pravda,* May 21, 1986, p. 4.
43. *Pravda,* February 26, 1982, p. 1, and February 24, 1985, p. 3; *FBIS,* February 14, 1986, p. 55; *Izvestiia,* July 21, 1984, p. 2; *Radio Free Europe/Radio Liberty,* RL 194/86 (May 15, 1986).
44. *Sovetskaia Rossiia,* May 30, 1982; *Radio Free Europe/Radio Liberty,* RL 468/82 (November 22, 1982).
45. *Literaturnaia Ukraina,* March 27, 1986; *FBIS,* May 6, 1986, p. S1; *Pravda Ukrainy,* March 18, 1986; *FBIS,* May 1, 1986, p. R4.
46. *FBIS,* May 30, 1986, p. U4, from TASS.
47. *New York Times,* January 28, 1988, p. 1; *Boston Globe,* December 24, 1988, p. 3.
48. *Moscow News,* no. 29 (1988), p. 10.
49. Bohdan Nahaylo, "Mounting Opposition in the Ukraine to Nuclear Energy Program," *Radio Liberty Research Bulletin,* RL 8/3472 (February 24, 1988), pp. 11, 14.
50. *L'Unita,* May 27, 1986.
51. Leonid Likhodeyev, *Moscow News,* no. 1 (1989), p. 5.

CHAPTER 4

Atomic Culture in the USSR: Before and After Chernobyl

Paul R. Josephson

The Chernobyl disaster brought into sharp relief the economic and safety problems that plague the Soviet nuclear-energy industry. Years of operating experience (with no major accidents) with reactors of large parameters located near large cities had convinced the public, scientists, and policymakers alike that any remaining technological, economic, or safety obstacles would soon succumb to the advantages of the Soviet system, its ideology, science, and planning. In fact, however, since the initial stages of attempts to utilize the energy of the atom for peaceful purposes in the late 1940s, a certain technological arrogance permeated the burgeoning nuclear-power industry and discouraged a more safety-conscious attitude on the part of engineers. The result has been the creation of a huge nuclear-power establishment with substantial institutional and technological momentum and little external control. This chapter examines the cultural, political, and economic context for nuclear power in the USSR from 1945 to the present, focusing primarily on the role of the scientific community in the development of the nuclear-power industry. It addresses the development of "atomic culture" and how this culture contributed to the problems facing the nuclear-energy industry in the 1980s, concluding with a brief discussion of the historical roots of the Chernobyl disaster and the state of nuclear-power engineering in the USSR in the post-Chernobyl period.

Atomic Culture in the Soviet Union

The 1920s are often seen as the golden age of Soviet society, a time of utopian and constructivist visions for the advent of communism. Many people anticipated the rapid construction of a "new Soviet man" based on the advantages of Soviet-style socialism, on large-scale, industrial mass production, and on the achievements of science and technology. Although obscured by other events of the late Stalin years, the post–World War II period shared many of these constructivist visions. In spite of tremendous obstacles encountered by the Soviet Union in rebuilding an economy and a population devastated by war, national achievements, especially in the area of science and technology, contributed to a rebirth of utopian views. A "cult of science," founded upon successes in nuclear physics and rocketry, stood at the center of these new visions. At this time, electrification based on the energy of the atom gave ideologues and scientists alike hope that communism would be achieved within their lifetimes.

Atomic power was incorporated into Soviet visions for the construction of communism in two stages. The first stage, from the late 1940s through the mid-1950s, involved the development of the social environment for the advance of nuclear energy in the USSR. In the immediate postwar years, in the face of significant technical problems and public concern over nuclear weapons and the threat of war with the West, Soviet physicists began to develop an "atomic culture" in the USSR. With the help of ideologues and science writers, they described in grandiose terms the potential for the application of nuclear energy throughout the economy. Acknowledging the need to build bombs because of "hostile capitalist encirclement" and "war mongering," they nonetheless stressed the peaceful uses to which this new energy would be put. Atomic culture was based on both reasonable and somewhat far-fetched visions of nuclear energy's potential. These ranged from use of radioisotopes in industry, agriculture, medicine, and biology to nuclear-powered automobiles, locomotives, airplanes, and rockets. All these visions were based on the assumption that atomic energy would accelerate the construction of communism. The visions were more utopian than scientific, helping to create an environment where technological arrogance and a false sense of the safety of nuclear power could thrive.

During the second stage, from the mid-1950s until the early 1970s, nuclear scientists and engineers struggled to put nuclear power on the political agenda and to overcome opposition to it that arose because of safety and economic reasons. But in the postwar environment of a "cult of science," the prestige, power, and influence of Soviet scientists in creating science policy grew manyfold. Policymakers and scientists alike came to see in such large-scale technologies as reactors the solution to the social and economic problems facing the USSR. This attitude toward technology, especially a belief in the infallibility of large-scale technologies, led to the development of a nuclear-energy industry based on the premature mass production of reactor vessels and components, and on economic rather than safety criteria as a basis for decisionmaking. Engineers were soon lulled into believing that reactors were safe enough to build in massive blocks near cities without full-scale containment. Ultimately, these utopian visions of atomic culture would haunt the nuclear-power industry at Chernobyl.

According to the prevailing ideology, use of atomic energy would exacerbate the contradictions inherent in the capitalist system; it would lead to wonderful, if not wondrous, applications in the economy and agriculture; it would be safe and economically viable, the danger of the bomb notwithstanding;[1] and it would serve military interests. Under socialism, atomic power was said to make possible the unprecedented growth of the productive forces and the control of man over the forces of nature,[2] including, for example, the use of peaceful nuclear explosions to alter the climate, create a "winter sun," melt the arctic snow, and turn deserts into lush gardens.[3] Soon, philosophers joined scientists in stressing the harmonious fit between nuclear power and Soviet ideology. The starting point for this assertion often included the trite rediscovery of Lenin's famous slogan "Communism equals Soviet power plus electrification of the entire country." More than ever before, increased capacity and production of electrical energy from gigantic, centralized grids were seen as vital to postwar economic and social programs.[4] The fact that communism and atomic energy were meant for each other was considered at least as important as practical need in the period of cultural preparation for atomic energy.

Most Soviet writers also drew the logical, if required, conclusion that "in the USSR Soviet scholars, of course, utilize all possibilities in order to place atomic energy in the service of socialist construction.[5] This led to an analysis of the potential of atomic energy from within the framework of "proletarian science": "The problem of atomic energy shows again clearly that there is no science 'in general,' pure, classless science. Science in the hands of a class which possesses it, is placed in the service of that class. In the hands of American imperialists, atomic energy is transformed into an instrument of inhuman destruction of the world's inhabitants."[6] In the USSR, in contrast, atomic energy would raise the productivity of labor, speed up technological progress, and improve the general welfare.[7]

By the late 1950s, these arguments took the standardized form that under socialism, as opposed to capitalism, energy research and development (R and D) serves the masses, not corporate monopolies, is for peaceful, not military purposes, and is thus safer than in the West and need not have the regulation required there. In fact, only under socialism was the rapid commercialization of atomic energy possible.[8] The notion that civilization was not ready for peaceful uses of nuclear power also had to be abandoned: In the socialist USSR, where "the progress of science and technology is tied to the building of communism . . . atomic energy in its turn opens new, grandiose perspectives in the matter of the creation of the material-technological basis of communism."[9] Finally, in the technological sphere, because of the unity between theory and practice in the USSR, it was indeed possible to build larger and larger reactors and to conduct tests on them, rather than to waste time in laboratory experiments.[10] Engineers claimed that this unique approach to reactor construction, the "prototype approach," set the USSR apart from the West.[11]

In his book on American culture at the dawn of the atomic age, Paul Boyer named one chapter "Anodyne to Terror: Fantasies of a Techno-Atomic Utopia" and discussed the attempts to recast atomic power in the United States in terms of its potential benefits for society.[12] In the USSR, as part of the cultural preparation for atomic energy, Soviet scientists presented similar utopian visions. In an effort to make atomic energy more palatable to a Soviet population with strong and relatively fresh memories of the destruction of World War II, popularizers of atomic energy stressed its potential peaceful applications in industry and agriculture and developed a peculiar iconography of the constructive potential of atomic energy.[13]

Although biological and medical uses stood at the forefront of Soviet visions of the future, no branch of the economy escaped atomic energy's magic wand of "modern alchemy." There were wide applications in agriculture, where the use of isotopes of phosphorus and carbon facilitated the study of plant physiology—the process of photosynthesis, the action of fertilizers, the role of viruses and bacteria, and so on. The author of one article also suggested the use of radioactive tracers for the study of bee husbandry and fishes, never considering the potential for radioactivity to move up the food chain into humans.[14] Others spoke with pride about the use of low-level radiation to prolong the shelf life of meat and the treatment of potatoes and other agricultural products,[15] a practice approved by the U.S. Food and Drug Administration in the mid-1980s but not in use because of widespread consumer opposition. In mining and metallurgy, similarly, Soviet engineers spoke hopefully about applications of gamma curretage to help in mineral prospecting, oil surveying, and coal monitoring and weighing, with especially great expectations for the Sixth Five Year Plan.[16] Radioactive isotopes had broad applications in all regions of the economy, including machine building, the chemical industry, textiles, communication, and construction.[17]

But of all the potential applications, atomic engines for transportation purposes excited the greatest expectations. "We have only just entered the century of atomic energy," one scholar wrote. "Many difficulties remain which it is necessary to overcome until portable, light, and easy to control powerful apparatuses with atomic motors are created." But progressive Soviet science and technology, and the leadership of the Party, would guarantee the utilization of atomic engines throughout the economy for the benefit of the masses.[18]

What were the technical reasons for faith in atomic motors for automobiles, boats, locomotives, submarines, airplanes, and rocket ships? First, atomic energy had limitless potential, a major asset since oil and gas reserves were limited and would run out someday. Second, the energy of the atom did not pollute; it did not burn oxygen as did conventional internal-combustion engines. What is more, volumetric considerations favored the atom—a few grams of uranium went as far as several tankers of gasoline. This permitted lengthy trips or flights without refueling. As one engineer wrote in *Novyi mir:*

> The silver "Victory" speeds rapidly along the broad superhighway. Snow-covered fields and winter forests sparkling with hoar-frost fly by. Behind are 300, 500, 700 kilometers. But the driver does not even think of stopping to refuel the car. He still has in reserve several grams of fuel, and this will suffice for several tens of thousands of kilometers of travel!! As the reader may have guessed, these conditions . . . may be achieved with the application of atomic energy.[19]

In spite of the recognition that very thick containment on reactors for radiation safety with a resulting increase in weight of the engines was necessary, concerns about nuclear-powered airplanes falling to the earth, for example, never entered into the discussions.

Finally, just like some scientists in the United States, Soviet scientists entertained the notion of using peaceful nuclear explosions (PNEs) "to increase man's control over the environment."[20] One engineer spoke of the use of controlled atomic explosions to fill deserts with water rapidly, to speed up strip-mining, and to build canals.[21] Another observed that "the application of atomic energy for peaceful construction permits us to correct the many 'mistakes' of nature." In one of the first popular discussions of plans to divert Siberian rivers, he argued that

> an explosion of the so-called Turgaiskie Gates will open the path of Siberian rivers to the south, to Central Asia and Kazakhstan. Here hundreds of millions of hectares of desert stretch out which are scorched by the burning sun. In the future, when Soviet engineers have brought water here, this parched land will become incredibly fruitful. By means of combined, directed massive throwing of the earth it is possible in the course of a few minutes to build gigantic dams, create entire mountain ranges or, alternatively, uncover at great depth deposits of ores. In our country there are huge reserves of still unconquered territory. The most vast of these . . . are the regions of permafrost. A decisive role in their transformation will belong to atomic energy.[22]

According to this view, only under socialism would it be possible to use peaceful nuclear explosions to bring water to the Sahara or build a huge hydroelectric-power station at the Strait of Gibraltar; however, the reasons for these conclusions are unclear.[23]

Although never addressing directly the potential environmental pollution that might result from PNEs, the government was always quick to point out safety measures it had taken to protect the population from the dangers of radiation. This involved not only various laws and regulations concerning exposure to radiation[24] but also the Soviet version of "duck and cover." A major monograph published by the Ministry of Health's Institute of Sanitary Education explained the destructive capacity of nuclear weapons in terms of heat, fire, shock wave, and radiation and the necessity of lying down immediately behind a fence, in a ditch, or along the side of a house in case of explosion and upon seeing a flash.[25] Underground fallout shelters of varying depth and thicknesses of steel or concrete could reduce radiation to under twenty-five roentgens (even fairly close to the center of the blast), offering protection to the Soviet citizen. In fact, the manual assumed a fairly high survival rate, offering suggestions for first aid and for washing radioactivity off the body. In seeming incongruity, a series of sketches in the same section of the monograph showed workers responsible for cleansing cities of radioactivity dressed in special suits and equipped with respirators. The book also failed to address the problems of water, air, and food contamination.[26]

In sum, Soviet scientists, and through them the populace, came to see nuclear power as a panacea for social and economic problems facing the nation. But the effort to convince the Soviet population of the benefits of atomic energy in medicine and biology, agriculture, and industry was only half the task. Once atomic energy had become part of the iconography of Soviet culture, Soviet nuclear physicists and engineers had to fight for its acceptance in the political and economic arenas. How did nuclear power get onto the political agenda? How were physicists able to overcome objections to atomic energy arising from economic and safety considerations? The major reasons for this success lay in the creation of a "cult of science" and in the increasing political power of scientists during the period of de-Stalinization.

The Politics of Nuclear Fission

Since the mid-1950s, Soviet scientists have contributed to and benefited from a "cult of science." This cult, initiated by postwar successes in nuclear-weapons research and development, and cemented by achievements in the peaceful uses of atomic energy and space exploration, was part of the general environment of de-Stalinization in which Soviet scholars, especially physicists, began to reclaim control over the scientific enterprise. They did this by demanding the right to commence new research programs (including those without immediate practical application), taking advantage of a sympathetic Party leadership to bring about a number of institutional reforms, and reasserting control over such areas of their own expertise as philosophy and fundamental science.

The cult of science is based on a reductionist belief that physics is the key to scientific and technological problems and an attitude that large-scale, expensive, and visible projects such as nuclear energy, Tokamak fusion reactors, and the Baikal-Amur Mainline (BAM) railroad should be at the center of national programs. A representative of the reductionist view of physics drew a direct link between atomic energy and achievements in Soviet society:

> As the leader of contemporary natural science which exerts a vital influence on all scientific disciplines, physics is called upon to play an outstanding role in the construction of communism. The assimilation of physical experimental methods in other natural sciences facilitates more successful and rapid progress of the latter, and this means more successful and rapid application of their achievements in the economy, in the development of health care and culture. The "daughters" of physics are radiolocation, reactive technology [jet engines], and atomic energy, which acquire all the more significance in the creation of the material basis of communism. This relates especially to atomic energetics which celebrated the advent of a new technological era. If before [1954] . . . different applications of atomic energy were indeed known . . . then the coming on line of the Soviet atomic electropower station—the only one in the world—serves as the most distinctive and prominent signpost . . . in the history of the peaceful, industrial utilization of atomic energy. The physics of

the atomic nucleus, not long ago "hatched from the egg," will lead to results that will call forth a true revolutionary transformation of the productive forces of society.[27]

Nuclear physicists were quick to use the postwar cult of science, with its emphasis on physics, to advance their programs.

Physicists soon became increasingly active participants in the domestic political arena. Having built in 1954 the world's first atomic-power station to generate electricity, an admittedly small 5,000-kilowatt (kw) channel-graphite reactor, and having grandiose plans for the development and application of atomic power throughout the economy, Soviet physicists pushed for expansion of nuclear R and D programs. At a session of the Academy of Sciences on the Peaceful Uses of Atomic Energy in Moscow in early July 1955, one Soviet nuclear physicist and engineer after another spoke about the necessity of promoting "industrial nuclear power" in the coming few years.[28] At the International Conference on the Peaceful Uses of Nuclear Energy held in August 1956 in Geneva they also described in detail the role of Soviet successes in advancing domestic scientific goals.[29] Until the 20th Communist Party Congress in 1956, however, discussions of atomic energy in such newspapers as *Pravda* and *Izvestiia* were for the most part technical, rather than political. But after I. V. Kurchatov appeared at the congress with the endorsement of Nikita Khrushchev, discussion of the potential of nuclear energy was elevated to a policy debate.

Khrushchev's major role in the development of nuclear power should not be overlooked. He recognized its value for both the Soviet economy and his own purposes. He supported reactor R and D with the same kind of vigor with which he supported large-scale technological development programs in agriculture (chemicalization, the planting of corn, the sowing of the Black Earth Regions) and space. He took a personal interest in nuclear energy, accompanying Kurchatov to Harwell, England, in April 1956, to visit the major British nuclear-research facility,[30] and participating in the Geneva Conference on the Peaceful Uses of Atomic Energy. It is clear that Khrushchev hoped to use Soviet scientific and technological successes to bolster his own position within the Party.[31]

At the Party congress Kurchatov, the father of the Soviet atomic bomb project, gave a short speech noteworthy for its support for a nuclear-energy program that bordered on scientific fantasy. He spoke about the increasing number of researchers and effort involved in atomic energy, a "strong, powerful, young, and capable army of scholars, engineers, and constructors" ready to solve the major tasks in the Sixth Five Year Plan (1956–1960). He called for the construction of 2,000 to 2,500 megawatts (MW) of atomic-power stations. Noting that they were significantly larger than those forecast in the United States or England, he explained, "Our atomic energy stations in the next five year plan are being built as part of a large experiment, conducted by the Government with the goal to find more technologically feasible and economical paths for the creation of atomic power stations."

This would help to define the scale for the seventh and subsequent five-year plans.[32]

Kurchatov next spoke of plans to build up to ten different kinds of experimental reactors with power ranging from 50,000 to 200,000 kw of fast and slow neutrons, with graphite, beryllium, heavy- and light-water moderators, and gas, water, and liquid-metal coolants. The Soviet effort to build industrial-size reactors and to determine parameters for serial production of those reactors as quickly as possible has been a trademark of the atomic-energy program since its first days. Kurchatov then focused on the directives of the Party "to develop projects for the creation of powerful nuclear-powered locomotives, rockets, airplanes, and even automobiles."[33] Atomic energy also figured in the speeches of Kurchatov and Khrushchev at the 21st (Extraordinary) Party Congress in 1959: Thus by the end of the 1950s Soviet scientists had succeeded in making nuclear power an issue of consideration by Party congresses.[34]

Although the Sixth Five Year Plan saw several of Kurchatov's ideas come to fruition, in most areas he and other physicists were well off the mark. The Sixth Five Year Plan envisaged the construction of nuclear-power stations of 400,000 to 600,000 kw in the Urals, near Moscow, and near Leningrad. Construction would begin in 1958, with completion of at least one reactor in 1959.[35]

In spite of the laudatory tone of articles in the major scientific and popular-science journals, successes were long in coming. Except for the application of isotopes in industry and agriculture, the Soviet nuclear-energy program met none of the ambitious targets set for the Sixth Five Year Plan. Construction delays and cost overruns plagued the nascent industry. Local opposition to nuclear power, and the low cost of fossil fuels, were also significant problems.

In response to the assertion that nuclear energy was not economically viable, the standard rebuttal was that nuclear energy would become cheaper, given the geographical imbalance between fossil-fuel resources and energy demand in the USSR, the limited nature of oil, gas, and coal reserves, and the safety of atomic energy. To render it more competitive with conventional sources of power generation, the engineering community made a number of fateful decisions. To make reactors more cheaply, engineers pressed for early "standardization and industrial assimilation."[36] One way to cut down on capital and generating costs associated with nuclear reactors was to use less steel and reinforced concrete. This practice persisted until quite recently in the construction of containment, which was not up to Western standards.[37] Engineers sought to commercialize nuclear power in larger and larger reactor units forecast on the order of 1,000 to 2,400 MW (a size that would never be licensed in the West); they sought to lay to rest concerns regarding fuel-cycle costs by pushing the creation of a network of breeder reactors; they adopted a plan calling for nuclear reactors to produce heat for industrial and domestic purposes significantly more cheaply than conventional plants;[38] and they continued to note the significant contributions to savings in the economy through the use of isotopes in industrial monitoring and quality control, metallurgy, catalytic processes, electrotechnology, radiation chemistry, and in biological and other research.[39] Thus, by the end of the 1950s the Soviet nuclear-power program had already begun to push for economy of materials and labor in the construction of atomic-energy stations (AES) and envisaged serial or mass production of stations and the application of radioisotopes throughout the economy, setting the stage for many of the difficulties that trouble the industry today.

In the 1960s, the "preparatory stage" for industrial nuclear power, the Soviets fixed upon the reactor types to serve as the mainstays of their program, putting many of the experimental reactors of the 1950s into mothballs and abandoning full-scale efforts to develop nuclear rockets, locomotives, and jets. They sought to build reactors in standardized form, using prefabricated components, although the parameters for today's reactors were not fixed until the 1970s. And they settled upon a program for nuclear power that extended to the end of the century. This program was based upon rapid commercialization of slow neutron reactors for the production of electrical power and of plutonium for the next stage of reactors. The second stage would involve the creation of a network of fast neutron breeder reactors, such as the planned (and later scuttled) Clinch River Breeder Reactor in the United States, sometime in the 1990s. Finally, in the first third of the twenty-first century, theoretical and experimental advances in controlled thermonuclear synthesis would lead to the creation of a network of fusion reactors.

After the initial enthusiasm of the late 1950s, however, for safety, fuel cycle, and economic reasons, the development of nuclear power took second place to development of fossil fuel in the Soviet national energy program. Fossil-fuel reserves were plentiful, although located in Siberia far from the population and the industrial center of the USSR. Moreover, because national economic growth was tied closely to increased electrical-energy capacity and production (and because atomic energy promised only long-term results, more expensive electrical power, and heavy capital investment), the Party focused on fossil fuels. The Third Party Program of the Communist Party of the Soviet Union (CPSU), promulgated at the 22nd Party Congress in 1961, left no doubt about the situation regarding atomic energy. Only "to the degree that the cost of the production of atomic energy is reduced will the construction of atomic electrical power stations be increased, especially in those regions with shortfalls of other sources of energy, or will the application of atomic energy for peaceful purposes in the economy, medicine, and science be expanded."[40]

Although supporters of nuclear energy spoke about economic benefits to the economy in the application of radioisotopes for production and control, medical, and agricultural purposes, they had to concede that at least for the near future the cost per kilowatt hour of electrical energy would remain higher for nuclear-power stations. This was true despite the fact that a few tons of uranium provided as much energy as thousands of tankers of oil and could reduce fuel-transportation costs from Siberia to the industrial and population centers of the European USSR. As a result, the Party failed to highlight the position of nuclear energy in national plans until the 24th Party Congress in 1971.

It is true that at this stage the nuclear-power effort encountered some resistance from those who were concerned about the potential hazards of low-level and catastrophic radiation releases from reactors. But the Soviet engineering community stressed the safety of their reactors and their concern for construction and operating personnel, dismissing the objections of those who opposed reactor construction.[41] It must be noted that the instances of vocal public opposition to nuclear power before Chernobyl were few. The "atomic culture" had succeeded in muting opposition and in creating the almost complacent attitude that the Soviets have adopted toward atomic energy. Eventually, Soviet engineers became so confident of the safety of nuclear reactors that by the mid-1960s they advocated the serial construction of blocks of three to five reactors at sites located no further than the "outlying regions of large cities," abandoning the earlier promise that stations would be built far from inhabited areas and underground to ensure the safety of the population.[42]

Technical and construction problems persisted during the period 1958 through 1972, however, and stations came on-line rather slowly.[43] The construction of these stations represented an achievement of the Soviet nuclear-energy industry, but the failure to complete construction rapidly troubled policymakers and discouraged them from committing additional resources to the program. Furthermore, in spite of increasing successes in the application of isotopes in the economy[44] and assertions that the growth of the nuclear-power industry and serial production of reactors had made nuclear power more economical,[45] some scholars still doubted the nuclear establishment's claims because of cost, fuel-cycle, and radioactive-waste considerations.[46] A prominent editorial in *Pravda* in 1968 criticized the burgeoning industry for being all too slow in improving the organization and production of equipment.[47] Nonetheless, reactor construction and operating experience convinced many that the potential for the industry had yet to be reached, especially in light of the fact that the United States was well on the way toward the construction of 100 power-generating reactors.

By that time, the nuclear-power industry had acquired substantial institutional and technological momentum.[48] And just as safety concerns had been laid to rest, at least in the minds of engineers, so too the economic question would be solved in favor of reactor development. The Soviet Union is energy rich: It possesses 40 percent of the world's fossil-fuel reserves, and 12 percent of its hydroelectric potential. But a tremendous energy imbalance exists. Seventy percent of Soviet energy consumption (and population) are located in the European part of the country, whereas 90 percent of the basic fuel resources are found in Siberia and Soviet Central Asia. The cost of transporting the energy thousands of kilometers from the east to the west, either in its primary form or as electricity—high-voltage power lines running for more than 7,500 km would be needed—is very high. This situation led Soviet planners during the Tenth Five Year Plan (1976–1980) to adopt an aggressive program of rapid commercialization of nuclear-power stations located near population centers of the European USSR, with the goal of producing 20 percent of Soviet electricity by 1990, although only 10 percent was achieved (60 percent in the Ukraine),[49] and 50 percent in the near future, based on a network of slow neutron reactors. This would be followed by the creation of a network of fast breeder reactors and ultimately by a series of fusion reactors to be built sometime after the year 2020.

With the endorsement of the Party, the growing nuclear-energy industry set out to build tens of 1,000-MW reactors, but failed to meet any goals. Because of the great capital investment needed for these reactors, and because fusion research proceeded more slowly than scientists had originally thought, the fusion-research program began to labor under budgetary and personnel shortages.

For example, at the 24th Party Congress in 1971, the Party approved plans for the construction of 6 to 8 gigawatts (GW) primarily of thermal nuclear-energy capacity, based on industrial, prefabricated construction where possible, and standardized production of components such as steam generators, pumps, and armatures.[50] These reactors would produce plutonium needed to fuel fast breeder reactors that would come on-line in the 1980s. A. M. Petros'iants, chairman of the State Committee for the Utilization of Atomic Energy, acknowledged that it was difficult to predict the ultimate mix of fast and slow reactors but recognized that the Soviet electrical-energy system would remain based on fossil fuel until the year 2000. However, because of the geographical imbalance between energy resources, industry, and people, the need for "huge blocks of atomic power stations" based on the construction of 2,000-MW and even 3,000-MW reactors of standard construction was clear. It did not matter if atomic "parks" of four or more reactor units were located near cities; atomic power was safe with respect to radiation, polluted less than coal, and in combination with cogeneration was cheaper than fossil fuel.[51]

Because of growing investment in fission nuclear power, fusion had become only a small, albeit integral, part of the program for expansion of the network of thermal and breeder reactors by the eve of the 25th Party Congress.[52] By the 26th Party Congress in 1981, in the face of massive investment in a large network of fission reactors throughout the European USSR, financial pressures were impinging upon the fusion program. But the Soviet commitment to nuclear power, both fission and fusion, had been established as a national priority.

In spite of the urgent need and established priority, however, the Soviet Union has experienced great difficulty in bringing reactors on-line in a timely fashion. Since the Ninth Five Year Plan (1971–1975), not one target date for additional capacity has been met; if anything the record is getting worse. Current nuclear-power capacity in the USSR is roughly 40,000 MW, with the Thirteenth Five Year Plan calling for an addition of 4 to 6 GW per year. So far, construction has reached only 1 to 2 GWs per year.

In sum, nuclear physicists were successful in getting government approval to begin an ambitious nuclear-energy program in the mid-1950s. The program included the construction of thermal, or slow neutron, nuclear-power stations, research and development on several experimental reactors, including fusion and fast reactors, and radioisotope development for application in industry and agriculture. Because of some opposition for safety and economic reasons, both from within the scientific community and from the population at large, the program failed to take off until the late 1960s, and the Party gave nuclear energy only passing attention at plenums and congresses. In the 1960s, nuclear power began to compete with conventional power in terms of cost. Some projections indicated that even large nuclear reactors—on the order of 500 to 1,000 MW—could be cheaper still. Furthermore, several years of operating experience had given nuclear engineers the freedom to assert that their "atomic giants" were indeed safer than oil- or coal-powered stations. They polluted less, and there had been no serious large-scale accident. And finally, Soviet citizens—from the average worker to scientists and policymakers—embraced the utopian visions of atomic culture with little question. By 1975, the Party was prepared to endorse an ambitious program for the serial production of nuclear reactors near the population centers of the western USSR.

From the start, nuclear scientists had pushed for rapid commercialization of reactors based on mass production of large, unitary reactors and associated components. Based on the notion that the first "Moskvich" car is expensive to produce, but that each subsequent vehicle is significantly cheaper, the USSR set out to establish a large-scale nuclear-power industry producing reactors serially by the early 1970s. This industry, an amalgam of fundamental and applied research institutes of the Academy of Sciences and the State Committee for the Utilization of Atomic Energy, construction trusts, enterprises, and ministerial institutes and associations, began to mass produce VVER-440, VVER-1000, and RBMK-1000 reactors by the end of the decade. Encountering little if any local opposition, and facing a legal environment conducive to bringing reactors on-line as quickly as the resolution of any construction or technical problems permitted, the nuclear-power industry rapidly developed the mind-set in which the Chernobyl disaster occurred.

The Chernobyl Disaster Revisited

The problems facing nuclear power in the USSR today, and the historical roots of the Chernobyl disaster, are a result of Soviet attitudes toward science and technology and the development of atomic culture.[53] Attitudes toward science and technology, especially the belief in the infallibility of large-scale technologies, helped to create an environment in which the shortcomings of the nuclear-energy industry were ignored. Based on notions of atomic culture that reflected the belief that reactor technology was inherently safe and that there was a technological fix for most problems, Soviet planners opted for premature selection of parameters, early prefabrication of VVER and RBMK reactors, and overly aggressive commercialization, primarily to lower costs. But these cost-cutting measures result in reducing the safety margin of Soviet reactors. The general ideological and philosophical environment in which nuclear-power engineering developed in the USSR encouraged a kind of "technological determinism," if not outright technological arrogance. The major factors involved were technological determinism in a peculiarly Soviet form; a belief in mass production as the highest form of technological culture; a conviction that technology and its makers were nearly infallible; and a fascination with things that were bigger rather than smaller, and faster rather than slower—like rockets and reactors.

Because of the common belief among Soviet policymakers, planners, scientists, and technologists in the infallibility and innate goodness of technology, the Soviets pushed ahead with rapid commercialization and mass production before conditions merited it, without adequate concern for such safety issues as siting, containment, and the development of an adequate legal framework. The drive for mass production of complex reactor technology was rooted in views of technology that developed in the 1920s. As we saw above, the utopian views about atomic energy that developed during the late 1940s and 1950s contributed to these beliefs. Then, in the late 1950s and 1960s, a fascination with mass production was married to nuclear power in an attempt to make atomic energy competitive with conventional sources of energy.

But what role did the fascination with mass production play in the Chernobyl crisis? Mass production of any sort inhibits the incorporation of design changes that may improve safety or efficiency but that have a higher cost. With prefabrication, each reactor becomes only as strong as its weakest point. Is each component up to par? Was each built with the care and materials befitting a complex and potentially dangerous billion-ruble technology? And if there were innovations in safety and efficiency, would planners introduce them at the risk of missing start-up targets and increasing total capital investment for the project? The experience of the Soviet nuclear-power industry indicates that the answer to some of these questions is no. Granted, Soviet attempts to mass-produce or prefabricate reactors of both the RBMK and VVER type had nothing to do with the immediate causes of the Chernobyl accident. But efforts at mass production reflected the belief that reactor technology was safe enough to be built with less than adequate containment and operated and supervised by nontechnical personnel.

In the late 1970s, in fact, Chernobyl was seen as a blueprint for future efforts at serial production of nuclear-power plants. After planners selected a pastoral site on the banks of a river, construction of four to six 1,000-MW reactor units began near Pripiat. As reported in *Ekonomicheskaia gazeta,* engineers at Chernobyl replaced the pouring of concrete as much as possible with prefabricated concrete and increased the number of mass-produced components to lower the labor intensiveness of atomic power. During the construction of the second block, "the industrial level of construction increased," with 1.5 to 2 times the usual amount of reinforced, prefabricated concrete, although "this [was] still insufficient." The goal was to have prefabricated material used in at least 70 percent of the construction of a typical power plant. "At this very [site] it is proposed in the future to raise still another ten blocks. There is a real possibility of organizing the mass production of AES. The Chernobyl AES site may serve as a paragon for this effort."[54] The Soviet nuclear-power industry now relies heavily upon prefabricated components.

As an indication of how much large-scale technologies are seen as a panacea for such economic problems as the geographic imbalance between fuel resources and population, Soviet engineers in the early 1980s approved several projects to build "mobile" and even "floating" nuclear-power stations for application in regions where because of climate or absence of fuel it is difficult to produce electrical energy from diesel or oil. The "Arbus," a 1,500-kw reactor for use in the far north, Siberia, and the far east, was built according to two different designs in the early 1960s: one with an organic coolant and moderator, the other a water-water model.[55] Later, engineers advanced a model of a floating 6,000-kw nuclear-power station to provide electricity for oil and gas exploration in the far north and far east.[56] The construction of these reactors reflected more than faith in the infallibility of technology. It suggested that "technological determinism"—technologies being developed because of the momentum provided by the institutions that work on them, in part simply because the technologies can be developed—also played a role in the Soviet nuclear-energy program.

The Soviet fascination with atomic-powered rockets and automobiles, and with mass-produced and floating nuclear reactors, indicates that as Soviet Marxism has evolved, it has taken on an increasingly technicist flavor. In the guise of two concepts, contemporary Soviet ideology sanctions the belief that science and technology are a panacea for social, economic, and political problems. First, science is considered "a direct productive force." As a result, scientists should be given control of their enterprise. They best know how to carry out "science," and accomplishments in science and technology are the clearest indication of successful economic development and sociocultural achievement.

Second, the Soviet fascination with the "scientific-technological revolution" also demonstrates the firm Soviet belief about science as a panacea, a vital aspect of economic growth, and a guarantor of the future. Representatives of the achievements of this "revolution" include new forms of production and automation, more powerful computers, spaceships and space stations, and fission and fusion reactors.[57] Many countries throughout the world—Japan, Korea, China, France, Germany, and the United States—share this Soviet fascination with science and technology, but a quasi-official Marxist ideology and a reductionist "cult of science" reinforce these beliefs in the USSR.

In two other important ways, safety philosophy and law and regulation of atomic energy, atomic culture contributed to the Chernobyl crisis. Soviet safety philosophy, as reflected in reactor construction and containment and in the legal framework for the licensing of nuclear-power stations, is based upon a strong belief in the overriding strengths of modern technology. For example, there is some question about whether Soviet engineers subscribe to the theory of "depth in defense" in reactor design. There has been a mismatch between application and Soviet writings in *Atomnaia energiia*, the main journal of the nuclear-power field, which suggested that the Soviets follow "depth in defense." Until quite recently Soviets used ordinary factory structures to house reactors and did not build proper containment vessels for them. They used conventional, rather than reinforced, concrete and less steel than U.S. reactors until the early 1980s. At that time containment was upgraded somewhat in response to the pressures of Soviet engineers on the nuclear-power industry, for reasons of safety and in order to compete with Western firms for contracts to construct reactors abroad. What is more, in the case of the RBMK, the reactor is designed for ease in refueling: It has a large number of plugs on the top; these, combined with the absence of Western-style containment, make it much more likely that radioactivity will be dispersed well beyond the reactor site in the event of an explosion. To this day, Soviet containment is not as comprehensive as Western, and the cost of retrofitting those reactors without adequate containment would be prohibitively large for the Soviets. However, public opposition to nuclear-power stations located close to population centers has led to the cancelation of ten reactors as of spring 1990 and to slowdowns in the construction of others.

The optimistic view of technology in the USSR has retarded the development of the legal framework for the control of nuclear energy. The vast majority of Western technologists agree that the government should regulate nuclear power. But as Donald Barry pointed out, in the USSR there is no formal licensing procedure in the strict sense for bringing reactors on-line, and no penalties for breaking laws regulating the construction, inspection, and operation of reactors. Indeed, "legal concerns are given virtually no expert attention in the Soviet Union and Eastern Europe. That is to say, the regulation of nuclear power in these countries is not so much lawless as it is lawyerless."[58]

Some would argue that legal, economic, geographic, and technical factors, and not "technological arrogance," led to the Chernobyl accident. They point to such articles as the well-known discussion of nuclear energy by Dollezhal' and Koriakin as evidence that there was skepticism and concern among energy specialists over the viability and safety of the Soviet nuclear-power program years ago.[59] They see this as an indication that a blindly proscience tradition began to wane some time ago. But these factors alone do not account fully for Soviet safety philosophy, the weakness of the legal tradition, or the premature prefabrication and mass production of nuclear reactors. The long-term historical experience of the Soviet Union with respect to large-scale technologies; the ability of scientists to put nuclear power on the political agenda with little opposition; technological momentum and decisionmaking based all too often on economic criteria; the Marxian tradition, which in its Soviet form is particularly scientistic; atomic culture—all of these factors helped create an environment in which the shortcomings of the Soviet nuclear-power program were ignored. In a few words, Soviet attitudes toward technology as a panacea and a symbol of national achievement explain why the USSR pursued nuclear power so aggressively, with disastrous results at Chernobyl.

Epilogue

The change of political climate in the Soviet Union may contribute to growing circumspection toward such large-scale technologies as nuclear reactors. Judging from books, plays, and short stories, statements of Soviet citizens, and official pronouncements, faith in technology has waned in the past fifteen years. To date, the policy of *glasnost'* has helped to develop in the Soviet public a more realistic attitude toward the potentials of science and technology and a greater awareness of their danger. For the first time in Soviet history, the media report the sinking of ferries, the crashes of airplanes and buses, and the cover-ups of man-made technological disasters that occurred in the past. Even the events surrounding Chernobyl were eventually carried rather openly and with little deceit. If Gorbachev's *glasnost'* creates a public with greater political sophistication, a public that opposes such large-scale technological projects as nuclear-power plants, then the industry will face a more fickle and intractable challenger to its plans.

At the same time, there are a number of reasons why atomic culture will slow attempts to make nuclear power safer. First, Soviet engineers have acknowledged that the cost of retrofitting RBMKs and building stronger containment vessels for all reactors is prohibitive. Changes in the operation of RBMKs have been mandated, but their continued operation reflects a belief that atomic energy is essentially safe. Moreover, efforts to save manpower and construction costs are endemic to the system.

In terms of changes in regulation, until recently one bureaucracy, the State Committee for the Utilization of Atomic Energy (GKUAE), was in charge of administration *and* promotion of nuclear-power research, development, and construction. In part because of economic pressures to meet and fulfill quite ambitious planning targets, the GKUAE prabably was "captured" by the industry it was meant to regulate and assumed promotional or advocacy (in addition to supervisory) functions. This meant that, unlike the case in the United States, there was no independent regulatory body that might have prohibited a poorly designed and inadequately reviewed experiment such as the one that caused Reactor No. 4 to explode.[60]

In response to the Chernobyl incident, and in an attempt to ensure that regulatory functions receive the proper weight, the Soviet Union has established a Ministry of Nuclear Power separate from the Ministry of Power and Electrification. Soviet officials merged the three bureaucracies responsible for nuclear safety, the State Hydrometeorological Committee, the Ministry of Public Health (and its State Sanitary Inspection and Sanitary-Epidemiological Administration), and the State Committee for Safety in the Nuclear Power Industry, into one organization and also fired and imprisoned a number of officials.[61]

The changes in the organization and management of the nuclear industry since Chernobyl have, however, done little to solve many of the problems facing nuclear power. Commitment to atomic energy in the form of the Atommash reactor factory, which is intended to produce eight pressure vessels and associated components for the VVER reactor type; tens of reactors currently under construction near population centers in the USSR, including RBMKs of the Chernobyl type; the operation of several liquid-metal fast breeder reactors, with the goal of bringing dozens on-line in the future; a large-scale fusion program (which, however, is currently belabored by budget, personnel, and technical problems); and strong economic incentives to continued construction as the importance of electrical-power generation for continued economic growth will put pressure on the industry to bring reactors on-line as rapidly as constraints on labor, materials, and safety allow. Yet an ever-growing environmental movement and rampant fear of radiation fed by *glasnost'* seem to have placed additional constraints on the nuclear-power industry.

However, technological determinism remains a major force in the contemporary Soviet Union, in part because the official ideology of the USSR, Soviet Marxism, is inherently technicist. Soviet leaders have revered science and technology since the first years of the Soviet state. Indeed, Gorbachev has surrounded himself with a handful of prominent science advisers. Faith in technology as the highest form of "culture," as the chief mode of modernization of the economy, and as a panacea for social and economic problems continues to hold sway. Atomic culture, which was built on forty years of achievements, is so deeply rooted in popular and scientific perceptions of the Soviet leadership in space exploration and nuclear physics that it will take more than Chernobyl to dislodge it. Inasmuch as atomic culture helped to create a Soviet population with tremendous faith in the potential and safety of atomic energy, it would seem that opposition to nuclear power, or at the very least objections to current construction and siting practices, will have to come from within the nuclear-engineering community. The increasing publicity given to natural and man-made disasters in the USSR probably will contribute to greater concern about technology's potential dangers. But above all else, constructivist and utopian visions of technology as a panacea for social and economic problems must give way to greater circumspection.

Notes

1. A number of physicists, including L. D. Landau, Ia. I. Frenkel', and S. I. Vavilov, published a series of articles in such journals as *Priroda, Smena, Ogonek,* and *Nauka i zhizn'* on the development of atomic theory from the 1890s and Becquerel, to Rutherford and Soddi's work on atomic structure, to the great potential energy in uranium and Soviet scientists' efforts to produce new isotopes with cyclotrons and to test materials and fuels for future reactors, using small, experimental reactors.

2. M. Rubinshtein, "Inostrannaia pechat' ob atomnykh bombakh," *Novoe vremia* 7, no. 17 (September 1, 1945), p. 18.

3. A. Morozov, "Razrushiteli," *Smena,* no. 9–10 (1946), pp. 11–12.

4. See Thomas Hughes, *Networks of Power* (Baltimore: Johns Hopkins University Press, 1983) for a discussion of the development of large, centralized electrical-power grids in the United States and Western Europe.

5. L. B. Ponizovskii, "Energiia atomnogo iadra," *Priroda,* no. 10 (1948), pp. 29–30.

6. G. A. Zisman, "Energiia atomnykh iader," *Nauka i zhizn',* no. 2 (1951), p. 24.

7. Ibid. See also V. A. Leshkovtsev, "Atomnaia energiia na sluzhbe amerikanskogo imperializma," *Nauka i zhizn',* no. 8 (1952), p. 44, for a discussion of the opposition to the development of nuclear power by U.S. oil and gas monopolies. In the USSR, according to this article, "atomic energy together with gigantic hydroelectric stations and different new sources of energy opens the richest perspectives for the furthest flowering of the country. For the benefit of humanity our scholars are working on the problems of the broadest application of atomic energy in the economy."

8. It was inevitable that the USSR would surpass the West in electrical-energy production, according to one writer, since in the West, atomic energy served only military purposes, and in the United States atomic energy lagged because of the opposition to it of the oil monopoly. In the socialist Soviet Union, this would not happen. Iurii Tytov, "Atomnaia energetika," *Literatur'naia gazeta,* October 2, 1958, p. 2.

9. V. S. Emel'ianov, "Mirnyi atom na sluzhbe kommunizma," *Novyi mir,* no. 10 (1961), pp. 37–43.

10. P. S. Neporozhnii, "Elektricheskaia reka," *Sovetskaia Rossiia,* June 11, 1957.

11. For a discussion of the "prototype approach" in the development of Soviet energy technologies, see Robert Campbell, *Soviet Energy Technologies* (Bloomington: Indiana University Press, 1980).

12. Paul Boyer, *By the Bomb's Early Light* (New York: Pantheon, 1985).

13. For a discussion of similar attempts in the United States to develop an "atomic culture" while avoiding discussion of the potential dangers of nuclear energy, see Daniel Ford, *The Cult of the Atom* (New York: Simon and Schuster, 1982).

14. A. M. Kuzin, "Mechenye atomy v biologii," *Nauka i zhizn',* no. 4 (1955), pp. 29–32.

15. E. S. Pertsovskii, "Energiiu atoma-pishchevoi promyshlennosti," *Nauka i zhizn',* no. 8 (1956), pp. 17–20; and B. A. Rubin et al., "Ispol'zovanie gamma-luchei pri dlitel'nom khranenii kartofel'ia," *Priroda,* no. 7 (1958), pp. 91–94.

16. Iu. P. Kurdinovskii, "Luchi, rozhdennye atomom," *Nauka i zhizn',* no. 3 (1956), pp. 17–21.

17. For a detailed discussion of these applications, see M. B. Neiman, "Primenenie radioaktivnykh izotopov v promyshlennosti," *Priroda,* no. 10 (1954), pp. 16–27.

18. R. G. Perel'man, "Atomnye dvigateli," *Nauka i zhizn'*, no. 1 (1956), p. 32.

19. P. Astashenkov, "Pervye shagi atomnoi energetiki," *Novyi mir,* no. 3 (1955), p. 181. Another article important for the popularization of atomic culture appeared in *Novyi mir* later that year. See V. Emel'ianov, "Rasskazy ob atome," *Novyi mir,* no. 8 (1955), pp. 219-34. On transportation and atomic energy see also Perel'man, op. cit.; A. Markin, "Atom na sluzhbe cheloveka," *Smena,* no. 1 (1955), pp. 18-19; and V. A. Mezentsev, "Na poroge atomnogo veka," *Nauka i zhizn',* no. 1 (1956), pp. 5-14.

20. For a fascinating discussion of the iconography of Project Ploughshares and attempts to end fears of military uses of the bomb through peaceful nuclear explosions in the United States, see Michael Smith, "Cultures of Procurement: Promotion of Weapons in the Nuclear Age," paper given at the Annual Meetings of the History of Science Society and Society for the History of Technology, Raleigh, N.C., October 30, 1987.

21. Mezentsev, op. cit., p. 7.

22. Markin, op. cit., p. 18.

23. Ibid.

24. See, for example, G. Duvankov, "Okhrana truda pri rabote s radioaktivnymi veshcnestvami," *Kommunist,* no. 3 (1956), pp. 67-70; and V. Emel'ianov, "Atomnaia tekhnika i progress promyshlennosti," *Otvety na voprosy trudiashchikhsia, vyp.* 67 (1956), pp. 15-21, both of which describe in great detail how laws, standards, and exposure rates are tightly monitored and controlled to ensure the safety of atomic workers in the USSR. For a detailed discussion of Soviet law and nuclear safety, see A. I. Ioirysh, "Pravovye problemy reaktornoi bezopasnosti," *Sovetskoe gosudarstvo i pravo,* no. 10 (1979), translated in *Soviet Law and Government* 19, no. 1 (Summer 1980), pp. 21-35.

25. E. I. Vorob'ev and U. Ia. Margulis, *Atomnaia energiia i protivo-atomnaia zashchita* (Moscow: Ministry of Public Health, 1956), pp. 46-47.

26. Ibid., pp. 67-68.

27. L. L. Miasnikov, "Lider sovremmenogo estestvoznaniia," *Nauka i zhizn',* no. 4 (1955), pp. 10-12. Another reductionist view of physics is that held by Oleg Pisarzhevskii, "Fizika i tekhnika," *Fizika v shkole,* no. 6 (1957), pp. 5-15.

28. N. A. Nesmianov, "Ispol'zovanie atomnoi energii v mirnykh tseliakh i sovetskaia nauka," *Vestnik akademii nauk sssr* [hereafter *VAN*], no. 7 (1955), pp. 3-14; "Ispol'zovaniae atomnoi energii v mirnykh tseliakh (na sessiiakh otdelenii Akademii nauk SSSR)," *VAN,* no. 8 (1955), pp. 34-46; and V. A. Leshkovtsev, "Sessiia AN SSSR po mirnomu ispol'zovaniiu atomnoi energii," *Fizika v shkole,* no. 6 (1955), pp. 7-15.

29. I. I. Novikov, "Mezhdunarodnoe nauchnoe sotrudnichestvo po mirnomu ispol'zovaniiu atomnoi energii," *VAN,* no. 9 (1955), pp. 47-61.

30. See *Atomnaia energiia* [hereafter *AE*] 1, no. 3, (1956), pp. 6-7 and 66-67, for photographs of the Harwell trip.

31. See also N. S. Khrushchev, *Khrushchev Remembers,* trans. Strobe Talbott (Boston: Little, Brown and Co., 1974), pp. 58-71, for a discussion of Khrushchev's relationship with the scientific intelligentsia.

32. *XX s"ezd KPSS. Stenograficheskii otchet,* vol. 1 (Moscow: Gospolitizdat, 1956), pp. 595-600.

33. For a discussion of some of these fantastic, futuristic projects, a number of which the United States also pursued, see Iu. N. Sushkov, *Atomnaia energiia i aviatsiia* (Moscow: Znanie, 1958); and A. P. Ermakov and A. G. Syrman, *Atomnaia energiia i transport* (Moscow, 1963); as well as the more popular R. G. Perel'man,

"Atomnye dvigateli," *Nauka i zhizn'*, no. 1 (1956), pp. 26-32. Kurchatov concluded his speech by mentioning the newly founded and promising program in controlled thermonuclear synthesis (fusion), based on the work of I. E. Tamm and A. D. Sakharov.

34. *Vneocherednoi XXI s"ezd KPSS. Stenograficheskii otchet*, vol. 2 (Moscow: Gospolitizdat, 1959), pp. 179-83. For a more detailed discussion of the Soviet fusion effort, see Paul R. Josephson, "The History and Politics of Energy Technology: Controlled Thermonuclear Synthesis in the USSR," *Report to the Congressional Office of Technology Assessment*, October 1986.

35. One reactor would be of the type of the Academy of Science 5,000-kw model: a graphite-moderated, enriched-uranium reactor, but sufficiently large so that less-enriched uranium could be used. Two other reactors would be water-moderated and water-cooled (the "water-water" reactor). A third model, a heterogeneous reactor with heavy-water moderator and gas coolant, was planned but never built. In addition, Soviet physicists began work on several experimental reactors of different fuel cycles, moderators, and coolants. Finally, a nuclear icebreaker, the "Lenin," was built. For discussion of achievements in nuclear power during the Sixth Five Year Plan, see I. F. Fainboim, "Atomnaia energiia v shestoi piatiletke," *Fizika v shkole*, no. 2 (1957), pp. 11-13; N. A. Nikolaev (deputy director of the Main Administration for the Utilization of Atomic Energy), "Budushchie atomnye giganty," *Trud*, November 22, 1957, p. 4; V. Emel'ianov, "Atomnaia energiia," *Krasnaia zvezda*, November 25, 1958; and various issues of *Atomnaia energiia*.

36. G. V. Ermakov (chief engineer of Glavatomenergo), "Pervyi gigant atomnoi energetiki," *Izvestiia*, June 19, 1957, p. 1.

37. A. N. Komarovskii, "Puti ekonomii stali v reaktorostroenii," *AE* 7, no. 3 (1959), pp. 205-15.

38. P. Anan'ev, "Nekotorye voprosy ekonomiki iadernoi energetiki," *AE* 6, no. 3 (1959), pp. 245-51; I. Vaisman, "Nekotoryye ekonomicheskie problemy atomnoi energetiki," *Voprosy ekonomiki*, no. 5 (1957), pp. 87-94.

39. Vaisman, op. cit.; A. V. Topchiev et al., "Primenenie radioaktivnykh isotopov v SSSR," *AE* 5, no. 3 (1958), pp. 321-33; A. Sokolovskii, "Izuchenie ekonomicheskoi effektivnosti ispol'zovaniia izotopov," *Voprosy ekonomiki*, no. 12 (1959), pp. 166-67. Sokolovskii calculated a savings of 500 million rubles for 1958 alone.

40. *XXII s"ezd KPSS*, vol. 1 (Moscow: Gospolitizdat, 1962), p. 279.

41. There is mention of local opposition to and fear of atomic energy in a number of articles, including: A. Petros'iants, "Atomnaia energiia na sluzhbe narodnogo khoziaistva," *Ikonomicheskaia gazeta*, November 3, 1962, p. 33; N. M. Sinev, "Atomnyi gigant na Donu," *Trud*, November 5, 1968.

42. A. Petros'iants, "Mirnyi atom sluzhit rodine," *Trud*, April 8, 1965, p. 2; Sinev, op. cit., and Markin, op. cit., p. 18.

43. In 1964 the Beloiarsk AES at 100,000 kw; in 1964 the Novovoronezh AES at 210,000 kw; the second block at Beloiarsk at 200,000 kw in October 1967; the BOR-60, an experimental breeder reactor at 12,000 kw, in December 1968; the second Novovoronezh reactor at 365,000 kw in December 1969; and a third block at 440,000 kw in December 1971, with several others under construction.

44. See A. M. Petros'iants, "Atom za rabotoi," *Pravda*, October 15, 1968, p. 3; A. I. Leipunskii, "Iadernaia fizika v smezhnykh oblastiakh nauki i v narodnom khoziaistve," *VAN*, no. 7 (1968), pp. 7-14; I. Morokhov, "Atom sluzhit miru," *Gudok*, November 16, 1967, p. 4.

45. Morokhov, op. cit.; and B. Filaretova, "Ekonomika atomnoi energetiki," *Ekonomicheskaia gazeta*, no. 35 (August 30, 1966), p. 18.

46. G. Kirillin, "Bor'ba za energiiu," *Ikonomicheskaia gazeta,* no. 14 (April 1968), p. 33.

47. "Atom—rabochii," *Pravda,* August 31, 1968, p. 1.

48. A. P. Aleksandrov, "Ispolinskii atom," *Izvestiia,* December 31, 1964, p. 3.

49. For a brief discussion of atomic energy in the Ukraine and problems of supply and production plaguing the industry, see David Marples, "Recent Developments in the Ukraine's Nuclear Energy Program," *Radio Liberty Report,* RL 405/85 (December 4, 1985). See also his *Chernobyl and Nuclear Power in the USSR* (New York: St. Martin's Press, 1986).

50. A. M. Petros'iants, "Atomnaia energetika v piatiletke," *Kommunist,* February 3, 1972.

51. E. Knorre and E. Rozental', "Budushchee iadernoi energetiki," *Pravda ukrainy,* September 30, 1971.

52. *XXV s"ezd KPSS. Stenograficheskii otchet,* vol. 1 (Moscow: Gospolitizdat, 1976), p. 136.

53. Many of the comments in this section are discussed in greater detail in my article, "The Historical Roots of the Chernobyl Crisis," *Soviet Union* 13, pt. 3 (1986), pp. 275-99.

54. "Chernobyl'skaia atomnaia," *Ekonomicheskaia gazeta,* February 6, 1978, p. 2.

55. See E. Maksimova, "Put' k Obninsku," *Izvestiia,* October 1, 1967, p. 5; A. M. Petros'iants, "Atomnaia nauka i tekhnika," *Trud,* October 24, 1967, p. 4.

56. See *AE,* no. 8 (1981), pp. 83-87.

57. See Erik Hoffmann, "Soviet Views of 'The Scientific-Technological Revolution,'" *World Politics* 30, no. 4 (July 1978), pp. 615-44, for a detailed discussion of these views.

58. Donald D. Barry, "Political and Legal Aspects of the Development and Use of Nuclear Power in the USSR and Eastern Europe," in *Soviet and East European Law and the Scientific Technical Revolution,* ed. Peter Maggs, Gordon Smith, and George Ginsburgs (New York: Praeger, 1982), pp. 159-80.

59. N. Dollezhal' and Iu. Koriakin, "Nuclear Energy: Achievements and Problems," *Problems of Economics* 23, no. 2 (June 1980), pp. 3-20. Originally published as "Iadernaia elektroenergetika: dostizheniia i problemy," *Kommunist* no. 14 (1979), pp. 19-28. It must be noted, however, that Dollezhal' and Koriakin advocated a more cautious approach to siting and containment; they did not oppose the Soviet program for commercialization of atomic energy. See Dollezhal', "Atomnaia energetika, nauchno-tekhnicheskie zadachi razvitiia," *VAN,* no. 7 (1978), pp. 46-61, which only a few months earlier spoke glowingly of the potential for serial production of RBMK reactors in even 2,400-MW units.

60. I found reference to a special council (*sluzhba*) for radiation safety with the right of veto over safety questions concerning peaceful nuclear explosions and atomic-power stations, but there is little information concerning the council's function, structure, history, or why it played no role in prohibiting the Chernobyl "experiment." See *Komsomol'skaia pravda,* November 1, 1969, p. 4.

61. Theodore Shabad, "Geographic Aspects of the Chernobyl' Nuclear Accident," *Soviet Geography,* no. 7 (1986), p. 504.

CHAPTER 5

Soviet Health Problems and the Convergence Hypothesis

Mark G. Field

> *An absurd situation was developing . . . we have the largest number of doctors and hospital beds per thousand . . . population, and . . . glaring shortcomings in our health services.*
>
> —Mikhail Gorbachev

After years of malign neglect, papered over by propaganda boasts of its superiority, Soviet socialized medicine has been officially diagnosed as seriously ill. In an almost masochistic fit of *glasnost'*-inspired candor, led by Dr. Evgenii Ivanovich Chazov, who was in 1987 the newly appointed health minister of the USSR, practically every aspect of the health service was described in need of restructuring, rebuilding, and reform. "The organization of our health protection," said Chazov, "is in a sad state."[1]

This is not to say that Soviet medicine was not found wanting earlier. In fact, criticism and complaints about it have been a fairly constant fixture in the Soviet media in the form of letters to the editor and articles by investigative reporters who usually confirmed what the letters said.[2] In 1985, the Health Ministry of the USSR received over 66,000 letters of complaints about the medical service, substantially more than in the preceding year.[3] But in most instances, the problems and the deficiencies were attributed to the actions (or inaction) of specific individuals characterized as irresponsible, corrupt, lazy, or inefficient. This "personalization of causality" had the triple advantage of (1) reaffirming that health care was basically sound; (2) allowing people to ventilate their anger and frustrations on specific targets; and (3) deflecting that anger away from the system and the regime responsible for it. The two preceding health ministers (B. N. Petrovskii and S. P. Burenkov) had been dismissed in a relatively short time, in the case of the former allegedly because of the poor showing of the Soviet Union in its infant-mortality rate (indeed, its rise), and in the latter case, supposedly because of foot-dragging in implementing a pay raise for health personnel,[4] whose salaries, even by Soviet standards, are abysmally low. I shall return to the income situation further on. Lately, another explanation has emerged for the problems in health (and elsewhere, I presume): that the situation began to unravel in the 1970s (for example, the rise of infant mortality between 1971 and 1974—after which publication of the data was discontinued for more than a decade).[5] The "1970s" is a euphemism for Leonid Brezhnev, who is thus posthumously blamed for what went wrong. Blaming former Soviet leaders like Stalin, Khrushchev, and Brezhnev is a favorite Soviet indoor sport of their successors. In the directives for the restructuring of the health service, issued in 1987 by the Party and the government, it was stated that in spite of tremendous achievements and the enormous advantages the Soviet health system enjoyed in resolving problems of health protection,

> an objective analysis demonstrates that these possibilities are not employed to their full measure. In the '70s and the beginning of the '80s negative tendencies began to appear and to grow in the activities of the organs and the institutions of health protection. The decrease in the economic growth of the country, the weakening of attention to questions of the protection of health led to a decline in the share of expenditures . . . in the state budget, a slowing down of the process of innovation in its material-technical base, in the mastering of new pharmaceuticals and methods of treatment.[6]

This was followed by a series of critical remarks about the style of work of the health administration, the rampant bureaucratism, corruption, indifference, irresponsibility, the serious mistakes in the admission to training, training itself, and licensing of medical personnel, the deficiencies in the payment levels for health personnel, the neglect of prevention, the insufficient attention to the protection of food, water, and the environment, the decrease in health consciousness of the population, the poor quality of care, particularly in the treatment of mothers and children, the inadequacy of equipment, the deficient supply of pharmaceuticals, and the mediocre if not largely irrelevant medical research and backwardness in comparison with the situation abroad.

Why Is There Concern Now?

The first question we might ask is why concern has suddenly been expressed formally and officially by people whose own medical care leaves little or nothing to be desired. It is, of course, an open secret that health care in the Soviet Union (like all other components of the standard of living) is stratified in many categories,[7] and it is, therefore, difficult, if not often useless, to speak of Soviet socialized medicine as a whole. One can refer to Soviet socialized *medicines*. The major concern of this chapter, however, apparently as well as of Gorbachev's appointed health officials, is the health care of the nonelites.

The following reasons may be suggested: The health service, as constituted at the end of the 1980s, is indeed in such poor shape that it helps to undermine the legitimacy of the Gorbachev regime, something that no amount of responsibility deflection is able to avoid; furthermore, the service continues to show a widening gap between propaganda claims and day-today reality, particularly in the rural areas and in Central Asia but also even in Moscow. According to the health minister, only 35 percent of rural district hospitals have hot running water, 27 percent have no sewerage, and 17 percent have no running water. The minister asked rhetorically, "What good are such hospitals for modern medical care?"[8] In Moscow, he said, women are reluctant to give birth "because of the disastrous conditions of the maternity hospitals—out of 33 such hospitals only 12 meet present-day standards and sanitary norms." As a result, while patients flock to the capital—the center of medical science—from all over the country, Moscow women go to the "backwoods, to Saratov" to have their babies.[9] At the same time, the increasingly embarrassing comparison with foreign nations, including even those of the Third World, makes the usual Soviet boasts of superiority seem hard to swallow. It must have taken courage for Chazov to announce publicly that the Soviet Union's infant mortality stood fiftieth in the world, after Barbados and the United Arab Emirates.[10] The backwardness of contemporary Soviet medicine at the clinical level has been confirmed by visiting foreign physicians. Thus Dr. Kenneth Prager, of the Columbia University College of Physicians and Surgeons, who visited the Soviet Union in 1986, reported that Soviet medical care was decades behind the West, particularly in its technology. He also remarked that the degree of sophistication with which the system dealt with such chronic and complex ailments as cancer and cardiovascular diseases was what one might expect of a developing nation, not one of the world's greatest powers.[11] This confirmed the earlier observations of Dr. William Knaus, who spent a year in the Soviet Union and had access to clinical facilities.[12]

But there is yet another aspect of major concern: the impact of illness and trauma and premature mortality upon people and society. This impact can be broadly defined as dual: The first is the expressive impact, that is, what morbidity does to the individual—personally, subjectively, emotionally—in terms of pain or discomfort. This aspect of illness is, of course, at the center of the clinical concern: It is the area of responsibility of the physician and therapist; it is what, for the public, medicine is all about (or should be). Furthermore, illness and trauma activate important psychologically regressive tendencies in the individual, leading to certain types of expectations concerning the supportive role of physicians and medical personnel. There are fairly constant complaints by Soviet patients about the rudeness, the indifference, the lack of compassion shown by doctors and nurses toward patients.[13] It should be noted that in most instances patients are automatically assigned to a physician (on the basis of residence or job), which means there is little incentive for physicians to please patients if they are not so inclined. In a survey, from 25 to 49 percent of patients questioned wanted to change their assigned doctor. In contrast, 70 percent of medical personnel opposed the idea of a free choice of doctors. One of their main reasons was the usual argument that patients are unable to evaluate a doctor's qualifications.[14]

The second impact is functional: the often incapacitating nature of morbidity for the role performance of individuals. In any society, each person has a series of obligations or functions not only in the occupational sphere but in many others as well. A mother who is ill and incapacitated may be unable to take care of her helpless child, a situation that may have tragic consequences. Thus, illness has economic, social, and sometimes military consequences. In the Soviet Union, time and again, we are reminded of the economic costs of temporary illness, that is, of those cases in which the individual is expected to return to work. For example, at the 18th Congress of Trade Unions of the USSR, the figure of 90 billion rubles per year was given an as estimate of the total losses inflicted upon the economy by what was said to be the "low effectiveness of public health."[15]

The individual is, of course, mainly preoccupied with the expressive side of illness. Society, however, and in this particular case, Soviet society, emphasizes illness's functional aspects.

Health and Society

Before proceeding further in an examination of the contemporary health and medical situation, it is important to make some statements of general (not only Soviet) relevance. First, one should note the roles that social, economic, political, and cultural factors play in shaping and maintaining the health service. That service is, as we shall see later on, not only the expression or the utilization of the state of the art—medical science and technology—but also a specific product of its social and cultural setting. It is only through that perspective that one can understand the nature of Soviet health care and its problems—and how it diverges from that of other countries, although the practitioners possess (in part) an identical knowledge of the etiology of illness and appropriate treatment modalities. This even helps us understand the role of Soviet physicians in the use or abuse of medicine for state-imposed purposes (psychiatry, for example, or the control of absenteeism through the delivery of sickness certificates).

Second, it is also necessary to realize that illness and mortality are, to a larger extent than commonly assumed, relatively impervious to the activities of the health-care system, particularly in a country that has gone through the initial phase of development, and where infectious diseases have, by and large, been brought under control. More important, in this respect, is the nature of social life, for example, the standard of living and quality of life (income, occupation, housing, availability of running water, sewers, education, infrastructure and communications, level of stratification and inequalities, social services, the environment). In addition to this list, we should add "voluntary health risks" against which medicine is largely ineffective (smoking, drinking, sedentary habits, overeating). It is, therefore, unfair to assign all the blame for illness and related problems to the health-care service alone.

Finally, before we turn to the specifically Soviet aspects of the problem, it is important to keep in mind certain aspects of health care observable almost everywhere and resulting from the nature of health knowledge and technology. Among the most salient trends are the following:[16] The increasing complexity of contemporary medical care leads to a growing division of medical labor and the proliferation of specialization and superspecialization, which necessitate the integration of all these narrow inputs into an acceptable clinical service. As a result of that complexity and the increasing size of medical-care facilities as well as their costs, a managerial organization emerges to handle both services and finances and introduces a new "bureaucratic" element in health care. Then, as medicine becomes increasingly scientific and technological, there is the growing problem of the alienation of the patient through the depersonalization of care.

In addition, as a result of the increased capacity of medicine to deal with a wide range of previously intractable conditions and the introduction of medical equipment that requires more labor and capital inputs, the proportion of the gross national product (GNP) spent by or allocated to the health service often grows at a faster rate than other sectors of society or of the GNP itself. This leads to at least two related problems or dilemmas: the opportunity costs incurred in nonhealth sectors owing to the growing share taken by health expenditures and the question within the health system itself of allocating scarce personnel and financial resources to the many claimants for these resources: clinical services (and for which conditions?), prevention, research (basic or applied?), and health education of the population. Moreover, as the technical capacity of medicine improves, a cultural lag appears between it and the ethical, moral, legal, and sometimes religious issues raised by that capacity. For example, when does one "turn the machine off"? Finally, in most countries the inequalities that result from class, ethnic, or other stratification and uneven distribution of wealth tend to be reflected in the quantity and the quality of care available to different groups, even where health care is paid from taxes and should ostensibly be equal for all. There are two aspects to this question: First, the upper, more educated, classes usually know how to derive more benefits from the medical establishment, even if it is available to all on an equal basis; and second, in some instances, tax moneys are used to support different categories of health care for different kinds of people, as is the case in the Soviet Union.

Major Health Problems of Soviet Society Today

Health care tends to be judged, whether entirely validly or not, by vital statistics: natality, mortality, life expectancy, morbidity, and so on. In these respects, and in its own terms, the Soviets have found their society's health care wanting. In particular, infant- and adult-male-mortality rates have risen to relatively high levels, the life expectancy of the male population has gone down,[17] and morbidity remains high enough to cause losses to industry that are deemed detrimental to the economy itself. The majority of the problems reported by the press, and confirmed by Chazov and those who echoed his views, seem to be inherent in the nature and structure of Soviet society.

More specifically, we can trace these problems to the following factors, and the list is far from complete: First, the obsession of the regime with increasing industrial production has led to a secondary or marginal priority for those sectors of the society that are not directly engaged in economic production: the health system costs money but does not immediately produce the output desired by the leadership or the population. The "functional" argument presented earlier would justify a higher priority for health care because it keeps the producers working or returns them to work after they have been temporarily incapacitated by illness or trauma. But apparently this argument has not been powerful enough to affect the position and the priority level of health care in the light of more pressing needs and probably because of a shortage in overall resources. The source of that problem is called the "residual principle of planning." What this means, to quote a Soviet source, is that "the health service got only what was left after the requirements were met of other branches which were once considered more important."[18] Apparently this approach has now been, or will be, superseded by a new one, in which health will be considered as the country's main wealth. This should lead to an improvement in the financing of medical care.

In the past, health care has been consistently underfinanced. Compared to most other industrial societies, the share of the Soviet national income or of the GNP that goes into the health sector has been small, and it tended to go down in the mid-1980s, not up. According to Chazov, that share was 4.1 percent in 1970 (down from 6.6 percent in 1965),[19] but was 4 percent in 1987, and if the late 1980s trends continue, it would fall to 3.9 percent by the end of 1990.[20]

By contrast, in most industrial nations, the share is from 6 to 12 percent of the GNP, with the United States at the high end. Thus, in these terms, most industrial societies spend about two to three times more of their national wealth on the health sector than the Soviet Union. Chazov's aim was to double the Soviet figure to about 8 percent by the year 2000, though a more realistic level would be 6.

Second, in addition to the "residual principle," which meant that when budget cuts had to be made, the health service got the brunt of them, it should be noted that the availability of financial resources alone is not necessarily sufficient to improve the service. It has often been difficult, if not impossible, for health authorities to spend their allocations because of the unavailability of either goods (medical equipment, spare parts, building materials) or the needed labor, often engaged in "higher priority" tasks.[21] As a result, millions of unspent rubles have had to be returned to the ministry, the planned institutions exist on paper only, and health facilities do not get needed maintenance. Thus often credit lines at the State Bank are as useful to hospital or clinic directors as $100 bills would be to someone stranded in the Sahara or on a desert island.

Third, the shortage of drugs and equipment,[22] just like that of other consumer goods, leads inevitably to a black or gray market that increases their costs and makes life even more difficult for those in low-income brackets or those whose occupations do not easily give them access to scarce goods and services that can be exchanged for what they need. In a case reported in the press, nurses in one provincial pediatric hospital stole medicines (mostly antibiotics), replaced the liquid (in ampules) with distilled water or dipheril-hydramine hydrochloride, and sold the ampules on the black market. This went on for two years before the nurses were caught. What amazed the reporter, however, was not so much the stealing but the fact that the pediatricians failed to notice that the substances they administered to their patients had no therapeutic effect.[23] Anyone who has been to the Soviet Union can testify to the lack of a culture oriented toward the welfare or interests of client or buyer. Except for the elites, the customer is usually more supplicant than king. The rudeness of waiters, hotel personnel, and office employees is legendary and can be matched by health-care personnel, from doctors to nurses to attendants.

Fourth, it has been said that the bureaucrats are major obstacles to *perestroika*. Bureaucracy has also invaded, with a vengeance, Soviet medicine, creating a large, centralized, unwieldy apparatus that is slow to react to new situations (as was the case with influenza epidemics of the 1970s or Chernobyl in 1986 or Armenia in 1988). And if we are to believe complaint letters, the bureaucratic mind-set, with its inflexibility and officiousness, also affects clinical personnel at all levels, not only health bureaucrats.

In the U.S. setting, the separation of state and medicine has assumed (as far as the American Medical Association [AMA] is concerned) the same kind of sacredness as the separation of church and state enshrined in the U.S. Constitution. The preamble to the Medicare Act states that "nothing in this law shall be construed to authorize any Federal Employee to exercise any supervision or control over the practice of medicine or over the compensation of any person providing health services."[24] The Soviet case is precisely a mirror image of that principle—the profession as an independent corporate group with political power was eliminated from the Soviet scene early in the history of the regime, and physicians have become state employees, in fact, bureaucrats, working for and paid by the state, under strict state supervision, and paid poorly. It is precisely this situation that enabled the regime to manipulate medicine, particularly psychiatry, to repress and control dissidents.[25] Dedication to service and placing the welfare of the patient first to a large degree disappeared, together with the disappearance of the profession and its professional ethic. In the Soviet context, the state, the Party, and the interests of the collective have priority.

Moreover, the general corruption that results from the scarcity of goods and services has, as we have seen in the case of scarce drugs, also penetrated health care. Surgeons, for example, in many instances reported in the press, do not operate, even in urgent cases, until a fee has been settled upon and paid by the patient, relatives, or friends.[26] These fees sometimes amount to hundreds of rubles.[27] This involves not only surgeons but also other health personnel, including attendants and nurses, who are especially poorly paid. Patients go to hospitals armed with sheafs of ruble notes to pay for every service: changes of linen, bedpans, medications, and so on. One begins to wonder whether the regime, aware of that situation, has not used it as an internal argument to pay health-care employees very poor salaries, or whether poor salaries in the first place have impelled personnel to accept and request money or gifts. The result (and the 1986 pay increases are not likely to change the situation very much since the average increase was 35.6 percent)[28] is that free and high-quality medical care (as guaranteed in the constitution) has often become a sick and very expensive joke.[29]

As Chazov indicated, the typical bureaucratic devices used in the economic realm to judge performance are also prevalent in the health system: the chase after quantitative indices and achievements and the neglect of quality. For example, because polyclinics are financed according to the volume of work (number of patient visits), there is pressure, as we shall see, to have doctors treat a very large number of patients. At the same time concern about the number of doctors and the number of hospital beds appears to be at the expense of worry about the quality of medical training and practice and the nature of these hospital beds.

Here again the revelations of Chazov[30] are interesting: Many doctors (around 10 percent) are incompetent, having been admitted to medical schools through bribery[31] and given diplomas without being able to perform the simplest medical procedures, interpreting an EKG, or delivering a child. In 1978, for example, it was reported that the director of a medical school in the Georgian Republic was sent to jail because 170 students from a class of 200 (85 percent) had been admitted subsequent to parental payments.[32]

Hospital beds are often beds, but no more. Chazov deplored the lack of adequate floor space and the absence of the equipment that is standard in hospitals the world over. For example, the official norm is 7 square meters per bed—but in fact there are only 4.2 square meters. In the Soviet Union 15 percent of the projected costs of a hospital is earmarked for equipment (the rest goes for bricks and mortar), whereas in the countries of Eastern Europe the figure is 40 percent.[33]

Thus hospital beds are often "just ordinary places to sleep"[34] located in completely unsuitable buildings, some dating back to the nineteenth century. "No wonder," added the minister, "that hospitals require weeks instead of days to cure certain minor illnesses." In the countryside, as we have seen, hospitals frequently do not have the most elementary sanitary facilities. More specifically, in an example from Turkmenia, a Krasnovodsk hospital for treating infectious diseases is located in a building that once was a stable! "The septic tanks (and, if you'll excuse the term, the open cesspools) are on a level with the ground water . . . epidemics of viral hepatitis don't die down in the summer months—on the contrary, jaundice cases are up 62 percent."[35]

At the same time, there is abundant evidence that in many instances, statistical reporting is inaccurate and "doctored" to make those responsible for performance look better. One professor of pediatrics reported, for instance, that in children's hospitals the death of an infant at age eleven months might be altered in the register to read one year and one month. Since the index of infant mortality is based on deaths *before* one year, that death would not affect infant-mortality statistics.[36] Many other instances of "cooking" the statistics to present a better showing have been reported in the press. For example, in Uzbekistan, cases have been brought to light of the concealment of babies' deaths by local hospitals. When records were straightened out, the infant mortality immediately quadrupled![37]

The stratification of medical care, noted above, has some direct implications on the quality and quantity of the care received by the population. Generally speaking, there are two networks for such care: the territorial network, available to the ordinary population and access to which is usually based on residence; and the closed, or special, network, reserved for a variety of population groups, based on occupation and rank, and of an ascending quality as one moves up the sociopolitical structure. At the apex of the medical pyramid are the facilities (such as the Kremlin hospitals and clinics) reserved for the top Soviet elites and their equivalents (either special sections of hospitals or freestanding medical facilities) elsewhere in the provinces. The upshot is that these special facilities drain an inordinate amount of resources and of personnel.[38] This explains why, in light of the plethora of physicians, ordinary medical facilities are crowded, inadequate, and often understaffed, and why physicians in these facilities have to see a patient every few minutes (sometimes as many as nine per hour). More than half of these few minutes are consumed by paperwork. For instance, Dr. G. Ivanov, from Leningrad, wrote to *Izvestiia* that he was so pressed for time that he had to make diagnoses and prescribe treatment as speedily as a jet pilot in aerial combat.[39] Another doctor complained that she went through her appointments without looking up at her patients. Her load was thirty-six patients in four hours, thus seven minutes per patient, again with more than half of that time consumed by paperwork.[40] (Most Soviet doctors have to write in longhand, as there are few dictating machines available.)

By contrast, according to recent Soviet information, half of the physicians in Moscow are employed in special, or closed, clinics and hospitals, where the load is considerably lighter, the pay better, and the work conditions easier and more pleasant. For the ordinary citizen, it is the familiar waiting in line like that in the grocery store, in the shops, at the railroad station, and practically everywhere else.

Health-care stratification is, as we pointed out earlier, a universal phenomenon. It does, however, create a problem when two glaringly dissimilar systems exist side by side, in light of the expectation by the population that they are entitled (Article 42 of the Soviet Constitution) to qualified medical care. It may be easier for a Soviet citizen to accept unequal pay and living conditions based on jobs and qualifications than unequal health care. This care, considering its expressive nature, discussed earlier, has a different resonance: It deals, after all, with life, with suffering, areas often of the deepest emotional significance. It is difficult for parents to accept their inability to find the antibiotic that may save their child's life when they know (or at least assume) that such medication is available in the special clinics for the elites and their children or at exorbitant and unaffordable black market prices. This inequality before illness and death is thus attributable to social and political conditions. It may be assumed that the poor showing in infant mortality originates, to a large extent, among the population that lives at or below the official poverty level. According to McAuley,[41] the poor constitute between 30 and 40 percent of the population. It may therefore be hypothesized that the concern of the Gorbachev regime with the health care available to nonelite citizens may have more than a strictly economic or functional aspect: In view of the expressive aspects of illness, the political and ideological implications may be just as important.

Finally, the Soviet Union suffers the whole gamut of other health-related problems that affect most societies today: the threat of an AIDS epidemic (though not yet comparable to the threat in the United States or Western Europe), the health implications of industrial pollution—where this has been considered secondary or tertiary to the needs of rapid industrialization and urbanization, the problem of alcohol-related diseases and mortality (including infant mortality), the growing drug abuse, and the increasing proportion of the aged in the population, that is, of individuals often with a multiplicity of health problems, many of which are intractable or difficult and costly to treat.

The Hypothesis of Convergence

The convergence hypothesis is that the increased industrialization of society after society around the world leads to a gradual resemblance of social systems because of the similarity in the means of production used in such societies and because of emulation. That kind of production has its own kind of imperatives, its specific time orientation, its need for discipline and a distinctive managerial structure, and a hierarchical system that extends well beyond the factory walls and the office and that creates a stratification system particular to the society. Convergence by emulation means that the availability of industrial models leads the less-developed or less-industrialized societies to attempt to copy already available patterns—more or less independently of the logic of industrial evolution.[42] Industrialization, wherever it is introduced, leads to change in the culture of the society and even in the character, or personality, of its people. Thus, convergence is a hypothesis of soft determinism. There certainly is plenty of available evidence to confirm, at least in part, that hypothesis. One might then posit precisely the same idea for the health-care services of different nations: the universality of medical knowledge and technology and of the "medical means of production" should lead to the same organizational structures. For example, the need to maintain aseptic conditions in the hospital operating rooms should lead to a universal blueprint of what a hospital is like, what kind of staffing it requires, what kind of administrative and managerial arrangements impose themselves.

And yet, an examination of the Soviet health-care system (and others around the world) suggests that the convergence hypothesis is not yet confirmed—there is often little convergence in spite of superficial similarities. A Soviet hospital is first and foremost a Soviet institution and secondarily a medical one. It seems that the medical reforms proposed by the Party and government in 1987[43] were aimed precisely at making the health-care system resemble its counterparts in advanced countries. But let us look at the main present divergences:

1. The percentage of the GNP going into the health-care system, contrary to the experience in the West, has decreased. As we have seen, less than half of what is presumably needed (8 percent of the GNP) is now allocated to the health system.

2. Technology is not an independent (and some would say demonic) force that inexorably imposes itself on the health system. It is possible, as the Soviet health system demonstrates, for a society to refuse to buy or build that technology because it is too expensive and there are higher-priority areas elsewhere for the use of the money. But here again, the international perspective complicates the situation for the Soviets: The knowledge exists, the equipment has been manufactured that deals more efficiently with morbidity and mortality. It becomes increasingly difficult to deny the availability of such equipment to the population. But so far, again with the exception of elites, this has been the case.

3. The health service has little independence; it is not really differentiated from the polity. It is state medicine, as pointed out earlier—and there is not a really autonomous medical profession that could apply pressure on the state and society for improving it, nor is there an articulate consumer movement. Perhaps the democratization that Gorbachev has mentioned alongside *glasnost'* and *perestroika* could lead eventually to an increasingly autonomous medical corps and more public involvement, but so far there is little indication of that. The reforms have been proposed by a small group at the apex of the ministerial health bureaucracy, with the prodding of the Gorbachev regime.

Conclusions

It seems fairly well established that a national health-care structure is the outcome of a dialectical combination of universal factors (such as knowledge and technology) and of particular elements (the culture of a specific society). This was well articulated by Shipler for the Soviet Union:

> The system of medical care expresses the full range of strengths and weaknesses of Soviet society; it is a model of the country's hierarchy, reflecting the instincts of authoritarianism, conservatism and elitism that pervades all areas of life. . . . Soviet medicine can be excellent and incompetent simul-

taneously, available in mediocrity to all and accessible in high quality only to the chosen or the canny or to those blessed by chance.[44]

To a large degree, the multiplicity of problems faced by the Soviet health service are also the problems of Soviet society. It is difficult to see how one set can be solved or resolved without the other. There is reason to be skeptical of the ability of the Soviet Union, as long as Soviet society does not change, to radically improve health care for the near future or even to finance the change in light of the rapidly deteriorating economic situation. Thus far, Gorbachev, in spite of the impressive rhetoric, has not accomplished very much. And the slowness of his reforms will be matched by the slowness of significant changes in medical care.

It will also be interesting, in the years to come, to see the degree to which the basic philosophical and ideological tenets of *perestroika* will percolate into the philosophy and the ideology of the health service. Certainly, in his pronouncements, Chazov echoed many of the themes of Gorbachev. One instance is his conditional support of a free choice of physicians, with the idea that good doctors would earn more money than the poor ones. He wants medical installations to justify, through an improvement of the quality of care, the funds allocated to them and thus the health-care system's impact upon illness and length of temporary incapacity. His measures also encouraged the private practice of medicine, although the setting up of such a practice continues to be hobbled and sabotaged by local bureaucrats.[45] The rise of cooperatives in the medical area is another signpost. These organizations, in effect, dispense medical care on a private basis. The best known is that of Svyatoslav Fedorov, a well-known ophthalmologist, who pioneered an operation that makes it possible for people who previously needed eyeglasses to see without them. Recently, however, medical cooperatives have been severely restricted in their scope of activities, and many have been forced to close.

Chazov suggested that the state cannot do it all and that there is a place for voluntary and community activities in health care; he even suggested a lottery to help the financing. As a matter of fact, charity organizations have appeared in the Soviet Union and in 1988 were placed under an umbrella structure called the "Soviet Health and Charity Foundation." Even more interesting, the USSR Health Ministry announced in June 1988 that the health authorities would accept "the voluntary assistance of religious believers in tending the sick in whatever form that help was offered."[46]

Time and again, the health minister deplored the technological backwardness of Soviet medicine and Soviet medical research, complaining for example that not a single Nobel Prize in medicine has been won by a Soviet scientist. His points of reference were Western industrial societies. In that respect he was a Westernizer and not a Slavophile in the Russian meaning of the term, eager like Gorbachev to direct reform from above. Instead of a romantic adulation of national Russian medicine and the use of folk remedies, he was dedicated to the introduction of the latest technological achievements. He did not claim that Soviet physicians are much more humane than their Western counterparts precisely because they do not have all that advanced technology and are therefore closer to their patients. Rather, he talked about the fact that so many doctors are incompetent and insensitive to the emotional needs of their patients.

There is no doubt that the structure of health care he wished for the Soviet Union tends to resemble systems of Western industrial societies. But these systems are moving targets. And it may also be suggested that in the West there are trends that, to some, are disturbingly similar to the situation in the Soviet Union: the increasing role of the polity in the organizing, financing, and controlling of health care (and in the United States the role of the large corporations in shaping the health services for their employees and workers);[47] the increasing bureaucratization and control over medical work and the activities of the physicians, in an effort to put a cap on medical costs; and the trend that some see toward the deprofessionalization or the proletarianization of the medical profession, as doctors increasingly are salaried and work in large organizations controlled by nonphysicians.

The study of Soviet health care has long been a neglected field in the West. The early enthusiasm elicited by the blueprint of socialized medicine has disappeared. Nevertheless, a look into that arrangement for health care may provide some interesting insights (duly qualified by the peculiarities of Soviet society) into the nature of the health problems in other societies. Its importance lies, to a great extent, in that it deals with the human resources of society, indeed its most important resource. Concern for health security, an area of marginal importance in the nineteenth century, has become a central problem at the end of the twentieth century and will continue to be so in the twenty-first.

The original design for Soviet socialized medicine reflected a grand vision, a progressive view. It is too bad that for a variety of reasons, some of which have been discussed here, the very milieu in which this vision was implanted could not sustain and nourish it. It remains to be seen whether a revised version of this blueprint, with a strong dose of the features that developed in the "capitalist" West, will lead to a design that will adequately and economically secure the health needs of the population in the next century, East and West.

Notes

1. "The Physician on the Threshold of the Third Millennium" (in Russian), *Literaturnaia gazeta,* April 29, 1987, p. 11, in *Current Digest of the Soviet Press* [hereafter *CDSP*] 39, no. 19 (June 10, 1987), p. 1. Dr. Chazov resigned his position in early 1990.

2. P. Beilin, "Chelovecheskii faktor" [The human factor], *Literaturnaia gazeta,* December 14, 1977.

3. A. Cherniak, "Complacency Reigns in the Collective" (in Russian), *Pravda,* September 15, 1986, in *Survey* 29, no. 4 (127) (August 1987), p. 164.

4. In the USSR Council of Ministers *Pravda,* January 4, 1987, in *CDSP* 39, no. 1 (1987), p. 19.

5. Mark G. Field, "Soviet Infant Mortality: A Mystery Story," in D. B. Jelliffe and E.F.P. Jelliffe, *Advances in International Maternal and Child Health,* vol. 6 (Oxford: Clarendon Press, 1986), pp. 25–65; and Christopher Davis and Murray Feshbach, *Rising Infant Mortality in the USSR in the 1970s* (Washington, D.C.: U.S. Department of Commerce, June 1980).

6. Proekt TsK KPSS i Soveta Ministrov SSSR, "Osnovnye napravleniia zdorovia naseleniia i perestroiki zdravookhraneniia SSSR v dvenadtsatoi piatiletke i na period do 2000 goda" [General trends in the health of the population and the restructuring of the USSR's public health care in the Twelfth Five Year Plan and for the Period up to the Year 2000], *Pravda,* August 15, 1987.

7. Christopher Davis, "The Organization and Performance of the Contemporary Soviet Health Service," in G. Lapidus and G. Swanson (eds.), *State and Welfare, USA/USSR* (Berkeley, Calif.: Institute of International Studies, 1988).

8. "Our Dialogue: The Science of Health" (Interview with Yevgenii Ivanovich Chazov, USSR health minister) (in Russian), *Sovetskaia Rossia,* July 5, 1987, p. 1, in *CDSP* 39, no. 27 (1987), p. 22.

9. "The Physician on the Threshold of the Third Millennium," op. cit.

10. Leonid Zagladskii, "The Child Fell Sick" (in Russian), *Literaturnaia gazeta,* no. 16, April 15, 1987.

11. Kenneth M. Prager, "Soviet Health Care's Critical Condition," *Wall Street Journal,* January 29, 1987, p. 28.

12. William A. Knaus, *Inside Russian Medicine* (New York: Everest House, 1981).

13. See, for example, D. Granin, "O Miloserdii" [On compassion], *Literaturnaia gazeta,* March 18, 1987, p. 13; Zh. Mindubaev, "The Line to the Physician" (in Russian), *Izvestiia,* November 14, 1984; and Zh. Mindubaev, "Someone Else's Pain" (in Russian), *Izvestiia,* February 26, 1985, p. 3.

14. E. Antipenko and R. Nesymova, "On Studying the Opinions of Patients About the Work of Polyclinic Physicians" (in Russian), *Sovetskoe zdravookhranenie,* no. 12 (1983), pp. 16–18.

15. "The Physician on the Threshold of the Third Millennium," op. cit.

16. Mark G. Field, "Introduction," in *Success and Crisis in National Health Systems: A Comparative Perspective,* ed. Mark G. Field (London: Routledge, 1989), pp. 1–21.

17. Alain Blum and Alain Monnier, "La Mortalité en Union Soviétique," *Population et Sociétés,* no. 223 (April 1988); and Vladimir G. Treml, "A Turning Point in the Availability of Soviet Economic Statistics," *Soviet Economy* 2, no. 3 (July–September 1986), p. 277.

18. "Health Care" in *USSR '88 Yearbook* (Moscow: Novosti Press Agency, 1989), pp. 264–269.

19. M. D'Anastasio, "Red Medicine: Soviet Health System Despite Early Claims Is Riddled by Failures," *Wall Street Journal,* August 18, 1987.

20. "The Physician on the Threshold of the Third Millennium," op. cit.

21. See for example, "Repair in the Old Way Creates an Artificial Deficit of Hospital Beds" (in Russian), *Meditsinskaia Gazeta,* March 20, 1982, p. 2.

22. Mark Popovskii, "Medicine for the Toilers" (in Russian), *Russkaia mysl'* (Paris), no. 3542 (November 8, 1984); and "The Individual Came to the Pharmacy," *Meditsinskaia gazeta,* December 14, 1984, p. 1.

23. O. Parfenova, "On Duty and Honor: Sisters Without Mercy" (in Russian), *Trud,* August 11, 1985, p. 2, in *CDSP* 37, no. 52 (1985), p. 22. ("Sister" means nurse.)

24. Robert Pear, "High Costs Deciding Who Controls Medicine," *New York Times,* October 18, 1987, p. E6.

25. Sidney Bloch and Peter Reddaway, *Psychiatric Terror: How Soviet Psychiatry Is Used to Suppress Dissent* (New York: Basic Books, 1972); Sidney Bloch and Peter Reddaway, *Soviet Psychiatric Abuse: The Shadow over World Psychiatry* (London: Gollancz, 1984); and S. Grigoriants, "Soviet Psychiatric Prisoners," *New York Times,* February 23, 1988, p. A31.

26. "Combat the Antipodes of Communist Morality" (in Russian), *Bakinskii Rabochi,* January 23, 1979, p. 2, in *CDSP* 31, no. 4 (1979), p. 13.

27. Granin, "O Miloserdii" [On compassion], op. cit.; and David K. Shipler, "Soviet Medicine Mixes Inconsistency and Diversity," *New York Times,* June 26, 1977.

28. "From Informed Sources: Medical Personnel and Wages" (in Russian), *Izvestiia,* October 22, 1986, p. 3, also in *CDSP* 38, no. 42 (1986), p. 26.

29. "The Debatable and the Indisputable" (in Russian), *Literaturnaia gazeta,* January 15, 1977, p. 13, also in *CDSP* 39, no. 2 (1977), p. 16.

30. "On the Most Vital Question in the Health Sphere: Formula for Health" (Interview with Chazov) (in Russian), *Pravda,* April 13, 1987, p. 3, in *CDSP* 39, no. 15 (1987), p. 19.

31. S. Bablumian, "Face to Face with the Law: Pseudo-Students" (in Russian), *Izvestiia,* September 11, 1981.

32. Craig Whitney, "In Soviet Bribes Help to Get a Car, Get an Apartment, and Get Ahead," *New York Times,* May 4, 1978, pp. 1, 22.

33. "The Physician on the Threshold of the Third Millennium," op. cit.

34. "Our Dialogue: The Science of Health," op. cit.

35. A. Kostikova, "Pay Daily Attention to Health Protection: Behind the Fence of Decisions" (in Russian), *Pravda,* February 7, 1987, p. 3, in *CDSP* 39, no. 6 (1987), p. 21.

36. V. Tabolin, "Consultation at the Cradle" (in Russian), *Sovetskaia Rossia,* October 23, 1987, p. 3.

37. M. Volkov, "Health Service—Mother and Child" (in Russian), *Pravda,* August 31, 1987, p. 25, in *CDSP* 39, no. 35 (1987), p. 25.

38. I. Borich, "For a Limited Circle—Polemical Remarks on Special Polyclinics and Special Hospitals" (in Russian), *Meditsinskaia Gazeta,* August 5, 1987, p. 2, in *CDSP* 39, no. 32 (1987), p. 21.

39. G. Ivanov, "Frankly" (in Russian), *Izvestiia,* February 7, 1986.

40. A. Paikin and G. Silina, "The Sector Physician" (in Russian), *Literaturnaia Gazeta,* September 27, 1978, p. 11, also in *CSDP* 30, no. 40 (1978), pp. 4–7; and Iu. Tomashevskii, "Bumazhnaia likhoradka" [Paper fever], *Izvestiia,* January 7, 1986.

41. Alastair McAuley, *Economic Welfare in the Soviet Union: Poverty, Living Standards and Inequality* (Madison: University of Wisconsin Press, 1979), chap 4, pp. 70–98.

42. T. Anthony Jones, "Modernization Theory and Socialist Development," in *Social Consequences of Modernization in Communist Societies,* ed. Mark G. Field (Baltimore: Johns Hopkins University Press, 1976), p. 34.

43. Proekt TsK KPSS i Soveta Ministrov SSSR, op. cit.

44. David K. Shipler, *Russia—Broken Idols, Silent Dreams* (New York: New York Times Books, 1983).

45. Iv. Bliev, "Private practice" (in Russian), *Meditsinskaia Gazeta,* June 8, 1988.
46. "Charity Playing a Larger Role in Soviet Union," *Soviet East European Report, Radio Free Europe/Radio Liberty* 6, no. 10 (January 1, 1989), p. 2.
47. Paul Starr, *The Social Transformation of American Medicine* (New York: Basic Books, 1982).

CHAPTER 6

Drug Abuse in the USSR

John M. Kramer

> *Until recently, we in the Soviet Union were firmly convinced that drug addiction was a problem only in other countries. There never had been or ever could be any social grounds for addiction here. But facts are facts: the number of our people who suffer from this terrible ailment is growing.*
>
> —Bakinskii rabochii

The "New Soviet Man," official commentaries traditionally declaimed, was a morally superior individual untarnished by "negative" phenomena, including drug abuse. These commentaries typically explained the existence of such phenomena under socialism as "vestiges of the past" or "remnants of capitalism" that were rapidly "withering away" as socialist society approached the millennium of communism.[1]

Commentaries on this subject as late as the mid-1980s claimed that in the Soviet Union "serious drug addiction does not exist," "no minors suffer from drug addiction," and "not a single case" of addiction to amphetamines, cocaine, heroin, or LSD had been recorded. The few individuals who had become addicts (officially estimated in 1985 to number between 2,500 and 3,000) primarily did so unwittingly while being treated with addictive drugs for chronic diseases. Finally, there was even a "tendency towards a decline" in the limited addiction that did exist.[2]

However, legal initiatives taken since the 1920s appear to belie these public pronouncements. Thus, the Criminal Code of the Russian Soviet Federated Socialist Republic (RSFSR) in 1926 established criminal responsibility for the "production and storage of cocaine, morphine, and other narcotic substances for sale without proper authorization" and for maintaining premises where narcotics were used or sold. In 1928, the USSR prohibited the free circulation of cocaine, its salts, hashish, opium, morphine, heroin, and other narcotic substances. These initiatives, a recent study explained, were taken to combat "an outbreak of narcomania" in the 1920s.[3]

An earlier version of this chapter appeared in *Problems of Communism*, March-April 1988, pp. 28–40.

Several initiatives in the 1930s also sought this end. In 1934, a joint decree of the All-Union Central Executive Committee and the USSR Council of People's Commissars prohibited sowing opium poppies and Indian hemp—except as state crops on authorized collective and state farms—on territory of the USSR. In accordance with this decree, the Criminal Code of the RSFSR established criminal responsibility for these acts. The USSR Council of Ministers issued in 1935 the decree "Charging the All-Union Inspectorate of the USSR Council of People's Commissars with Observing and Overseeing the Circulation of Opium and Other Narcotic Substances."

The next set of initiatives against drug abuse did not appear until the 1960s. In 1966 the USSR Supreme Court and its counterpart in the Russian Republic convened plenary sessions that examined, inter alia, legal issues involved in the prosecution of individuals accused of manufacturing and distributing "narcotics, harsh acting substances, and poisons."[4] Their concern may have been prompted in part by reports of a "large number of drug users" in the military, particularly among soldiers serving in Central Asia.[5]

In 1972, the *Principles of Criminal Legislation of the USSR and the Union Republics* was amended to include under "grave crimes" the "theft, manufacture, acquisition, or possession of narcotics for the purpose of sale, and/or the sale of such substances." The Russian Republic in the same year decreed that narcotics addicts had to undergo specialized treatment for their condition. Those addicts who "evade treatment or continue to take drugs after treatment, who violate labor discipline, public order or the rules of socialist communal living" were subject to "compulsory treatment and labor re-education" in medical and labor-therapy institutions for terms of one to two years. Then, in 1974, the USSR Supreme Soviet issued a decree, "On Intensifying the Struggle Against Drug Addiction," that specified a series of measures to combat addiction.[6] Finally, in 1975 the USSR Supreme Court, in a plenary session, again examined the issue of drug addiction. The court did so, one commentary explained, "not because the scale of drug addiction has become menacing in any way, but because . . . this poison must be killed in its infancy."[7]

Officials in the republic of Georgia—when compared to their peers in other republics—appeared particularly concerned about drug abuse. As early as 1967 officials there asked: "Why were hemp and poppies being grown in areas of Georgia where they had not been sown in the past? Why were many young people with no ties to the criminal world and no previous convictions turning up among drug addicts? Why were there a growing number of crimes—thefts, speculation, extortion—committed for a single purpose: to obtain money immediately?"[8]

In 1967, the republic's Ministry of Internal Affairs (MVD) and the Komsomol established a special commission to study the extent of, and provide proposals to combat, drug abuse in Georgia.[9] In 1977, researchers in Georgia conducted the first known empirical sociological study in the

USSR of individuals officially considered abusers of drugs.[10] The study, whose findings were not published until 1987, provided data on the age, sex, family background, educational and occupational status, and drug-related activities of the individuals surveyed. The study found, inter alia, that among its sample the consumption of opium-based derivatives occupied "first place"—thereby refuting claims still made in official media that consumption of such drugs was "practically unheard of" in the USSR.[11]

The ascension to power of Mikhail Gorbachev as general secretary of the Communist party initiated a dramatic change in the official attitude towards drug abuse. Official media, reflecting the general secretary's campaign for *glasnost'* ("openness"), have carried numerous revealing accounts—frequently employing lurid language—portraying drug abuse (or "narcomania" as Soviet sources themselves often refer to it) as far more widespread in the USSR than previously admitted.

For example, an official in the USSR MVD claimed that in some areas of the Soviet Union illegal drugs were so available, "it's as if home-brewed beer flowed out of the water faucets." A reporter for *Literaturnaia gazeta*, after recounting how when visiting the United States she was warned always to carry money for drug addicts who might accost her, observed, "Now, as we see, this misfortune also has overtaken our country." It is thought that organized criminal gangs control the lucrative trade in illegal drugs. Gang leaders, "whose bodyguards sleep by their beds," who "keep hundreds and thousands of rubles under their doormats," and who "have hundreds of lives on their conscience," rarely are apprehended by the authorities.[12]

Two factors account for this *glasnost'*. First, the phenomenon—albeit its precise dimensions remain unknown—appears sufficiently serious to merit an official response that previous silence on the subject only inhibited. As one source argued: "Concealing an illness will not make it go away; it will only drive it inward. We have come to realize that openness is needed in the struggle against drug addiction; that we must look truth in the eye, no matter how unsavory that is."[13] More broadly, this circumstance is part of Mikhail Gorbachev's overall campaign for *glasnost'* in discussing and combatting social pathologies—alcoholism, corruption, prostitution—that he perceives are undermining the moral fabric of Soviet society.

Scope of the Problem

Soviet accounts of drug abuse undoubtedly employ hyperbolic language. However, as Soviet sources themselves readily concede, no one knows the actual dimensions of the phenomena they describe.[14] Western countries also encounter this problem. For example, an official with the United States Institute of Drug Abuse asserted that "you just can't trust the numbers" when assessing drug abuse in U.S. society.[15]

Several factors create this situation. First, terminological imprecision is common in much of the extant literature on drugs both within and without the USSR. Terms such as *abuse, addiction, dependency,* and *misuse* have no universally accepted definitions and often are employed interchangeably.[16] Soviet sources frequently exhibit this imprecision by referring to all drugs—regardless of their pharmacological properties—as "narcotics" and all users as "addicts."[17] Indeed, one Soviet official argued that to make any distinction among drugs is a "pernicious practice" because all drugs are "dangerous."[18]

The Standing Committee on the Control of Narcotics of the USSR Ministry of Health—officially the principal coordinating body charged with controlling production and use of narcotic and psychotropic substances in the USSR—applies its own terms to these phenomena.[19] According to E. A. Babaian, chairman of the committee, the term *narcomania* describes a "state induced by the use of narcotic substances" and is employed when "nonmedical use occurs of a substance which by law is classified as a narcotic substance." In contrast, the term *toxicomania* describes the "damage to health" that is induced by the nonmedical use of a substance "which has not yet been juridically recognized as being narcotic."[20] Unfortunately, these words themselves are not without terminological imprecision. For example, how precisely does one define—and what criteria are employed to measure—that "state" that narcomania induces or the "damage to health" that toxicomania describes?

To mitigate, if not eliminate, terminological confusion, the World Health Organization in 1965 proposed to substitute the term *drug dependence* for *drug addiction* in discourse about the subject.[21] Similarly, the United States National Commission on Marijuana and Drug Abuse recommended (notwithstanding the title of the commission itself) that the term *drug abuse* be deleted from public discussion: "The term has no functional utility," the commission claimed, and "has become no more than an arbitrary codeword for that drug use which is presently considered wrong."[22] Although this observation has merit, the present study employs the term *drug abuse* because a term that emphasizes "drug use which is presently considered wrong" has utility for the social scientist who studies public policy and the values of both elites and masses contained therein. Then, too, most individuals possess a commonsense—albeit imprecise—understanding of behavior that constitutes "drug abuse."

Second, in any society drug abusers for both personal and professional reasons often seek to conceal their condition. They do so especially in the USSR, where even casual drug users are registered with the police and often subject to severe legal penalties. Indeed, proponents of less draconian sanctions contend that current law serves only to discourage drug abusers from revealing their condition publicly and availing themselves of requisite medical treatment and counseling services.[23]

Third, only since 1988 has the USSR published even incomplete data on the extent of drug and toxic substance addiction nationally and in the union republics. Furthermore, the dictates of *glasnost'* notwithstanding, Soviet officials appear ambivalent about how candidly they should discuss this issue. A. V. Vlasov, then minister of the USSR MVD, typified this ambivalence in a *Pravda* interview. After conceding that "keeping silent" about drug abuse only exacerbated the problem, the minister nevertheless advocated limits on public discussion to avoid "stimulating unhealthy curiosity and interest" in the subject.[24]

However, the available materials on drug abuse do permit several generalizations. First, official statistics about drug abuse—which include only those individuals registered with the police and medical institutions—substantially understate the extent of the phenomenon. Thus, the minister of public health of the Russian Republic contended that it is "naïve" to believe official statistics reporting only one or two drug addicts in many oblasts of the USSR.[25] Nevertheless, drug abuse is unlikely in the foreseeable future to supersede alcoholism as the preeminent social pathology in the Soviet Union. Second, in contrast to findings in an earlier study on this subject,[26] the phenomenon now appears, albeit to different degrees, among all socioeconomic groups and educational levels in the population. In 1988 workers (*rabochie*) constituted more than 60 percent of all individuals registered with drug-addiction clinics. It remains unclear whether this figure accurately reflected the incidence of addiction among different socioeconomic groups or indicated only that workers were more likely than individuals from other groups to be registered with drug-addiction clinics.[27] Third, drug abusers acquire and consume drugs in ways similar (although not identical) to those in the West. They steal them, produce them themselves, and purchase them illegally from drug dealers and often legally from pharmacies and other medical institutions. To support their habit, they engage in sundry illegalities ranging from prostitution to armed robbery. Users sniff glue, swallow amphetamines, barbiturates, and cough syrups with a high codeine content, smoke marijuana and hashish, inject themselves with heroin, etc. In contrast, the consumption of narcotic drugs appears far less prevalent in the Soviet Union than in many Western countries.

In 1988, 52,000 individuals were officially registered as drug addicts in the USSR. Individuals under the age of thirty (including 14,000 minors) made up 62 percent of this group and females, 12 percent. Approximately 80,000 individuals were recorded as "using," but not addicted to, "narcotics."[28] Toxic substance abuse also has become a "serious problem." In 1988, 22,000 individuals, including 13,000 minors, "used" these substances.[29] Although national statistics on drug-related deaths have not been published, one report stated that such deaths are "far from unique."[30]

Table 6.1 provides data on individuals registered at medical institutions with a diagnosis of drug or toxin addiction. These data indicate that in 1987, compared to 1986 and 1980, the number of such individuals per 100,000 population in the USSR increased by approximately 25 and 60 percent, respectively. In 1987, Turkmenia possessed the dubious distinction of having (by far) the highest such index among the union republics. The 1987 index in Ukraine, Kirgizia, and Kazakhstan also exceeded the national

TABLE 6.1
Individuals Registered at Medical Institutions with a Diagnosis of Narcomania or Toxicomania (per 100,000 Population)

	1980	1985	1986	1987
USSR	13.6	14.9	17.1	21.5
Union republics				
Armenia			7.9	6.3
Azerbaidzhan			7.8	11.1
Belorussia			3.2	4.8
Estonia			5.9	10.3
Georgia			17.2	17.7
Kazakhstan			19.5	26.5
Kirgizia			32.7	29.0
Latvia			12.3	19.0
Lithuania			7.2	10.1
Moldavia			5.7	8.0
Russia			13.4	17.9
Tadzhikistan			6.2	9.1
Turkmenia			152.3	129.9
Ukraine			24.9	32.4
Uzbekistan			15.5	20.8

Sources: For the USSR--*Narodnoe khoziaistvo SSSR v 1987* (Moscow: Finansy i Statistika, 1988), p. 549. For the union republics--*Argumenty i fakty*, no. 13 (1989).

average. In contrast, the index in the Armenian, Belorussian, Estonian, Lithuanian, Moldavian, and Tadzhik Soviet Socialist Republics (SSRs) was half the national average or less.

These data must be assessed cautiously. First, they indicate only the number of addicts registered with medical institutions, not the number of addicts in the USSR. The latter figure undoubtedly far exceeds the former because, as noted, many addicts avoid registering with the police and undergoing medical treatment. In informal talks with representatives of the United States Drug Enforcement Agency in 1988, Soviet officials estimated that in the USSR there were currently 150,000–200,000 drug "addicts" (three to four times the number of officially registered "addicts") and that the number of drug "abusers" increased by 50 percent annually.[31]

Second, Soviet officials provide vague and even incorrect definitions of what constitutes an "addict," "user," and a "narcotic." The head of the Main Administration for Criminal Investigation of the USSR MVD reported that registered addicts are "people whom doctors officially consider sick." Users are individuals who consume "narcotics" in "one way or another or have already tried them . . . but whom doctors do not consider sick." Hashish is the principal "narcotic" consumed by a "majority" of individuals in both categories.[32]

Such materials are of limited utility. They do not indicate what criteria doctors employ to determine how and when a person is sufficiently "sick" to merit the appellation "addict." Similarly, a category that includes individuals who "use" narcotics "in one way or another or have already tried them" reveals little about the actual incidence of drug abuse. Finally, to consider hashish—which produces no physical and, usually, no psychological dependence—as a "narcotic" is, at best, a debatable proposition.[33] To make no distinction between hashish and narcotic substances (e.g., opiates), which produce both physical and psychological dependence, is inaccurate.

Third, the number of "addicts" registered at medical institutions may reveal more about the zeal, effectiveness, and honesty of officials in registering and reporting these individuals than it does about the actual incidence of drug abuse in different union republics. For example, one can hypothesize that drug abuse has been a serious problem in Moldavia: The Presidium of the USSR Supreme Soviet heard a report on this subject in 1988.[34] Yet according to Table 6.1, Moldavia in 1986 had the second lowest, and in 1987 the third lowest, number of registered addicts per 100,000 population of any union republic. The aforementioned report of the USSR Supreme Soviet also asserted that there is "great concern" about "the struggle against drug addiction, especially among young people" in the Russian and Uzbek SSRs—but registered addicts in both republics were below the national average in 1986 and 1987. Similarly, one suspects that the extremely low figure for registered addicts in Tadzhikistan in comparison to other Central Asian republics presents a misleading picture of the extent of drug abuse there. Yet other officials may seek to demonstrate their zeal in the fight against drugs by *inflating* the number of registered addicts in their republics. Turkmenia, with its disproportionately higher number of registered addicts than the national average, may provide a relevant example of this circumstance. Such behavior would parallel that displayed by officials in other "campaigns" against social pathologies and deviant life-styles.[35]

Data on the socioeconomic background and drug-related activities of known drug users come principally from two polls in the republic of Georgia, one conducted in 1977 and the other in the mid-1980s.[36] A comparison of the respective samples indicates that in the 1980s drug users were far more likely than their counterparts in the 1970s to be female, young, well educated, affluent, and raised in families with both parents present. The 1980s poll provided data on the occupational status of its sample (see Table 6.2).

Finally, the polls provide data on the usage of drugs. Individuals in the 1977 sample typically began to use drugs while in prison. In contrast, in the following decade users were far more likely to have become acquainted with drugs from friends and acquaintances at home and at school. This circumstance suggests that illicit drug use by the 1980s may have spread

TABLE 6.2
Occupational Status of Drug Users in the Georgian SSR (mid-1980s)

	Percent (n = 1760*)
Industrial workers	46.4
Employees (*sluzhashchii*)	29.3
Collective-farm workers	4.5
Housewives	2.7
Soldiers	0.4
Other occupations	16.7
Total	100.0

*Approximately.

Source: Compiled from data in *Sovetskoe gosudarstvo i pravo*, no. 7 (1987), p. 65.

to a broader segment of the general population than was the case in the previous decade. The incidence of drug use differed little between the two samples: Over 80 percent of the individuals in each sample consumed drugs at least once a day and a majority of them did so at least twice a day. However, the polls did find a significant difference in the types of drugs that users consumed. Opiates occupied "first place" among drugs consumed by the 1977 sample. In the later sample, hashish held this status, although opiates continued to be among the "most consumed" of narcotic substances.

Unfortunately, the absence of comparable national statistics prevents an assessment of how representative these samples of drug users are throughout the Soviet Union (or even in Georgia itself). In turn, this circumstance demonstrates the impossibility of making definitive generalizations about the overall dimensions of drug abuse in the USSR.

The Causes of Drug Abuse in the Soviet Union

Soviet sources sometimes appear perplexed that the New Soviet Man would even want to abuse drugs. Reflecting these sentiments, one source contended: "Drug addiction. It does not seem to make sense for our contemporaries, our countrymen, to suffer from this disease. The social causes that drive Western young people into a drugged haze do not exist in the USSR. If over there inability to find work or the hopelessness or excesses of life force young people to seek escape from reality, in our case we have to seek the roots elsewhere."[37]

Most commonly, Soviet commentaries identify a cluster of personal factors—boredom, curiosity, escapism, hedonism, the desire for acceptance by one's peers—motivating resort to drugs.[38] In the opinion of a senior official in the USSR MVD, youths take drugs primarily out of curiosity aroused by sensationalist publications and "idle" conversations among their peers on this subject.[39] In particular, many Soviet youths seek to emulate the hedonistic life-styles, including the use of drugs, allegedly glorified in Western films. "Such films need not be banned, but people must be taught to interpret them correctly and critically," a Soviet source cautioned.[40] Reportedly, many individuals turn to drugs to escape from the trials and travails of their daily lives. "Shortcomings" in the family often promote this circumstance. Broken homes, excessive drinking by parents, and the absence of warm and loving bonds among family members are all seen as driving youths to seek solace in drugs.[41] Then, too, drug abuse among certain ethnic groups (particularly Muslim peoples of Central Asia) for which the consumption of drugs is embedded in the traditional culture supposedly represents a "vestige of the past."[42]

Official policy is said to promote drug abuse at times, albeit unintentionally. Thus, official reticence about drug abuse supposedly increases resort to drugs, because many drug users are unaware until it is too late of the pernicious physical and mental consequences of their actions. Calling for a comprehensive campaign to alert the citizenry to the dangers of drugs, a prominent drug-treatment specialist contended that the public must understand that to use an illicit drug even once "can lead to tragedy."[43]

Other sources have argued—without providing compelling evidence in substantiation—that Mikhail Gorbachev's campaign to combat alcoholism unintentionally fostered drug use among individuals who sought substitutes to satisfy their craving for vodka.[44] Soviet policy in Afghanistan may unwittingly have had similar consequences. Published accounts reported widespread use of hashish and sundry opiates among Soviet troops in that country. It is said that upon their return to the Soviet Union many of these veterans continued their drug habit in part to erase memories of the war.[45] A senior coach of the USSR Track and Field Team recently revealed that the enormous pressure to succeed in international athletic competitions, especially the Olympics, sometimes leads participating athletes to illegally use anabolic steroids and other performance-enhancing drugs. Soviet officials punished nearly 300 athletes for using banned substances in the three years preceding the 1988 Olympic Games.[46] Official policies have even been indicted for creating "moral losses" and a "moral vacuum" that promote drug abuse: "If one thinks that upbringing is only a task of schools, family, slogans, and brilliant lectures by intelligent teachers, one can make a dangerous mistake. Unfortunately, we haven't avoided this mistake. Economic miscalculations, discrepancies between words and deeds, and wishful thinking have brought moral losses and created a moral vacuum. Drug addiction has sprouted from this ground."[47]

Although these explanations may all have some merit, the nascent state of the etiology of drug abuse in the USSR is obvious. To be sure, Western specialists as well advance numerous—and conflicting—physiological, psychological, and sociocultural hypotheses to explain drug abuse.[48] The unique physical and psychological makeup of each individual probably precludes any definitive explanation for the phenomenon. Nevertheless, both Soviet and Western researchers agree that drugs can become a placebo for adolescents seeking to cope with the emotional insecurities and vulnerabilities typical of their stage in life.

Acquiring Drugs

Individuals so inclined can acquire drugs in multiple ways. Frequently, they purchase drugs from professional traffickers in this trade. For example, more than 70 percent of the drug users surveyed in Soviet Georgia in 1977 indicated that they acquired drugs principally by this means.[49] The head of the Main Administration for Criminal Investigation of the USSR MVD, reversing long-standing official silence on the subject, charged in 1988 that a "Narco-Mafia" of organized drug dealers and pushers dominated the illicit trade in drugs in the Soviet Union.[50] A. A. Gabiani, head of the Laboratory of Criminal Sociology in Tbilisi of the USSR MVD, estimated that in the republic of Georgia alone this illicit trade approached 40 million rubles annually.[51] Not surprisingly, law-enforcement officials responsible for combating this illegality—especially local cadres of the MVD—at times succumb to its financial enticements and themselves become corrupt and "caught in the clinging web that is the drug trade."[52] This circumstance helps explain how many drug traffickers ply their wares openly when they and their activities are known to the authorities.[53]

The vast areas where poppies and hemp grow wild or are cultivated either legally by collective farmers or illegally by "hundreds of thousands" of households are a major source of raw materials for drugs.[54] The poppy harvest is supposed to be reserved exclusively for the production of legal drugs and for culinary purposes. However, it is freely admitted that much of the crop is sold on the black market to organized drug manufacturers and individuals who produce opium-based derivatives from it. Collective farmers often more than double their incomes through the lucrative trade in poppies.[55] A deputy minister of the USSR Ministry of Agriculture called the growth of wild hemp (from which hashish is produced) the "problem of problems" in the spread of drug abuse and admitted that his ministry has been "powerless" to stop it. This same official estimated that more than 50 percent of the hemp and poppy crop grown legally on collective farms remains in the fields after harvesting and becomes a fertile source of drugs for both local users and illegal drug producers.[56]

Pharmacies, hospitals, and other medical establishments provide another source of drugs for illicit use. It has been reported that such institutions have become the principal source for illicit drugs of 30–40 percent of the drug abusers in Leningrad, Moscow, and the Baltic republics.[57] They acquire the drugs by stealing them or using fraudulent prescriptions or by purchasing stolen drugs from personnel employed in these institutions. Supposedly, pharmacies exercise strict control over the fulfillment of prescriptions, but according to one law-enforcement official, to believe they actually do so is "wishful thinking."[58] Then, too, a thriving trade has developed between medical personnel and drug abusers in which the latter acquire drugs for cash and/or for coveted consumer goods, including, if one report is accurate, even automobiles.[59] Ironically, such practices seem to have increased recently as drug abusers respond to stricter controls over the cultivation of poppies and hemp by seeking alternative sources for drugs.[60]

Smugglers, either amateur or professional, also supply drugs for domestic consumption. Among the thousands of foreign tourists and students who annually visit the USSR, some bring drugs with them to sell or give to local friends and acquaintances.[61] Professional traffickers either smuggle drugs directly into the Soviet Union or ship drugs from Asia and the Middle East via the Soviet Union to Western Europe and the United States. In the latter case, some drugs inevitably filter down to the domestic market.

No published estimates exist on the volume of drugs smuggled into the USSR. Soviet sources themselves usually contend that strict controls at borders over the movement of both goods and individuals substantially limit the extent of smuggling. Several accounts from the past few years dispute this. One source—while providing no data on volume—has admitted that smuggled drugs do enter the USSR through "chinks" in its customs service. Another source, perhaps hyperbolically, charged that insufficient personnel and equipment in the customs service had made Soviet borders "virtually open" to drug traffickers. This source also contended that "casual unscrupulous people" among the ranks of customs officials abetted the illicit trade in drugs.[62] Furthermore, the USSR has concluded a bilateral agreement with Great Britain to combat international drug trafficking and has joined Interpol, the international police organization, for the same purpose.[63] The agreement with Great Britain represents the first accord of its kind between the USSR and a Western state.

Finally, abusers satisfy their habit through the use of commodities obtained legally. They inhale volatile substances (e.g., glue and paint remover), they swallow brews of legitimate medicines mixed with alcohol or strong teas, and they produce synthetic or semisynthetic drugs from available chemicals and other ingredients.[64]

Definitive generalizations cannot be made about expenditures on illicit drugs in the USSR. However, the data available do suggest that for many individuals these expenditures each month substantially exceed the average monthly wage of a Soviet worker. In the 1977 poll of drug users in Soviet Georgia, 44 percent of those surveyed reported monthly expenditures on drugs of 300–500 rubles and 36 percent reported comparable expenditures of over 500 rubles. A similar survey conducted by the USSR MVD found that in its sample (whose size and composition was unpublished), 22 percent spent from 1,000 to 3,000 rubles and 8 percent spent from 300 to 500 rubles each month on drugs.[65]

Drug users resort to assorted illegalities to acquire these sums. According to the head of the Main Administration for Criminal Investigation of the USSR MVD, 40,000 crimes "stemming from drug addiction" annually are committed in the Soviet Union. Nevertheless, "drug-related crimes" reportedly have declined by 25 percent—but in comparison to what year remained unspecified. Presumably, most violations involve the illicit production or distribution of drugs or assorted illegalities—theft, prostitution, the use of forged prescriptions—to acquire money for, or directly obtain, drugs. To these ends, drug addicts are said to be responsible in "some regions" for upwards of 60 percent of all burglaries of apartments.[66] Even murder is not unknown in the drug trade: "We are seeing drug possession, payment for drugs, and large debts as motives for murder. Incidents of this kind are primarily taking place in Central Asia.[67]

The Response

The Soviet Union, by acknowledging the magnitude of the problem, has now taken (however belatedly and hesitantly) the necessary first step to combat drug abuse. Since 1986, the USSR Supreme Soviet, the USSR Supreme Court, and the procurator general of both the USSR and the Russian Republic have all held official sessions on this subject.[68] In 1988, the USSR Ministry of Public Health began publishing *Voprosy narkologii*, a quarterly journal devoted to research on drug and alcohol abuse.[69] The Komsomol in 1987 established a commission to combat social pathologies—including drug abuse—among young people.[70] Members of the Institute of Public Opinion of the Georgian SSR MVD even published an open letter that claimed that drug abuse represented a "serious latent threat to . . . the physical and moral health" of the Georgian people; the letter called upon the citizenry "to apply their whole attention, strength, and knowledge" to combat it.[71] Of course, not everyone shared this assessment of drug abuse. Many personnel in the MVD charged with combatting drug abuse allegedly still believed that "in some parts of the country there is absolutely no drug abuse whatsoever." This "delusion," as one source characterized it, helps explain why these personnel worked "slowly" and did a "poor job" in the performance of their duties.[72]

Numerous Soviet sources have made it clear that the battle against drug abuse has just begun.[73] Reflecting their still nascent state, antidrug initiatives often are subsumed under institutions and policies concerned primarily with problems of alcoholism and mental health rather than specifically with drug abuse. Considerable debate also exists among specialists regarding the most effective means to combat drug abuse.

Punitive measures predominate among initiatives that have been undertaken. The director of a drug clinic expressed the rationale for such initiatives: "The drug addict is a socially dangerous person. . . . What we need is strict police control, registration, official hospital treatment and complete frankness about the issue. If you want to be a full fledged member of society, prove it by your actions."[74]

Legal strictures against drugs reflect these sentiments. Under the Criminal Code of the Russian Republic, the illegal manufacture, acquisition, storage, and transport of narcotic substances with intent to sell or actual sale are punishable by deprivation of freedom for up to ten years (with or without confiscation of property). These same acts when committed without intent to sell entail deprivation of freedom for up to three years or, in the case of recidivists, for up to five years. The criminal code also specifies criminal liability for the planting or cultivation of forbidden crops that are considered to contain narcotic substances (e.g., poppies and several types of hemp), the setting up or maintaining of places for the use of narcotics, and the habitual consumption of narcotics.[75]

The republic of Georgia specifies even harsher penalties for several of these acts.[76] Activities associated with intent to sell, or the actual sale of, narcotic substances entail deprivation of freedom for up to fifteen years with confiscation of property. Persons using or attempting to use narcotic substances without a doctor's prescription are subject to arrest for terms of ten to fifteen days. The criminal codes of Kirgizia and Uzbekistan contain similar provisions against the use of narcotics, whereas in all other union republics the action is an administrative offense usually punishable by fine. Turkmenistan until November 1987 maintained criminal penalties—prison terms for up to one year or corrective labor for up to two years—for the use of narcotics.[77]

Between 1985 and 1987, an average of 28,600 individuals were convicted annually for sundry "narcotic-related" crimes.[78] Without providing precise figures, one source indicated that many of these individuals were indicted for "little things" involving the possession and/or use of illicit narcotic substances.[79] "Some" 500 individuals were also indicted "recently" for stealing drugs from facilities of the USSR Ministry of Public Health. In one instance, five nurses who were convicted of this offense with intent to sell received prison terms of up to thirteen years.[80] Typically, the sentence for individuals convicted of the illegal manufacture, acquisition, storage, and transport of narcotic substances with intent to sell is deprivation of freedom for one to two years.[81]

Critics express considerable dissatisfaction with these measures. One criticism alleged that legal strictures have done little to deter drug abuse either because judges are overly lenient in applying existing sanctions or, paradoxically, because the sanctions themselves are insufficiently stringent.[82] Ironically, other critics charged that judges were overly harsh in their actions. In particular, these critics opposed the common practice of applying criminal sanctions entailing deprivation of freedom to individuals convicted of possession for personal use of small quantities of drugs, including hashish and marijuana.[83] According to A. A. Gabiani, incarceration can turn casual drug users into hardened addicts by placing them in prison conditions where illicit drugs are readily available and fellow inmates themselves often are addicts.[84] Official policy appears to be moving toward decriminalization of casual drug use. Reportedly, the USSR MVD no longer institutes criminal proceedings against people for possession of small quantities of illicit drugs or if they voluntarily turn themselves in to the authorities.[85]

Moreover, guidelines issued in 1987 by the USSR Supreme Court imply that judges should treat less harshly individuals convicted of possession for personal use or sale of hashish, marijuana, and other nonnarcotic drugs.[86]

The USSR MVD receives considerable criticism for its alleged laxity in enforcing legislation against drugs.[87] In the opinion of its former minister, the agency exhibits "serious shortcomings" in this work, its criminal investigation units are "weak" and their initiative "low," and its local cadres do little to expose participants in the illegal drug trade. Although the police annually uncover "tens of thousands" of drug-related crimes, drug dealers and pushers make up only a small percentage of individuals apprehended. One estimate, which provided no information on its method of computation or the specific drugs involved, indicated that police confiscate "no more" than 15 percent of the illicit drugs in the USSR.

Several factors account for these failings. As noted, on occasion "the poacher has been appointed gamekeeper": That is, officials charged with the enforcement of antidrug legislation have themselves become corrupted by, and participants in, the illegal drug trade. Even honest policemen often are ineffective in combatting drug-related illegalities because they receive almost no specialized training for this task.[88] Furthermore, the police often lack the most elementary equipment, including motor vehicles and devices to determine the quantity and type of drug that an individual has consumed, to perform their duties effectively.[89]

Efforts to reduce the size of, or limit access to, the poppy and hemp crop—despite several well-publicized campaigns to these ends[90]—have proven particularly ineffective: "We attack it wherever we can; we cut it, burn it, treat it with herbicides, and plow it under. We made all the farmers promise to work to exterminate it. And we created special units to fight it. . . . But all of these measures are not very effective."[91] Concern for the impact on the environment of plowing under huge areas or spraying them with highly toxic herbicides has also impeded efforts to reduce the hemp and poppy crop.[92] To date, specialists from the United States have been unable to fulfill a request from the Soviet Union to develop a special herbicide that would destroy only hemp plants while leaving surrounding vegetation unharmed.[93] Efforts by Soviet specialists to develop new varieties of hemp with minimal narcotic content have been equally unsuccessful.[94] Available evidence suggests that the decision to discontinue legal cultivation of certain types of poppies (and rely upon importation to meet demand for culinary and medicinal purposes) will not appreciably limit the availability of illegal drugs.[95]

Dissatisfaction with punitive measures has led some specialists to argue that abuse of drugs (although not their sale or distribution) is a medical, not a legal, problem and should be treated as such. Reflecting this attitude, a senior official in the USSR MVD commented that "society does not gain when, instead of trying to treat a patient, we send him to a corrective labor camp."[96]

To encourage drug users to seek therapy, officials have pledged that those doing so voluntarily would incur no criminal liability (although they would be registered with the police and had to undergo therapy).[97] Authorities in Moscow have established a "hot line" for drug users that dispenses advice and counseling in times of crisis.[98] "If you have a problem or face a difficult moment, telephone us," read a small advertisement about the service in *Vecherniaia Moskva*. "Secrecy is guaranteed," the advertisement asserted. However, a proposal to prohibit drug "addicts" from marrying until they successfully completed therapy to end their addiction seemed unlikely to encourage voluntary resort to treatment.[99] A similar observation applied to the requirement that those undergoing voluntary treatment had to register with the police. As one drug-treatment specialist contended (plausibly), "You'll agree that hardly anyone is likely to seek advice when they know they will be immediately registered with the police."[100] The USSR Supreme Court recently instructed that courts were "obliged" to "consider" compulsory treatment for drug addicts who refuse voluntary treatment. Addicts undergo such treatment in "closed-type therapy and labor rehabilitation centers" run by the police. Inmates receive wages for labor performed, but those who attempt escape are subject to prison terms of up to one year.[101]

Reportedly, of individuals officially registered as drug addicts in 1987, 40,000 underwent voluntary, and 4,000 compulsory, medical treatment for their addiction.[102] This indicated that in 1987 over 80 percent of the registered addicts underwent either voluntary or compulsory drug-addiction therapy. Officials also claimed that some 15,000—or almost 40 percent—of the individuals who underwent voluntary treatment had "stopped using narcotics."[103]

One should assess these claims cautiously. First, the Russian Republic minister of public health reported that in 1986 only 25 percent of the registered drug addicts in the USSR received any medical treatment whatsoever for their condition.[104] Indeed, in 1988 only 31 hospitals and 410 clinics in the USSR provided treatment for abuse of drugs.[105] Second, few, if any, treatment programs for drug abuse anywhere can boast the rate of success that the Soviets claim for theirs. Third, it may be premature to claim permanent success for treatment when, as Soviet sources frankly admit, many so-called cured addicts soon resumed their habit.[106] Finally, considerable evidence exists that drug-treatment facilities and procedures are woefully inadequate to their task.[107]

The Russian Republic minister of public health was outspoken on this latter subject.[108] In his opinion, there were "no physicians in the USSR who [knew] how to treat drug addicts properly" (in part, because medical schools offer no training in this area). The addicts who were treated usually received a "high speed" treatment of seven or eight days that has proven largely ineffective. The minister himself recommended that treatment extend for "at least" sixty days with continued close supervision of the addict upon completion of formal therapy. The minister also felt "in no uncertain terms" that the alcohol-abuse clinics where drug addicts typically received treatment had proven unsuited for this purpose. His overall assessment of drug treatment was blunt: "As yet, there is no effective therapy for drug addiction" in the USSR. To help remedy this condition, the head of the Main Administration for Criminal Investigation of the USSR MVD recommended that drug treatment specialists in the Soviet Union examine—and, wherever feasible, adopt—the practices of their counterparts in other countries.[109]

Efforts to alert the population to the dangers of drugs constitute another body of measures. Succinctly providing the rationale for such measures, one source commented that to combat drug abuse "we need at least minimal information" about the threat that it poses.[110] Typically, these measures have been overly heavy-handed and didactic. Documentaries about drug abuse with such titles as "Children of Vice," "Pain," and "Business Trip to Hell" have appeared on television. An article entitled "A Warning," describing the horrors of drug addiction, appeared in a mass-circulation weekly. At one point, a young addict called the individual who supplied him with drugs "My Mephistopheles" and added that "as a rule, drug addicts are a cowardly but inquisitive lot."[111] Three million copies of an informational pamphlet about drugs, "Beware of the White Cloud," were printed for Soviet schools.[112] The authorities have encountered resistance to their efforts to speak out about drugs. Thus, a physician reported that he was "exasperated" by the "many people" who refused to discuss the problem. In one instance, a conference of educators prevented doctors from addressing them about drug abuse "on the pretext that there were more important problems and the topic was not appropriate for a wide audience."[113]

Finally, the USSR began to cooperate with both capitalist and socialist states to combat drug abuse. This cooperation—although limited—reversed the traditional official attitude that saw drug abuse as a problem principally for capitalist states and of little concern to the USSR. Although the Soviet Union is a signatory to both the 1961 United Nations Uniform Convention on Narcotics and the 1971 United Nations Convention on Psychotropic Substances, its fulfillment of their obligations has been mostly perfunctory.[114]

Now, as noted, the USSR has membership in Interpol and has concluded a bilateral agreement with Great Britain to combat international drug trafficking. Soviet specialists have visited France, Great Britain, and the United States to coordinate multilateral efforts to this same end. Reportedly, the Soviet Union has shared intelligence with the United States and other Western nations that has resulted in the seizure of illegal drugs and the arrest of traffickers. The USSR proposed that such cooperation be formalized in an agreement between itself and the United States Drug Enforcement Agency.[115] In 1988 the latter agency, responding to a Soviet request, began to train Soviet personnel in drug-enforcement skills.[116] The USSR also was an active participant in the 1987 United Nations–sponsored conference on drug abuse held in Vienna.[117] Finally, most Eastern European states participated in two conferences to discuss cooperative efforts among themselves to interdict international drug trafficking.[118]

Of course, the most controversial aspect of this subject is the U.S. allegation that the Soviet Union and other socialist states engaged in drug trafficking to earn hard currency and undermine the moral fabric of Western societies. One study, coauthored by a defector who had been a senior officer in the Czechoslovak armed forces, asserted that the Soviets began to realize the potential efficacy of the "drug weapon" when they discovered widespread use of drugs among U.S. troops during the Korean War. Reportedly, this discovery led Soviet analysts to conclude that drugs could be employed as a long-term strategic weapon to cripple capitalist societies, especially the United States, Canada, France, and West Germany. Nikita Khrushchev was said to have justified the morality of this strategy by asserting that "anything that speeds the destruction of capitalism is moral."[119]

Not surprisingly, the USSR itself denounced these allegations as falsehoods perpetrated by its ideological opponents to embarrass it.[120] A senior official of the U.S. Department of State told a Congressional hearing in 1985 that although there were indications that "certain of the Communist countries have engaged to some degree in facilitating narcotics trafficking," he did not have evidence of a "Communist conspiracy to use drugs to undermine Western democracies or our own society in particular."[121]

Chto delat'?

The USSR has taken the necessary first step to combat drug abuse by acknowledging the danger this phenomenon poses to society. More sophisticated and realistic initiatives have appeared, including efforts to decriminalize the casual use of (especially nonnarcotic) drugs. Another example is the greater willingness of the USSR to cooperate with—and seek assistance from—other states to combat drug abuse. Finally, specialists are engaged in a vigorous debate about how best to combat drug abuse.

Overall, however, efforts to date to combat the drug problem have been limited and mostly ineffectual. Although the assessment of a Western source that the Soviet Union began to combat drug abuse "in the nick of time" because the phenomenon was "spreading with the speed of an epidemic" appeared hyperbolic,[122] this chapter makes clear that drug abuse has become—and will remain—a serious social problem affecting many segments of Soviet society. Requisite measures to mitigate this situation may create déjà vu among Western readers, whose own societies confront many of the same imperatives:

1. Augment the quality and quantity of research on this subject and publicly disseminate all results obtained therein.
2. Separate initiatives to combat drug abuse from those concerned primarily with alcoholism and mental health.
3. Permit *glasnost'* to permeate all discussions and efforts to alert the citizenry to the dangers of drug abuse and eliminate the overly didactic and alarmist rhetoric that characterizes present discourse on the subject.

4. Enhance control over access to drugs from pharmacies, medical institutions, and the poppy and hemp crop.
5. Apply, where appropriate, the other countries' experiences that have proven effective in the fight against drugs (e.g., emulate the example of Poland, where private citizens and institutions are active participants in efforts to combat drug abuse[123]).
6. Broaden cooperation with other governments and international institutions to interdict international drug trafficking, to participate in multilateral research projects on drug abuse, and engage actively and productively in joint efforts to control a problem that truly respects no international boundaries.

None of these initiatives represents a panacea to eradicate drug abuse—indeed, no such panacea is likely to be found either under capitalism or socialism. Nevertheless, the USSR can learn from the experiences and, one hopes, avoid the mistakes of its capitalist counterparts in the fight against drugs. Failure to do so may well find the USSR in a Sisyphean endeavor to combat "narcomania."

Notes

1. Among the few previous analyses of this subject in English were E. A. Babaian, "Control of Narcotic Substances and Prevention of Addiction in the USSR," *Bulletin on Narcotics,* January-March 1979, pp. 13-22; David E. Powell, "Drug Abuse in Communist Europe," *Problems of Communism,* July-August 1973, pp. 31-40. For a more recent analysis of drug abuse, see John M. Kramer, "Drug Abuse in Eastern Europe: An Emerging Issue of Public Policy," *Slavic Review,* Spring 1990, pp. 19-31.
2. *New Times,* no. 22 (May 1984), p. 27; Radio Moscow, April 4, 1985, in *Foreign Broadcast Information Service-Soviet Union Daily Report* [hereafter *FBIS-SOV*], April 8, 1985, p. R3.
3. *Sovetskoe gosudarstvo i pravo,* no. 1 (1987), in *Soviet Law and Government,* Summer 1988, p. 26. All materials on antidrug legislation in the 1920s and 1930s were drawn from this source.
4. *Izvestiia,* March 3, 1966, and November 26, 1966.
5. *Literaturnaia gazeta,* October 26, 1988.
6. *Vedomosti Verkhovnogo Soveta SSSR,* May 31, 1972, item 176; *Vedomosti Verkhovnogo Soveta RSFSR,* August 31, 1972, item 870; *Vedomosti Verkhovnogo Soveta SSSR,* May 1, 1974, item 275.
7. *Literaturnaia gazeta,* October 15, 1975. The report on the session itself was carried in *Izvestiia,* October 9, 1975.
8. *Izvestiia,* August 12, 1986.
9. *Radio Liberty Research Bulletin,* no. 204 (May 25, 1987).
10. For a detailed analysis of the results of this study, see *Sovetskoe gosudarstvo i pravo,* no. 7 (1987), pp. 64-69.
11. Ibid., p. 66. In contrast, a broadcast on Radio Moscow asserted that in the USSR the consumption of opiates such as heroin and morphine was "practically unheard of except for foreign films"; see Radio Moscow, August 30, 1986, in *FBIS-SOV,* September 3, 1986, R4.

12. *Komsomol'skaia pravda,* June 8, 1986; *Literaturnaia gazeta,* August 20, 1986; and *Izvestiia,* August 12, 1986.

13. *Bakinskii rabochii,* August 26, 1986.

14. See, for example, the interview with the minister of public health of the Russian Republic in *Literaturnaia gazeta,* August 20, 1986.

15. Quoted in *Washington Post,* August 11, 1986.

16. For an extended discussion of this circumstance, see Second Report of the National Commission on Marijuana and Drug Abuse, *Drug Abuse in America: Problem in Perspective* (Washington, D.C.: Government Printing Office, 1973), pp. 121–140. Another treatment of this subject was R. L. Hartnoll, "Current Situation Related to Drug Abuse Assessment in European Countries," *Bulletin on Narcotics,* January-June 1986, esp. pp. 71–76.

17. "Narcotics" medically are defined as central nervous system depressants with analgesic and sedative properties. Under U.S. federal law, narcotics are considered to be addictive drugs that produce physical and psychological dependence and include opium and its derivatives, heroin, morphine, codeine, and several synthetic substances that can produce morphine-type addiction. Under this conception of narcotics, hashish and marijuana would be excluded. See Robert O'Brien and Sidney Cohen (eds.), *The Encyclopedia of Drug Abuse* (New York: Facts on File, 1984), p. 183.

18. *Sotsialisticheskaia industriia,* September 16, 1987. The official was head of the Main Administration of Narcology of the USSR Ministry of Public Health.

19. Babaian, op. cit., pp. 18–19, provided a detailed explication of this issue.

20. Ibid., p. 18.

21. The World Health Organization defined "drug dependence" as follows: "a state, psychic and sometimes also physical, resulting from the interaction between a living organism and a drug, characterized by behavioral and other responses that always include a compulsion to take the drug on a continuous or periodic basis in order to experience its physiological effects and sometimes to avoid the discomfort of its absence." Besides being convoluted, this definition is terminologically imprecise as well. For a discussion of this imprecision, see Second Report of the National Commission on Marijuana and Drug Abuse, op. cit., pp. 126–127.

22. Ibid., p. 13.

23. As one source explained, "It's no secret that if dozens of addict-treatment institutions were created, people would be afraid to go to them for treatment for fear that criminal charges would be brought against them"; see *Izvestiia,* October 3, 1986.

24. *Pravda,* January 6, 1987. Another example of this circumstance involved the repeated but unsuccessful efforts by correspondents of *Izvestiia* to obtain an allegedly public document detailing the antidrug program of the Moscow City Soviet. Calling the situation a "strange approach to *glasnost',*" the writers added, "A document that is not secret has, for all practical purposes, been closed to the public. Specifically, the editors were unable to obtain a copy of the document"; see *Izvestiia,* November 23, 1987.

25. *Literaturnaia gazeta,* August 20, 1986. For the expression of similar sentiments, see *Pravda,* February 18, 1988.

26. Powell, op. cit., p. 40, found that drug abuse was restricted primarily to the progeny of the middle and higher classes resident in urban areas.

27. Data on workers who were registered drug addicts from *Trud,* August 3, 1988.

28. TASS, March 26, 1988, in *FBIS-SOV,* April 5, 1988, p. 49.

29. *Izvestiia,* June 27, 1988.
30. Ibid., May 30, 1987. Another source added, albeit without providing empirical data in substantiation, that "group deaths" of children have occurred from sniffing sundry volatile substances. See ibid., June 20, 1986.
31. *Washington Post,* July 20, 1988.
32. *Izvestiia,* May 13, 1987.
33. The pharmacology of hashish was discussed in O'Brien and Cohen, op. cit., pp. 117–119.
34. *Izvestiia,* March 10, 1988.
35. For an accusation that the fight against drugs has assumed the character of a "campaign" similar to those against alcoholism and unearned income, see *Moscow News,* no. 34 (1988), p. 13.
36. All materials on these polls were drawn from *Sovetskoe gosudarstvo i pravo,* no. 7 (1987), pp. 64–69. See also *Zaria vostoka,* February 20, 1987; *Sotsiologicheskie issledovaniia,* no. 1 (1987), pp. 48–53.
37. *Moskovskaia pravda,* June 11, 1986.
38. For a typical exposition of this argument, see *Sovetskoe gosudarstvo i pravo,* no. 5 (1988), p. 86.
39. *Literaturnaia gazeta,* August 20, 1986.
40. *Kommunist Tadzhikistana,* August 1, 1986.
41. For a typical exposition of this argument, see *Bakinskii rabochii,* August 26, 1986.
42. Examples of this argument include *Izvestiia,* October 3, 1986, and *Kommunist Tadzhikistana,* August 1, 1986.
43. E.g., polling data from the Georgian SSR indicated that 90 percent of the drug users surveyed "did not know about the pernicious consequences of narcotics when they reached for the poison the first time"; see *Izvestiia,* August 12, 1986. A similar argument was made in *Uchitelskaia gazeta,* January 10, 1987. The statement by the drug-treatment specialist that any illicit drug use could lead to tragedy was reported by Moscow Domestic Service, December 15, 1987, in *FBIS-SOV,* December 18, 1987, p. 42.
44. See, for example, *Komsomol'skaia pravda,* June 8, 1986; *Moskovskaia pravda,* June 12, 1986. However, the deputy head of the Main Administration for Criminal Investigation of the USSR MVD asserted that no definitive data established a link between increased consumption of illicit drugs and Gorbachev's anti-alcoholism campaign; see *Literaturnaia gazeta,* August 20, 1986. Lending credence to this assessment, numerous reports indicated that the Gorbachev campaign encountered serious obstacles and did little to reduce the overall consumption of alcohol in the USSR. Indeed, it is far more likely that the campaign stimulated the consumption of *samogon,* "moonshine," rather than illicit drugs. On the problems encountered in the anti-alcoholism campaign, see, for example, *Izvestiia,* October 3, 1987.
45. *Sobesednik,* no. 2 (January 1988). Interviews with Soviet soldiers who had served in Afghanistan made clear "that obtaining hashish, opium, or other narcotics from the local Afghan population was no problem at all" for these soldiers; see *Literaturnaia gazeta,* October 26, 1988. For an overall discussion of drug abuse in the Soviet military, see *Krasnaia zvezda,* November 28, 1987.
46. *Moscow News,* no. 50 (1988), p. 15. This source asserted that similar practices also occurred in school athletics: "Drugs are also well known to some victors in school competitions."
47. *Sobesednik,* no. 40 (September 1986).

48. A compilation of these theories appeared in O'Brien and Cohen, op. cit., esp. pp. 274–279.

49. *Zaria vostoka,* February 20, 1987.

50. This official elaborated: "No matter what we call it, the Narco-Mafia or an organized criminal group . . . coherent professional group crime does exist and has for a long time"; see Moscow Television Service, February 19, 1988, in *FBIS-SOV,* February 26, 1988, p. 62.

51. *Sotsiologicheskie issledovaniia,* no. 1 (1987).

52. *Pravda,* February 18, 1988. This circumstance was not surprising given the report by the minister of the USSR MVD revealing widespread corruption among ministerial personnel. The minister stated that between 1983 and 1985 approximately 160,000 employees in the agency were dismissed "for violation of law and order, for their being unable to attend to their duties"; see TASS, March 26, 1988, in *FBIS-SOV,* April 5, 1988, p. 48.

53. The head of the Main Administration for Criminal Investigation of the USSR MVD made this charge in *Pravda,* February 17, 1988. A similar accusation was made in *Literaturnaia gazeta,* January 14, 1987.

54. *Izvestiia,* October 6, 1987, carried the comment that "hundred of thousands" of households illegally grew poppies and hemp.

55. *Komsomol'skaia pravda,* June 8, 1986.

56. *Literaturnaia gazeta,* August 20, 1986.

57. As reported by the head of the Main Administration for Criminal Investigation of the USSR MVD in *Izvestiia,* February 29, 1988.

58. *Literaturnaia gazeta,* August 20, 1986. However, enhanced security measures have, according to one report, "sharply reduced" the theft of drugs from pharmacies; see *Pravda,* February 17, 1988. These measures included connecting almost all pharmacies to centralized burglar-alarm systems and at many stores an additional (but unspecified) "two or three lines of defense"; see *Izvestiia,* February 29, 1988.

59. For reports of such practices, see *Sovetskaia Rossiia,* August 6, 1986. For the assertion that passenger cars are among the goods bartered in this trade, see *Sobesednik,* no. 40 (September 1986).

60. *Pravda,* February 17, 1988.

61. For an accusation that such practices occur, see Moscow Domestic Service, January 29, 1988, in *FBIS-SOV,* February 2, 1988, p. 63.

62. The comment regarding "chinks" in the customs service came from *Pravda,* February 3, 1988. This appeared to be a problem especially in the Turkmenian SSR, which borders on both Afghanistan and Iran: "The situation is worsened there by the closeness of the state border. It becomes necessary to check on the border areas and close all loopholes to prevent the taking of narcotics into the republic from outside"; see TASS, April 15, 1988, in *FBIS-SOV,* April 19, 1988. *Izvestiia,* May 30, 1988, charged that Soviet borders were "virtually open" to traffickers and that "casual unscrupulous people" filled the ranks of the customs service.

63. See Reuters, September 16, 1988, for details of the agreement between the USSR and Great Britain to combat international drug trafficking. The secretary general of Interpol provided the assessment that the USSR would soon join this organization, in part, to combat international drug trafficking: "I see it as only a short time before the Soviet Union applies to join *Interpol.* They are beginning to acknowledge that they have a problem." However, a spokesman for the USSR MVD, while confirming Soviet interest in joining *Interpol,* said it was premature to think this would occur "soon"; see TASS, April 22, 1988, cited in *Radio Liberty Research Bulletin,* no. 77 (April 22, 1988).

64. On these practices, see *Izvestiia,* March 26, 1988.

65. *Zaria vostoka,* February 20, 1987; *Izvestiia,* May 13, 1987.

66. All data in this paragraph were provided by the head of the Main Administration for Criminal Investigation of the USSR MVD. His comments appeared in *Izvestiia,* May 13, 1987; *Pravda,* February 17, 1988; *Izvestiia,* February 29, 1988.

67. *Izvestiia,* February 29, 1988.

68. For reports of these sessions, see, respectively, *Izvestiia,* January 1, February 29, and March 5, 1988; *Sovetskaia Rossiia,* December 26, 1986.

69. Rubrics under which articles were published included: "Biological Aspects of Narcology," "Diagnosis," "Clinical Narcology," "Epidemiology," "Guidelines for Practitioners," and "Practical Notes." Articles published in the first several issues examined both physiological and sociological aspects of drug and alcohol abuse.

70. Moscow Domestic Service, January 29, 1988, in *FBIS-SOV,* February 2, 1988, p. 63.

71. *Zaria vostoka,* February 10, 1987.

72. These remarks came from the head of the Main Administration for Criminal Investigation of the USSR MVD; see *Izvestiia,* February 29, 1988.

73. E.g., one source asserted that drug abuse has demonstrated an "uncommon ability" to resist efforts to eradicate it; see *Pravda,* February 17, 1988. In the opinion of another source, "we have virtually no means of combatting this evil"; see *Komsomol'skaia pravda,* March 3, 1988. For the expression of similar sentiments related to antidrug initiatives in Moscow, see Moscow Domestic Service, December 15, 1987, in *FBIS-SOV,* December 18, 1987, p. 41.

74. *Ogonek,* no. 8 (February 1988).

75. For a detailed discussion of antidrug legislation in the USSR, see *Meditsinskaia gazeta,* April 9, 1986. The relevant articles in the Criminal Code of the Russian Republic are Nos. 224-226.

76. *Sovetskoe gosudarstvo i pravo,* no. 7 (1987), pp. 67-69, provided an extended analysis of this legislation. The relevant article in the Criminal Code of the Georgian SSR is No. 252.

77. TASS, November 19, 1987, cited in *Radio Liberty Research Bulletin,* no. 473 (November 20, 1987).

78. The USSR State Committee for Statistics reported that in 1985, 1986, and 1987 there were, respectively, 25,600, 33,600, and 26,800 individuals convicted for such offenses; see *Argumenty i fakty,* November 12, 1988, p. 6.

79. *Izvestiia,* February 29, 1988.

80. *Pravda,* February 17, 1988, and *Meditsinskaia gazeta,* April 9, 1986.

81. This figure came from a survey of court practice reported in *Sovetskoe gosudarstvo i pravo,* no. 7 (1987), p. 69.

82. For example, A. A. Gabiani reported that courts in Soviet Georgia "frequently" applied to drug dealers (even including "organized criminal dealers of narcotics") the less-stringent sanctions intended for those who only used, but did not sell, narcotics. The courts took "the path of least resistance," in Gabiani's opinion, because they did not want "to trouble themselves with the complex procedures for demonstration of guilt in the sale of narcotics"; see ibid., pp. 67-68.

83. See, for example, the commentary in *Moscow News,* August 19, 1987.

84. *Sovetskoe gosudarstvo i pravo,* no. 7 (1987), p. 67.

85. *Izvestiia,* February 29, 1988.

86. The guidelines instructed courts to consider in such cases not only the quantity of drugs involved but also the "characteristics of the varying kinds of

narcotics in terms of the degree of their effect on the human body"; see *Izvestiia,* January 1, 1988. Another source reported that recent amendments and supplements to the criminal law on drug addiction established standards for "smaller quantities of drugs"—although the source did not indicate what drugs came under the new standards; see Moscow Television Service, January 11, 1988, in *FBIS-SOV,* January 19, 1988, p. 64.

87. All information in this paragraph was drawn from interviews with the minister of the USSR MVD and the head of the Main Administration for Criminal Investigation of the USSR MVD published in, respectively, *Pravda,* January 6, 1987, and *Izvestiia,* February 29, 1988. The latter official provided the estimate of the amount of illicit drugs confiscated in the USSR.

88. *Komsomol'skaia pravda,* June 8, 1986.

89. See *Pravda,* January 6, 1987, and *Izvestiia,* February 29, 1988. The head of the Main Administration for Criminal Investigation expressed concern that without proper diagnostic equipment MVD personnel might commit sundry illegalities in apprehending drug users and might even charge innocent people: "A diagnosis must be made, and sometimes we have to get into risky areas—areas bordering on the illegal—because of a lack of elementary equipment. Fortunately, internal affairs agencies have so far not committed *any gross violations* of socialist legality in their efforts to combat drug addiction. But it is extremely dangerous to operate blindly, and it is possible that a person will be wronged for no reason; see *Izvestiia,* February 29, 1988 (emphasis added).

90. In one such operation—code-named "Poppy 86"—the police reportedly detained 300 drug traffickers and 4,000 drug dealers and destroyed poppies and hemp growing wild on thousands of acres of land; see *Pravda,* January 6, 1987. For a description of a similar operation—code-named "Black Poppy"—see *Selskaia zhizn,* August 18, 1987. As noted, such initiatives seemingly have done little to deter drug abuse as users quickly found alternative means to satisfy their habit.

91. *Izvestiia,* June 30, 1986.

92. This according to the head of the Main Administration for Criminal Investigation of the USSR MVD; see *Izvestiia,* February 29, 1988. In contrast, the minister of the USSR MVD argued that concern for the environment should not impede efforts to eradicate wild hemp and poppies; see *Pravda,* January 6, 1987.

93. *Izvestiia,* February 29, 1988.

94. This effort is proceeding "slowly," according to the minister of the USSR MVD; see *Pravda,* January 6, 1987.

95. TASS, February 16, 1988, in *FBIS-SOV,* February 24, 1988, p. 54, carried an announcement of this decision. Reportedly, this decision was "not reached easily," as several agencies argued that the poppy had too many economic uses to ban its cultivation; see *Izvestiia,* October 6, 1987. Available evidence indicates that drug users have responded to the ban on poppy cultivation by consuming other types of drugs. One source contended: "The results were not as expected. Many addicts have started using chemical compounds, medicines, and tranquilizers. There has been a sharp rise in substance abuse"; see *Trud,* August 3, 1988.

96. *Literaturnaia gazeta,* August 20, 1986. For expressions of similar sentiments, see, for example, *Izvestiia,* August 12, 1986, and *Komsomol'skaia pravda,* January 11, 1987.

97. *Moskovskaia pravda,* June 12, 1986.

98. As quoted in Agence France-Presse, August 22, 1986, in *FBIS-SOV,* August 22, 1986, p. R6.

99. This proposal was made in a roundtable discussion of initiatives to combat drug abuse, as published in *Sovetskoe gosudarstvo i pravo*, no. 8 (1987), p. 138.

100. *Ogonek*, no. 8 (February 1988).

101. The instruction from the USSR Supreme Court was reported in *Izvestiia*, January 1, 1988. See *Pravda*, January 6, 1987, for a discussion of the policy of compulsory treatment of drug addicts. *Washington Post*, January 7, 1987, also treated this subject.

102. TASS, February 16, 1988, in *FBIS-SOV*, February 24, 1988, p. 54, and *Izvestiia*, February 29, 1988.

103. Moscow Television Service, February 19, 1988, in *FBIS-SOV*, February 26, 1988, p. 62. On this subject, also see TASS, February 16, 1988, in *FBIS-SOV*, February 26, 1988, p. 62.

104. *Literaturnaia gazeta*, August 20, 1986.

105. *Trud*, August 3, 1988.

106. See, for example, *Sovetskoe gosudarstvo i pravo*, no. 8 (1987), p. 137, and *Literaturnaia gazeta*, August 20, 1986. One study found that "at best" only 10 percent of the treated addicts were permanently cured of their habit; see *Ogonek*, no. 8 (February 1988).

107. Thus, the head of the Main Administration for Criminal Investigation of the USSR MVD, after citing the data on the numbers who purportedly have voluntarily undergone successful treatment for their addiction, asserted that the "effectiveness of addiction treatment and the monitoring of treatment proper remain urgent questions"; see *Izvestiia*, February 29, 1988.

108. The following discussion was drawn from the interview with the minister published in *Literaturnaia gazeta*, August 20, 1986.

109. As reported by TASS, February 16, 1988, in *FBIS-SOV*, February 24, 1988, p. 55.

110. *Komsomol'skaia pravda*, June 8, 1986.

111. On the television documentaries about drug abuse, see *Izvestiia*, August 12, 1986. The article "A Warning" appeared in *Nedelia*, January 12, 1986, in *FBIS-SOV*, January 17, 1986, pp. R2-3.

112. The contents of the pamphlet were discussed in *Uchitelskaia gazeta*, January 15, 1987. For a highly critical assessment of the work of educational institutions in alerting their students to the dangers of drugs, see *Sovetskaia Rossiia*, December 26, 1986.

113. *Sovetskaia Rossiia*, August 31 and December 26, 1986. At times, parents have resisted efforts by teachers to inform them of the drug-related activities of their progeny. For examples of such behavior, see *Sobesednik*, no. 4 (September 1986).

114. For an analysis of these conventions by a Soviet author, see L. N. Anisimov, *Narkotiki: Pravovoi rezhim* (Leningrad: Izdatel'stvo Leningradskogo Universiteta, 1974), pp. 34-54, 63-72.

115. *Washington Post*, July 20, 1988, provided details of the proposal. The director of the Drug Enforcement Agency asserted that such cooperation would bring "minimal" benefits to the United States, but the proposal should be considered because "the drug problem is an international problem and the more countries that cooperate the better for all of us"; *Washington Post*, February 21, 1988, provided information on multilateral efforts involving the Soviet Union and Western states undertaken to 1988 to interdict international drug trafficking. See *New York Times*, May 1, 1988, for a recent example of Soviet assistance facilitating the seizure by British authorities of 3.5 tons of hashish.

116. *Washington Post,* February 21, 1988.

117. *Sotsialisticheskaia industriia,* September 16, 1987, discussed the participation of the USSR in the conference.

118. The first conference, involving representatives from all states of Communist Europe (except Yugoslavia) plus Cuba and Mongolia, met in Sofia, Bulgaria, in May 1987. For details of the meeting see Bulgarska telegrafna agentsiia (BTA), May 12, 1987, in *FBIS-East Europe Daily Report,* May 14, 1987, pp. AA2. The second meeting took place in June 1988 in the USSR. The participants, the respective ministers of internal affairs from Bulgaria, Czechoslovakia, Hungary, Poland, and the USSR, met to discuss "problems connected with the anti drug struggle." The participants signed a protocol "on cooperation in the sphere of combatting drug addiction." They also agreed to hold "regular meetings of this kind in the future." See *Izvestiia,* June 27, 1988, for details of this meeting. There has been no published explanation of why representatives from the German Democratic Republic (GDR) and Romania did not participate in these deliberations.

119. Joseph Douglas and Jan Sejna, "International Narcotics Trafficking: The Soviet Connection," *Journal of Defense and Diplomacy,* December 1986, pp. 20–25. Before his defection, Sejna was secretary of the Czechoslovak Defense Council and chief of cabinet at the Ministry of Defense.

120. Moscow Television Service, December 18, 1986, in *FBIS-SOV,* December 22, 1986, p. R12. Similar allegations were made in *Krasnaia zvezda,* December 19, 1986.

121. From the "Prepared Statement" of Clyde D. Taylor, deputy assistant secretary of state, Bureau of International Narcotic Matters, U.S. Department of State, inserted into the record of *International Terrorism, Insurgency, and Drug Trafficking: Present Trends in Terrorist Activity,* Joint Hearings before the Committee on Foreign Relations and the Committee on the Judiciary of the U.S. Senate, May 14, 1985 (Washington, D.C., U.S. Government Printing Office, 1985), p. 119.

122. *Radio Liberty Research Bulletin,* no. 70 (February 19, 1987).

123. Kramer, op. cit., discussed these initiatives in detail.

CHAPTER 7

Drinking and Alcohol Abuse in the USSR in the 1980s

Vladimir G. Treml

Introduction

Excessive drinking, alcohol abuse, and alcoholism have been a part of Russian and Soviet life for a long time. There is little doubt, however, that in the 1970s the alcohol problem reached a crisis level unprecedented in the history of the country. For years the leadership, professionals in the health, social, and law-enforcement fields, and the public were not particularly concerned with heavy drinking and alcohol abuse. This complacency could be explained by the absence of reliable information about the magnitude of the alcohol problem, the fact that per capita consumption of state-produced alcohol in the USSR (i.e., excluding homemade vodka-like moonshine, or *samogon*) was lower than consumption in a number of other countries, and the widely shared belief that "drinking is an integral part of Russian life." At the same time, periodic antidrinking campaigns satisfied those few in the leadership and the public who were aware of the problem. By the early 1980s adverse effects of heavy drinking on national health, mortality, public order, and labor productivity were, however, becoming too visible to be dismissed as insignificant. It is, therefore, not surprising that Gorbachev started his radical restructuring of the Soviet system with a far-reaching antidrinking campaign.

The early phases of Gorbachev's antidrinking campaign have been analyzed by this author elsewhere.[1] This chapter will therefore offer only a brief summary of these issues and developments and then discuss the course of the campaign at the end of the 1980s as well as some more controversial topics that have been subject to less research.

It must be stressed at the outset that any description and analysis of the alcohol problem in the USSR is greatly handicapped by the absence of comprehensive and reliable data. Publication of detailed statistics on production and consumption of alcoholic beverages in liters and in value terms ceased in the USSR in the late 1920s–early 1930s along with other statistical series on demography, health, welfare, and deviant behavior. The traditional Soviet policy of blanket suppression of adverse social data was modified under Gorbachev's *glasnost'* and some aggregate data on consumption of alcoholic beverages and statistics on alcohol-related morbidity and mortality started to appear in standard statistical sources.[2] At the same time a greater amount of general, descriptive, and anecdotal evidence concerning alcohol abuse is being published in newspapers and journals. But the Soviet public and Western analysts are still very much in the dark concerning most basic data on drinking and its impact on their society.

The difficulty, caused by the absence of reliable statistics, of analyzing various adverse effects of alcohol abuse is compounded by certain biases found in the Soviet literature, particularly materials dealing with such phenomena as alcohol abuse, crime, divorce, and suicide. All Soviet literature, be it large-circulation propaganda pamphlets and speeches of the leadership or technical and scholarly studies on the subject of alcohol abuse, offers description and analyses of empirical data mixed with elements of prescription and indoctrination. Professionals and the authorities share the belief that one of the most effective ways of combatting heavy drinking and alcohol abuse is to convince the public that drinking leads to moral degradation, crime, violence, suicide, disintegration of the family, disruption of professional advancement, spread of venereal disease, and other perils. Recognition of these tragic consequences of alcohol abuse will, it is hoped, force the public to abstain from alcohol. Injection of these elements of intimidation into specialized studies is of doubtful utility because it leads Soviet social scientists and specialists on alcohol abuse to overstate their case, distort their analysis, offer simplistic interpretation of complex phenomena, and, ultimately, mislead each other and policymakers. There have been some outstanding Soviet specialists on alcohol who offered balanced, scholarly, and insightful analyses.[3] Unfortunately, for a long time these specialists had to work without statistical information, their writings were heavily censored, and political and medical authorities paid little attention to what they were saying.

Soviet Drinking and the Dimensions of the Alcohol Problem in the Early 1980s

Basic statistics on consumption of alcohol per person aged fifteen and above are summarized in Table 7.1. The absolute level of consumption of alcohol per person and the rate of increase in the 1960–1980 period were clearly high and alarming, but taken by themselves, they did not necessarily suggest a true crisis. Other countries, such as France, Spain, Portugal, Italy, and the United States, have experienced similar or even higher rates of increase in drinking in some years and have recorded higher absolute levels of per capita alcohol consumption. We must examine Soviet patterns of drinking, ethnic differences in per capita consumption, and other aspects of Soviet alcohol culture to form a comprehensive picture of the alcohol problem.

The data broken down by republics on consumption of state-produced alcohol per person are given in Table 7.2. The differences in consumption levels among republics are striking. It should be pointed out, however, that

TABLE 7.1
Consumption of Alcohol in the USSR: Liters of Absolute Alcohol per Person 15 Years Old and Older

	State	Samogon	Total
1960	5.56	2.89	8.45
1970	9.67	3.13	12.80
1975	11.18	2.61	13.79
1980	11.58	3.13	14.70
1984	11.22	3.39	14.61
1985	9.59	2.48	12.07
1986	5.75	3.83	9.58
1987	4.44	5.15	9.59
1988	4.84	4.88	9.72
1989	5.81	4.30	10.11

Note: Here and elsewhere total figures were derived by converting liters of different alcoholic beverages (vodka, wine, cognac, champagne, beer) to pure alcohol depending on their content. Rough estimates of *samogon* are discussed in Chapter 7. Consumption of homemade wine and beer, stolen industrial alcohol, and alcohol surrogates is not included.

Source: Data for different beverages are from *Narodnoe khoziaistvo SSSR* and *Vestnik statistiki* for various years.

the data shown in Table 7.2 are not based on nationalities—the data for which are not available. All available fragmentary evidence indicates that differences in per capita consumption among nationalities would be even greater.

Per capita consumption data are a poor, and often a misleading, index for the overall adverse effect of alcohol abuse for intertemporal and particularly for regional and international comparisons. In addition to per capita consumption the following factors should be considered:

- The composition (mix) of alcoholic beverages: The higher the share of strong beverages (40 percent alcohol content) the stronger are the immediate negative effects—accidents, crime, disturbances of public order, violence, fatal poisoning, and cardiovascular problems.
- The patterns and frequency of drinking: As a rule regular consumption of moderate amounts of alcohol produces fewer negative health and social effects than irregular or periodic drinking of large quantities, or "alcoholic binges." Part of the pattern is the relationship between alcohol and food intake. Alcoholic beverages consumed during or immediately after meals produce fewer adverse effects than alcoholic beverages consumed without meals.

TABLE 7.2
Consumption of Legal Alcohol by Republics: Liters of Absolute Alcohol per Person 15 Years Old and Older (Selected Years)

	1984	1985	1987	1988
USSR	11.18	5.78	4.40	4.85
RSFSR	13.44	6.67	5.05	5.55
Ukraine	7.95	4.78	3.73	4.07
Belorussia	12.81	7.31	6.31	6.73
Uzbekistan	6.05	3.30	2.09	2.18
Kazakhstan	11.43	5.69	4.84	4.89
Georgia	5.20	2.87	2.37	2.46
Azerbaidzhan	3.44	2.13	1.49	1.50
Lithuania	14.33	8.50	6.30	6.68
Moldavia	7.85	2.83	2.31	2.64
Latvia	13.35	8.31	5.87	6.14
Kirgizia	9.45	3.69	2.94	3.28
Tadzhikistan	4.05	1.70	1.22	1.58
Armenia	6.17	4.34	3.24	2.44
Turkmenia	6.67	3.69	2.75	3.25
Estonia	14.80	9.43	7.60	7.91

Source: Based on retail trade sales as reported in *Vestnik statistiki*, no. 6 (1989), p. 60.

- Age and sex of drinkers: Other things being equal, adverse health effects of drinking are related to age and sex. The younger the age of the drinker, the more severe the long-term effects; heavy drinking contributes significantly to cardiovascular and other medical problems of the elderly. Drinking is also extremely dangerous for pregnant women.

It cannot be overemphasized that the alarming figures on alcohol abuse in the USSR are explained not only by the relatively high levels of per capita consumption in the country but also by the unfortunate fact that the patterns of drinking of a large share of the population (particularly Slavs and Baltic nationalities) are extremely unhealthy. In this regard I will distinguish five[4] separate broadly defined national groups (see Tables 7.3 and 7.4):

- *Slavs* (RSFSR, the Ukraine, and Belorussia) on the average consume more than the national average of alcohol. State-produced alcoholic beverages are supplemented with large quantities of *samogon* and smaller quantities of homemade wine. Rates of growth of per capita consumption in the 1960–1980 period were much higher than in the

TABLE 7.3
Alcoholism by Republics (per 100,000 Population)

	Number First Diagnosed as Alcoholics		Number of Alcoholics Registered	
	1984	1988	1984	1988
USSR	206	154	1560	1598
RSFSR	243	198	1875	2000
Ukraine	228	148	1709	1619
Belorussia	257	143	1757	1758
Uzbekistan	69	33	472	436
Kazakhstan	172	126	1222	1278
Georgia	39	29	327	282
Azerbaidzhan	23	16	278	241
Lithuania	158	133	1575	1602
Moldavia	274	206	1679	1838
Latvia	275	213	1777	2013
Kirgizia	105	62	868	742
Tadzhikistan	71	28	478	425
Armenia	20	11	262	175
Turkmenia	39	47	496	433
Estonia	185	114	1316	1490

Note: Official data on newly diagnosed alcoholics and the total number of registered alcoholics are probably grossly understated.

Source: From *Vestnik statistiki*, no. 6 (1989), p. 61.

rest of the country. In the early 1980s vodka and *samogon* constituted more than 60 percent of total alcohol consumption. Women drink, on the average, about 35 to 45 percent of the level of average consumption of men. Drinking by the majority is irregular, with a large share of total alcohol consumed in periodic "binges," and without food intake. Levels of alcohol abuse, disturbances of public peace, incidence of alcoholism, alcohol-related accidents and traumas, fatal alcohol poisoning, and other forms of alcohol-related mortality are, on a per capita basis, two to three times higher than in the rest of the USSR.

- *Baltic nationalities* (Lithuania, Latvia, Estonia) consume on the average only slightly less than Slavs. The two main differences are that consumption of *samogon* is low and that vodka constitutes less than half of total alcohol consumed. The 1960–1980 rates of growth of per capita consumption were as high as those in Slavic areas. Women drink about 35 to 45 percent of the level consumed by men. Drinking is more regular than among Slavs, and most of drinking is done with meals. Alcohol-related mortality and alcoholism are only slightly lower than among Slavs, but other manifestations of alcohol abuse such as

TABLE 7.4
Alcohol-Related Mortality by Republics (per 100,000 Population)

	1980	1984	1985	1986	1987
USSR	19.0	17.2	14.4	8.3	7.40
RSFSR	26.4	23.0	19.3	10.6	9.10
Ukraine	16.8	17.3	14.6	9.2	9.20
Belorussia	13.3	15.3	12.1	8.2	8.50
Uzbekistan	1.5	1.5	1.2	1.0	0.60
Kazakhstan	6.8	6.1	5.8	3.8	3.10
Georgia	2.4	3.1	2.3	2.5	1.80
Azerbaidzhan	1.9	1.1	1.1	0.7	0.50
Lithuania	25.9	25.3	19.2	12.2	11.20
Moldavia	14.3	19.5	16.0	9.7	7.80
Latvia	18.8	11.5	11.4	7.4	5.10
Kirgizia	8.0	6.4	4.6	2.1	2.40
Tadzhikistan	1.9	1.6	1.4	1.0	1.10
Armenia	1.0	0.5	0.5	0.2	0.20
Turkmenia	2.5	1.7	1.6	1.2	0.06
Estonia	21.2	21.5	18.4	11.4	10.40

Note: The Soviet definition of alcohol-related mortality is rather restrictive. It covers only alcohol psychosis, chronic alcoholism, alcoholic cirrhosis of the liver, and accidental fatal poisoning by alcohol. The last term is particularly ambiguous -- does the "accidental fatal poisoning" exclude the cases of Russian *opoy*, that is, voluntary (nonaccidental) consumption of a critical quantity of alcohol in a short span of time? A second related ambiguity concerns the term "alcohol." Does it mean ethanol manufactured for human consumption or does it cover technical alcohols (including methanol), alcohol-containing fluids, antifreeze, after-shave lotions, and other alcohol surrogates? I was told privately by a Soviet specialist that accidental fatal poisoning by alcohol surrogates is excluded from the mortality statistics although, in fact, these liquids were consumed as alcohol substitutes and should be classified with alcohol-related mortality.

Source: From *Vestnik statistiki*, no. 6 (1989), p. 62.

disturbances of public peace, accidents, and crime are much lower than the USSR level.
- *Moldavians* are ranked third among heavy drinkers, consuming about 80 percent of the per capita USSR level. *Samogon* is virtually unknown, but large quantities of homemade wine are consumed. Vodka accounts for only 23 percent of total alcohol consumed. Alcohol-related mortality and levels of alcohol abuse are substantially lower than in the rest of the USSR. However, for reasons that have not been addressed in the literature, rates of alcoholism per 100,000 of population are the highest in the country—1.33 times the national and 1.14 times the Slavic level.
- *Central Asia* (Uzbekistan, Kirgizia, Tadzhikistan, and Turkmenistan). Reflecting the alcohol proscription of Islam, the national groups of Central Asia show little evidence of alcohol abuse. Average consumption per person is about half the USSR level and almost without

samogon. Rates of growth in per capita consumption in the 1960–1980 period were much lower than in Slavic areas. Women's consumption is probably about 15 to 20 percent of the level of alcohol consumption of men. Drinking is more regular than in Slavic areas of the country. Incidence of alcoholism is low (about one-third of the USSR level) and the rate of alcohol-related mortality is even less—about 14 percent of the USSR level.
- *Transcaucasus* (Georgia, Azerbaidzhan, and Armenia) shows little evidence of alcohol abuse. Consumption of alcohol is less than half of the USSR level, and vodka constitutes only 20 percent of total alcohol consumed. Production of *samogon* is virtually unknown, but rural households produce homemade wines and strong brandy. Women drink at the level of about a quarter of male consumption. Drinking is regular and accompanies meals. Levels of alcohol abuse are very low. Incidence of alcoholism and of alcohol-related mortality are about ten times lower than the national averages.

It should be apparent from the above description that heavy drinking and adverse effects of alcohol abuse are concentrated, by and large, among Slavs and Baltic nationalities and that antidrinking programs should be designed to affect these regions. Another important conclusion is that most adverse effects of heavy drinking stem not so much from the absolute level of per capita consumption but from the mode of drinking. Accordingly, the best approach to the alcohol-abuse problem in the USSR would be to design programs that educate people about drinking in moderation and in a civilized manner, avoiding periodic binges, and using alcohol with meals. This was essentially the position of a group of prominent Soviet specialists termed proponents of "civilized drinking" in the 1970s and the early 1980s. Unfortunately, this position was completely discredited in the early stages of Gorbachev's antidrinking campaign.

Measuring the Effect of Alcohol Abuse in the USSR

The Soviet Union is a country of heavy drinkers. According to one leading specialist, G. Zaigrayev, clinically defined alcoholics constitute between 3 and 4 percent of the total adult population; heavy drinkers (*p'yanitsy*), 9–11 percent; moderate drinkers, 70–75 percent; with the rest of the population being either nondrinkers or people who would drink only in exceptional cases.[5] On the eve of Gorbachev's campaign, about 4.3 million people were officially classified as chronic alcoholics registered by health authorities.[6] Because of shortages of health facilities, however, this number appears to be too low. According to Zaigrayev's percentages, the true number should be between 6 and 8 million; according to other specialists the country has between 5 and 7 unregistered alcoholics for each registered one.[7]

Probably the most alarming index of change in the adverse effect of alcohol abuse is mortality. Life expectancy of men (measured at birth) rose to a relatively high, for the Soviet Union, level of 66.1 years in the 1964–1965 period and then started to decline, reaching 62.3 years in the 1980–1981 period. Female life expectancy displayed a less alarming trend, but it also declined from 73.8 in 1968–1969 to 72.5 in 1980–1981.[8] Most Soviet and Western demographers agree that increasingly heavy drinking has contributed significantly to an upward curve in male and female mortality (including infant mortality associated with drinking by expectant mothers) and decreasing life expectancy in the USSR[9] as well as to morbidity. Without offering a detailed demographic analysis, I can briefly describe some specific issues. Mortality from alcohol poisoning increased from 12,500 deaths in the early 1960s to 50,000 in the late 1970s.[10] In the early 1980s about 13,000–14,000 people were killed and 60,000 injured in traffic accidents caused by drunken drivers, and these rates have been steadily increasing.[11] Accidents and resulting traumas at work and in homes appear to have been high and increasing. One Soviet study reported in the early 1970s that drinking and alcohol abuse reduced labor productivity by 10 percent[12] and the situation must have deteriorated in recent years. Soviet specialists stress the strong correlation between heavy drinking and cardiovascular and other somatic problems, suicide, divorce, rape, homicide, and other violent crimes. Unfortunately, comprehensive and documented data describing these phenomena are rarely available.

Causes of the Alcohol Problem and Heavy Drinking

Alcoholism, heavy drinking, and changes in per capita consumption of alcohol over time are very complex multidimensional phenomena that are difficult to explain fully even with complete historical, demographic, and socioeconomic data. The paucity of information on various aspects of drinking in the USSR makes the task all but impossible. Thus we can only list certain factors that seem to have affected alcohol consumption in the USSR and that have contributed to the rapid and uninterrupted growth of consumption per capita between the 1950s and the 1980s.

Alcohol has been an important part of Russian life for centuries, and thus the well-established alcohol tradition must be listed as one of the primary background factors in the analysis of heavy drinking in the USSR.[13] There are some specific factors that have contributed to increased drinking and alcohol abuse in the period under investigation. The relationship between state alcohol policies and drinking requires a special study; in this chapter I can offer only a brief summary.

Khrushchev, Kosygin, Brezhnev, Andropov, and other Soviet leaders apparently recognized, at least partially, the dangers of increasing drinking, but there is no evidence that a sustained, long-term antidrinking program was ever seriously considered by any of them. The media and specialized publications continued to stress the dangers of alcohol, but these publications had hardly any effect on the drinkers. The most salient fact, however, is evident from the data in Table 7.1. The state, which has a complete monopoly over production and distribution of alcoholic beverages, continued to supply the population with alcohol in increasing quantities. In the thirty years between 1955 and 1984 the total production of beverages (with contents converted to pure alcohol) was cut only in the four years of antidrinking campaigns. These cuts were rather small, and in each case the growth in production was resumed about a year later.[14] The reversals of promised cuts in production were always dictated by short-term fiscal considerations—the state revenues from alcohol were too high to allow any cutbacks. The state continued to supply the people with growing quantities of alcohol, thus making increasing per capita consumption possible.

Since the mid-1950s the Soviet people have enjoyed a moderate, albeit uneven, growth in real income and an even more rapid growth in money income and state transfer payments; there was also a gradual decrease in the length of the workweek without a commensurate increase in the availability of income-elastic goods and services and of residential housing. Availability and diversity of entertainment and leisure-time facilities as well as consumer leisure goods have been particularly lagging. The everyday life of the Soviet people, especially in rural areas and small and medium-sized towns has been, simply put, dull. Most television and radio programs, newspapers, periodicals, and books are relatively serious and their purpose is to educate, indoctrinate, and enlighten, rather than simply to entertain the reader or to help him to relax. Thus, drinking has increasingly become the only generally accepted way of spending one's leisure time and discretionary income.

Drinking by women and by minors has been increasing throughout the world, and the USSR is no exception. Soviet popular and specialized literature is full of evidence of this phenomenon. Apparently, more women have been consuming increasing quantities of alcohol per capita, have been caught in the sobering-up stations network, and have become alcoholics. The age at which minors have had their first experience with alcohol has been lowered, and per capita consumption by those under fifteen has increased. Unfortunately, as with most other Soviet information on drinking and alcohol abuse, the evidence presented in the literature is undocumented, based either on samples of unknown size and location or on small samples, making generalization and quantitative evaluation impossible.

The growth in drinking by women can be explained by several factors. The first is demographic: Heavy war losses created a marked and lasting male-female imbalance in the USSR, and it is not surprising that some of the 20 million women left without husbands and families at the end of World War II took to drink. High mortality rates among men in the 20–45 age group and an increasing rate of divorce, both of which can be connected to alcohol abuse, continue to increase the pool of women without families, who are more likely than other women to become heavy drinkers.

The second factor, which is probably equally important and also has a similar adverse effect on drinking by minors, is the changing mix in the supply of alcoholic beverages. In the mid-1950s Soviet authorities concluded that the consumption of vodka had a stronger negative impact on health than did other beverages and decided to change the mix of beverages in favor of wine and beer. This policy had limited success. Consumption of vodka did not decline on a per capita basis. In fact, it grew rapidly from 3.4 liters of absolute alcohol in 1960 to 5.6 liters in 1984. However, per capita consumption of grape and fruit wine and of beer did grow much faster: In 1955 vodka accounted for 74 percent of total alcohol consumption; this share dropped to 50 in 1983. It is difficult to say how this change in the mix of beverages affected the hard-drinking Soviet men, but it backfired in terms of overall level of drinking in the country. Women and minors, as a rule, prefer wine to vodka, cognac, and other strong beverages. And the average liter of pure alcohol in the form of vodka was priced somewhat higher than one liter of pure alcohol consumed in the form of grape or fruit wine, making wine more affordable to women and minors, who had lower earnings than men. Accordingly, the continuously increasing availability of wine must have contributed to growing consumption of alcohol by women and minors.

The growth of the "second economy," focusing on production of large quantities of *samogon* for home consumption and for sale, has also contributed to the spread of drinking. The second economy plays an equally important role in contributing to the spread of drinking by circumventing various government restrictions on sale and consumption of alcoholic beverages.[15] Since the late 1950s the authorities have attempted to control heavy drinking and alcohol abuse by a variety of restrictive measures such as prohibiting the sale of alcoholic beverages in certain establishments or locations (near schools, factories, hospitals), by limiting the hours of sale of vodka and other strong beverages, and by placing strict rules on sales in state retail trade. Most, if not all, of these restrictions have little or no effect on the drinking public because second-economy operators working as middlemen, or intermediaries, would buy alcoholic beverages in large quantities and resell them at a premium to drinkers in restricted places or during prohibited hours. A majority of sales personnel in liquor stores and restaurants are also always ready to disregard restrictions for a fee and to sell alcoholic beverages during off-hours, to obviously intoxicated customers, or to minors.

In concluding this summary of causes of heavy drinking in the USSR and particularly in seeking connections between alcohol and Soviet institutions and policies, I must repeat the persistent regional differentiation in per capita consumption of alcohol and in levels of alcohol abuse. It is quite clear that people in Central Asia and the Transcaucasian republics have a much smaller alcohol problem than the rest of the country. Any generalization establishing a given factor, for example, the dullness of everyday life in the USSR or the availability of low-price wines as leading to higher levels of alcohol abuse, must be tempered with the observation that these factors do not have similar effects on Muslims or wine-drinking Georgians and Armenians.

Gorbachev's Antidrinking Campaign

Gorbachev's antidrinking campaign was launched in May 1985. The minimum legal drinking age was raised to twenty-one. Existing restrictions on sales and consumption of alcoholic beverages and penalties and fines for being intoxicated and disorderly were increased and new ones were introduced. The industry was ordered to reduce production of all alcoholic beverages and to phase out completely production of fortified fruit wines; the number of stores and restaurants selling or serving liquor was drastically cut.[16]

The emphasis of the new legislation was clearly on restrictions, punishment, and sanctions. The whole complex of medical and social issues—treatment, hospitalization, medicine, and pre- and posttreatment counseling of alcoholics, habitual drinkers, and their relatives—was barely mentioned. Party and state resolutions depicting the alarming picture of alcohol abuse in the country suggested that one cause of excessive drinking lay in the drabness and boredom of everyday life, exacerbated by the inadequacy of entertainment, rest, and relaxation facilities.

One unfortunate aspect of the antidrinking campaign was its timing. It was launched too early in the *perestroika* period, that is, before the emergence of *glasnost'* policies. Thus, at least in the first three years, the campaign was conducted in the characteristic "administrative," or "directive," style that was seen in so many Soviet campaigns in the past. The orders were given from above and all lower Party and state organizations and institutions had to follow them without question and, in fact, competed with each other in meeting and exceeding the targets posted by the center. The media allowed no dissenting opinions on the nature and the progress of the campaign, high unanticipated costs of the campaign were not discussed, and side effects were ignored, while its successes, such as reduction in drinking or improvements in health and public order, were frequently exaggerated.

Many elements of Gorbachev's antidrinking campaign were not new—similar measures such as stiffer penalties, more restrictions, higher prices, and projections of reduced production of alcoholic beverages—had been introduced during the previous antidrinking campaigns. In the past, restrictions, penalties, and higher prices stayed on, but projected cuts in production were reversed in a year. This time, however, authorities continued to apply the pressure, and production and sale of alcoholic beverages were cut relentlessly for the next three years. Compared with 1984, production of alcoholic beverages was cut by 14 percent in 1985, by another 40 percent in 1986, and by 22 percent in 1987. As the result, consumption per person aged fifteen and older was reduced from 11.22 liters of pure alcohol on the eve of the campaign in 1984 to 4.44 liters in 1987, or by some 60 percent (see Table 7.1). It must be stressed that this in itself was an unusually impressive feat—except for instances of introduction of total prohibition or periods of war, no country had ever achieved such a reduction in alcohol consumption in a span of less than three years.

The media started a virtual "blitz" describing in vivid colors the dangers of alcohol and high social, health, and economic cost of heavy drinking and alcohol abuse. Monitoring of the progress of the campaign was also entrusted to the media—newspapers reported arrests of workers who had been drinking on the job and dismissal of Party and state officials for drunkenness and investigated and reported on violations of newly introduced regulations of liquor trade. Vigilantes searched through the sociological, legal, and medical literature published in the past and castigated authors who had not condemned alcohol abuse in sufficiently strong terms.

A new organization, the All-Union Volunteer Temperance Society, was founded with the full support of the leadership; its membership soon reached 11 million and later 14 million; it had 7,200 paid staff members.[17] The society and its journal "Culture and Sobriety" became the rallying point of an uncompromising abstinence movement. The editorial policy of the journal was to stress that any amount of alcohol was detrimental to health and that the only solution to the drinking problem of the country was total prohibition. The journal attacked and succeeded in silencing, at least for the first three years, the group of prominent Soviet sociologists and legal and medical specialists in alcoholism who rejected total abstinence and called for "civilized drinking," such as Boris and Mikhail Levin, G. Zaigrayev, E. Babaian, and Yu. Lisitsyn. On this and on many other issues the positions and policies advocated by the Temperance Society were often dogmatic, simplistic, and naïve, but until the middle of 1988 the society clearly dominated the course of the campaign[18] and should carry the blame for its excesses and partial failure.

One uncertain element in the 1985 antidrinking campaign was the issue of government revenues. In the early 1980s excise (turnover) taxes on retail sales and profits from production and imports of alcoholic beverages, accounting for some 13–14 percent of the Soviet state budget, constituted one of the most important sources of state revenues. Not surprisingly, fiscal considerations always played an important role in the state's alcohol policy. In fact, losses of alcohol revenues were primarily responsible for reversals of earlier antidrinking campaigns.

In contrast to earlier campaigns the antidrinking measures announced in May of 1985 did not include price increases. Some three months later, in what now is recognized as a major policy error, prices of all alcoholic beverages were raised by about 20 percent[19] and again by about 30 percent in August of 1986.[20] As the result the price of one liter of vodka rose from about 10 rubles on the eve of the campaign to a very high 20 rubles by the end of 1986. Prices of all other alcoholic beverages were also raised at different rates. International comparisons of the purchasing power of wages are fraught with methodological problems, and Soviet-Western comparisons are even more difficult because of difference in the distribution of free state services. Nevertheless, we can get some rough idea of the cost of alcohol relative to earnings in different countries from Bush.[21] In the following tabulation the average price of one liter of vodka is expressed in hours of an industrial worker's time necessary to purchase it:

Munich	2.0 hours
London and Washington	2.6 hours
Paris	3.2 hours
Moscow	19.0 hours

The price of vodka was clearly excessively high, and it is difficult to understand how the drinkers could afford alcohol. Higher prices combined with lower production open the floodgates for *samogon,* which, as we will see below, ultimately doomed the first phase of the 1985 campaign.

Because of the campaign, there were a number of adverse effects and disruptions in the economy. These disruptions were particularly costly because of the abruptness with which the campaign was started and the simplistic nature of many policies. Reduction in sales of alcoholic beverages produced large increases in cash in the hands of the population. This excess cash, cumulatively estimated at some 49 billion rubles in the 1984–1988 period,[22] contributed to inflationary pressures in legal and underground markets. Long waiting lines in front of the reduced number of liquor stores angered the shopping public.[23] The police were mobilized to enforce the laws and regulations governing distribution and consumption of alcohol, to increase the policing of streets, factories, and roads, and to combat growing production and sale of *samogon.* It is possible that some cuts in crime rates observed in 1986–1987 may be explained by the transfer of the police resources to the antidrinking campaign.

Drastic cuts in production of alcoholic beverages led to the closing down of a large number of producing and bottling plants and the need to retrain and reallocate workers. Some 16 percent of vineyards, including thousands of hectares of table grapes, were destroyed by overzealous enforcers of the antidrinking campaign, and wine-research institutes and wine-processing plants were closed.[24] Effects of cuts in wine production were concentrated in wine-producing republics—Moldavia, Azerbaidzhan, Georgia, and Armenia. Because these republics have much lower levels of alcoholism and alcohol abuse than the Slavic areas of the country, the senseless destruction of vineyards and dislocations in the wine industry were particularly frustrating for the population.

During the course of the antidrinking campaign the state budget lost approximately 28 billion rubles in tax revenues.[25] It is worth noting that by the time of the reaction to the campaign in 1988 the leadership included losses of alcohol revenues alongside the cost of the Chernobyl disaster and of the earthquake in Armenia as among the major disruptions threatening the success of *perestroika.*

Illegal home production of *samogon* jumped from approximately 1.7 billion liters in 1984, to 2 billion in 1986, and 2.7 billion in 1987.[26] Thus while the consumption of legal alcohol per person was cut by almost 60 percent in the 1984–1987 period, consumption corrected for *samogon* was reduced by only 35 percent (see Table 7.1). Even a 35 percent cut is rather substantial, but it is clearly not the level of reduction the authorities were hoping for and were willing to sustain given the high budgetary losses. The police redoubled their effort in combatting illegal home production, but the task was clearly hopeless.

The huge increases in illegal home production frustrated not only the authorities but the nondrinking public as well. The main ingredient in *samogon* is sugar, and the growing demand of home distillers led to shortages and formal rationing of sugar throughout the country. By 1987 the scarcity of sugar became so great that it was transmitted to the market for candy and confectionery products, thus angering the consumer even further.[27]

It is difficult to evaluate the impact of the antidrinking campaign on labor productivity, social conditions, and health in the first three years. Basic demographic indicators improved. Male life expectancy at birth increased from the low point of 62.4 years in 1984 to 63.3 in 1986 and to 65.1 in 1987; murder dropped from 9 per 100,000 to 6, and suicide from 30 to 19 per 100,000 in the same period.[28] Mortality and morbidity rates dropped. Some selected measures such as indexes of industrial and traffic accidents caused by drinking and certain types of street crime showed moderate improvements. The number of people diagnosed as alcoholics was cut from 206 in 1984 to 154 per 100,000 in 1988. In fact, some demographic improvements occurred so fast that one begins to have doubts about the validity of statistical data. For example, is it possible that male life expectancy increased by 0.9 years and that suicides dropped by 13,000 in 1985 as the result of eight months of the enforcement of new antidrinking measures? Reduced drinking, increased social pressures on heavy drinkers, and stricter police controls must ultimately have a positive effect on health. But such improvements can hardly be expected in eight months or one year from the start of the campaign. It is possible that some of the dramatic improvements, particularly in 1985 and 1986, were overstated either by Goskomstat or by lower-level reporting units.[29] We will need much more verifiable statistical data to be in a position to assess fully the results of the first three years of the campaign.

Retreat from 1985 Campaign Goals

It appears that by summer 1988 the authorities decided that the immediate and high costs of the antidrinking campaign were far exceeding potential future benefits. The Politburo discussed the course of the campaign in July 1988. Speakers at the June Party conference referred to "high economic and political cost of the antidrinking campaign"—an unusually strong statement. For several months the leadership was uncertain of the course to take. Critical reports began to appear in the press. Restrictions on sales of alcoholic beverages were eased selectively and some liquor stores closed since 1985 were reopened.

Finally in October 1988 the Central Committee issued a statement expressing its dissatisfaction with the progress of the antidrinking campaign; the full text of the Central Committee memorandum describing the failures of the campaign was published in January 1989.[30] While reiterating its support of general goals of the campaign, the Central Committee blamed overzealous local Party and state organizations for excesses in the campaign. The Central Committee noted the "excessively rapid reduction in production of alcoholic beverages and liquidation of the productive base of the alcohol industry" and directed the retail trade network "to eliminate, as soon as possible, conditions responsible for long waiting lines in front of liquor stores." Increased production of *samogon,* widespread speculation in alcoholic beverages and corruption of trade officials, rapid increase in drinking of alcohol surrogates such as after-shave lotions and industrial glues, and increased incidence of poisonings were also listed among the negative results of the campaign. Price increases and the loss of alcohol revenues in the state budget were not mentioned in the memorandum. The statement of the Central Committee also called for a more balanced approach to the alcohol problem, declaring both the position of "prohibitionists" (i.e., the policy advocated by the Temperance Society) and of "civilized drinking" as invalid.

The reversal of the policy of cuts in alcohol production started in 1988. Compared to 1987, the total consumption of alcoholic beverages measured in pure alcohol rose by about 10 percent in 1988 and jumped 21 percent in 1989. As the result, by mid-1989 consumption per person aged fifteen and older was 5.78 liters; that is, it had returned to the 1986 level (see Table 7.1). This trend continued through 1989 and into 1990; the state's need for additional revenue clearly has helped to bring about more and more drinking.

Gorbachev's antidrinking campaign has so far affected people's lives and incomes, state and local finances, day-to-day operations of the MVD, and interrepublican income to a much greater extent than other *perestroika* reforms. It can only be regretted that the Soviet system in the pre-*glasnost'* days distorted the design and the execution of the antidrinking measures. Had the campaign been started a few years later, the results could have been quite different. But the campaign was clearly associated with Gorbachev's name, and the reversal of 1985 campaign goals was widely interpreted in the country as a major embarrassment to the general secretary, who, beset with other difficulties facing *perestroika,* simply could not sustain the momentum of the campaign. His commitment to temperance or, as some would say, his stubbornness and lack of realism forced the campaign much further along than past campaigns. In the long run some of the measures introduced in May 1985 could not fail to produce positive results. Will Gorbachev get credit for it, or will the setbacks of 1987 and 1988 be used by his opponents to weaken his position? It is too early to tell. At this time the consensus in the Soviet Union seems to be that Gorbachev has lost this one.

Notes

1. V. Treml, "A Noble Experiment? Gorbachev's Anti-Drinking Campaign," in *Soviet Society under Gorbachev,* ed. M. Friedberg and H. Isham (Armonk, N.Y., and London: M. E. Sharpe, 1987), pp. 52–75, and "Gorbachev's Anti-Drinking Campaign: A 'Noble Experiment' or a Costly Exercise in Futility?" in U.S. Congress, Joint Economic Committee, *Gorbachev's Economic Plans,* Pt. 2 (Washington, D.C.: Government Printing Office, 1987), pp. 297–311.

2. The newly released data essentially cover the years 1985–1988, with some selected production and consumption statistics going back to 1960. Historical series are not available. No data have been released on such vitally important aspects of drinking as per capita consumption and frequency of drinking broken down by age, sex, urban and rural areas of residence, and the nationality of drinkers, expenditures on alcohol by different income groups, reliable price information and price indexes, confinements of habitual drinkers in various police facilities, excise taxes on alcoholic beverages, state alcohol revenues, and the like. Data on the relationship between drinking and other types of deviant behavior such as crime, suicide, and divorce found in the literature are fragmentary, undocumented, and often ambiguous.

3. The following important names and their representative works must be mentioned in this connection: E. Babaian and M. Gonopol'skii, *Uchebnoe posobie po narkologii* (Moscow: Meditsina, 1981); B. Levin, "Sotsial'nyi portret alkogolika," in *Mnenie neravnodushnykh* (Moscow: Nauka, 1972), pp. 63–133; Yu. Lisitsyn and N. Kopyt, *Alkogolizm,* 1978; B. Segal, *Alkogolizm* (Moscow: Meditsina, 1967); B. Segal, *Russian Drinking: Use and Abuse of Alcohol in Pre-Revolutionary Russia* (New Brunswick, 1987): I. Strel'chuk, *Ostraia i khronicheskaia intoksikatsiia alkogolem* (Moscow: Meditsina, 1973); and G. Zaigrayev (ed.), *Profilaktika p'ianstva i alkogolizma* (Moscow: Iuridicheskaia Literatura, 1983).

4. In the absence of data by nationalities, the groups are identified by republics. Kazakhstan was omitted from the comparison because demographically it must be viewed as two separate demographic entities. Urban areas are essentially populated by non-Kazakhs, whose drinking patterns are very similar to those of Slavs. Rural areas are populated by Kazakhs: Their drinking is similar to that of other Central Asian groups.

5. "Za trezvyi obraz zhizni," *Kommunist,* no. 11 (1987), p. 37.

6. *Vestnik statistiki,* no. 6 (1989), p. 56.

7. V. Bokhovkin et al., *Kommunist,* no. 7 (May 1989), p. 49.

8. *Naselenie SSSR 1987: Statisticheskii sbornik* (Moscow: Goskomstat SSSR, 1988), p. 351.

9. See M. Feshbach, "The Soviet Union: Population Trends and Dilemmas," *Population Bulletin,* no. 37 (August 1982), p. 34. Feshbach's estimates were broadly confirmed by the demographic data subsequently released in the USSR.

10. See V. Treml, "Death from Alcohol Poisoning in the USSR," *Soviet Studies* 34, no. 4 (October 1982), pp. 488–490, and "Fatal Poisonings in the USSR," *Radio Liberty Research Bulletin* 50 (December 1982), pp. 1–12. Deaths from the traditional Slavic *opoy* (acute alcohol poisoning caused by a rapid ingestion of a critical quantity of alcohol) increased from about 12,500 in the early 1960s to 50,000 in the late 1970s. This translated into a rate of 19.5 deaths per 100,000 population (comparable rate for nineteen countries for which data are available is 0.3 deaths).

11. Treml, "A Noble Experiment?" op. cit.
12. S. Strumilin and S. Sonin, *Ekonomika i organizatsiia promyshlennogo proizvodstva,* no. 4 (1974), p. 38.
13. For an excellent analysis of the background of the Russian alcohol culture see Segal, op. cit. Important contributions to understanding of the causes of Russian and Soviet drinking, particularly in the 1960s and 1970s when Soviet authorities denied the existence of the alcohol problem, were also made by M. Field and D. Powell, "Alcohol Abuse in the Soviet Union," *Hastings Center Report,* October 1981, pp. 40–44; W. D. Connor, *Deviance in Soviet Society: Crime, Delinquency and Alcoholism* (New York: Columbia University Press, 1972); "Alcohol and Soviet Society," in *Beliefs, Behaviors, and Alcoholic Beverages,* ed. M. Marshall (Ann Arbor: University of Michigan Press, 1979), pp. 433–449.
14. Production was cut by about 4 percent in 1958, 2 percent in 1972, 1 percent in 1977, and 3 percent in 1982; see V. Treml, *Alcohol in the USSR. A Statistical Study* (Durham, N.C.: Duke University Press, 1982), p. 16, and various annual issues of *Narodnoe khoziaistvo SSSR* (Moscow: Goskomstat SSSR).
15. V. Treml, "Alcohol in the Soviet Underground Economy," *Berkeley-Duke Occasional Papers on the Second Economy in the USSR,* no. 7 (December 1985).
16. *Pravda,* May 17, 1985, pp. 1–2, and B. A. Stolbov, ed., *Zakonodatel'stvo v bor'be s pianstvom i alkogolizmom* (Moscow: Iuridicheskaia Literatura, 1985).
17. The data are from different issues of *Trezvost' i kul'tura.* Evidence reported later in newspapers cast some doubt on the voluntary nature of the society. It appeared that all employees of some enterprises and organizations were signed up by management and learned about their membership only when presented with requests for annual dues of 2 rubles. Nevertheless, the anger and frustration of non- and moderate drinkers about the extent of alcohol abuse in the country were so great that millions had probably joined the society voluntarily.
18. See Treml, "A Noble Experiment?" op. cit., pp. 56–60.
19. Radio Moscow, August 26, 1985.
20. *Pravda,* August 1, 1986, p. 2.
21. K. Bush, "Retail Prices in Moscow and Four Western Cities in October, 1986," *Radio Liberty Research Bulletin,* RL Supplement 1/87, January 21, 1987, p. 26.
22. *Vestnik statistiki,* no. 6 (1989), p. 55.
23. According to Goskomstat's survey of thirty large regions in summer 1988, waiting lines in front of liquor stores averaged between 200 and 800 people; they had to wait between one-and-a-half and three hours before they could make their purchase (ibid.). According to a Central Committee memorandum published later, "tens of billions of man-hours were lost in waiting lines"; see "O nekotorykh negativnykh iavleniiakh v bor'be s p'ianstvom i alkogolizmom," *Izvestiia TsK KPSS,* no. 1 (1989), p. 48.
24. D. Melikov, *Sotsialisticheskaia industriia,* September 17, 1987, p. 2; and Yu. Chernichenko, *Ogonek,* no. 33 (August 1987), pp. 12–24.
25. Estimated by the author as the difference between total alcohol-tax collections on the eve of the campaign in 1984 and each of the years in the 1985–1988 period. Much higher figures cited by Gorbachev (*Pravda,* July 27, 1986, p. 2; *Izvestiia,* October 2, 1987, pp. 1–2) and other authorities referred to total losses in state trade revenues from sale of alcoholic beverages.
26. Author's estimates. See Treml, *Alcohol in the USSR,* op. cit., pp. 47–66, for the methodology of estimation. Production of *samogon* in the late 1970s–early 1980s estimated by the author was confirmed by V. Bazhenov, *Literaturnaia gazeta,* May

29, 1985, p. 11. Changes in production of *samogon* in the 1980s were estimated on the basis of changes in sales of sugar. Some Soviet authors estimated production of *samogon* at much higher levels than the author. See B. Iskakov et al., *Na puti k trezvosti*, ed. B. M. Levin et al. (Moscow: Sovetskaia Sotsiologicheskaia Assotsiatsiia, 1987), p. 25. Official Goskomstat statistics showed production of *samogon* "from sugar only" as 1.6 billion liters in 1984, 1.8 billion liters in 1986, and 1.2 billion liters in 1988; see *Narodnoe khoziaistvo SSSR v 1987 godu* (Moscow: Goskomstat SSSR, 1988), p. 422, and *SSSR v tsifrakh v 1988 godu* (Moscow: Goskomstat SSSR, 1989), p. 87. The low figures reported by Goskomstat are difficult to accept, especially because they show an increase of only 200 million liters between 1984 and 1986. Sales of sugar, which remained relatively stable in the early 1980s, increased by 785,000 metric tons in 1986 and by 780,000 metric tons in 1987 and most Soviet authorities interpret these increases as caused by *samogon* producers. These changes in sugar sales were clearly inconsistent with Goskomstat *samogon* estimates.

27. "V Tsentral'nom Komitete KPSS," *Pravda*, October 28, 1988, p. 1.

28. *SSSR v tsifrakh*, op. cit., pp. 132–140.

29. One example of puzzling statistics is seen in the following: According to several Soviet sources, deaths from cardiovascular problems were reduced by about 107,000 in 1986 and this remarkable improvement was attributed to the antidrinking campaign. However, subsequently published mortality data showed that this number breaks down into 49,000 fewer male and 58,000 fewer female deaths. Since heavy drinking and alcohol-related mortality is much more prevalent among men than women, these mortality data and their relations to the antidrinking measures appear rather doubtful; see V. Treml, "Was 1988 a Year of Demographic Disasters?" *Report on the USSR* 1, no. 22 (June 2, 1989), pp. 1–3.

30. "O nekotorykh negativnykh," op. cit., pp. 48–51.

CHAPTER 8

Equality of Opportunity

Walter D. Connor

Introduction

Five years into the "Gorbachev era," few aspects of Soviet life remained untouched by the policy controversies, freewheeling discussions, legislative activity, and political changes that led to the tumultuous year of 1989. In what would be the first year of a (U.S. presidential) "second term," Gorbachev pushed through a reformed election process that produced a new, contentious Congress of People's Deputies and a new Supreme Soviet, not so toothless as the old—placing in some question the political prerogatives of both Party *apparatchiki* and state-ministerial functionaries. He has done more in this regard than even the most optimistic observers of Soviet affairs might have predicted. However, he has been luckless in some ways as well. The economy stubbornly fails to improve its performance. Ethnic conflicts and tensions—an aspect of Soviet reality about which Gorbachev has seemed, on the whole, to be less "musical" than other aspects—have erupted into violence. The wave of strikes in Siberian, Ukrainian, and Arctic mines in July 1989, whose ultimate echoes are yet to fade, presented a challenge to the very design of state power itself. Whether Gorbachev would turn this crisis to his long-term political benefit, as he has done with smaller ones, was a question whose answer depended heavily on his ability—or "luck"—in dealing with some of the economic and social problems in which the crisis was rooted.

The Soviet scene, then, shows continuing tension between the new directions and the old patterns and practices—a society is not reshaped overnight, even under *perestroika* and *glasnost'*. The Gorbachev program implied changes that would cut deep into the lifeways and customary world of Soviet citizens: a world that is materially threadbare by Western standards but that has afforded basic security and certainties, to which many citizens had grown quite used. Gorbachev has been unable to offer immediate and significant increases in general affluence as a trade-off for renouncing some of the old security. This has bred reluctance among many to part with old ways. For others, the various promises of *perestroika,* thus far unrealized, have only increased feelings of malaise.

In this context, the issue of *equality of opportunity* in Soviet economy and society has loomed large among social controversies unleashed by *glasnost'* and *perestroika*. Socialism is, in a sense, "about" equality—it cannot avoid the issue. *Soviet* socialism, at the ideological level, has accepted the differentiation of abilities ("from each according to his abilities, to each according to his work") and a differentiation of reward as well (at least until the time when general abundance could allow distribution according to need). Such principles, of course, could accommodate either steep or gradual scales of differentiation, and did: In Stalin's time, the former (in conditions of very low general living standards); since then, more of the latter.

Nor has the concept of "reward" always focused on the material sphere. Soviet ideological prose has often emphasized the moral equality of all "socially useful labor," the "prestige" of any work well done, the "honor" that attached to factory hand as to academic, to miner as to surgeon. In the absence of any threat of unemployment, motivating effort in a generally poor society by any combination of material and nonmaterial stimuli has, however, been a complex matter. The Soviet economy shows the effect of a "low-effort" syndrome—one of the problems with which *perestroika* seeks to cope, with policy instruments as yet not proven equal to the task.

It has been, in effect, equality of opportunity, rather than result, that has been emphasized in Soviet official ideology. Whether "striving" has really been encouraged in state ideology or accepted in "folk" culture is another matter. But the notion that Soviet citizens have, or should have, equal opportunity to develop their minds and skills has been underlined in various ways. At times of rapid economic growth, the spectacle of peasant and worker sons ascending educational and occupational ladders to professional or managerial careers gave a good deal of credence to equality of opportunity. Even if the reality, technically speaking, was one of an *increased* (but still unequal) supply of opportunities as the structure of occupational demand changed under rapid industrialization, the result was the extension of opportunity to many who would have been denied it under a more stagnant economy.

Large-scale "bursts" of occupational mobility, however, cannot outlast the economic processes that underlie them. For some time, as growth fell to still-respectable levels under Khrushchev and the earlier Brezhnev, then into the late Brezhnevian *zastoi* (stagnation), Soviet society has been in a process of stabilization, of a concretization of groups, patterns, and structures. In the end, what developed, in the views of Western analysts as well as of many of the architects of *perestroika,* was a public mind-set that, if anything, reversed socialist principles of meritocratic distribution. Though there is evidence that many sought to "rise" through the certification that comes with higher education, what came most generally to be valued was, first, the security of employment at low effort the system afforded and, second, the apparently egalitarian structure of economic reward that saw few rising very high above a common level and few falling visibly below it. "Success," one might argue, had come to be defined as having, pretty much, what one needed and was entitled to—within a broad social assumption that everyone needed, and was entitled to, roughly the same things. This, for many, was "social justice."

Enter Mikhail Gorbachev, with a new, explicit, and thoroughgoing diagnosis of Soviet ills that related many of them to this concept of justice. It is with the notion of success that we begin, to move on later to two areas where opportunity and its distribution are matters of current concern, and then to some more general thoughts about the Gorbachev agenda and the notions of "social justice" widely diffused in Soviet society that reform seeks to alter.

Opportunity, Equality, and Success

That there has been a heavy material dimension in the official notion of success in Soviet society is clear. Since Stalin's denunciation of *uravnilovka* (egalitarianism) in the heat of the First Five Year Plan, the implication has been that mechanical egalitarianism is unsocialist, that "to each according to his work" is an *equitable* principle. Expectations of material reward for high-quality effort and results found legitimation in Soviet popular literature in the Stalin era,[1] a time when rewards were certainly very unequal. The Khrushchev years saw some relief from the overall material poverty of Stalin's time but, along with it, a somewhat populist-idealist denigration of the search for material reward[2] and an emphasis on *communal* forms of consumption as the channel through which overall material progress would be realized in a communist future, which the utopian Khrushchev saw impending before century's end.

With adequate economic performance through its first half, and declining-to-stagnating growth rates in its second, the Brezhnev era exhibited somewhat contradictory tendencies. A "creeping egalitarianism" in the salary/wage area prevailed overall, to be denounced roundly with the coming of Gorbachev. Corruption and its resultant profits for some operated as a de-equalizing factor, in fact suggesting to many people that the period was one of pronounced *inequality* if compared with their images of earlier times in Soviet history.[3] Brezhnev-era social policy also allowed more by way of the "privatization" of consumption than had the Khrushchev period. Automobiles, other expensive consumer durables, and co-op apartments were more in evidence as differentiators of a household's place in the material hierarchy. Indices of material success, if not nearly as blatant as in the West, were growing more visible to many. But for others, a secure life amid a rough equality seems to have been the predominant impression. It would not be easy to get the relative proportions straight.

The social policy of *perestroika* has set itself against this sort of egalitarianism, castigating it as rooted in a destructive *envy,* a negative egalitarianism that puts a price on evident success, that longs to hammer down the nails that "stick up." Andrei Amalrik, the dissident who asked, in the late 1960s, whether the USSR would "survive until 1984" put the matter well, if harshly, in characterizing an instinct for leveling down among

Soviet citizens. To the "average Russian," "freedom" meant "not the possibility of securing a good life for himself but the danger that some clever chap or other will make good at his expense"; the notion of justice involved the wish that "nobody should be better off than me"; and if the "average Russian" faced hardships greater than his neighbor, "what he thinks about is not to try and get himself organized as well as his neighbor but to arrange somehow or other so that his neighbor too is as badly off as himself."[4] It is amusing to remember now that some Westerners viewed these words as those of a sour, "unpatriotic" dissident who found fault with the *people* as well as the regime. Amusing, especially, because Amalrik sounded little different from Gorbachev's economic reformers. As Leonid Abalkin, a deputy prime minister charged with shepherding *perestroika* policies, put it, "we are indeed fond of counting the money in someone else's pocket."[5]

The reformers have found some of the roots of economic stagnation in the old-style confidence in getting paid regardless of the quality of one's efforts or results; in the parity between lazy and industrious workers; and in the ready assumption that those who had desirable goods somehow acquired them in dishonest ways. They diagnosed egalitarian attitudes as a major socioeconomic barrier in the path of a *perestroika* that should ultimately yield a more abundant life for all.

But theirs has not been the only voice heard or attended to. Participants in the continuing discussion who might be considered tepid on reform (no one is "against" it) cited a need for fair limits on inequality, the necessity of a basic material security for all, and the avoidance of the negative example of a work-and-acquisition-driven Western capitalism as elements of the Soviet social contract, which *perestroika* must preserve. Those on the egalitarian, "welfarist," side were tapping some deep feelings. Few indeed are their opponents, who favor a freer play of market mechanisms, of economic "levers," of *success* expressed as deserved, though unequal, economic reward of which one can be proud, who have not, still, shown some sensitivity to the issues raised by new, implied definitions of "failure" as the reciprocal of success. Unemployment—in the Soviet context, a very controversial possibility—has been an especially explosive topic. Nikolai Shmelev, the economist who argued in a 1987 *Novyi mir* article[6] that unemployment with benefits was potentially better than stockpiling lazy, destructive workers, later backpedaled on the point.[7] Other economists, relying on the absorption capacity of an expanding service sector, have stressed that *perestroika* represents a way of *guaranteeing* full employment. In this, they have shown political judgment, whatever their economic instincts. If unemployment comes, it will be seen as a major social problem, not as a policy instrument.

For the present, the tensions inherent in new definitions of success and failure are more evidently dramatized by inequalities between employed citizens. Three dimensions, at least, are involved here:

- State-sector employment versus cooperative or "private" (individual labor activity) enterprise as sources of income
- Earned versus "unearned" income
- State-sector inequalities in salaries/wages

The first, as we shall see, predictably emerged as an issue almost as soon as Gorbachev's opening to new forms of enterprise began. The second crosscuts the first; "second economy" activities that were long common though illegal and now are legalized have been characterized as sources of "unearned" income even if the intelligence, energy, and sweat invested in them were far more than Homo sovieticus put into his state-sector job. The third has emerged in wage and salary policies formulated in 1986–1987 that finally promise to favor educated, white-collar professionals (whose work shows results) over the blue-collar work force and to make a greater differentiation among the latter as well. The raises implied are to be financed, however, by "results"—by the enterprise's income—rather than out of the state budget, as before.

Selling differentiated material success as "legitimate" requires renewed attention to equality of opportunity. Some writers, notably the economist-sociologist Tatiana Zaslavskaia, have dealt at length with the aspects of Soviet life wherein inequality of opportunity works its effects: rural/urban and small town/large city distinctions, situational factors in local-labor-market structures, enterprise-based inequalities in earning potential, and regional inequalities in the availability of goods and services for the same amount of rubles.[8] Dealing with all of these sources of differentiation is a massive order indeed—many of them are inherent in the organization of industrial society in general. Yet if society is to become more "competitive," it is important that the competition be seen as "fair."

This is, altogether, a more complicated notion than it seems. Various factors in Brezhnev's time moderated the degree to which life seemed competitive and material success appeared evident. Endemic shortages, "rationing by queue," the massive pileup of unspendable rubles in savings institutions and mattresses, all limited ability to predict living standard from salary or wage level. Nor, leaving out of consideration for the moment medium-to-large illegal incomes and a very small legally "rich" segment of the society, were salary and wage scales so differentiated as to agitate egalitarian sentiments. Shortages of durables and of many food items with fixed state prices also meant that many of those *with* money paid more than the stated price for much of what they acquired. The trade-off of effort, even with money in hand, to find desired items—the "opportunity cost"—versus doing without them, with less effort, also must have affected some calculations. All in all, given the security at a low level that the system afforded—something most citizens understood as security, rather than poverty—the race to achieve was one many saw no reason to join, if they even perceived that it was being run.

For those who were aware of a race, however, its venue was clear. As in other industrial societies—and more so given the bureaucratic, nonentrepreneurial nature of the Soviet economy—education was for a long time a major route to elevated economic reward and to the status, bureaucratic access, and/or interesting work that, in Soviet conditions, often meant as much or more than salary. We turn, therefore, to an examination of some patterns of access ("opportunity") to this good.

Education and Opportunity

A generation has passed since Vladimir N. Shubkin inaugurated his research on educational aspirations and outcomes—how "youth starts out in life."[9] That time has seen other researchers follow in the same mode, throwing considerable light on the dynamics of *unequal* access among Soviet high-school graduating classes (typically, tenth-graders) to higher education.

Shubkin's initial research, carried out in Novosibirsk in 1963–1964, yielded results too well known to recount in detail here. Suffice it to indicate that the findings included: (1) a fair similarity in aspirations (for continuing on to higher education, against going immediately to work) across different social origin groups; (2) radically different outcomes for those same origin groups (urban, nonmanual workers' children managed to continue into some form of postsecondary education at a high rate (82 percent) versus less than 14 percent of farm workers' children, with blue-collar-workers' offspring in between). The lineup at the start of the race was anything but even.

Third, Shubkin's research—and that of others who followed—found what were, on the whole, *high* aspirations. By the early to mid-1960s, a much larger share of the seventeen-year-old population was to be found in the final grade of academic secondary school than there had been in Stalin's time, when a majority exited school with six to eight years of formal schooling. Independent of social origin, youthful educational and occupational aspirations had been encouraged by a more inclusionary policy with respect to secondary education. But the desires thus developed, that is, for admission to an institution of higher education (VUZ), for the sort of job prospects that followed on higher education—were "out of sync" with state policy and with the supply of such jobs the Soviet economy could provide.

As the share of seventeen-year-olds finishing academic secondary school increased, so too did the gap between higher-education aspirations and the degree to which they could be satisfied. Although tenth-grade numbers expanded greatly, classes in universities and institutes grew, but not by nearly so much. Meanwhile, parental aspirations for children also were on the rise. In 1965, a study of parental aspirations among employees at the Uralmash industrial complex near Sverdlovsk showed, not surprisingly, that among intelligentsia-parents, 99.6 percent wanted their children to be "specialists"—so, however, did fully 84.8 percent of worker-parents.[10]

The numbers suggest increasing frustration. Estimates indicated that in 1950–1953, 65 percent of high-school graduates entered higher education (representing a quite small share of the total age group); by 1960–1963, around the time of Shubkin's study, this fell to 33 percent, and it had fallen further to 19 percent by 1970-1973.[11] By 1984-1985, about 16 percent were continuing into higher education. Over time, the preselection dynamic had changed radically as well. In 1965, about four in ten eighth-grade students continued into ninth and tenth grades of academic school; only these were eligible to appear in Shubkin's data. By the early to mid-1980s, almost three-quarters passed into either the academic school (60+ percent) or a diploma-granting combined trade and academic school (around 14 percent)—the SPTU, or *srednee proftekhuchilishche*.[12] If not all of these were likely aspirants to higher education, many were.

The gradual development of the SPTU, combining trade-school training and the diploma—if not the education—of ten years of academic school, set the stage for disagreement among Soviet specialists on education. As larger shares of the relevant age groups continued into the ninth and tenth grades or entered SPTU, were "cultural" effects likely to counteract the elevation of aspirations? Were desires for the VUZ still as pronounced as in past years when tenth-graders typically came from economically and educationally "elite" households? Certainly, some decline in aspirations among this less exclusive and larger percentage of the age cohort was expectable and did occur. One specialist cited a 46 percent figure for higher-educational aspirations for tenth-graders in 1977, contrasting it to an "80-90 percent" aspiration rate in the 1960s, and reported data for studies in five cities showing rates ranging from 58.2 to 47.8 percent.[13] (One Soviet scholar combined estimates of tenth-graders seeking higher education and "specialized secondary," paraprofessional-type, education and estimated that between 85 and 94 percent of tenth-graders had some further educational aspirations as late as the 1977-1980 period.[14])

Whatever the precise reality, these were figures still far in excess of what could be satisfied given the places available in postsecondary education. It was urban, well-educated families with commensurate occupational status who did best at seeing that their children obtained the scarce places in the VUZy.

The inequalities of the sort that Shubkin first revealed and other Soviet sociologists continued to explore were deeply rooted in earlier, and reflected in later, education. Parental educational and occupational levels and economic returns from work constituted in some cases assets, in others liabilities, for children. Less-educated, poorly paid, low-job-status parents saw their children drop out of school for the world of work earlier and more often opt, after eight years of academic schooling, for a nondiploma, lower-level trade school (*proftekhuchilishche,* or PTU), rather than continuing for the last two years of the academic track and eligibility for VUZ entrance exams. But this sorting process left many with aspirations hard for the system to accommodate.

How should education policy be altered to cope with those white-collar, professional aspirations, in a largely blue-collar USSR? How should that policy be steered in the direction of reducing the "labor shortage" of the late Brezhnev years, which was compounded by the reluctance of seventeen-year-olds to enter the labor force rather than pursue further schooling?

One answer—a prospectively harsh one—was the educational reform of 1984. This broad-gauged but short-sighted set of measures, a child of the end of the Brezhnev era, offered an administrative solution that proved controversial and was ultimately abandoned, long before it might have worked its way to altering patterns of long standing. The SPTU—the combined academic and trade school—was, by the reform's language, to double its intake, effectively halving the intake of the "pure" academic school.[15] Eighth-graders, previously free to choose, would now be "streamed," in a never quite clearly specified process. Twice as many would receive the supposedly "equal" academic training of the SPTU and with it the vocational training lacking in academic schools. (The latter, by the early 1980s, were sending most of their graduates, willy-nilly, into the world of work, since they could not meet the increasing competition for VUZ admission.)

Who would be selected, who not? Here, again, equality of opportunity was likely to be poorly served. The same resources, generally parentally determined (dress, demeanor, verbal facility, and parental "clout"), that sorted winners from losers in the higher-education competition would probably work to reduce the share of working-class and peasant children in the upper grades of the academic school. If workers' children were, after eighth grade, mainly tracked into the SPTU, where the trajectory was toward entering the world of work (without the distinction of having taken, and failed, VUZ entrance examinations), this was probably exactly what planners and officials wished.

The "reform," however, was not to work. Complaints about its administration mounted,[16] and the numbers actually redirected seemed to be small. By the third year of Gorbachev's rule, it was clear that the SPTU performed neither its academic nor its vocational-training functions well. Its deficiencies were attacked openly by the chairman of the State Committee on Vocational-Technical Education,[17] and the death knell was sounded by Egor Ligachev at a special Central Committee meeting on education on February 17–18, 1988.[18]

The rationale for abandoning such "tracking" did not, however, include its role in reproducing social inequality—at least not that connected, per se, with educational certification. If anything, this laissez-faire policy was likely to intensify some aspects of social self-selection that led to unequal outcomes.

One possibility discussed was a reduction of compulsory schooling to nine years, leaving those who went only this far without the diploma that allowed one to compete for VUZ entry.[19] It was perhaps indicative that the chairman of the newly created State Committee for Public Education said in March 1988 that "we are planning to abandon the drive toward a compulsory secondary education for all. If a young man or girl wants to learn certain skills and become a high-class worker, it's only to be welcomed."[20]

Without overinterpreting this statement, one can read in it an implication that educational "upward mobility" is not to be actively promoted among those who are not "naturally" oriented toward long academic training. This, in turn, can cut two ways. Current thinking, in the age of *perestroika,* dictates that many specialties requiring a degree have been greatly underpaid—and policy is to raise the pay in most of these. Thus, educational certification may generate higher returns than in the past, and access to these may be more *unequally* distributed.

However, the logic of *perestroika* also dictates more of the "market," more room for entrepreneurship and its rewards, and less restriction of opportunities to the bureaucratic-organizational paths where educational credentials are typically needed. We turn, now, to this new area where opportunity for material reward has expanded—and proven very controversial.

Opportunity and Risk: Cooperative Enterprise

For his economic program, Gorbachev, breaking with the near-total statist tilt of Soviet economic practice, in 1986 introduced legislation to legalize both "cooperative" enterprise and solo, independent work ("individual labor activity"). We will deal here only with the former, since it is by far the more significant.

The cooperatives make for an interesting story—too long to tell here, except in brief—and rich with indications that the philosophy underlying their legalization and encouragement ran counter to many ideas of "social justice" and of what Soviet life should be. The beginnings were not auspicious; whereas late 1985–early 1986 saw some discussion that indicated "enabling" legislation might be on the way, the first fruits were a decree and resolution in May 1986 against "deriving unearned income,"[21] which led, in summer 1986, to what one economist called a "pogrom against private hothouses, gardeners and feedlots"[22]—activities in the farm sector that were, generally, legal. This phase probably reflected a combination of compromise on matters of policy conflict and, for the reformers at least, a "clearing of the decks" for the proenterprise moves to come. These followed: a draft law on cooperatives[23] in October and a decree on individual labor activity in November.[24] Cooperatives got under way under the provisional legislation, as did individual entrepreneurs. At the local level, where licensing took place, there was evidence aplenty of bureaucratic resistance and restriction,[25] leaving the central authorities in the uncharacteristic posture of demanding legal support for the rights of entrepreneurs,[26] and reminding local authorities that the rules meant that all that was not specifically prohibited was permitted.[27]

The "final" law on cooperatives—more liberal than the draft—was published in June 1988.[28] It came at the end of rather complex wrangling over taxes—both those to be paid by cooperatives as "corporate" entities and those to be paid by the member-workers of such as individuals. In the dispute, concerns about promoting the development of cooperatives via low tax rates on retained income (after wages to members and workers) conflicted with Finance Ministry concerns about increasing tax receipts; and varying conceptions of "social justice" warred in setting tax rates for individuals.[29] Eventually, a corporate tax regime setting a maximum of 40 percent of the gross, but leaving the individual republics to set rates lower if they wished, was adopted.[30] Still too high in the view of many reform economists, the arrangement allowed for the possibility, as one source noted, that the Baltic republics, whose Western traditions and front-line status in both political and economic reform made them hospitable to entrepreneurship, might well set their rates low and become tax havens for cooperatives doing business in several republics.[31]

With regard to individuals, a new draft income-tax law published in April 1989[32] established parity of rates between state-sector and cooperative workers, leaving the (very) modestly progressive old rates in effect up to incomes of 701 rubles per month, and then escalating in a series of steps to a marginal top rate of *50* percent for "superearners" in the 1,500 and over rubles per month category. (This replaced a version that had been rejected earlier that had singled out co-op workers earning over 500 rubles per month, imposing on them a higher set of rates that escalated to a top marginal rate of *90* percent on wages over 1,500 rubles monthly.[33]) With average blue- and white-collar state-sector pay at around 215 rubles in 1988, only a small segment of the population was likely to be affected, but the parity of rates signified some victory for the advocates of reform—and for those in cooperatives and individual labor, a number that if one counted as half-time privateers about 1.6 million moonlighters who also held state-sector jobs, reached an estimated 3.5 million "full time equivalents" in 1989.[34]

For participants, the cooperatives have meant: (1) more autonomy in work life, (2) the chance to deploy entrepreneurial skills and talents, (3) a closer linkage between the "results" of work efforts and money earned, and (4) the prospect of quite high earnings, given all the gaps in consumer and service sectors to be filled.

All of these are objectives of *perestroika* (for the state sector as well as for the private sector). All of them, however, have also proven unfamiliar, "alien," to a goodly segment of the Soviet population. Moral disapproval, suspicion, and a rather uncomfortable environment have awaited those who chose to take advantage of these new opportunities. Autonomy, after all, has hardly been a major officially approved value in the Soviet system. Much of what might be adjectivized as "entrepreneurial" in the West has been denominated "money-grubbing," "speculation," and simply criminal in the Soviet context, during many pre-Gorbachev decades.[35]

This attitude found early expression in bureaucratic resistance and foot-dragging at the local levels where cooperatives and individual operators were to be licensed and registered. Despite "authoritative" demands by Moscow officials that citizens' newly established rights in these areas be protected by law, lest citizens be left to defend themselves,[36] visceral reactions to would-be entrepreneurs coming "out of the woodwork" and fears of miscalculating which way the political winds would ultimately blow moved local officials to erect many barriers. The cooperatives *have* grown but not yet triumphed. Although the worsening economic situation of 1988–1989 added sharpness to public discourse about fairness, equality, and the bare sufficiency of living standards in general, the cooperatives and the "entrepreneurs" who have flocked into them would be controversial in any case.

A major bone of contention (as implied in the earlier discussion of setting tax rates) is the clear potential for high earnings for those cooperators who find a niche of unfulfilled demand in a nascent market. The early experience of Gorbachev-era cooperatives' finding product lines profitable in a goods-starved economy generated complaints, for example, from a tractor driver who objected that makers "of bra-fasteners" earned 100 rubles per day, while he earned only 2–3 rubles per day whenever his tractor was under repair.[37] Another case involved a plastic-costume-jewelry co-op that earned nearly 500,000 rubles in its first four months: Nervous local officials declared the earnings "illegal" and closed it down.[38] One co-op, engaged in making pantyhose, did so well that its four workers generated 200,000 rubles over a four-month period—Croesus-like returns compared to Soviet wage/salary scales—and "shut down" voluntarily in anticipation of police attention. (It received a clean bill of legal health—promoting a pro-*perestroika* commentator to observe that the "main 'culprit' " was the shortage.[39])

Exercising the new rights to seek economic opportunity via cooperative enterprise, one runs into a good deal of social resistance, based on reality, suspicion, and perception. Let us take an honest founder-manager-employee of a cooperative. He/she will make more money than a state employee, often much more. This is accomplished by "producing" a good or service in demand, and typically in short supply, and charging a "market-clearing" price for it or by operating literally as an "entrepreneur," a middleman, getting goods, moving them to the customer, and pocketing a markup.

On the down side, our honest cooperator may be thought a "crook"—some racketeers have founded cooperatives and used them to "launder" reported co-op income, money acquired over a long period from illegal operations. He may be victimized by crooks—in Moscow and other cities, "protection" rackets seem to be flourishing—or by angered citizens who vandalize or burn his shop (as happened in Ashkhabad in 1989, leading to the arrest of around 100 rioters).[40] He may be blamed for shortages of goods in state stores, a distrustful and frustrated public assuming that the availability of the "same" good at higher prices in the co-ops means that they have been transferred from one sector to the other. He will be blamed for the "high" prices he charges, in the face of the quasi-monopoly many co-ops enjoy in the particular locality and sector of the goods- and service-starved economy in which they operate—with few understanding the logic that *more* co-ops, *more* supplies, will eventually promote the competition that can break monopolies. On the whole, the Soviet citizenry does not "understand" the market logic that drives the cooperatives; if they understood it, it is likely that many would not, on the whole, accept it as a *moral* justification for how the co-ops work and how much they earn.

"Success," in a material sense, is thus available to those who take advantage of the opportunity cooperative enterprise offers. It is a new channel of opportunity, one effectively barred to no Soviet citizen. Even with the encouragement offered by the state as such, however, those who pursue this channel, by doing so, indicate that they are atypical of the Soviet citizenry in general. They are exposed on two sides: Whereas the state per se encourages such activity, some leaders express, especially at the current time of perceived decline in living standards, reservations that indicate that they were never really comfortable with "enterprise" at all. *Not* all leaders see cooperatives as Gorbachev and his close associates and advisers do. Moreover, those who are involved in cooperatives are exposed to a public whose conceptions of "justice" do not easily make room for what cooperators do, why they do it, and what they gain from it.

Redefining "Social Justice"

Policies that are likely to affect opportunities, that focus attention on success and its opposite, and that are presented to the public by a political leadership that speaks a language of impending crisis are likely to generate concern and controversy. The Soviet public is long habituated to a certain structure of employment, security, price levels, on the one hand, and used to enduring long lines, shortages, poor provision of many services, as part of the "natural" environment, on the other. An order so familiar was regarded by many as not only normal but also "just." Whether because it "worked" or because Soviet citizens' experience provided no real knowledge of concrete alternatives, it was a noncontroversial way of life, and most assumed it would endure. *Perestroika*'s attack on old ways of living and working is a mixed bag from this viewpoint. Is unearned income a violation of social justice? At a general level, the general secretary and the millions will surely agree: Who could disagree? But when recipients of unearned income are identified, and it is not just "speculators or profiteers" that are pointed to, but also workers in large state-sector factories in heavy industry who receive their wages while producing little or producing goods for which the economy has no use, opinions will differ.

What to Gorbachev is *vyvodilovka* (wage-padding) is surely to many citizens what the "security" guaranteed by the socialist order is all about. In official discourse, *vyvodilovka* is a bad word. But in the popular consciousness, "topping up" the pay of the poorly paid categories of workers and employees, to compensate for (1) wage rates that are "too low," (2) output norms that are "too high," or (3) children and dependents that are "too many," is good practice, "only fair." It guarantees the (expected) minimum to which, most would agree, everyone is entitled. There is a fundamental decency in this notion; there is also, of course, inefficiency. Is the pay packet the place to take care of problems of low skill ratings, many dependents, and so forth, or should there be some other form of individualized welfare payment that will not reduce the "stimulus" effect of wages? Soviet citizens, who receive the vast amount of their cash incomes through work, their "benefits" (housing, education, medical care, utilities) free or nearly so, with little money involved, are not so sensitive to this question as the economists of the Gorbachev leadership. *Vyvodilovka* is a greater problem for the latter: For the former, or many of them, it is an element of "social justice."

The Brezhnev era and most of the post-Stalin period, however, saw policy drift in an egalitarian direction. If people grew used to this, if an egalitarian psychology grew deep roots, they are ones Gorbachev and the reformers seek to tear up. *Uravnilovka* is now a target of policy, and attacking it, even if it is seen as socially just, is the business of *perestroika*. The attack takes two forms. The first is to convince "sober, hard-working" citizens that egalitarianism hurts them by rewarding the drunkard or slacker at roughly the same level—that it is unfair, unjust. This requires that enough people come to think of themselves as hard-working, and of others as not, and to lose "sympathy" for them. It requires that, in reality, enough people *do* work hard enough to be worth rewarding. It is a desensitizing, disuniting appeal, if one assumes that *uravnilovka* represents a widely shared value. A works hard and well; B does not. Both are paid the same. A is being robbed by B; B is stealing from A, however tolerant their mutual relationships may have been. This is all very good—but how many Soviet citizens (1) believe, deeply, that they are "A" or, more important, (2) believe that state policy (in wages and work) will correctly distinguish them as "A" and others as "B"?

The second form is to blame "B," in his/her millions, for the general impoverishing of the society and economy. It is to connect laziness, too much security in one's wages, the "right not to work hard," with the lack of goods, the shortages of services, the woeful state of things. "B" people are seen as robbing the whole society, and robbery can hardly be social justice. Poverty is its fruit.

Whether Gorbachev will succeed in this dramatization of economic evil, this A-versus-B scenario, is unclear. The script legitimates differentiation, the feeling that one is "better" than another if one works better; that, being better, one is entitled to greater reward. It means to encompass the honest cooperator as well as the worker in the state factory. It tells the public to worry, not about *high* incomes, but about unearned incomes—the latter reduce the opportunities of the industrious to earn more. As those opportunities are expanded, Soviet society may grow more unequal, but the impetus to hard work in the state or the cooperative sector should make it more affluent overall as well.

The problem is that, in most citizens' eyes, the society is already growing visibly more unequal—thanks to the cooperatives—while it is, if anything, growing poorer. From grumbling in shopping queues, to letters to newspapers, to the many strikes that, in the first half of 1989, preceded the massive miners' strikes in the Kuzbass, Donbass, Kazakhstan, and the far North, a common thread has been the perception that some are doing very well, but most are doing worse.

Social and economic policy in a USSR moving, however fitfully, toward a more-market-type economy faces other problems as well. The reform economists have diagnosed as one of the economy's major problems its traditional emphasis on "material production"—manpower, fuel, and raw-material-intensive heavy industry—which has proven wasteful, retrograde, and ultimately a brake on economic progress. Material production is thus slated for streamlining in personnel terms, and the nonproductive service sector for expansion. Such a policy also has implications for those who have been, in the past, "winners" in wage terms and for those who have been "losers." As one economist put it, in the first months of *perestroika* in 1986, in the Party's theoretical journal *Kommunist:* "The interests of acceleration of socioeconomic development demand that future average wages in the leading branches of the nonproductive sphere be on par with wages in material production. In our view, this is one of the fundamental issues of economic policy."[41]

The problem is that wage parity would be quite new. Heavy, metal-eating industry has always been better paid than consumer industry; (male) steel-workers and miners have always outearned (female) rank-and-file doctors. The state long defended this in terms of the "national economic significance" of heavy industry. But now, the weakness of service and consumer industries has been diagnosed as a brake on the whole economy. Relatively, this means a loss of advantage to those who work in heavy industries and are traditionally well paid. It is also those who work in these (often unprofitable) industries who are threatened with layoffs or job transfers if their enterprises are closed. No wonder this looks less than fair to some. A worker from Krivoi Rog complained that in the past, "we" were told that society needed "workers who produce material assets, not clerks."[42] Now, he and others are being told something different—the "opportunity" to earn high wages with virtually total job security in heavy industry is not to be a permanent feature of the economy. In the Soviet economy, such reversals of relative advantage are not accomplished by the "market" but by decree. Many workers in what the West would call "sunset" or "smokestack" industries are unlikely to see justice in such decrees or in the government that issues them.

Policy must also deal with a number of seemingly petty questions, ones that seem petty if one's viewpoint is that of a market economy, but that are not if one is working within the quite different Soviet context. In the early phases of *perestroika,* for example, most would accept that the money a collective farmer made by selling private-plot-produced vegetables, eggs, and other prosaic items on the market was "earned." But some would have argued that a similar farmer, raising flowers in a self-built hothouse on the same plot and reaping the large returns these "decorative" items command, was collecting something beyond the "earned."[43] Was the farmer who grew food doing what he was supposed to, he who grew flowers somehow taking advantage, abusing opportunities the state afforded him by way of the private plot? Some clearly thought so. In the southern republics, climate conditions and soil combine to give the farmer the ability to produce fruit and melons, at great profit. Is only some of this earned via work? Should his profit be reduced by a differential rent charge? Should the state concern itself with this? Many Soviet citizens would answer yes to all three questions; so do some reform economists.[44] Even though events have rendered most of these concerns outmoded, for cooperatives engage in a multiplicity of activities, it is not the case that people find the reality acceptable.

"Opportunity," then, is a controversial matter. It runs, ultimately, into the less-attractive side of Soviet egalitarianism, as a large segment of the population understands it. Not only should no one be allowed to sink too low, but also no one should, even by his or her own efforts, be allowed to rise too high. Were the popular response to the economic success stories of the cooperators an attempt to emulate them, *perestroika* might well be said to have taken root. But it is more likely that the predominant attitude, a somewhat chilling one, is that of a woman who, contrasting her modest circumstances with that of an acquaintance who, by growing and selling spring vegetables, made extra money and bought some of life's good things: "I don't want to live like her—I want her to live like me."[45]

Conclusion

Given the rapidity of change in so many areas of Soviet politics and society and the uncertainty of the outcome, conclusions of any sort are difficult, if not totally out of place. Equality of opportunity and its place in the Soviet scheme of things, considered from the angles of opportunity for education and "enterprise," have been my concern here. *Perestroika* has brought nothing fundamentally new in the structuring of educational opportunity. Forces emerging in the inequality of households and families, present in any society, have worked in the past to make educational access unequal. The educational reform of 1984 seemed to aim, for labor-allocation purposes, at introducing administrative procedures that on the whole would have made access even more unequal. *Perestroika* has rejected this, but with what seems to be an attitude of "benign neglect," a rejection of administrative intervention on behalf of "equalizing" opportunities as well as the reverse.

Perestroika has provided new opportunities for "enterprise"—on the whole a controversial move. If one argues that the earlier Soviet system virtually totally closed off (legal) opportunity to exercise entrepreneurial drives and abilities for those who had them, then now these opportunities have been provided. Are they "equal" opportunities? In a formal-legal sense, surely. But for rank-and-file Soviet citizens, lacking those drives and abilities and taught to regard them as wrong for so long, there are two objections. First, these are opportunities given to people who are, by taking them, "wrong." Secondly, these opportunities detract from the other equality that so many Soviet citizens connect with social justice—a rough equality of result. It is this concept of equality that the convinced reformers struggle against—with indifferent success thus far. That struggle can better be waged when and if the economic results promised by *perestroika* begin to be achieved. But in 1990, as both the alarms sounded by reform economists about the near-collapse of retail trade and the epidemic of labor militancy show, the promise is further away than ever. At the core of the public mood there looms a conviction that the opportunity to live even a minimally acceptable material life is "unequally" denied to most and granted to only a few. Of such tensions are political crises made.

Notes

1. Vera S. Dunham, *In Stalin's Time: Middle Class Values in Soviet Fiction* (Cambridge: Cambridge University Press, 1976).
2. See Murray Yanowitch, *Work in the Soviet Union: Attitudes and Issues* (Armonk, N.Y.: M. E. Sharpe, Inc., 1985), pp. 42–45.
3. See Donna Bahry, "Politics, Generations and Change in the USSR," Soviet Interview Project, Working Paper, No. 20, Urbana-Champaign, Ill. September 1986, mimeo., p. 37.
4. Andrei Amalrik, "Will the USSR Survive until 1984?" *Survey*, no. 73 (Autumn 1969), pp. 62–63.
5. *Trud*, October 9, 1987, p. 2 (trans. in *Foreign Broadcast Information Service* [hereafter *FBIS*], October 26, 1987, p. 52).
6. See Nikolai Shmelev, "Avansy i dolgi," *Novyi mir*, no. 6 (1987), pp. 142–158.
7. See *Sovetskaia kul'tura*, October 17, 1987, p. 3.
8. This discussion follows Tatiana I. Zaslavskaia, "Tvorcheskaia aktivnost' mass: sotsial'nye reservy rosta," *EKO (Ekonomika i organizatsiia promyshlennogo proizvodstvsa)*, no. 3 (1986), pp. 3–25.
9. V. N. Shubkin, "Molodezh' vstupaet v zhizn'," *Voprosy filosofii*, no. 5 (1965), pp. 57–70.
10. Ia. M. Tkach, "Roditeli o sud'bakh svoikh detei," *Protsessy izmeneniia sotsial'noi struktury v sovetskom obshchestve* (Sverdlovsk: Ministerstvo vysshego i sredne-spetsial'nogo obrazovaniia RSFSR, 1967), pp. 147–150.
11. See Murray Yanowitch, *Social and Economic Inequality in the Soviet Union* (White Plains, N.Y.: M. E. Sharpe, Inc., 1977), p. 80, and sources cited therein (n. 38).
12. The 1984–1985 data and estimates are drawn from M. N. Rutkevich, "Reforma obrazovaniia, potrebnosti obshchestva, molodezh'," *Sotsiologicheskie issledovaniia*, no. 4 (1984), p. 24.
13. G. A. Slesarev, *Demograficheskie protsessy i sotsial'naia struktura sotsialisticheskogo obshchestva* (Moscow: Nauka, 1978), pp. 155–167.
14. See V. N. Turchenko, "Vazhneishaia sostavliaiushchaia proizvoditel'nykh sil," *EKO*, no. 12 (1983), pp. 87–88.

15. See *O reforme obshcheobrazovatel'noi i professional' noi shkoly: Sbornik dokumentov i materialov* (Moscow: Izdatel'stvo politicheskoi literatury, 1984), p. 42.
16. *Sovetskaia Rossiia,* October 24, 1986, p. 2.
17. *Pravda,* December 29, 1987, p. 3.
18. See *Pravda* and *Izvestiia,* February 18, 1988, pp. 1-4.
19. See *Uchitel'skaia gazeta,* August 22, 1987.
20. Radio Moscow World Service (English), 0310 GMT March 26, 1988 (*FBIS,* April 5, 1988, p. 49).
21. *Pravda,* May 28, 1986, pp. 1-2.
22. Shmelev, op. cit. (trans. in *Problems of Economics* 30, no. 10 [February 1988]), p. 17.
23. *Ekonomicheskaia gazeta,* no. 43 (October 1986), pp. 15-16.
24. *Pravda,* November 1, 1986, pp. 1, 3.
25. See, e.g., *Izvestiia,* December 12, 1987, p. 5; and *Izvestiia,* May 16, 1987, p. 2.
26. *Izvestiia,* September 10, 1987, p. 3.
27. *Pravda,* December 20, 1986, p. 3.
28. *Pravda,* June 8, 1986, pp. 2-5; see also John Tedstrom, "The New Law on Cooperatives," *Radio Liberty Research Bulletin,* 246/88 (June 10, 1988).
29. See, generally, John Tedstrom, "Soviet Cooperatives: A Difficult Road to Legitimacy," *Radio Liberty Research Bulletin,* 244/88 (May 31, 1988), and "New Draft Law on Income Taxes," *Radio Liberty Report on the USSR,* no. 24 (1989), pp. 8-10.
30. *Sotsialisticheskaia industriia,* February 21, 1989, p. 2 (*FBIS,* March 6, 1989, p. 93).
31. *Moscow News,* no. 10 (1989), p. 4 (*FBIS,* March 16, 1989, pp. 85-86).
32. *Ekonomicheskaia gazeta,* no. 17 (1989), p. 3.
33. Tedstrom, op. cit.
34. *Pravda,* April 23, 1983, cited in *Radio Liberty Report on the USSR,* no. 18 (1989), p. 26.
35. See Konstantin Simis, *USSR: The Corrupt Society* (New York: Simon & Schuster, 1982).
36. *Izvestiia,* September 10, 1987, p. 3.
37. *Izvestiia,* February 27, 1988, p. 3.
38. *Izvestiia,* December 12, 1987, p. 5.
39. Shmelev, in *Trud,* April 24, 1988, p. 1.
40. *Pravda,* May 3, 1989, p. 6.
41. S. Shabalin, "Sotsial'noe razvitie i ekonomicheskii rost," *Kommunist,* no. 14 (1986) (trans. in *Problems of Economics,* October 1987, p. 34).
42. *Izvestiia,* February 13, 1988, p. 3.
43. See, e.g., the comments of V. V. Naidenov, deputy procurator-general, on Moscow Radio, 1100 GMT, November 23, 1986 (*FBIS,* November 26, 1986, pp. S1-S8).
44. The reformist Zaslavskaia showed a sensitivity to this; see Zaslavskaia, op. cit.
45. V. Z. Rogovin, "Sotsial'naia spravedlivost' i sotsialisticheskoe raspredelenie zhiznennykh blag," *Voprosy filosofii,* no. 9 (1986), p. 17.

CHAPTER 9

Perestroika and the Rebirth of Charity

Mervyn Matthews

One of the less-expected consequences of Gorbachev's advent to the general secretaryship of the CPSU has been the reintroduction of the idea of charity into Soviet public life. The change has already attracted a great deal of attention in both Soviet and foreign media. Charity is, however, a vague concept, and a full account of its development would require a lengthy study. My aim here is merely to summarize, perhaps more systematically than has hitherto been done, such advances as can be distinguished in the years between 1985 and 1988. A more detailed review will certainly be needed as more information becomes available. It is as yet much too early for definitive assessment.

The history of charitable activity before and immediately after the Bolshevik takeover has not, to my knowledge, been properly studied, and even generalization about it is difficult.[1] Charity had, of course, a long and honorable history under the czars: Nineteenth-century literature is replete with references to individuals and entire movements that were devoted to charitable causes. There is also no doubt that the Revolution, and the massive social turbulence that followed it, disrupted traditional attitudes and greatly inhibited charitable practice.

The Bolsheviks did not prohibit personal charity by any specific decree (to do so would have been impossible), but many of their early policies were extremely effective in this respect. Non-Bolshevik public organizations were closed, and the various churches, formerly a major vehicle for such work, were persecuted. Later, under the infamous decree of April 8, 1929, on religious associations, church charity was specifically prohibited.[2] The suppression of the "exploiting" classes, the sequestration of private assets, and the impoverishment of people who might formerly have had money to spare meant the destruction of the main sources of benefaction.

Of course, the new leadership did not leave an entirely empty space. Some charitable work was undertaken by organizations concerned with the physically handicapped and the injured. Party, state, and social bodies would at times organize help for their members according to the political and material exigencies of the day.[3] The 1920–1921 famine prompted direct appeals for urgent assistance, both at home and abroad. Nevertheless, Bolshevik ideology interpreted the socialist state as a protective, charitable institution that scarcely needed support from well-meaning individuals. The social-security system that began to appear in the 1920s was always held to be (despite its massive shortcomings) a sufficient arm of support.

But behind these considerations lay uglier principles. Particularly after Stalin came to power, the state apparatus actually *created* widespread distress and deprivation. The USSR, surrounded by "capitalist enemies," was said to have a duty to suppress without mercy internal "enemies of the people." The fact that these opponents came to number millions is a grotesque irony of Soviet history. Apart from this, successive Soviet leaderships retained a profound distrust of personal initiative and of any social activity that was not specifically authorized by the state. The calamity of World War II brought no change in official attitudes.

Even the Russian language was modified to reflect official connotations. The words for charity (in an active sense) and charitableness (in a passive one) are respectively *blagotvoritel'nost'* and *miloserdie. Filantropiya* may be used in a more general sense. A cursory survey of successive Soviet dictionaries and encyclopedias by the *Moscow News* journalist Vitalii Tetriyakov revealed that the first edition (1927) of the *Great Soviet Encyclopedia,* which, he claimed, had the longest article on charity, defined *blagotvoritel'nost'* as "foreign" to the social system of the USSR. The word was still "bourgeois" in the prestigious Academy of Sciences dictionary published in 1981.

Against so unpromising a background, efforts to encourage charity as a positive, spontaneous social movement have required many catalysts. First among them is, no doubt, the existence of poverty and need throughout the country. Hardly less significant is the new atmosphere, if not of freedom, at least of what might be termed "permissibility," together with the understanding that official suppression of personal initiatives is no longer inevitable. I may add here Gorbachev's interest in the "human factor" and his emphasis on eliciting positive social responses. The policy of *glasnost',* for all its shortcomings, encouraged the revelation and discussion of social problems, particularly through investigative journalism. New definitions of the poverty threshold, putting it as high as 100 rubles per capita a month, revealed how widespread deprivation was. The groups most likely to suffer (pensioners, invalids, the denizens of public homes, single parents, and poor families) were delineated with even greater clarity.

Such public admissions were backed by a recognition that (given current economic difficulties) poverty was going to be a problem for many years to come. The stagnation, or fall, in living standards in the 1980s inevitably hit poorer people harder than others, increasing social misery. Demographic change meant that the number of pensioners would grow and constitute an ever-larger contingent of the population. Another catalyst was the new, critical attitude toward the failures of the state social services (bad organization, bureaucratic indifference, and corruption). The apparently fundamental realignment of relations between church and state, to the benefit of the former, inevitably raised the question of charitable work, an integral part of most religious belief.

Another factor was the encouragement of private enterprise and cooperatives, as embodied in the laws of November 1986 and June 1988: Such activity lends itself to advantageous adoption by charitable institutions. Fortuitous disasters, particularly the Chernobyl explosion, the mass exodus of Armenians and Azerbaidzhanis from one another's territories, the Armenian and Tadzhik earthquakes, all called for massive charitable response. One might further posit, after so many barren years, the buildup of a psychological potential for involvement, mediated by concerned and prominent individuals. Beyond all of these factors, it is hard to imagine a movement so widespread operating without very specific directives from the Politburo or Central Committee of the Party. It must reflect Gorbachev's expressed wish for more popular involvement in the solution of social problems.[4]

Categorization of charitable institutions and activities, insofar as they can be currently discerned, is by no means easy, but I intend to deal with the topic under four broad headings. These are the modification of existing apparatuses to facilitate charitable activity; the extension of social-security benefits; the new, broadly based public charities, operating with various degrees of state approbation; and the activities of various religious bodies. Each is a study in itself, but my intention here is to provide only a fair overview.

Some Bureaucratic Adjustments

Before the present movement began, the managements of productive enterprises and, indeed, local social-insurance offices were ill adapted to accommodating spontaneous charity, undertaken either by their own employees or on behalf of them. Administrative obligations were usually restricted to observance of labor and social-security regulations rather than the encouragement of charitable initiative. With *perestroika,* one can perceive a number of statutory changes designed to facilitate such initiative. Let us begin with the enterprises.

The statute for productive enterprises that came into force in September 1987 differed considerably from that of March 1974, in that (among other things) the 1987 statute contained an entirely new section on the "social development" of workers and employees. This meant, primarily, improving working conditions, housing, catering, and the regulations on the labor of women and minors. However, a separate paragraph indicated the need to "care constantly for war and labor veterans, pensioners, invalids and children; surround them with attention and help; create conditions necessary for involving able-bodied pensioners and invalids in suitable jobs, and in the life of the collective; provide them with available medical services, etc., rest and recreation." The enterprise should "participate in building homes for the aged and the sick, effect trusteeship over them, and also over children's homes and hostels, providing them with material and financial assistance."[5]

In like fashion the March 1988 model charter for collective farms significantly exceeded its 1969 predecessor in provision for the needy. Rank-and-file members of the farm had, it will be recalled, been prohibited from joining the agricultural workers' trade union and thus excluded from union benefits such as labor protection, social-security rights, and so on. This ban was lifted under Brezhnev, and by the end of the 1970s the overwhelming majority of farm members were unionized. The new charter contained specific reference to the supportive functions of the farm-union committee. A new section devoted to "social development" also required farms to observe legislation on working women, families, and minors; reduce heavy physical labor; provide homes for old people; and help with housing in the farm itself.[6]

In 1984, departments of labor and social affairs were set up in rural soviets. Ultimately subordinate to the USSR State Committee for Labor and Social Affairs (usually abbreviated to Goskomtruda), they had formerly existed only in the towns.[7] Now they were to monitor not only farm labor and pay but also social security, farm-supported amenities, child care, catering, and schools. The work of these departments has, it seems, been little illustrated in published sources, but the economic independence proposed for agricultural enterprises may increase their importance as a monitoring device. It was planned that living standards in rural areas would rise more quickly than in the towns, anyway.

The encouragement of some private enterprise is likely, as noted, to further charitable causes insofar as it facilitates money-making activities, either with the participation of, or on behalf of, persons in need. Some charities have been quick to establish their own cooperatives. However, I believe that on the whole the cooperative movement is socially differentiative in its impact. The extra demands it places on inadequate supplies and the transfer of resources to high-priced output are probably hostile to the interests of the poorest people in Soviet society.

As for change in the sphere of social-security administration, a reading of *Sotsial'noe obespechenie,* the journal of the RSFSR Ministry of Social Security, revealed a new concern with charitable initiative. Specifically, after January 1987, Social Help Sections were opened in local offices. The staff were authorized to help people (primarily invalids and the elderly) at home, this being, if not a new, at least an unusual practice. Red Cross personnel were also brought in to help. According to V. Kaznacheev, the minister, by 1988 all invalids living alone in the RSFSR—some 170,000—were to be covered by this service. Instructions were also issued on establishing day and long-stay centers for pensioners.[8]

The total number of persons in need was, however, far greater. According to Maria Kravchenko, a prominent official of the USSR office of Goskomtruda, in 1988 there were about 10 million single elderly people and invalids in the country as a whole. More than 700,000 of them needed permanent daily help, and 400,000 lived in public homes and hostels. In Moscow, by September 1987, there were 42,000 unattached old people living alone, of whom 11,000 were quite helpless. About 9,000 had been registered at social-help sections.

The development of the new sections was not without problems. The work was hard, and each member of the staff was expected to look after up to ten people. The pay was only 90 rubles a month (one of the lowest rates for state jobs), so it was not easy to find suitable applicants. Moreover, there were kinds of help that the staff did not normally provide: They would do some shopping and contact laundry services, but not clean or sit and talk to their charges.[9]

Caring for the destitute had long been part of the work of the Red Cross and Red Crescent. There are indications that also they have been required to upgrade these activities. I was told in an interview with O. M. Sidorov, chairman of the RSFSR Committee, that local commissions formerly made small one-time grants averaging 25–30 rubles to around 35,000 needy people annually. The development of charitable activity would involve a doubling of this number, more contact with the social-security offices, and an increase in staff, for which money had been made available. The main problem (again) lay in attracting people at the traditionally low wage rates.[10]

Another change of a bureaucratic order concerned the establishment, in December 1986, of an All-Union Organization for Veterans of War and Labor.[11] This move was supported by the trade unions, the Komsomol, Goskomtruda, a number of ministries, the national Societies for the Blind, Deaf and Dumb, and the Red Cross. The principal task of the organization appeared to be the integration of invalids and pensioners into suitable working environments. However, other aims included educating the young in a spirit of patriotism, improving housing conditions, social and medical services, and leisure amenities, and defending invalids' rights and voicing their interests. In January 1988 it took over the *Veteran* insert of *Sotsial'noe obespechenie* and began to publish it as a separate, much-enlarged monthly magazine. The RSFSR organization of the All-Union Organization for Veterans of War and Labor had its inaugural conference in October 1988, by which time it claimed 16,164 "primary" organizations and 376,000 members.

An interesting overview of developments in the sphere of social security was provided by Maria Kravchenko in *Izvestiia*.[12] The changes, she said, addressed "the broader task of solving the problem of material provision of old people, invalids, and others who cannot work, in a comprehensive manner . . . the further development of all forms of assistance for old people, and perfecting the system of family grants." The efforts of the social services were to be concentrated in two directions: increasing help at home as much as possible; and setting up territorial social-service centers in which pensioners and invalids could stay permanently or temporarily, as well as constructing more homes.

Things are bad in this respect . . . homes containing 17,000 places could be built from the funds unused in the last three five-year plan periods. The situation is no better with the construction of special houses with all domestic services and work-rooms for single, elderly citizens—only eighteen have been built! . . .

Solving this problem should be a priority for social security organs and local soviets. We also hope that the press will help. . . . At the present time there are one and a half thousand enterprises, shops and work sectors designed for employing invalids. About 150,000 invalids are in them. That's extremely few. . . . As a result of the transition to self-financing and profit-making there is a reduction in work-places everywhere. . . . Large enterprises are hardly likely to create special sectors or workshops for invalids. In our view the answer lies in creating small enterprises and employment centers oriented to serving them. . . .

Local soviets should look into the matter. . . . We set great store by the republican societies for invalids now being established. They could help not only in finding work and professional instruction, but also in organizing leisure activities. . . . There are changes for the better. Take the work of the social security organs in Lithuania. The staff there do not wait for people to come to them with complaints or explanations. They regularly organize outside meetings, and invite the heads of organizations to come along and decide questions on the spot. With the help of the press, radio, television they give information about their plans and new benefits, and they bring up serious problems for discussion. However, this is not done everywhere. There are many complaints of indifference, heartlessness, and formal attitudes to labor veterans and invalids.

Direct Improvements in Social Benefits

A thorough reform of the systems of pensions and benefits was to be one of the more important social dimensions of *perestroika*. State assistance for pensioners, invalids, and poor families had been developing (albeit slowly) since the Khrushchev pension reform of 1956. The proposals put forward were, however, very contentious, and by the end of 1988 no revised general law had gone through. Social-security rules are complex, and for present purposes we need to note only the more significant improvements following Gorbachev's advent to power.[13]

The standard minimum old-age pension (the bedrock, as it were, of the system) remained unchanged at 50 rubles a month. But in May 1985 the relatively small numbers of persons who were not entitled to a formal retirement pension, and in receipt of maintenance payments instead, had their mite increased to 30 rubles. By the same enactment the collective farmers' minimum retirement pension was raised to 40 rubles, and local soviets were allowed to make small allowances to pensioners "in acute need," provided that the personal income of such persons did not exceed 50 rubles a month. In January 1987 the basic minimum rates for invalids were raised to between 30 and 50 rubles, according to age and category of disability.

In November 1985 a mechanism was at last introduced to allow small percentage-point augmentations of retirement pensions as the years went by. The problem here lay in the old practice of fixing a pension once and for all in accordance with former earnings, regardless of the fact that the wage paid for a given job would generally rise with time. Thus persons retiring successively from the same job would get ever-larger pensions, and overtake their predecessors, before being overtaken themselves. The new measure, however, covered only pensions under 60 rubles that had been set ten years or more previously. Other improvements included the removal of a tax on pensioners who continued to work a household plot, some free transport, a 50 percent reduction of the cost of pensioners' medicines purchased in pharmacies, and somewhat easier access to the 12-ruble grants already available for needy families.

As may be appreciated, the level of benefits remained low, and such raises as occurred at best alleviated the plight of those in greatest need. By the late 1980s a 50-ruble minimum, for example, was scarcely enough to nourish even the most parsimonious individual. Beyond this, suggestions that the pension system should be made *more differentiated* and the apparent abandonment of plans to increase the state minimum wage to 80 rubles augured ill for the lowest earners. Presumably the improvements authorized reflected the capability of the state treasury, balanced against the obligation of caring for an aging population: Between 1980 and 1987 the total number of pensioners of all kinds increased from 50.2 to 57.7 million.[14]

The authorities have renewed efforts to improve the provision of accommodation for various categories of homeless. Decrees passed for the USSR and RSFSR in January and March 1987 and June 1988 demanded that local soviets pay more attention to homes for the elderly and invalids. This included proper implementation of improvements stipulated in 1985, the fulfillment of construction plans, better catering, medical services, living conditions, and full staffing. Further decrees, of August and November 1988, called for improvements in the running of children's homes, and the opening (evidently at the suggestion of the new Children's Fund, discussed below) of homes run on a foster-parent basis. The high divorce rate goes some way to explaining this development.[15]

Two "Official" Charities

The spirit of *perestroika* brought into being new charitable funds, which, though state approved and highly centralized, were genuine enough in their aims and enjoyed widespread public support. The first I shall describe is the Lenin Soviet Children's Fund. Its establishment followed several years of growing public concern about disadvantaged minors, including the million or so children in care (in state instiutions or foster homes) and those who had been driven from home. Between 1985 and 1987 several systematic investigations of children's homes were undertaken; a laboratory was set up under the USSR Academy of Sciences to study practices current in them; and certain pedagogical institutes began (for the first time) to offer courses to train the staff of children's homes. This concern was also reflected by numerous articles in the press and some public meetings. A leading figure in the movement was A. A. Likhanov, writer and editor-in-chief of the youth newspaper *Smena*.[16]

Following approval by the Central Committee of the CPSU, the Children's Fund held its inaugural conference in Moscow on October 14, 1987. Described in its statutes as a "self-governing public agency," it was to base its activities on nationwide public support, but be centralized in the traditional Soviet mold. An all-union conference of representatives was to meet once every five years and elect a board and an auditing commission. The board in turn was to convene at least once a year and elect a presidium to manage current activities. A chairman and deputy chairman had executive rights within this framework, though the basis of their electivity was not spelled out. With regard to decisionmaking, the terms of the statute were vague, but the basic mechanism was a simple majority vote by a show of hands. The Children's Fund was supposed to be self-financing, though administrative support (mainly in the form of premises) was expected from local authorities.[17]

Less expected (given the aims and size of the organization) were the absence of specific reference to Party involvement; the emphasis, apparently genuine, on independence; a provision for the fund to develop its own productive activities; and the explicit encouragement of foreign contacts and foreign sources of income. The text suggested that the Soviet authorities had abandoned their former reluctance to solicit help from the capitalist world.

Official approval meant that the fund's bureaucratic development was relatively fast. In December 1988 the head office was located in rooms in the Yunost Hotel in Moscow. An administrative officer, E. M. Rybinski, told me in an interview that local bodies had been set up in nearly all oblasts, *krai*s, and republics. The board contained 57 representatives (1 from each organization represented at the founding conference). The full-time apparatus comprised 5–6 persons at the republican level, 2–3 persons at the oblast level, and 40 people in Moscow (making a total of 500–600). The bulk of the Children's Fund's work was done by about 10,000 unpaid activists; the full-time staff, he asserted, were paid not from public contributions but from other income. This included returns from the fund's new journal *Sem'ia* and several commercial cooperatives, among them a clinic, a family-services unit, and a milk-processing center.[18]

The functions of the fund, as listed in the statute, included providing additional help for children's and young people's homes, assistance in the case of natural disaster, support for large families and talented, but underprivileged, children, fund-raising, developing its own financial basis, and participating in international movements. According to Rybinski, the fund had some 43 million rubles in its account, acquired from collection, publishing, concerts, and other fund-raising activities.[19] Its work is conducted in the aura of its own publicity; links are maintained with children's organizations in Austria, the United States, Holland, Mongolia, and Bulgaria.

The fund gives priority to helping orphans. It has already provided 237 motor vehicles (buses, minibuses, and trucks) for children's homes. There were plans to build, in the course of 1989, thirty children's villages. It is encouraging foster parentage and extra support for children with cancer and for the mothers of large families. It was also very much involved in alleviating the consequences of the Armenian earthquake. Thirty tons of clothing were collected for the victims and a million rubles' worth of equipment sent into the province. The fund has undertaken to construct a school there at its own cost. Through it some 3,500 Moscow parents offered to take in children from the disaster areas. The fund has also been concerned with the problem of high infant-mortality rates in Central Asia, and with the assistance of the Ministry of Health, it sent 2,000 medical personnel to work in maternity wards in the region for two months.

The establishment of a broadly comparable organization—the Soviet Fund for Health and Charity—is best viewed in the context of growing public concern over the well-being of vulnerable adults. Shortly before Gorbachev came to power, this found some expression in Yuri Andropov's drive against alcoholism. *Glasnost'*, however, provoked broader criticism of public-welfare standards and the inability of the public services to respond. Other consequences were the publication of previously unavailable health statistics, the promulgation of a new statute on health, and plans for a reorientation of the health service.

To judge from a report in *Izvestiia,* groups of volunteers and associations with names like "Charity," "Participation," and "Concern" sprang up in Leningrad, Gorky, Tbilisi, Kemerovo, and Dnepropetrovsk. In April 1988, a draft statute for the fund was published, and an inaugural conference was held in Moscow on September 16 (nearly two years after the foundation of the All-Union Organization for Veterans of War and Labor). A prominent eye surgeon, Dr. S. N. Fedorov, was named chairman.[20]

The statute of the Fund for Health and Charity in many respects resembled that of the Children's Fund, stipulating a similar apparatus and functions.[21] In this case twenty-nine all-union organizations and thirty republic ministries were listed as founding members; apart from organizations for the disabled, they included the USSR Academy of Medical Sciences, the Red Cross and Red Crescent, various state committees, the Novosti Press Agency, the main artistic unions, and representatives of the churches. Local departments were opened, with their own revision commissions, down to the autonomous republic, oblast, and *krai* level. Below that, participatory commissions could be set up in virtually any local organization or collective.

The fund was to be guided by "the principles of socialist humanism, self-management, collective leadership, the initiative and independent work of public activists, *glasnost'*, and concern for public opinion." A major object, in the words of its chairman, was to "supplement [state] measures . . . for example, rendering medical, social and other assistance to a home for elderly and disabled citizens and to disabled war and labor veterans who live alone." Other needy categories mentioned in the statute were the families of men killed while on military service and the victims of catastrophe. More generally, the fund was to promote public health, social security, physical education, sport, and charitable service. It was to discourage alcoholism and smoking; propagate health through the publication of a journal and handbooks; and improve working and living conditions. It was to cooperate with, and attract contributions from, other organizations, collectives, and individual citizens at home and abroad and to participate in international information exchanges. It was to encourage staff in the health and social-service sectors to work better; it was also to hold fund-raising activities, including lotteries, and accept gifts and foreign currency. It had the right to rent buildings, equipment, and other property; it could involve itself in capital construction, create, and close its own enterprises and organizations.

It remains to be seen how both of these funds will develop, particularly in their relations with the less-stratified charitable organizations we shall consider next. During my interview at the RSFSR Red Cross I was told that a merger with the Fund for Health and Charity was not out of the question.

The *Miloserdie* Groups

Public desire to help the needy resulted in the formation of numerous local support groups that were largely independent of the giant funds just considered. The local groups seemed to be motivated as much by a real concern with moral regeneration as with offering practical help. The press was soon involved in both publicizing their concerns and promoting appropriate reaction to it. In fact it is possible to perceive, in this respect, a distinct change of editorial policy in a number of leading newspapers, involving the adoption of letter columns and publication of hitherto unthinkable articles about social need. Thus, *Pravda* was able to boast that its "Mutual Help Club," or column, started in 1986, had led to numerous charitable responses among readers. The feeling of collectivity, an interest in social matters, and a readiness to help others, which was characteristic of socialism, had been in some degree lost and required resuscitation.[22]

Of the towns involved, it would appear that Leningrad took the lead. The independent *Miloserdie* organization started there attracted widespread public attention and served as an exemplar for others. The background to its establishment was as follows.[23] In 1973 Lyubov' Begovaya, a teacher of nursery-school attendants at a Leningrad pedagogical college, decided that her charges should learn more about the trials of children during the Leningrad blockade. This eventually led her to set up a museum and contact former college teachers who had lived through those years. But the majority of them, she found, were "living alone on small pensions, in great need of care and help." It was a visit to the museum that apparently prompted the prominent writer Danill Granin to involve himself in charity. He too wished not only to help the needy but also to change people's attitudes toward social misfortune.

Yet it was (as he said) only "after April 1985" that he was able actively to pursue these aims. On March 18, 1987, he published an article entitled "On Charity" in *Literaturnaia gazeta,* and it was subsequently broadcast nationwide. The gist was that the practice of public charity needed to be resurrected and channeled through legally recognized social organizations. The text attracted many letters. The publication of Granin's appeal indicated considerable high-level support, and he even discussed the matter with Mikhail Gorbachev.

It is interesting, incidentally, to speculate how far the responses of leading public figures like Granin were influenced by the efforts of dissidents, from the mid-1960s, to collect modest funds for political prisoners. This was another practice with a long history in Russia, one that had been suppressed under Stalin. From about 1970 on, Aleksandr Solzhenitsyn was said to have donated part of his royalties to such causes, and after his exile in 1974 he established his own Russian Social Fund to aid political prisoners. It was administered in the USSR by Aleksandr Ginzburg and, after his arrest, by Ekaterina Svetlova.[24]

The Leningrad *Miloserdie* organization had its founding conference and adopted its statute in April 1988. Granin was elected chairman of its board. By June 1988 its membership had risen to some 6,000 schoolchildren, pensioners, Party members, believers, representatives of informal groups, Komsomol members. There was plenty for them to do—the number of people needing help was estimated at 2,000 to 3,000 per district, or up to 50,000 for the city as a whole. The organization ran its own premises and boasted 13 sections.[25] Subsequently there were reports of branches being set up in other towns. An all-union meeting of local societies was called in Leningrad on December 9, 1988, at which no fewer than 53 organizations were represented.

If the Leningrad *Miloserdie* has been successful, its success was not achieved without effort. The movement at first provoked palpable hostility among local officials. Granin mentioned in particular the health authorities who, fearing complaints about conditions in public homes and hospitals, did not want to allow volunteers in. But the need for help was so acute that some directors welcomed popular involvement (a point I shall return to below).

The story of the Moscow *Miloserdie* group, at least insofar as it can be determined, presents some noteworthy contrasts. Its formation is said to have been prompted by the receipt in June 1987 of a letter to the youth journal *Sobesednik.* Written by the members of a youth cooperative called "Master" Social Services, it contained an offer to work out a mercy/charity program for the whole of the USSR.[26] The staff of the journal, led by the journalist Marina Mulina, responded a few weeks later by organizing a Saturday "help day" for old and sick people in the Sverdlov District, where the editorial office was located. A list of several hundred addresses was obtained, evidently from the local social-security department. Outsiders were invited to join in by means of advertisements posted in the streets.

The initial response was disappointing: Only four young men came, one of whom was a believer. "But why not?" wrote the commentators. "The operation was open to everyone, anyway." A leading Moscow hippie listened to their invitation and refused to participate. The International War Veterans Department in the Zheleznodorozhny District Komsomol office also refused, but some Afghan veterans came voluntarily. A deputy to the local soviet lent his car to deliver groceries. The visitors found a number of heartrending cases: Old people who had not been out for years on account of broken elevators, who were obliged to pay relatives and friends to shop for them, who lived on mixtures of children's soup and water, who lacked essential domestic facilities.

As a result of publicizing the Saturday operation, however, *Sobesednik* received a large number of letters and proposals. Those listed in a subsequent article included the creation of "initiative groups" at enterprises, institutes, and journals, with the help of the Komsomol: the establishment of old people's social clubs; invitations to students to provide personal services and company for old people, invalids, and orphans. In December 1987, the journal provided *Miloserdie* activists with a room and a telephone.

By December 1988 (when I visited their premises), the group was engaged in a fairly extensive program. It included helping old people at home, organizing social evenings and excursions, visiting two nurseries for orphaned children, and providing regular help at one home for the aged and occasional help at four others. There was a formal link with the district Komsomol, and about 300 people were participating more or less regularly.

The organizers, however, were disappointed with the progress. They attached great importance to independence and the avoidance of bureaucratic control: This caused difficulties. They had not been able to register as a recognized public organization, despite meetings in the Moscow Party and local government offices, as the authorities wished them to merge with the Fund for Health and Charity. This failure meant that they did not have the rights of a juridical body and could not have their own bank account or write contracts. I was told, incidentally, that a similar merger proposal had been made to the Leningrad *Miloserdie* and had also been rejected. The best path for advance lay, according to the Moscow organizers, in finding powerful local backers, preferably people with a high public profile.

The Involvement of the Churches

The churches in the Soviet Union were, as I noted, deprived of their charitable function by the decree of April 8, 1929. To judge from published comment, the official church hierarchies at first played a secondary role, behind intellectuals, journalists, and indeed their own believers, in the reactivation of charitable work. Such caution accorded, of course, with the humiliating stance they had been obliged to adopt since the Revolution. Leading churchmen were said to have made quiet appeals to do charitable work in "the years of stagnation"; but these had simply been ignored.[27] Now that the movement has gotten under way, the involvement of church leaders seems to be more assertive.

Information is patchy, and a great deal has no doubt gone on behind the scenes. A highly significant event occurred in August 1987 when Mother Teresa visited Moscow and Kiev and was awarded the "Fighter for Peace" Gold Medal by the Soviet Committee for the Defense of Peace. Her stay and her activities in the Third World were given considerable publicity in the Soviet press. Later there were suggestions that her order might be permitted to set up its own charitable institution in the USSR. A number of authoritative religious figures, including Orthodox bishops, published articles in the central press, particularly in the months prior to the celebration of the millennium of Russian Orthodoxy. The immensely important meeting between Mikhail Gorbachev and Patriarch Pimen on May 29, 1988, in connection with the celebrations, set the seal of approval on church efforts to engage in charitable activity.[28]

It would appear that the official religious hierarchies tended to act independently of one another. In September 1987, the Moscow Orthodox clergy made a formal approach to the Main Health Administration of the City Council, possibly the first such action that ever had a real chance of success.[29] In June 1988, a prominent official of the USSR Ministry of Health at last acknowledged the Orthodox clergy's request and declared that local institutions would gladly accept believers' help. Beyond this it seems that priests were authorized by the Patriarchate to contact institutions individually.

Early in 1988 the All-Union Council of Evangelical Christians contacted the CPSU Central Committee and the USSR Council for Religious Affairs, and their approach was said to be "fully understood." In March 1988, some fifty members of the Moscow Baptist community started helping at two gerontological wards of the Kashchenko Psychiatric Hospital, and a special church service was dedicated to the cause of charity in September.[30] Subsequently there were reports of Seventh Day Adventist involvement. The three most usual channels were official church representation in the administrative bodies of the new national charities; gifts of church money to existing funds; and individual assistance at local homes and hospitals. In addition, one must, of course, remember that charitable help was already common among parishioners, though it was not normally registered and of dubious legality.

The Church of Vsekh Skorbyashchikh Radost' in Moscow has been used to publicize the official movement, and my own observations there deserve some attention. I was told that following a telephone call from the Patriarchate in September 1988, the senior priest, Father Boris (Guznyakov) formed a group of up to sixty parishioners for regular visits to three institutions (a home for retarded children, a psychoneurological hostel, and a home for labor veterans). A clinic hospital was to be added in January 1989. To quote a notice prominently displayed on the church door:

> The help comprises caring for the sick, feeding them, cleaning their rooms, etc. The timetable varies: about 30 parishioners visit homes 3-4 times a week, and the same number do so about once a week. A group of parishioners do general cleaning on Thursdays. Some people in this group can help only once a month, but their labor brings happiness and comfort to the lonely and poor.
>
> This help has been gratefully received by the managements of the homes. They cooperate in every possible way with the parishioners and priests who have, over the last three months, offered communion to over 250 patients in the homes for the elderly. The church also gives financial help, particularly to the children's home. The number of persons engaged in visiting is growing constantly.

This church would also seem to have a fair potential for financial assistance, since in the previous year it had been required to make a donation of 60,000 rubles to the Soviet Committee for the Defense of Peace. As was made clear to me, access to the homes brought priests the welcome right to give communion to the inhabitants. Formerly each request had to be approved separately by the hospital authorities, and press comment has indicated that refusal was frequent.[31]

The acute need for help in these institutions became apparent to me after a brief (and it must be said) restricted visit to the psychoneurological hostel that the church supported. It was listed for frequent visits by foreign delegations and therefore presumably one of the most desirable of its type. Nevertheless, the director revealed that it was 55 percent understaffed. A shortfall of this measure (which was common) meant that the staff carried a double work load. The low rates of pay for nursing staff and onerous duties attracted only those who could not get better jobs.[32] It is commonly understood that staff in such places make ends meet by pilfering food from the kitchens. The cumulative impact of such difficulties on a nationwide scale cannot but be deleterious, and horror stories of neglect and ill-treatment abound. Many a director must have been delighted to have any extra help he could get, especially if it was unpaid.

It is strange that (despite such efforts) up to the beginning of 1989 the authorized Christian journals contained virtually no reference to the charity movement. Similarly, the official publication of Soviet Islam gave no hint of Islamic response, though the faith clearly requires almsgiving and help for the unfortunate. The potential for Islamic involvement in charity is great, and there are already indications of increased activity. These will evidently deserve careful monitoring. Annual donations in the form of the *zakyat* have been preserved in the USSR, and some Soviet mosques have offices to receive it.[33]

Conclusions

The development of Soviet charity, as outlined here, should be regarded as an extremely positive phenomenon. Given the widespread nature of poverty and the inadequacies of the social services, there seems to be a strong likelihood of this development continuing. The only obvious alternative, if social needs are to be met, is a massive injection of state funding. Yet current economic trends make this improbable. Between 1985 and 1987, expenditure on social security, family aid, and collective-farm social funds apparently rose only from 15.1 percent to 15.2 percent of the USSR national budget, which may well have meant a fall in real terms. Public charity is a cheap and fairly innocuous way of supplementing this disbursement.[34]

However, Soviet reality also presents obstacles to charity: Some are common to other lands; some are more specifically Soviet. Without adopting too negative a stance, I believe these should be mentioned in order to conclude. The first is the natural reduction of public response as time goes by. There is little reason to believe that Soviet citizens are less charitable by nature than the citizens of other lands, despite the dreadful conditioning of their past experience. But initial enthusiasm may also tend to wane as the intractability of the problems becomes apparent. If one believes that "sociological laws" exist, one can say that such a law operates as much in the Soviet Union as elsewhere. The bureaucratization of some movements and the involvement of discredited political organizations in others may further dampen enthusiasm.

The involvement of the churches may evoke distrust in some quarters. The USSR has a history of active denigration of religious belief and a nationwide apparatus for atheist propaganda. Many people, apart from bureaucrats, will object to the clergy—if not to believers—acquiring an active role in areas from which they were formerly banned.

Another obstacle lies in the very nature of Soviet bureaucracy. The societies of the West have easily accommodated free markets and regard state administration as generally undesirable. By contrast, Soviet society has always been highly administered; people are used to it; and informal charitable groups may well, as a result, find themselves at a sort of psychological disadvantage. In more practical terms, any group (in a provincial town, let us say) could find it extremely difficult to hold out against the opposition of a determined local Party secretary.

The voluntary nature of some movements may gradually be subsumed by bureaucratic control: Some people believe that this threat already emanates from the Fund for Health and Charity. The mere fact that charitable activity is supposed to be personal and voluntary may mean that it will attract rather independently minded people, who always provoke official hostility. A prominent churchman recently found officials of the Children's Fund strong in their interest in cash, but weak on personal warmth.[35] Relations between the new charitable organizations can be less than entirely amicable. Also, it seems unlikely that Soviet charity (just like that of other lands) will remain entirely free from corruption and dishonesty.

The arguments on both sides are many and inconclusive. The future of the movement, I would suggest, looks promising but by no means certain. Apart from everything else, past experience shows that virtually any policy can be abandoned or robbed of its content by a simple decision of the Soviet leadership. Public charity, too, could suffer this fate. Though it is too diffuse and, I believe, too apolitical to depend wholly on the future of the Gorbachev leadership, the official political line will undoubtedly affect its development.

Notes

1. Some remarks on this topic may be found in my book *Poverty in the Soviet Union* (New York: Cambridge University Press, 1986), pp. 141-145. It is noteworthy that even when writing those lines (1985), I did not anticipate the extent of the change that Gorbachev's policies would entail.

2. "On Religious Organizations," decree of April 8, 1929, in Mervyn Matthews, *Soviet Government, A Selection of Official Documents* (London: J. Cape, 1974), p. 63. Later legislation, including the 1975 revision of this decree, retained earlier restrictions.

3. The Societies for the Blind, Deaf and Dumb, the Red Cross, and the Red Crescent, founded betweeen 1922 and 1926, are probably the best known. The Lenin Fund for Aid to Children's Homes and the Friends of Children Society (according to *Izvestiia*, July 7, 1987) existed in the mid-1920s but were closed down in the 1930s.

4. See the comments in his report to the 19th Party Conference (July 1988), section 7; no such comments were made in his report to the 27th Party Congress in February 1986; see also the decrees of the Central Committee of the CPSU, USSR Council of Ministers, and All-Union Council of Trade Unions of May 14, 1985, and January 22, 1987; *Spravochnik partiinogo rabotnika*, no. 26 (Moscow: Politizdat, 1986), p. 479; no. 28 (Moscow: Politizdat, 1988), p. 382.

5. Such activities, of course, presupposed a healthy financial balance. See *Resheniya partii i pravitel'stva po khozyaistvennym voprosam*, vol. 10 (Moscow: Politizdat, 1976), p. 166 (article 111); *Spravochnik partiinogo rabotnika*, no. 28, op. cit., p. 339 (article 13).

6. *Vestnik agroproma, ezhenedel'noe prilozhenie*, December 2, 1988, pp. 1-5.

7. Their statute was published in *Ekonomika sel'skogo khozyaistva*, no. 7 (1984). Some apparent strengthening of the USSR State Committee for Labor and Social Affairs needs to be mentioned in this connection. This body was set up as long ago as 1955 as an ersatz Ministry of Labor. Although its main function was the control of recruitment, placement, and direction of labor throughout the country, its Moscow office also evidently served as a coordinating body for the republican Ministries of Social Security. Its local organs were simply committees or departments "for labor" until 1987, when the committee was given union republican status, and the local organs too acquired the second half of the title. See also *Vedomosti verkhovnogo soveta RSFSR*, no. 36 (1987), article 1296; no. 38 (1987), article 1360.

8. See the joint decree of January 22, 1987, in *Spravochnik partiinogo rabotnika*, no. 26, op. cit.

9. See M. Kravchenko; also, *Sotsial'noe obespechenie*, no. 10 (1987), p. 2; no. 10 (1988), p. 5; *Sobesednik*, no. 39 (1987), p. 10.

10. See also *Izvestiia*, April 21, 1988.

11. *Bolshaya sovetskaya entsiklopediia, Ezhegodnik* (1987), p. 23; *Veteran*, weekly supplement to the newspaper *Trud*, various numbers; *Sotsial'noe obespechenie*, no. 11 (1988), p. 5. The all-Russian conference of this organization was supposed to convene once every five years; in the interim its affairs were handled by a presidium under the chairmanship of A. V. Deryugin, himself a war invalid and hero of the Soviet Union. Its establishment evidently enjoyed massive local support and was in this respect belated. The All-Union Organization for Veterans of War and Labor was not (like the "funds" to be discussed below) primarily a money-raising organization.

12. *Izvestiia*, April 29, 1988.

13. Convenient accounts of the complex rules may be found under the relevant headings in A. Ya. Sukharevskii (ed.), *Iuridicheskii entsiklopedicheskii slovar'* (Moscow, 1987).

14. See also the discussion in my book *Patterns of Deprivation in the Soviet Union* (Stanford, Calif.: Hoover Institution Press, 1989).

15. Legislation in other republics and at local levels remains to be explored. Apart from the references given in note 4 above, see *Sobranie postanovlenii Soveta Ministrov SSSR*, no. 9 (1987), article 39; *Sobranie postanovlenii Soveta Ministrov RSFSR*, no. 4 (1987), article 39; no. 21 (1987), article 132; no. 15 (1988), article 78; no. 23 (1988), article 136.

16. For a selection of articles on this problem see translations in *Current Digest of the Soviet Press* 39, no. 27 (1987), p. 21; no. 32 (1987), p. 2. According to a report in *Uchitel'skaya gazeta*, August 15, 1987, between 1976 and 1985 the number of children in care grew by one-third and reached 1 million, of whom 300,000 lived in institutions and 700,000 with foster parents. Only 4 to 5 percent of them were orphans, the remainder being victims of broken marriages.

17. *Statute of the Lenin Soviet Children's Fund* (Moscow: Novosti Press Agency, 1987).

18. This journal was launched in January 1988. Rybinski appeared to be reluctant to provide documentation about the fund, though it was available in his office. The information given herein may have been incomplete.

19. This figure was provided without further detail and hardly accords with the 125 million rubles mentioned in the *New York Times*, December 25, 1987. There are several possible explanations for the discrepancy.

20. *Izvestiia*, September 17, 1988.

21. Draft proposal for the Soviet Fund for Health and Charity, *Izvestiia*, April 26, 1988; a meeting of the organizing committee was reported in the Radio Liberty, *Soviet Media Actualities*, no. A-344 06, July 14, 1988.

22. *Pravda*, July 7, 1988. See also columns in *Izvestiia, Trud, Literaturnaia gazeta, Sem'ia, Moscow News*, etc. By the end of 1988 dozens of items of this kind had appeared, merging, of course, with articles on poverty, homelessness, and delinquency. I base my remarks only on the central and republican periodicals available in the West. Local Soviet newspapers cannot normally be subscribed to abroad.

23. Details from a mimeographed publicity leaflet dated June 10, 1988.

24. See M. Scammell, *Solzhenitsyn* (London: Hutchinson, 1984), p. 874, and indexed entries. Also A. Solzhenitsyn, *The Oak and the Calf* (London: Collins and Harvill, 1980), p. 321. It is significant that the statute of the new memorial society

for rehabilitating the victims of Stalinism, established in the USSR in January 1989, allows for the collection of donations and assistance for individuals (*Ogonek*, no. 4 [1989], p. 29).

25. The sections included: hospital work, sick children, social projects, the Phoenix Club, dispatch and home help, technology for invalids, help for veterans, home technology, prisons and labor colonies, advice on establishing new groups by place of residence, healthy living and psychophysiology, Komsomol youth group, publicity/propaganda, and ecology.

26. *Sobesednik*, no. 33 (August 1987), p. 10.

27. *Ogonek*, no. 38 (1985), p. 32.

28. For a number of references see *Radio Liberty Research Bulletin*, RL 62/88 (February 16, 1988); RL 179/88 (April 27, 1988); and *Sem'ia*, May 7 and June 10, 1988.

29. *Ogonek*, no. 38 (1985), p. 32.

30. *Information Bulletin of the All-Union Council of Evangelical Christian-Baptists*, no. 10 (1988), p. 2. Many other references to such activities can be located.

31. *Meditsinskaya gazeta*, March 30, 1988.

32. For selected rates of pay see my book *Poverty in the Soviet Union*, p. 36.

33. The journals I have in mind are *Zhurnal Moskovskoi Patriarkhii* and *Bratski Vestnik*, which Michael Rowe kindly perused on my behalf. The Islamic journal is *Moslems of the Soviet East*. See also M. B. Piotrovski and S. M. Prozorov (eds.), *Islam—Slovar' ateista* (Moscow, 1988), p. 77. Clerics seem to find the editorial offices of the popular press more receptive, but church publications will no doubt follow suit.

34. See *Narodnoe khozyaistvo SSSR v 1987* (Moscow: Finansy i Statistika, 1988), p. 588. I draw this general conclusion from discussions of Soviet inflation rates and the fact that published figures may be exaggerated. Of course, the Soviet state has a sad tradition of tolerating socially harmful practices by way of supplement to low pay, as theft in the food-services sector demonstrates. For instance, the state-approved wage rates in many service branches are obviously insufficient to maintain the average worker's family.

35. *Meditsinskaya gazeta*, March 30, 1988.

CHAPTER 10

Aging and the Elderly

David E. Powell

Unfortunately, the notion of respect for old age has still not found a place in our re-structuring efforts [perestroika].

—*Sobesednik*

An old Russian saying holds that *starost' ne radost'*—old age is no joy. Given the dreadful history of Russia and the Soviet Union, one can easily understand why this sentiment arose and why it has endured. During the czarist period, the landed aristocracy (and toward the end of czarist rule, the merchant class) lived exceedingly well, largely at the expense of the rest of the population. For most people throughout most of Russian history, life resembled what Thomas Hobbes described as the state of nature—solitary, poor, nasty, brutish, and short.

The Revolutions of 1917, which promised major improvements in health, education, and welfare, did so, but at terrible cost. Political freedoms were curtailed to a degree unimaginable even during the cruelest periods of the autocracy, while living standards and the overall quality of life dropped sharply, especially during the Stalin era. Peasants were forcibly uprooted from the land and placed in collective or state farms, while industrial workers suffered under the five-year plans with their all-but-impossible quotas and demands for "labor discipline." A 1932 law stipulated that persons who failed to appear for work without a valid reason could be dismissed, deprived of the right to use a ration card, and evicted from the apartment that had been allocated by their place of employment.[1] More generally, life under Stalin meant shortages of consumer goods and foodstuffs, desperately crowded housing, little or no leisure time, strict travel restrictions and residency requirements, and a virtual atomization of society.

Since the dictator's death in 1953, the quality of life has improved substantially. Although the USSR is hardly a welfare state in the West European sense of the term, housing is now more readily available and less crowded, disposable income has increased significantly, and consumer goods are much more plentiful—especially in the cities, but in much of the countryside as well. People today can move about the country more freely, have much more leisure time, and—if Mikhail Gorbachev manages to succeed in his ambitious program of *perestroika*—have a chance to enjoy "the good life."

And what of the members of the older generation? How can we evaluate *their* quality of life? What can we say about their current situation, their concerns, and the way the government responds to them? In the following pages, we will examine these questions, focusing especially on matters affecting the physical and financial well-being of senior citizens. In doing so, we will follow the lead of Western gerontologists, who distinguish between the "young old" (men and women between the ages of 60 and 75) and the "old old" (those who are over 75). As we shall see, the situation of the elderly represents a social problem of considerable magnitude: Large numbers of these individuals are not well taken care of, and some have been left in a precarious position.

Life Expectancy

Before World War I, female life expectancy in the Russian Empire was 33; for males, the figure was 31. After gaining power, Lenin and his followers set about changing that. They invested considerable effort in improving the country's infrastructure—dams, water-purification facilities, irrigation canals—they also constructed thousands of hospitals and trained millions of doctors, nurses, and paramedics. This complex of measures helped to raise male life expectancy to 66 by the mid-1960s; for women, the peak was 74, a level reached in the same years.[2]

During the period between the mid-1960s and the early 1980s, however, male life expectancy fell by at least four years; among females, it dropped by one year. These developments were so disturbing that the USSR Central Statistical Administration published no new data on life expectancy for a decade and a half—from 1971-1972 to 1985-1986. The drop, associated with an immense upsurge in alcohol consumption and a virtual epidemic of cardiovascular disease, appears to have ended, and life expectancy today is once again moving upward—even if at a very slow pace. In 1988, the average for the country's population was 69.5 years, less than the figure of 70 that prevailed from 1963-1964 to 1971-1972, but better than it had been in recent years.[3]

The Gender Gap. There are sizable differences in the life expectancy of men and women throughout the country. This pattern, which existed long before the Great October Socialist Revolution in 1917, grew more striking during the first seven decades of Soviet power. As increments in life expectancy among men began to level off in the late 1950s (rising from 64.4 years in 1958-1959 to 64.7 years in 1968-1971), the figure for women continued to increase at a more satisfactory pace (from 71.7 to 75.5 years during this same period).[4] In fact, the gap between female and male life expectancy grew for several decades: In 1926-1927 it was 5 years (47 for women, 42 for men), in 1958-1959 it reached 8 years (72 for women and 64 for men), and in 1981 the difference was a full 10 years (74 for women versus 64 for men).[5] As recently as 1984–1985, the Soviet statistical authorities put the gap at a decade (73 for women, 63 for men), but more recent reports indicate that it has narrowed to 8.8 years (73.6 for women, as against 64.8 for men).[6]

Regional Disparities. There are also major differences in life expectancy among people living under different climatic conditions, between urban and rural populations, and—related to these two variables—among groups differing with respect to socioeconomic status, access to medical care, and "overall cultural level and health standards."[7] For example, life expectancy in the northern and eastern reaches of the USSR is lower than in the European part of the country. The explanation for this phenomenon involves many factors, the most important of which undoubtedly is the harsh climatic conditions prevailing in the North and East. Other considerations include poor housing and transportation, nutritional deficiencies, and an inadequate public-health infrastructure in these regions (too few hospitals and doctors, a lack of medical specialists, shortages of diagnostic equipment and medicines, and remoteness even from provincial centers).

For many of the same reasons, life expectancy in urban areas is higher than in rural areas. The differences are less palpable than one might expect, since city dwellers, who have more and better medical services available to them, are also more apt to experience the harmful consequences of "modernization," such as environmental pollution, hypertension, depression, obesity, and an increased incidence of various chronic diseases.

Ethnic Differences. While life-expectancy figures for the country as a whole remain low, there are significant differences among ethnic groups, thereby making the demographic picture more complicated. Thus, the 1970 census (the last to publish comprehensive age-related data) reported that 11.8 percent of the USSR's population was 60 years of age or older. Far higher figures—the highest in the country, in fact—were reported for Latvia (17.3 percent), Estonia (16.8 percent), and Lithuania (15.0 percent). In contrast, a relatively small proportion of the population of Central Asia was 60 years of age or older: The lowest figures reported, 7.2 percent and 7.5 percent, came from Turkmenia and Tadzhikistan, respectively.[8]

These disparities are not an expression of differences in life expectancy per se. Instead, they can be explained by three other factors: (1) historical and cultural patterns, especially the extremely low birthrates prevailing in Estonia and Latvia, along with the extraordinarily high birthrates one finds in the "Muslim" parts of the country; (2) vast differences in urbanization, industrialization, and educational levels in these two areas, as well as equally sharp differences in the quantity of medical care and the quality of sanitary-hygienic practices; and (3) the overall character of the infrastructure that has been erected during the past century in the sphere of public health.

More generally, the nation as a whole has undergone a distinct "graying" in recent decades. On the eve of World War II, 8.9 percent of the population was of pension age—60 for men, 55 for women. By the time of the 1959 census, this figure had risen to 12.2 percent, and by the 1970 census it reached 15 percent. Today, men and women of pension age constitute 16.9 percent of the country's population, and their number is expected to increase to 17.8 percent by the year 2005.[9] With good reason, then, the USSR is regarded by United Nations demographers as an "old" country.

Medical Care

For decades—until the era of *glasnost'*—Soviet propagandists spoke rhapsodically about the wonderful quality of medical care available in the USSR and of the regime's solicitude toward people who had reached retirement age. Year after year, official spokespersons asserted that health care was free and readily available to all, that their country had trained more physicians and built more treatment facilities than any other in the world, and so on. "Only the first socialist state," because it was guided by collectivist and humanistic principles, they said, could guarantee high-quality care from cradle to grave.

At the same time, they cited the fact that people could retire at such an early age as evidence of the privileged position of the older generation, as well as the progressive character of Soviet society. Other arrangements designed to ease the lot of the nation's elderly have been adopted over the years in such areas as health, housing, and transportation, as well as in the form of direct economic aid. Since 1936, the constitution has stipulated, "Citizens of the USSR have the right to material security in their old age,"[10] and an elaborate network of old-age pensions and other retirement benefits supposedly ensures that they do.

How valid are these claims? The Soviet government has, to its credit, trained millions of doctors; at present, they far outnumber those in the United States and other countries—1,255,600 in 1988, as compared with 612,400 in the United States. The regime has also constructed large numbers of hospitals and clinics, and every year it adds thousands of hospital beds to the total. Here, too, the numbers are quite impressive: In 1988, there were 3,763,000 hospital beds in the USSR, as against 1,261,000 in the United States.[11] These contrasts would appear especially striking in view of the fact that the Soviet population is only 15 percent larger than that of the United States.

There is also an elaborate program for the prevention and early detection of disease, which undoubtedly has improved the population's access to medical care and increased public understanding of how hygiene, sanitation, nutrition, and exercise contribute to good health. Because of such measures, the authorities have brought under control many of the life-threatening diseases that had affected infants and young children, and it has all but eliminated cholera, smallpox, and certain other infectious diseases that had periodically decimated the country's population.[12]

But health-care conditions in general, and the situation of older men and women in particular, are much less desirable than official rhetoric

TABLE 10.1
Mortality Levels in the USSR, 1958-1987
(Deaths per 1,000 Population)

	Male	Female
1958-1959	8.1	6.8
1960-1961	7.8	6.6
1962-1963	7.9	6.9
1964-1965	7.6	6.7
1966-1967	8.0	7.0
1968-1969	8.6	7.4
1970-1971	8.9	7.7
1972-1973	9.2	8.1
1974-1975	9.7	8.4
1976-1977	10.3	8.9
1978-1979	10.7	9.3
1980-1981	11.1	9.6
1982-1983	10.9	9.6
1984-1985	11.2	10.3
1986-1987	9.9	9.8

Source: *Naselenie SSSR 1987, Statisticheskii sbornik* (Moscow, 1988), pp. 320-321.

would suggest. Indeed, the past several decades have witnessed a dramatic increase in mortality levels among both men and women. This shift reflects not only the overall aging of the Soviet population but also widespread alcohol abuse and alcoholism (especially among men), increased cigarette smoking, an inadequate diet, too little physical exercise, and a number of other problems associated with contemporary Soviet life. Male mortality rose from 8.1 per 1,000 in 1958-1959 to 11.2 in 1984-1985. During the same period, the figure for women rose from 6.8 per 1,000 to 10.3 (see Table 10.1). Although conditions appear to have improved in the very recent past (a development probably associated with Gorbachev's anti-alcohol campaign), the situation today remains very troublesome.

More important for our purposes is the sharp increase in mortality among older persons: Among men 60-64 years of age, it rose from 25.4 per 1,000 in 1958-1959 to 32.6 in 1984-1985 (see Table 10.2). Among men who were 70 or older, it increased from 74.7 to 98.4. For women, the same phenomenon could be observed: among those 60-64 years of age, it rose from 12.6 per 1,000 to 14.1, while among those aged 70 or more, it increased from 58.7 to 71.4. Although age-specific mortality among the elderly has decreased somewhat since Gorbachev came to power, the overall trend during the past thirty years has been decidedly negative. The consequence is highly paradoxical: Increased mortality among older persons, an erratic and problematical pattern of changes in life expectancy—and a population that, as a whole, continues to age with each passing year.

How can we explain the retrograde movement—a veritable crisis—in well-being among senior citizens? The answer is at once extremely simple

TABLE 10.2
Age-Specific Mortality Among Older Persons in the USSR, 1958-1987
(Deaths per 1000 Population)

	50-54		55-59		60-64		65-69		70 and Older	
	Male	Female	Male	Female	Male	Female	Male	Female	Male	Female
1958-1959	11.9	5.5	17.8	7.8	25.4	12.6	35.3	19.8	74.7	58.7
1960-1961	11.3	5.2	17.0	7.6	25.3	12.3	35.3	19.0	73.3	58.2
1962-1963	11.5	5.4	17.4	7.7	26.5	13.0	37.0	19.9	78.7	62.6
1964-1965	11.9	5.4	16.5	7.4	26.2	12.6	36.0	18.9	75.9	58.9
1966-1967	12.1	5.4	17.3	7.7	27.1	12.4	38.1	20.2	79.2	60.3
1968-1969	12.8	5.4	18.8	8.2	28.1	12.7	41.1	21.3	82.3	60.9
1970-1971	13.6	5.7	19.2	7.8	28.3	12.5	41.1	20.4	92.7	69.0
1972-1973	13.4	5.5	20.0	8.3	28.2	12.5	41.8	20.7	94.2	69.8
1974-1975	14.0	5.6	20.3	8.6	29.1	12.7	42.6	20.7	93.6	67.9
1976-1977	15.0	5.8	21.0	8.8	31.1	13.3	43.9	21.2	95.0	69.2
1978-1979	15.9	6.1	22.1	8.9	32.2	13.8	45.0	21.6	95.5	69.0
1980-1981	16.3	6.1	22.4	9.0	32.9	14.1	46.0	21.7	96.8	69.7
1982-1983	16.5	6.1	22.3	9.0	31.8	13.7	47.8	22.8	93.1	66.8
1984-1985	17.0	6.3	22.8	9.3	32.6	14.1	47.9	23.2	98.4	71.4
1986-1987	13.4	5.3	20.3	8.5	29.4	13.2	43.2	21.8	95.5	70.0

Source: *Naselenie SSSR 1987, Statisticheskii sbornik* (Moscow, 1988), pp. 320-321.

and highly complex. Numerous failings in the health-care delivery system—poorly trained and indifferent personnel, shortages of medicines, and medical equipment that is outdated, inadequately maintained, and of inferior quality—affect the elderly more severely than they do other strata of society. Not only are older people more likely than other citizens to become ill; in addition, for many decades they have been a casualty of the government's obsession with increasing industrial and agricultural output.

Throughout most of its history, the Soviet regime has had a decidedly instrumental attitude toward medical questions. Officials have been far less concerned with promoting feelings of "subjective well-being" than with keeping people on the job.[13] While contributing to widespread cynicism among doctors and despair among patients, this attitude has also had unfortunate implications for the allocation of health-care resources.

Over the past three decades, government expenditures for health care, relative to other expenses, have declined steadily. In 1960, 6.6 percent of all budgetary allocations went to health care. By 1970, the figure had dropped to 6.0 percent; in 1975, it was 5.3 percent, and by 1980 it had fallen to 5.0 percent. Even in the latter part of the 1980s, health-care allocations continued to plummet: In 1985, they represented 4.6 percent of the country's GNP, and in 1987, they were a mere 4.4 percent.[14]

This trend can be explained in large part by shifting patterns of investment. During the same three decades, central planners allocated a smaller and smaller proportion of available investment capital to public health—indeed, to the entire "nonproductive" sphere of the economy. In

1960, some 35 percent of total investment went to health, education, housing, and social welfare; the figure for the end of the 1980s was only 26.7 percent.[15]

Although absolute figures have, of course, increased over the years, the relative decline in health-care expenditures indicates clearly that this sphere is less and less a priority concern. Indeed, Dr. Evgenii Chazov, who was minister of health, complained in mid-1988 that the USSR ranked number 75—out of a total of 126 countries—in the percentage of gross national product allocated to health care.[16] Sad to say, *perestroika* has done very little to improve matters: In 1989, the State Committee on Statistics concluded that "there have been no substantial changes. . . . [The] medical service is still characterized by a lack of amenities in hospital premises, a lack of modern equipment . . . a shortage of medicines and linen, and poor food service."[17]

Older men and women are a major component of the "nonproductive" sphere. Although, as we shall see, a fair number of them are employed in industry or agriculture, their overall contribution to the national economy is quite modest. Far more apt than the average citizen to suffer from one or another chronic (and therefore expensive) ailment, they are seen primarily as an economic liability rather than as an asset. Thus, they receive only the most limited attention from the authorities.

Placing limits on capital investment means failing to carry out repairs on old hospitals and polyclinics, cutting corners in the construction of new ones, and a reluctance to encourage innovation in the pharmaceutical industry. Even in Moscow, Leningrad, and other major cities, buildings belonging to the public-health system are old and dilapidated. Hospitals located in the less-developed republics of Central Asia and the more remote rural areas of all republics are especially badly off. Most hospitals in Central Asia lack running water, heating systems, and indoor plumbing: In Uzbekistan, 46 percent of all hospitals do not even meet the state's minimum requirements for sanitation and hygiene. Conditions in rural hospitals throughout the country are equally grim: More than a fourth lack sewage-disposal facilities, half are without running water, and two-thirds have no hot water.[18]

Shortages of medicines and medical equipment also represent a major barrier to effective medical care, especially to the older men and women who are most in need of such items. For many years, Soviet industry has been unable to satisfy the demand for medical goods or to produce many of the medicines commonly available in the West. Thus, even though output of medicines increased by 6 percent in 1989, it was enough to meet only 40 percent of the country's needs. Imports of medicines rose, too, but this added volume met only another 35 percent of the total required.[19]

Part of the problem here is the system of central planning: Generally speaking, it takes ten years to bring a new piece of medical equipment from the first stages of design to actual production. Such delays, along with serious deficiencies in quality control, mean that 80–85 percent of domestic production in this field is not up to world standards. In addition, there is a "catastrophic" shortage of disposable equipment such as scalpels, catheters, devices for performing blood transfusions, and syringes. (Demand for disposable syringes is some 3 billion per year, but only 192 million were produced in 1989.[20])

Recent economic reforms may have served only to make things worse. With the decentralization of decisionmaking, some enterprises now refuse to produce medical equipment: Profit margins on such items are very small, and a number of plants actually had to sell them below cost. Managers are no longer willing to do so. "Before the shift to financial autonomy, we could use 'strong-arm tactics,'" one official observed, "but now enterprises decide for themselves what they will produce."[21]

In 1988, the USSR Council of Ministers adopted legislation aimed at speeding up the development and production of the most urgently needed products. Even if the most optimistic assumptions turn out to be warranted, however, these items will not begin to appear until 1993–1995. We are not speaking here of exotic or expensive products: In mid-1988, it was calculated that the country was short 1,000 operating tables, 5,000 surgical lamps, and 100,000 bactericidal lamps—not to mention the items noted above.[22]

Perhaps the most serious issue—one that the Gorbachev administration seems to find especially troubling—involves devising a way to assess healthcare programs. Central planners traditionally have focused on quantitative indicators—the number of people employed in this sector, the number of square meters added to buildings, the number of beds added—as a measure of quality health-care delivery. In doing so, they have largely ignored the fact that Soviet physicians are poorly trained, that instruments and diagnostic devices are out-of-date, that pharmaceuticals are of poor quality and often unavailable when needed, and that official rules and regulations make it all but impossible to deliver quality care. As Chazov observed in 1988, "We were proud that we had more physicians and more hospitals than any other country in the world, but we kept quiet about the fact that with respect to average life expectancy, we ranked 32nd in the world."[23]

Because of the government's quantitative approach to health-care evaluation, one finds massive evidence of indifference on the part of doctors and nurses. "Care" for patients has been sacrificed. Physicians, like other workers and employees, are assigned certain quotas; in order to fulfill (or, if possible, overfulfill) their plan, they simply do not have the time to be solicitous of their patients. According to William A. Knaus, an American physician who worked for the U.S. government in the USSR and who interviewed numerous public-health experts in that country, Soviet doctors are required to see eight patients each hour (nine for surgeons). This rigid schedule allows them a mere seven minutes per consultation. Furthermore, surveys have shown that the average polyclinic physician "needs at least five minutes to fill out the forms for the patient's medical record, his trade union, and to excuse the patient from work." Thus, the health-care provider actually has only two minutes to discuss symptoms, perform a physical examination, discuss the prognosis, offer advice, and discuss medications or the possible need for further tests.[24]

This arrangement, which emphasizes quantity rather than quality, has come in for considerable criticism since the policy of *glasnost'* was introduced. Leading medical authorities have condemned the phenomenon of "paper fever," complained that they have to make diagnoses and prescribe treatments too quickly to guarantee proper care, and criticized the practice of training ever-greater numbers of doctors, just to "put them to work scribbling."[25] One physician, from the city of Tula, asserted that the emphasis on quantitative indicators was more self-defeating than helpful. In *Izvestiia,* he wrote, "It is practically impossible to extract information about the effectiveness of treatment from all the numbers. Has the patient's health improved? Stayed the same? Deteriorated? There is no way of knowing."[26]

Hospitalization

The exceptionally high figures for hospitalization in the USSR—Knaus remarked that people in the Soviet Union "are among the most hospitalized in the world"—are by no means evidence of solid medical care for the population in general or for the elderly in particular. One of every four Soviet citizens is hospitalized every year. This circumstance is explainable only in part by the prevalence of troublesome medical conditions and illnesses. According to a high-ranking official of the USSR Ministry of Health, "Many patients are not properly examined before being sent to the hospital. The polyclinic doctor decides the illness is not interesting or that he doesn't understand the problem. He sends the patients to the hospital, knowing that his colleagues will find out what's wrong."[27]

Furthermore, figures on hospitalization rates do not have the same meaning in the USSR that they do in the West. Indeed, they probably say as much about popular attitudes toward these institutions, and about the competence of Soviet doctors and nurses, as they do about the physical well-being of the citizenry. In rural areas, for example, people of all ages and social strata are especially reluctant to be hospitalized. They recognize that the quality of personnel, services, and equipment is vastly inferior to that which are available in the larger cities. This is true in virtually all countries, of course, but the consequences in the USSR are particularly striking. According to Knaus, "Some of the small rural hospitals are empty 180 days or half the year, while hospitals in cities like Yerevan and Tbilisi remain overcrowded."[28]

Among older persons, popular feelings toward the prospect of being hospitalized range from uneasiness and anxiety to fear and outright refusal to seek admission.[29] Studies carried out in the USSR have shown that among people 60 years of age or older, the older one is, the less likely he or she is to be hospitalized. (In the United States and other developed countries, the reverse is true: The "old old" are far more likely to spend time in a hospital than the "young old.")

The explanation for this unusual circumstance is not that socialism imparts a special sprightliness to older men and women. Rather, it seems to involve a number of other elements: (1) the role of tradition and the continued strength of the family, at least in rural areas, (2) an attitude of fatalism among the elderly toward the issue of death and dying, (3) popular distrust of public-health institutions and health-care providers, and (4) the reluctance of hospital administrators to offer care for the "old old."

Old people everywhere recognize that infirmity is an inevitable concomitant of aging; they can handle some illnesses, at least for a while, but eventually they wear out, physically or psychologically. For some of these individuals, knowledge of this fact—that the end is coming—is reason enough not to seek medical intervention, but rather to rely on the care of family and friends. Other elderly persons, who have spent a lifetime trying to cope with poor medical care, fear that they would be more at risk inside than outside a hospital, and thus remain at home. Still others seek admission (or their families do) but are denied a bed and have no choice but to remain at home.

The circumstances surrounding denial of access to a hospital are sufficiently ghastly to warrant amplification here. Each hospital in the USSR is assigned a specific "death quota," that is, a figure that, if exceeded, would trigger investigations, boards of inquiry, and if deemed appropriate, the imposition of various penalties. The precise number of "acceptable" deaths in each institution is based on the size of the hospital and the types of patients it treats.

To avoid such sanctions, hospital administrators employ a number of tactics, of which two are especially common. In some cases, they will instruct admitting physicians to refuse ambulances with dead-on-arrival cases. In others, they encourage the families of terminally ill patients to take the individual home so that death will occur outside the hospital. The result, of course, is that the most seriously ill old people, those most at risk of dying, are also most apt to be denied admission to a hospital.[30]

The "young old," primarily people in their 60s, are especially likely to seek and gain admission to a hospital; in fact, during any given year, members of this age-group are three times as likely as the average citizen to be hospitalized.[31] But as one grows older, the likelihood that he or she will be hospitalized—even for a serious illness or injury—steadily declines. Approximately 10 percent of all persons aged 60–69 with medical problems that warrant hospitalization are cared for at home. Among those 70–74 years of age, the figure is 20 percent; for those in the 75–79 age bracket, it is 33 percent; and for those 80 years of age or older, it rises to 50 percent.[32]

Older people are also more likely to seek medical aid outside the hospital setting. Thus, more than 50 percent of all home visits by doctors are to people over the age of 50, even though this group represents only 22 percent of the country's population. Similarly, men and women of retirement age are three to five times more apt to turn to the *Skoraia medit-*

sinskaia pomoshch' (Emergency First Aid Service) than people who are currently in the labor force. In contrast to the situation with respect to hospitalization rates, though, the figure rises as one goes from those 60–64 years of age to increasingly older age cohorts.[33]

But older persons who call the *Skoraia* do not always get the help they need. Doctors, nurses, and ambulance personnel employed by the service give priority to younger people, even if a call involving an elderly person comes in earlier. Informed citizens, when telephoning for emergency medical assistance, are said to conceal the fact that the individual in need is an older man or woman. As one doctor acknowledged candidly, *Skoraia* personnel "are held strictly accountable if they fail to respond quickly to a call concerning a young patient."[34]

Older people are often treated like second-class citizens at neighborhood polyclinics, too. Thus, a Soviet journalist offered a poignant description of an elderly woman who was crying when he came to visit her. In response to his expression of concern, she explained why she was weeping: "I had just barely succeeded in dragging myself to the [local] polyclinic and waited in line. Eventually, the doctor said, 'Why are you here? I don't even have time to examine the younger patients.' " The various ministries and departments responsible for helping pensioners, the journalist added, are simply not motivated by feelings of "humanism, philanthropy, and charity" and thus do not provide "social justice."[35]

At-Home Care

Fully aware of the vulnerability of very old men and women, Soviet public-health officials have for years developed plans, passed decrees, and issued exhortations explaining how best to help them. Today, for example, government regulations require that 130 hospital beds be set aside for geriatric patients for every 1,000 people over the age of 60. There is also supposed to be an elaborate network of outpatient centers for geriatric patients. But almost everywhere around the country, these and other medical facilities for senior citizens exist only on paper, and anyone who is very old and, at the same time, seriously ill will find it difficult to receive care on either an out-patient or an in-patient basis.[36]

Thus, the "old old"—most of whom suffer from some sort of chronic condition requiring constant supervision and few of whom are very mobile—must be cared for at home. In choosing this approach, the regime is able to serve two purposes. First, it permits those who have reached an advanced age and are infirm to live out their lives in familiar surroundings. This arrangement helps to ease their psychological distress and may even contribute to the healing process. Second, the policy makes sense from the economic point of view. According to a 1984 estimate, the cost to the state of providing services to a single pensioner living at home was 120–150 rubles per year. In contrast, per capita expenditures for constructing a nursing home were approximately 5,000–6,000 rubles, and maintenance costs were an additional 1,000 rubles a year.[37]

At-home care is largely the responsibility of family and friends, much as it has been for centuries. Such arrangements are the custom in Central Asia, the Transcaucasus, and certain other areas where families are multigenerational and adhere to well-established traditions. It is rare to find anyone requiring or asking for institutional care in such communities. Elsewhere, however, especially in the more urbanized parts of the country, the younger generation has moved away from notions of filial piety. Partly as a response to this shift in attitudes and behavior, the constitution (Article 66) now stipulates, "Children are obliged to care for their parents and to help them."

Studies have shown that this constitutional norm, like many others, bears only the faintest resemblance to reality. According to the gerontologist V. D. Shapiro, whereas 64 percent of all working pensioners provide financial assistance to their children, a mere 5 percent receive such assistance from their children. Among nonworking pensioners, the situation is much the same. Despite their less-secure financial situation, 26 percent manage to give money regularly to their offspring (who are, of course, adults). Only 10 percent of the children, however, help support their parents.[38]

In the past few years, officials in some cities and towns have begun to provide not only medical care but also other services to old people living at home. Social-security agencies, local factories, and other enterprises, as well as increasing numbers of volunteers, have pooled their resources in this effort. As might be expected, most of the persons requiring such assistance live alone, have no family, and receive very small pensions (some receive none at all). A few, ignored or abandoned by their children, are awaiting admission to an old-age home. All of them, however, have the same sorts of needs—companionship, medical attention, and help with such mundane concerns as shopping, laundry, transportation, and personal hygiene.[39]

The network of "social assistance units" has been developed most fully in Moscow. Each of the city's thirty-three boroughs has set up at least one of them, and by 1988 there were eighty-seven in all. But they provide services for only some 5,000 people. (More than 40,000 pensioners live by themselves in the capital; of these, 6,600 are believed to require some form of at-home assistance.)[40] Another 8,000 or so individuals living elsewhere in the Russian Republic have access to such arrangements, as do a few individuals residing outside the RSFSR.[41]

For the system to develop further, for it really to ease the situation of the elderly, several steps will have to be taken. In particular, more local initiative will be needed, as will more effective coordination among government agencies and—now that it has become possible—significantly more public-private cooperation. Whether it is even realistic to contemplate such changes is far from clear. To date, initiative and cooperation have not been a prominent feature of the Soviet administrative system. One hopes that the Gorbachev reforms will bring improvements in this sphere.

Nursing Homes

Generally speaking, senior citizens in the USSR live in conditions that Westerners would find unacceptable. Take, for example, the matter of housing. A 1982 survey carried out among elderly persons in Moscow, Sverdlovsk, and Ivanovo and Lvov provinces found that 90 percent of villagers, along with 30 percent of urban dwellers, lived in premises that had no running water. Similarly, 94 percent of those residing in rural areas, and 57 percent in urban areas, had neither a bath nor a shower. With respect to lack of sewage disposal, the figures were 92 percent and 33 percent; and for no central heating, they were 80 percent and 31 percent.[42]

Nevertheless, almost all men and women who reach retirement age, whether or not they are gainfully employed, continue to live in the same apartments or homes where they had been residing. Surveys have shown that virtually all older persons, regardless of their health, want to live with their children. A small number would prefer to live alone, and only a handful express a desire to live in a "home for labor veterans," as Soviet nursing homes are known. A typical study of popular attitudes toward such institutions found that only 1.4 percent of people between the ages of 60 and 75 expressed a desire to live in one.[43]

Their attitude appears to be the product of three factors. (1) The tradition of the three-generation family unit, common in rural areas, continues to seem "natural" to large numbers of urbanites—most of whom are recent migrants, or the offspring of recent migrants, from the countryside. (2) There continues to be a shortage of old-age homes, and those that are in use tend to be of a design poorly suited to the needs of older persons, are maintained inadequately, and are overcrowded. (3) Although elderly widows and widowers experience intense feelings of loneliness, not many of them wish to live with strangers, even if the latter are in the same position.

Though they are few in number, elderly bachelors or widowers are more apt than women who are their age to wind up in a "home for labor veterans." Soviet scholars have found that the various social roles performed by women (as mothers, grandmothers, and housewives) make it relatively easy for them to adapt to their new lives—even though they are cut off from their jobs and the network of friends and colleagues with whom they worked. Men generally find the phenomenon of isolation more troublesome; the small number who manage to outlive their wives face the added difficulty of shopping, preparing meals, and taking care of themselves in other ways—responsibilities for which few males in the USSR, especially those who are advanced in years, are prepared.[44]

In any event, only a very small number of older people, primarily the frail elderly, live in nursing homes; there they receive little more than custodial care. Admission to such an institution is considered "an exceptional measure of social support for an elderly person." It is mandated when "he cannot take care of his own basic needs and is unable, either physically or psychologically, to lead an independent life, and his close relatives (if he has any) are not in a position to arrange constant care for him."[45]

Roughly half the inhabitants of these institutions are actually incapacitated or confined to bed. The rest are in poor health, cannot take care of themselves, and have no family to support them. As a group, they are overwhelmingly from the "old old" population: Almost half (49.5 percent) are 80–89 years of age, and another fourth (29.4 percent) are between the ages of 70 and 79.[46] Those who received pensions before their admission continue to do so, but they are required to surrender 90 percent of their income to pay for their maintenance.[47]

In 1979, there were said to be about 1,500 old-age homes, and 360,000 men and women lived in them. By 1986, the number of occupants had shrunk to 327,000. Another 90,000 persons were on waiting lists, and an unknown number had not even bothered to apply, for they knew how difficult it would be to gain admission.[48]

The number of places set aside in "homes for labor veterans" has not kept up with the increase in the number of very old people, especially those who live alone. In 1960, when Nikita Khrushchev was in power, there were 5 beds per 1,000 elderly persons; the figure rose to 6 in 1965, remained there until the early 1980s, but has since fallen back to 5.[49] During the past several decades, however, the number of "old old" and other elderly people living alone, that is, the pool from which residents of nursing homes are drawn, has increased dramatically. In 1970, 4.7 million persons 60 years of age or older lived alone in various parts of the country. By 1984, the figure had risen to approximately 7 million,[50] and the projected figure in 1988 was 9 million.[51]

Even if more such institutions were available, however, it is unlikely that many citizens would choose to move into one. The existing network of old-age homes consists largely of dilapidated old structures. Special furniture, wheelchairs, and emergency-care medical equipment are almost unheard of, and the buildings lack even the most basic amenities. Residents are, in the most awful sense of the term, simply "warehoused"; government resources are directed elsewhere, while private energies (of the kind so helpfully deployed in the United States) are not coordinated in any sort of organized system of charities.

The authorities periodically promise to upgrade these facilities but actually have done little to implement their own decisions. In January 1987, the Party Central Committee, the USSR Council of Ministers, and the All-Union Central Council of Trade Unions adopted a resolution calling for improvements in services to the elderly. This document promised, inter alia, to increase the number of nursing homes and to outfit them with modern equipment, furniture, and furnishings.[52] Since the decree was promulgated, there has been no significant change of the kind outlined in it.

Economic Status and Concerns

Pensions

The number of persons receiving old-age pensions has increased dramatically, especially since Stalin's death in 1953. Much of the growth can be explained by legislative changes adopted in 1956 and 1965, although the rapid rise in the number of people of pension age also has been a major factor. In 1941, a mere 200,000 people received pensions;[53] by 1961, the number had risen to 5.4 million. In 1976, it reached 29.4 million, increasing to 34 million in 1981 and to more than 43 million by the end of 1989.[54]

But the major laws in effect until 1989—the Law on State Pensions (1956) and the Law on Pensions and Benefits for Collective Farmers (1964)—provided retirees with far less money than they needed. Even with occasional increases over the years, benefits did not even keep up with increases in the cost of living. In 1989, the USSR Supreme Soviet adopted a law with the revealing title, "Emergency Measures for the Improvement of Pension Security and Social Maintenance of the Population." Its main purposes were to eliminate inequities in the system—collective farmers were not even eligible for pensions until 1964, and as recently as 1987, the average *kolkhoznik*'s pension was only 63 percent of the average state pension—and to provide additional support for all retirees. The new legislation provides for an increase in the minimum old-age pension to 70 rubles a month, up from 40 rubles for *kolkhozniki* and 50 rubles for former state employees. According to one estimate, the new rules affect some 8 million of the former and 12.5 million of the latter.[55]

Still, average pension levels are quite low, and there continues to be an upper limit of only 120 rubles a month—not very much in a country where the average monthly wage is about 240 rubles. Although conditions should improve, the typical retiree today lacks the wherewithal to meet anything more than his or her most basic needs. In 1988, the average monthly pension for those who had been workers or office employees was 86 rubles; for collective farmers, it was only 54 rubles. As Prime Minister Nikolai Ryzhkov observed, "These sums are not even what one could call modest."[56]

Another law, scheduled to come into effect in 1991,[57] is supposed to raise benefits still further sometime in the early 1990s. It will do so in two ways. First, it will adjust the mechanism for calculating pensions, increasing benefits to 55 percent of earnings from the current figure of 50 percent. A second change is designed to reinforce the first. At present, as long as a person has put in the requisite number of years (twenty-five for men, twenty for women), he or she will receive a pension. But the size of the award does not vary with the number of years he or she worked. Under the new system, for every year worked beyond the twenty/twenty-five-year threshold now in force, retirees will be paid an additional 1 percent of earnings over and above the basic pension norm.[58]

But the promise of increased pensions will prove to be nothing more than promises unless the decline in the country's overall economic performance is arrested. Any hope for improved living standards assumes that the economic "stagnation" (*zastoi*) of the Brezhnev era, as well as the crises that the USSR has experienced thus far under *perestroika,* will come to an end. As an observer for TASS put it in early 1990, "Without a significant correction to improve the country's economic situation, without an accumulation of social wealth, prospects for an adequate pension fund are nothing more than self-delusion."[59]

The Question of Poverty

In 1956–1957, Soviet scholars specializing in the field of social security established a definition and a measure of "poverty" in their country.[60] The term they used was *maloobespechennye* ("under provided for," rather than "poor"); families whose per capita monthly earnings were less than 25–30 rubles were included in this category. For our purposes, what is most relevant is the overlap between the elderly population and citizens whose income defined them as *maloobespechennye*. The average pension did not reach 25–30 rubles per month until 1960, which means that at least 50 percent of all old-age pensioners received monthly payments putting them below the poverty line. According to estimates prepared by the British economist Alastair McAuley, the average collective-farm pension in 1965 was approximately 13 rubles a month, and the vast majority of elderly *kolkhozniki* and *kolkhoznitsy* actually received the minimum pension—12 rubles a month.

In the mid-1960s, a new definition of poverty was adopted, largely because inflation had altered the structure of incomes and prices. The threshold below which individuals were considered "under provided for" was set at 50–56 rubles, but only at the end of the 1970s did the average pension actually reach this level. Thus, more than half of all retirees had to live on incomes that were held below the poverty line, and until recently, average pension levels were barely above the statutory minimum.

At the end of the 1980s,[61] the official poverty line was an income of 75 rubles; according to Soviet economists, 43 million people lived below that level. (In 1989, the State Committee on Statistics suggested that a more realistic definition was 100–110 rubles a month per person. If adopted as the official standard—and a combination of higher inflation and greater *glasnost'* is a strong argument for it—this change would increase the number of individuals living in poverty to about 105 million, or more than a third of the country's population.) Because average pension levels are so low, it appears that a *majority* of pensioners currently receive benefits that put them below the poverty level.

To be sure, some of the elderly can count on financial support from their children. As we have seen, however, the number is not great—perhaps 5–10 percent of retirees receive aid regularly. Furthermore, senior citizens who are poor tend to save less than do those who are more prosperous (studies have shown that households with a per capita income of less than 75 rubles a month save less than 1 percent of their income). This amount is hardly enough to live on, much less tide them over in times of crisis. As William Moskoff pointed out, "The poor save less because they earn less, and they receive lower pensions because they have earned less in the past." Unless social-security benefits are increased, these individuals will face increasing difficulty. Even now, the condition of some borders on the desperate: They are "caught in the double trap of having low pensions with which to support themselves and no backstop in the form of savings to compensate for these low pensions."

But attempts to alleviate the problem of poverty among this segment of the population often collide with "old thinking" within the bureaucracy.[62] Indeed, many officials continue to deny that a problem exists. One journalist who raised the question at the Chief Social Security Administration (a unit of the USSR State Committee on Labor and Social Questions) was told pointedly, "There's no such problem here, because it's not supposed to exist."

Perhaps the government does not even want to know how bad the situation is; at present it is not trying to gather data on this topic. Furthermore, statistics on social problems, far more abundant since Gorbachev came to power, shed little light on the links between poverty and old age. One source of difficulty is the fact that although begging is a criminal offense, men over 60 years of age and women over 55 are exempted from the law. The police generally confine themselves to chasing elderly beggars away, viewing them as something of an eyesore or public nuisance. (In rare cases, such individuals may be sent to a hospital for treatment or be placed in nursing homes or institutions for the disabled.)

Nevertheless, one can certainly find pathetic-looking old people near the entryways and exits of churches or mosques, asking for money or looking mournfully at parishioners. Even in downtown Moscow, men and women wait in pedestrian underpasses or public parks, asking for handouts. Many have been abandoned by their children and grandchildren; others do not qualify for pensions or receive only paltry sums; still others cannot find a space in a "home for labor veterans." One such person, asked by a Soviet newspaperman why she was begging, declared: "My children won't help me, and I don't get a pension because I didn't put in enough years. They won't take me at the old people's home; they say there isn't any room."

Pensioners in the Labor Force

Since January 1, 1980, men and women of pension age, who have been employed in certain occupations, have had the option of having their pension raised by 10 rubles per month for every additional year they work *after* becoming eligible to retire. (The law does, however, place a ceiling of 150 rubles on pension benefits for individuals who choose this scheme.[63]) Persons who have maintained an unbroken record of employment at any enterprise for fifteen years are eligible for a 10 percent increase in their pensions, while anyone with twenty-five or more years of uninterrupted service may receive an additional 20 percent, on top of the 10 percent granted for fifteen years of uninterrupted work. (Women with children are eligible for the extra 20 percent if they put in twenty or more years without interruption at the same plant.[64])

This elaborate array of financial incentives has had a definite effect on labor-force participation rates among older workers. Even though the available evidence is sketchy, it appears that the principal factor inducing men and (to a lesser degree) women to continue working is the promise of more income. The desire (or need) to continue earning money is cited by slightly more than half the males questioned in several surveys; the figure for women ranges from about one-fourth to two-fifths. In contrast, the decision *not* to work seems to hinge on nonfinancial considerations. The most important of these is the desire to avoid heavy physical labor, but the lack of opportunities to work part-time or to work at home also pushes people toward retirement as soon as they become eligible.

Not surprisingly, women approach the work-retirement decision with a very different mind-set from that of their male counterparts. In particular, women tend to retire in order to deal with family responsibilities, for example, to take care of grandchildren or to liberate children and/or grandchildren to study, work, or enjoy additional leisure.[65]

At the present time, more than one of every three pensioners is employed. Most of these men and women have full-time jobs, while a few work part-time; some continue in the same position they occupied before reaching retirement age, while others have moved on (either voluntarily or involuntarily) to another job. Almost all of these individuals decided to continue working without interruption, even though they could have retired; only a handful left the labor force, reconsidered their decision, and returned to work.

Virtually all pensioners who want to continue working after "retirement" have had to take full-time jobs, either staying on at their regular place of employment or seeking a position elsewhere. Very few have the opportunity to work part-time, whether a few hours a day or a few days a week. Various surveys of pensioners with jobs have put the number working at home at less than 1 percent of the overall sample; even fewer—between 0.3 and 1 percent, it is estimated—enjoy a reduced workday or workweek.[66] According to one estimate, only 9,000 out of a total of 2,000,000 working pensioners in the Russian Federation—less than 0.5 percent—are employed part-time.[67] A more comprehensive and detailed survey of Muscovites, carried out in 1973–1975, drew a picture that was only slightly more encouraging. According to the investigators, fully 86 percent of all working pensioners in that city had to put in a full day, even though 58 percent of the sample expressed a desire to work part-time.[68]

Whether the shortage of part-time jobs (including at-home employment) results in a net gain to the labor force (because workers who would prefer to work part-time must work full-time) or a net loss (because individuals who would like to work part-time cannot do so) is unclear. What is absolutely certain is that existing programs and policies do not meet the needs of older men and women.

Throughout the country, more and more men reaching 60 and women reaching 55 are deciding to continue working. According to the 1970 census, 12.4 percent of all pension-age people had jobs. Five years later, the figure had almost doubled, and it now exceeds one-third of all age-eligibles.[69] In the larger industrial cities, whose populations tend to be a good deal older than the national average, the rate of increase has been especially high. Perhaps most strikingly, in recent years, more than 60 percent of all new pensioners have chosen to work, rather than to retire,[70] so we can expect the total number of working pensioners to rise still further.

For the foreseeable future, financial considerations are likely to play an increasingly important role in the work-retirement decision. Even with the recent passage of "emergency" legislation to increase benefits, pension levels remain quite low. Since 1956, the year of a major reform in social-security arrangements, the average wage has doubled. Over the same period, the average pension has also increased, but at a much slower pace, and the maximum old-age pension has remained virtually the same. Thus, in 1956, the highest pension was more than 1.5 times the average wage; today, the average wage is roughly 3 times the average pension and approximately twice the maximum pension.[71] In view of growing evidence of inflation in the USSR, prudent men and women who reach retirement age are unlikely to feel secure with only the promise of a pension.

Concluding Remarks

One of the best ways to assess the health of a society, a Soviet journalist wrote, is to look at how it treats its elderly.[72] An examination of the situation of older men and women in the USSR today, the kinds of programs that have been devised to make their lives easier—focusing on their physical and financial circumstances—leaves an observer with a feeling of profound disquiet. Decades of failed economic programs, inadequate social-security arrangements, and a health-care system far more interested in keeping people at work than in providing quality care of the elderly, have conspired to offer most senior citizens little more than financial and medical insecurity. They, like the rest of the population—indeed, like Gorbachev himself, his program of *perestroika,* and the Soviet political and economic system more generally—face a decidedly uncertain future.

Notes

1. See Robert Conquest, *Industrial Workers in the USSR* (London: Bodley Head, 1967), p. 99.
2. *Narodnoe khoziastvo SSSR v 1985 g.* (Moscow: Finansy i Statistika, 1986), p. 547.

3. *Narodnoe khoziaistvo SSSR v 1988 g.* (Moscow: Finansy i Statistika, 1989), p. 30.

4. *Itogi Vsesoiuznoi perepisi naseleniia 1959 goda,* SSSR, Svodnyi tom (Moscow: Gosstatizdat, 1962), p. 85; *Vestnik statistiki,* no. 2 (1974), p. 95.

5. *Vestnik Moskovskogo Universiteta,* seriia 6, no. 1 (1981), p. 59.

6. *Argumenty i fakty,* no. 18 (1987), p. 7; *Narodnoe khoziaistvo SSSR v 1988 g.,* op. cit., p. 30.

7. This paragraph and the one following are derived from *Vestnik Moskovskogo Universiteta,* op. cit., p. 59.

8. V. I. Kozlov, *Natsional'nosti SSSR: Etnodemograficheskii obzor,* 2nd ed. rev. (Moscow: Finansy i Statistika, 1982), pp. 197-198.

9. See Stephen Sternheimer, "The Graying of the Soviet Union," *Problems of Communism* 31, no. 5 (September-October 1982), pp. 81-82; *Planovoe khoziaistvo,* no. 11 (1988), p. 114.

10. Article 120 of the 1936 Constitution; Article 43 of the 1977 Constitution.

11. Soviet figures are taken from *Narodnoe khoziaistvo SSSR v 1988 g.,* op. cit., pp. 220 and 222. The U.S. figures, the most recent available, are for 1987. See *Statistical Abstract of the United States,* 110th ed. (Washington, D.C.: U.S. Dept of Commerce, Bureau of the Census, 1990), pp. 101, 105.

12. See L. L. Rybakovskii (ed.), *Naselenie SSSR za 70 let* (Moscow: Nauka, 1988), p. 135.

13. See Mark G. Field, *Doctor and Patient in Soviet Russia* (Cambridge, Mass.: Harvard University Press, 1957). See also Field, "Medical Care in the Soviet Union: Promises and Realities," in Horst Herlemann (ed.), *Quality of Life in the Soviet Union* (Boulder, Colo.: Westview Press, 1987), pp. 74-78.

14. *Narodnoe khoziaistvo SSSR v 1985 g.,* op. cit., p. 560; *Pravda,* November 18, 1986.

15. *Narodnoe khoziaistvo SSSR v 1985 g.,* op. cit., p. 365; *Narodnoe khoziaistvo SSSR v 1988 g.,* op. cit., pp. 553, 554; *Izvestiia,* December 18, 1989.

16. *Pravda* and *Izvestiia,* June 30, 1988.

17. *Pravda,* January 28, 1990.

18. See Chapter 5. See also *Sovetskaia Rossiia,* July 5, 1987; *Pravda* and *Izvestiia,* June 30, 1988.

19. *Pravda,* November 9, 1989.

20. *Washington Post,* January 11, 1990.

21. Christopher M. Davis, "The Organization and Performance of the Contemporary Soviet Health Service," in Gail W. Lapidus and Guy E. Swanson (eds.), *State and Welfare USA/USSR* (Berkeley, Calif.: Institute of International Studies, 1988), p. 102; *Sotsialisticheskaia industriia,* September 11, 1988.

22. *Pravda* and *Izvestiia,* June 30, 1988.

23. Ibid.

24. William A. Knaus, *Inside Russian Medicine* (New York: Everest, 1981), pp. 219-220.

25. *Izvestiia,* January 7 and February 7, 1986.

26. *Izvestiia,* June 13, 1986.

27. Knaus, op. cit., p. 343.

28. Ibid., pp. 342-343.

29. The following section is based on V. Kogan, "Odinokie prestarelye—problemy i puti ikh sotsial'nogo obsluzhivaniia," in D. I. Valentei et al. (eds.), *Naselenie tret'ego vozrasta* (Moscow: Mysl', 1986), pp. 107-131.

30. See Knaus, op. cit., p. 108.

31. Dmitri F. Chebotarev and Nina N. Sachuk, "Union of Soviet Socialist Republics," in Erdman Palmore (ed.), *International Handbook on Aging* (Westport, Conn.: Greenwood Press, 1980), p. 408.

32. M. Potekhina and V. Turchaninova, "Meditsinskaia pomoshch' pozhilym liudiam," in D. I. Valentei et al. (eds.), *Zdorov'e pozhilykh liudei* (Moscow: Mysl', 1978), pp. 41-42.

33. Ibid., p. 43.

34. *Sobesednik*, no. 48 (1986).

35. Ibid.

36. Kogan, op. cit., pp. 124-125; E. G. Azarova and A. E. Kozlov, *Lichnost' i sotsial'noe obespechenie v SSSR* (Moscow: Nauka, 1983), p. 186; *Izvestiia*, September 19, 1986.

37. Kogan, op. cit., p. 36.

38. V. E. Gordin, *Chem starost' obespechim* (Moscow: Mysl', 1988), p. 58.

39. Ibid.; *Pravda*, May 21, 1985; *Meditsinskaia gazeta*, November 25, 1987; *Sem'ia i shkola*, no. 9 (1989), pp. 31-33.

40. *Sotsial'noe obespechenie*, no. 5 (1987), p. 25; E. G. Tukhkov and M. L. Zakharov, *Sotsial'noe obespechenie i obsluzhivanie pensionerov* (Moscow: Nauka, 1988), pp. 159-160.

41. *Sovetskaia Rossiia*, May 28, 1987; Gordin, op. cit., pp. 409-410.

42. Gordin, op. cit., pp. 63-64.

43. A. V. Dmitriev, *Sotsial'nye problemy liudei pozhilogo vozrasta* (Leningrad: Nauka Leningradskoe otdelenie, 1980), p. 59, n. 14. See also Chebotarev and Sachuk, op. cit., pp. 409-410.

44. Dmitriev, op. cit., pp. 56-57, 64-65, and 68-70; Stephen Sternheimer, "The Vanishing *Babushka:* A Roleless Role for Older Soviet Women?" in Herlemann, op. cit., pp. 133-149.

45. V. A. Acharkan, *Obespechenie veteranov truda v SSSR* (Moscow: Nauka, 1985), p. 86.

46. Kogan, op. cit., p. 33; Gordin, op. cit., pp. 67-68.

47. Mervyn Matthews, *Poverty in the Soviet Union* (Cambridge and New York: Cambridge University Press, 1986), p. 52.

48. *Moskovskie novosti*, no. 4 (1988), p. 12.

49. Calculated from figures in Matthews, op. cit., p. 5; Kogan, op. cit., p. 31; Chebotarev and Sachuk, op. cit., pp. 409-410.

50. *Sovetskoe gosudarstvo i pravo*, no. 12 (1986), p. 8; M. Ia. Sonin and A. A. Dyskin, *Pozhiloi chelovek v sem'e i obshchestve* (Moscow: Finansy i Statistika, 1984), p. 163.

51. Gordin, op. cit., pp. 59-61.

52. *Pravda*, January 23, 1987.

53. Alastair McAuley gave a figure of 225,000. See his "Social Policy," in Archie Brown and Michael Kaser (eds.), *Soviet Policy for the 1980s* (Bloomington: Indiana University Press, 1982), p. 157.

54. *Sobesednik*, no. 48 (1986); *Pravda* and *Izvestiia*, November 3, 1989.

55. See D. J. Peterson, "Supreme Soviet Adopts Emergency Pension Measures," *Report on the USSR* 1, no. 33 (August 18, 1989), pp. 7-9.

56. *Pravda* and *Izvestiia*, November 3, 1989. See also *Vestnik statistiki*, no. 6 (1988), pp. 10-11.

57. *Ogonek*, no. 7 (1989), p. 32.

58. *Pravda* and *Izvestiia*, November 3, 1989. See also *Vestnik statistiki*, no. 6 (1988), pp. 10-11.

59. *Trud,* January 3, 1990.
60. This and the following paragraph are derived from McAuley, op. cit., pp. 150-162, and Mervyn Matthews, "Aspects of Poverty in the Soviet Union," in Herlemann, op. cit., pp. 51-52.
61. This and the following paragraph are derived from William Moskoff, "The Aged in the USSR," *Report on the USSR* 1, no. 37 (September 15, 1989), pp. 7-9, and *Pravda* and *Izvestiia,* November 3, 1989.
62. The following discussion is drawn primarily from *Argumenty i fakty,* no. 40 (1989), p. 4.
63. *Pravda,* October 2, 1979.
64. *Sotsialisticheskaia zakonnost',* no. 11 (1983), pp. 54-55. See also T. Anthony Jones and William Moskoff, "Pensioners in the Soviet Labour Force: The Limits of Monetary Inducements," *Soviet Studies* 39, no. 1 (January 1987), pp. 88-90.
65. William Moskoff, "Part-Time Employment in the Soviet Union," *Soviet Studies* 34, no. 2 (April 1982), pp. 279-280.
66. A. G. Novitskii and G. V. Mil', *Zaniatost' pensionerov: sotsialno-demograficheskii aspekt* (Moscow: Finansy i Statistika, 1971), p. 94; A. G. Novitskii, "Istochnik formirovaniia zaniatosti s rezhimom nepolnogo rabochego vremeni i v poriadke nadomnichestva," in A. Z. Maikov and A. G. Novitskii (eds.), *Problemy nepolnogo rabochego vremeni i zaniatost' naseleniia* (Moscow: Statistika, 1975), p. 60; *Kommunist,* no. 2 (1980), p. 54.
67. A. G. Novitskii, "Dopolnitel'nyi istochnik rabochei sily sfery obsluzhivaniia," in *Narodonaselenie: naselenie i trudovye resursy* (Moscow: Statistika, 1973), p. 59.
68. *Sotsiologicheskie issledovaniia,* no. 1 (1976), p. 110.
69. *Sotsialisticheskii trud,* no. 12 (1987), p. 80. See also V. P. Belov (ed.), *Trudosposobnost' pensionerov po starosti: voprosy stimulirovaniia i organizatsii ikh truda* (Moscow: Tsentral'nyi nauchno-issledovatel'skii institut ekspertizy trudosposobnosti i organizatsii truda invalidov, 1975), pp. 6, 141.
70. Jones and Moskoff, op. cit.
71. *Ekonomika i organizatsiia promyshlennogo proizvodstva,* no. 5 (1978), p. 29, and no. 7 (1988), pp. 7-8; *Ogonek,* no. 7 (1989), pp. 31-32.
72. *Sem'ia i shkola,* no. 9 (1989), p. 33.

CHAPTER 11

No End of a Problem: *Perestroika* for the Family?

Peter H. Juviler

Rulers, experts, groups, and individuals see "social problems" from their own points of view. For them all, though, a "problem" is something in people's behavior or relations that calls for change. Rarely if ever can a social problem be solved without causing new conflicts. Often "solving" a problem may be the lesser of two evils. Family problems are no exception.

In their approaches to family problems, the first Soviet leaders vacillated between need of the family and distrust of it. They put need ahead of distrust by the mid-1930s.[1] Today both women and the government, in their own ways, see conflicting interests in women's working and their staying home to have more children and look after the family. Both women and the government are torn between family stability and free choice. "Katya," for example, represents the two of every three Soviet women who stick with their marriages. She wants at least two children but can cope with only one. She is determined come what may to end her second pregnancy. Her choices in family planning are unenviable. Katya's husband, Ivan, a man in his own way devoted to his wife and daughter, sighs, nods in assent, and settles back into his *Ogonek* magazine to read more frank complaints about *perestroika*.

Perestroika connotes for its Soviet sponsors a comprehensive renewal of Soviet society by freeing human potential.[2] Yet the complications in Katya and Ivan's family life and workplace connected with *perestroika* seem to drain as much as release their "human potential." The couple's life has become more than ever a study in contrasts between new public words of concern and hope and the growing difficulties of everyday life. For Ivan and his wife *perestroika* means more interesting reading (for Katya, when she has a chance), modest increases in family benefits, but more complications at home and at work.

Family problems in their present forms reflect at once the shift of work—and working women—out of the family and the special destructiveness of Stalin's "revolution from above" in 1928–1934. Family breakup and drops in birthrates spelled demographic crisis in the 1930s. Stalin exacted a toll of millions of casualties during agricultural collectivization.

He brutally dispossessed peasant farming families and spurred a rural-urban flight and women's recruitment into the labor force. Stalin then called in 1935 for "strengthening the family" as society's demographic wellspring. This meant between 1936 and 1944 a largely coercive program of banning abortions, curbing divorce, and limiting the recognition of paternity only to registered marriage. A double burden of work and homemaking as well as the responsibilities of extramarital parenthood fell increasingly on women's shoulders.[3]

Stalin's successors saw the solution to problems of family infertility and instability in a less-compulsive accommodation. They allowed greater freedom of reproductive and marital choice, and they increased pronatalist incentives. Despite the "stagnation" and political repression of the Brezhnev period, families could look on it as a period of reform and betterment, as one on the whole alleviating (if not eliminating) *their* problems of daily life, choice, and material security.[4]

But decreasing family size and rising rates of divorce during the 1960s and 1970s betokened problems of illegitimacy and single-parent families, conflicting pulls of work and home, unresolved tensions of married life. This chapter reviews the impact of *perestroika* on problems of family size and issues of ethnic differences, women's role conflict, family health, abortions, family instability, the new beginnings of family and women's advocacy, and the turn to family enterprise.

Family Size: "Social and Personal Interests"

A party decree in 1930 under Stalin put an end to "harmful utopian schemes" of eliminating the family, calling them premature in the light of both resources and attitudes. But diehard collectivists, seeing selfish individualism as the enduring problem in the family, held fast to the idea of communal upbringing until Khrushchev conclusively repudiated it in 1961.[5] Brezhnev echoed the 1966 International Covenant on Social and Economic Rights in his 1977 Constitution, putting the family "under protection of the state."[6]

Today if the populace and the Communist party agree on one thing, it is that *perestroika* should leave the family intact as source and upbringer of coming generations. The problem has been how best to motivate the family to do these things.[7] The USSR Supreme Court under Brezhnev ordered Soviet jurists to keep in mind the CPSU's commitment to protecting the family, "in which social and personal interests blend harmoniously."[8] Moscow's social interests center on bringing birthrate patterns into line with economic and political needs. Whereas the Chinese government wants fewer babies, the Soviet government wants more of them. One hears from a demographer that "we have begun to leave democratic stagnation behind. National birthrates are rising."[9]

The rise in birthrates began, however, under Brezhnev, not Gorbachev, and quite possibly because of his pronatalist measures of 1981. These measures came about after a heated debate among more- and less-feminist points of view; it was decided that women should be encouraged to spend more time as mothers and less as workers. That men should help more hardly entered the debate. A 1981 Party decision initiated increases in various family grants, maternity leaves, and allowances. Brezhnev's reforms in family law, leaves, and allowances had as their aim bolstering the family to perform its task of procreation, upbringing, and mutual support.[10] The present government stands by this position.

The population expert Murray Feshbach called the policy "remarkably successful."[11] The decline in birthrates stopped, and birthrates began to increase in the 1980s. More children have been born recently than at any time since before World War II, not only in an echo of the postwar baby boom but also because a higher proportion of fertile women have begun to have two or three children instead of one or two.[12]

The extended maternity leave has proved to be popular. Ninety-two percent of women working and studying who became mothers in 1983 availed themselves of the right to a year's partially paid leave and half-year's unpaid leave to care for their children, a rate of use of extended leave about five times higher than before the partial pay began to apply in 1981.[13] Every one of the many Soviet mothers asked by this writer explained that she now feels increasingly obligated to avail herself of the modest new incentives and stay home a year or two with her new child because of the poor upbringing and risks of infection in the huge Soviet child-care network.[14]

The modest demographic turnabout in the 1980s appears to have vindicated noncoercive approaches to shaping family choices. But it leaves unanswered the question of how far to differentiate among nationalities in family policy.

Family Allowances and Ethnic Differences

Demographers have debated for years whether funds for family support should differentiate among nationalities. Should allowances be raised for small families? These are typical of non-Moslem regions and ethnic groups. Their children have been most easily absorbed into the urban work force.

During Brezhnev's time, the government rejected as un-Leninist and discriminatory Russian suggestions to redistribute family incentives from large to small families, in effect, away from Central Asia and parts of the Caucasus. But since the 1970s fears of the growing regional "disproportion" in population growth have kept alive the issue dividing demographers and officials: Should family allowances not peak at levels of two or three children instead of ten children? That would mean persons of Moslem descent and other nationalities favoring large families would lose benefits; the benefits would shift to families of European nationalities.[15]

A tally of Mother Heroine awards (medals, cash, and allowances) to mothers who had raised at least ten children showed that 87 percent of them went to Central Asia, a region with 10 percent of the Soviet population. Awards per 100,000 population reached 66.3 in Tadzhikistan, compared with 0.7 in the Ukraine, 1.4 in the RSFSR, 0.4 in Latvia![16]

Moslem women of Central Asia expect to have about three times as many children as do Russian women: Turkmen women, on the average, anticipate more than six children, whereas Russian women anticipate fewer than two.[17] Soviets forecast that more Moslems will be born than non-Moslems by the early twenty-first century. Birthrates among Soviet Europeans have not risen high enough to avoid a milder version of Western Europe's failure to reproduce itself.[18]

All political considerations aside (which they are probably not in fact), the shift in the center of population gravity eastward stirs fears about the "quality" of the future labor force, given the relatively low level of training and urbanization of the Moslem families. "Sociologists note the low territorial and social mobility of large families," wrote demographer Anatoly Vyshnevskii, chief researcher of the USSR Academy of Sciences Commission for the Study of the Labor Force and Natural Resources, in the Party journal *Kommunist,* "and sometimes the conservative role they play in handing down social relations and structures, social consciousness. One must keep all this is mind when assessing the recent noticeable increases in birthrates in the republics of Central Asia and Kazakhstan."[19]

Moslem rural life entails not just a separateness from the modern urban economy (outside of farming industrial crops like cotton). It entails also special restraints on the advance of women, the persistence of practices like bride price and polygamy, as well as the virtual confinement of women in some families. An investigative reporter looking into "cruel" customs in Central Asia reported that forty girls in Tadzhikistan had ended their lives by self-immolation in 1986, according to the Ministry of Internal Affairs, because their families would not let them go to school or wanted to force a marriage on them, or after having been beaten by their husbands.[20]

Also asserting that "demographic problems require a fundamentally different approach," Yurii Riurikov followed quite another tangent but one still disadvantaging non-Europeans. He envisaged rewarding families according to their offspring's creativity and development of their potential.[21] Both Riurikov's and the other proposals for combatting birthrate "disproportions" mean a redistribution in favor of the best educated, most accomplished, and most talented families. In the case of Riurikov's proposals to reward creativity, not only the Moslems but also the less advantaged generally might object.

Regional differentiation has begun to appear in the two lowest-fertility areas, Latvia and Estonia. These republics have been allowed to provide additional birth incentives to young families.[22] Baltic-Russian relations within those republics are affected by the Balts' fear of inundation by younger, and therefore more fertile, Russian immigrants. A proposal for additional benefits to families one of whose members had lived in Estonia a stated number of years (e.g., five or fifteen) favored nonimmigrant, that is, Estonian families, over Russian families. This evoked angry protests on the part of Russian immigrants.[23] In response, Estonians sought limits on immigration and citizenship rights tied to past residence in the republic.

Women's Conflicting Roles

"Who was I? Yevgeniya Albats, a journalist," wrote a Moscow correspondent assigned to cover her own pregnancy. "But a wife too, wasn't I? Of course I was, and that entailed cooking, laundering, house cleaning. Yet inside me, in my heart of hearts, I was before all else a journalist."[24] Albats wrote not one word about any help from her husband in the round of prenatal preparations. In her society, on the average, women put in nearly three times as much housework each week as men do.[25]

Perestroika has brought increases in family benefits such as child-care leaves, extra assistance to poor families and large single-parent families, and a minimum for child support. The new benefits hardly make a dent in the material difficulties of life among the numerous Soviet poor.[26] Whatever their incomes, mothers' living standards and motivations to have more children will depend not just on direct incentives, such as maternity and child-care leaves, and modest income supplements. The real meaning of "the equality of women and men" and "the protection of motherhood" emerges out of the totality of maternity rights, social attitudes, living standards, and a mother's burdens that daily difficulties increase.[27] Albats wrote with disdain about the 35-ruble monthly pay on extended leave when "a baby carriage costs more." Moscow is the best-supplied Russian city, but the clothes at the special shop for expectant mothers fell dismally short of the promise in the booklet issued Albats by the Ministry of Health—no nursing bra that fit, no cotton panties. "The doctors tell me to move about as much as possible," Albats wrote, "and I do move, from one drugstore to another," in search of a few-kopek pacifier.[28]

Such difficulties daily aggravate women's leading problem in family life—its conflict with their work outside the home.[29] Soviet women are either studying or almost fully employed, at the highest rate for industrialized countries. Women make up more than half the Soviet labor force overall and less than half only in the least-industrialized border republics.[30]

Soviet experts and the public continue to debate as they have for years how best to resolve women's conflict between work and family obligations. Nonfeminists blame juvenile crime and delinquency on working women's neglect of their children. People inclined more to a feminist perspective suggest better child care as a solution, meaning better-staffed and more-hygienic facilities. The head of the Soviet Women's Committee (a government-sponsored organization) blamed delinquency not on women but on economic backwardness and violations of labor laws protecting women (laws restricting their work on night shifts, calling for flexible-time and part-time jobs, and so forth). These women's advocates hardly appreciate the new symbols of women femininity, beauty pageants. Nor will they agree with the sixteen-year-old winner of Moscow Beauty '88 that Soviet beauty pageants differ from Western ones "because we have *perestroika*."[31]

The government in the 1980s, whether under Brezhnev or Gorbachev, has inclined toward encouraging women to stay home more with young children. For Gorbachev the issue was not whether women should do this but "how to enable women to return to their purely womanly mission."[32] That is a "mission impossible" and, like the TV exploits, achieved at no small cost in effort and ingenuity.

When her family was poor, a Soviet mother and part-time head librarian told this writer, "we believed that explained our everyday difficulties which were bad enough. But when our incomes increased above most other people's, I still found myself spending hours waiting in lines and hunting all over for basic necessities." "Every day," one read in *Ogonek* magazine, "more goods disappear which once were plentiful. We can't get razor blades to shave with, soap to wash with, paste to clean our teeth with, nothing." For the librarian such scarcities meant that "no matter how hard we work or how well we earn, life remains difficult, especially for us mothers."[33]

The Family's Health Imperiled

Albats pointed to the extra and debilitating strain associated with maternity, at a cost in health and premature births. Shortcomings in her prenatal care lead us to the general question of health care for the family.

Albats received prenatal care at her district "women's consultation" clinic, where each wait lasted long enough to permit her to read through a long article in a thick journal. The laboratory assistant drew blood samples with a reusable syringe. Albats fervently hoped she was a good lab assistant and properly sterilized the reusable syringe used to draw blood from Albats for testing, opposite a sign about AIDS and its transmission. "But what if she's not?" Every pregnant woman is supposed to be tested for AIDS. But the USSR Public Health Ministry's Chief Department of Medical Care and Hygiene for Children and Mothers "had no idea how the test was being administered." She noted that the department should have been especially concerned about supplies of disposable syringes in the USSR, a world leader in rates of viral hepatitis.[34]

Lack of disposable syringes, plus the failure of medical personnel to sterilize reusable ones, has been implicated in the infection with AIDS of at least forty-one children and eight mothers in a children's hospital of Elista in the Kalmyk Autonomous Republic in 1988[35] and the infection with AIDS of at least ten more children in Volgograd.[36] The AIDS infections mean for families of the afflicted a price, not only in health and lives, but also in the burdens and costs of special care, the misery of ostracism, "and a blank wall of malevolence, suspicion and hostility."[37]

The careful reader could learn even before *glasnost'* about bad medical care and a lethally polluted and irradiated physical environment taking their toll of people's health.[38] The discussion of these problems became more open after *perestroika* began in 1985. The USSR minister of health at the time, Dr. Evgenii Ivanovich Chazov, pushed a more vigorous response to the crisis in Soviet health care. A trigger for his concern seemed to be the high Soviet mortality rate, back in print after more than a decade of secrecy.[39]

The writer A. A. Likhanov, head of the Soviet Children's Fund, a public organization founded under governmental aegis in October 1987 to help children and the family and protect children against abuse and threats to their health, deplored Soviet infant-mortality rates (up to age one year), 25.4 deaths per 1,000 live births—2.5 times U.S. rates, 5 times Japanese.[40] This understates the problem. Soviet rates are actually at least 15 percent higher by standard international calculation, that is about 29, or 3 times the U.S. average and 6 times the Japanese.[41]

Infant-mortality rates reflect the backward conditions of care and sanitation in regions like the Turkmen Republic of Central Asia. It registered the highest republic rate of infant mortality, 58.2, in 1987. The lowest rate, 11.3, obtained in the Latvian Republic.[42]

According to Likhanov the infant-mortality rates were "an obvious sign of social injustice and neglect, striking evidence of obsolete approaches to child care," cultural backwardness, and poor hygiene.[43] The Soviet press carries evidence of what makes Soviet efforts to stem infant-mortality rate no better than fiftieth in the world, behind Barbados and the United Arab Emirates: The government diverts resources to elite medical care and defense spending;[44] heavy pollution and alcoholism take their toll.[45] Drug addiction receives growing mention both as a threat to health and as a symptom of parents' estrangement from their children.[46] Every year thousands of mothers reject their children, leaving them in the scandalously bad and often brutal care prevailing in 80 percent of the state homes for orphaned and abandoned children.[47]

Abortions: The Lack of Informed Choice

Abortions pose a special health issue in the USSR, land of the world's highest abortion rates by far. Among groups practicing family planning, approximately 2.5 abortions take place for every live birth.[48] Illegal abortions still occur in huge numbers despite the lifting of the ban on abortions in 1955. They reach as high as 80 percent of all abortions in some parts of the country. Reports on the situation appear often now in the mass-circulation press. People ranging from skilled doctors to quacks perform the abortions for various fees, under many levels of medical care.

The Soviet press conveys some of the background of such illegal abortions. Sometimes the patients are hoping for better treatment than in the grim state abortion clinics.[49] They may wish to keep their abortions secret and avoid the humiliation and gossip that may come from leaks in the formal procedures of medical leave and passage through the abortion clinic.[50] Sometimes they had illegal abortions after expiration of the three-month time limit (now extended). Abortions that are self-inflicted or performed by unqualified persons may have tragic results. Soviet specialists estimate that about 80 percent of abortions, with their risks of medical damage to the woman, would not have taken place had effective means of contraception been widely available. Decades after the relegalizing of abortions, Soviet health authorities have as yet provided no effective and widely available substitute for them in family planning.

But a long-overdue extension of the period of pregnancy during which nontherapeutic abortions may be induced legally responds to this epidemic of illegal abortions. An order of the USSR Ministry of Health has extended the limit on nonmedical abortions from three months to twenty-eight weeks of pregnancy (longer than the six-month limit of protection for abortion rights under the 1973 U.S. Supreme Court decision). The mother seeking an abortion after the third month must state why, but the grounds are broad and respond to the rise in pregnancies of very young teenagers, and cases of hardship, ranging from family size, penal convictions, and death of one's husband to "other real life situations that, objectively speaking, make the birth of a child undesirable," in the words of a health official.[51]

Family Breakdown

One in three Soviet marriages ends in divorce. The Soviet national divorce rate of 3.4 remains the highest of any other industrialized country except the United States. The 950,000 divorces annually leave 700,000 children in single-parent families. Among European and urbanized populations in the USSR every second marriage on the average ends in divorce—just where birthrates are lowest.[52]

Experts who think that somehow legal limits and bonds can "strengthen the family" argue for longer waiting periods between application and marriage than the present two-week minimum (in dubious cases the maximum is three months, at the civil registry's discretion) and for tougher divorce law. Opponents of compulsion counter that longer waiting periods are just not feasible because half the young brides are pregnant. Erecting obstacles to divorce will simply lead to a return to the unofficial divorce and de facto remarriage practiced in the past. One remedy the opponents urge is for the government to implement constitutional rights to preferred work and housing. This, they say, would reduce the gender imbalance, which tends to destabilize families. A gender imbalance in rural areas, for example, comes about because women flee from unpleasant living and working conditions. The perennial lack of urban housing for newlyweds leaves them the alternatives of married life in dormitories or crammed in with parents. Moreover, young couples are ill prepared for marriage.[53]

The unstable mix of Soviet marriages outside of the Caucasus, Central Asia, and regions of traditionalist nationalities is likely to last and to confound any attempted *perestroika* in family therapy, as long as men tend to drink heavily and abuse and deceive their wives, and as long as women tire of unrewarding unions and assert their financial independence. Seventy percent of divorce proceedings are initiated by women.[54]

Couples divorcing by consent and without minor children may register their breakup at the civil registry office, after a three-month wait, upon a 50-ruble payment. In other cases those suing for divorce must turn to the courts. The court may delay divorce, imposing a reconciliation period of up to six months. No-fault grounds for divorce center on evidence (easily found) that the family "has broken down beyond repair." Court-assigned divorce-registration fees vary from 50 to 250 rubles.[55] The government's perennial message to the courts dealing with divorce cases is that they are to stop "underestimating the importance of court proceedings in the cause of strengthening the family and holding parents more responsible for their children's upbringing."[56]

New Beginnings in Family and Women's Advocacy

Citizens, said one commentary on family size, should cast off "medical paternalism," and stop being only passive recipients of health campaigns and to channel their growing dissatisfaction with medical care into concerted action through "new democratic forms of organization," for promoting family planning, family interests, and health.[57] Stopping a ministry from building a polluting factory may prove easier than goading health authorities into a genuine *perestroika* of medical care, especially as long as women lack a vigorous independent voice. *Glasnost'* has encouraged independent organizations for virtually everything but feminist issues.

Children's Fund staff and volunteers set out to help abandoned and abused children generally and to promote family health and well-being, to the point of joining in to help send emergency medical teams to Central Asia.[58] Since 1988 the fund has published a hard-hitting weekly, *Sem'ia* (Family), carrying exposés on everything from one grandmother's struggle to help a foster child in the face of local red tape and indifference, to the abysmal condition and equipping of the central pediatric hospital of the Russian Republic.[59] The Children's Fund is prochild and profamily, not necessarily profeminist. Nor is it fully independent.

The absence of a prominent independent women's organization contrasts with the existence of hundreds of independent organizations formed to advocate nonfeminist causes. The independent press lacks feminist publications. An exception to this is the Leningrad feminist journal, *Readings for Women,* founded in 1988. It takes up issues like abortion and women's family burdens as well as hush-hush subjects like wife battering and rape.[60] But women's advocacy remains notably scarce—not because Soviet women are passive. After all, they appear among the leaders of many of the thousands of other independent organizations in the USSR. Torn between self-protection and self-assertion, women tend to shun feminist action.

The Soviet Women's Committee has begun to speak out for women at last, upbraiding, for example, male officials in ministries in which 3.5

million women work under unhealthy conditions violating labor law. Both women traditionally inclined toward family issues and more feminist women have joined a growing number of protests and meetings against working conditions that jeopardize the health of women and their infants. Women unknowingly are exposed to harmful industrial chemicals and herbicides.[61] Four million women work night shifts—twice as many as men do. Hundreds of thousands of women toil at heavy manual labor. Zoya Pukhova, chairperson of the Soviet Women's Committee, faulted her own organization: "The court doesn't know of a single appeal to the prosecutor to take legal action in a violation of labor laws."[62] How many women eventually will be working in family enterprises (other than the peasants' garden plots)?

What Role for the Family Enterprise?

When Stalin turned to collectivization, four out of five families lived off their own family enterprise. Most of them worked the family farm. Now only a small number of Soviet families depend on family enterprise for their main living. Soviet power eliminated most private enterprise by the mid-1930s. Decades of compulsory collectivism reinforced popular prejudices against private gain.

I myself remember one frustrated restaurateur stating over Moscow television, "People would rather our staff got paid 150–200 rubles a month and stole the rest, than that they earned better than others, say 350 to 500 rubles, by dint of hard and productive work." A Soviet housewife complained to me about the scarcity of cooperatives and private enterprise to date and exclaimed: "The sin of Russians is our envy—our envy of others' making a profit. But if we keep this up, we'll never bring private market prices down. We've got to let that market grow if life is to become bearable." Russia's past casts a shadow over the goals of *perestroika* to revive a private economy, to restore family enterprise through individual or cooperative labor activity and, on the farms, the family-contract system and, thereby, private family farming.

Soviet food shortages grew more troublesome and politically dangerous as *perestroika* faltered soon after its introduction. Hence the importance of Soviet efforts to stimulate food production under the Soviet version of the Chinese contract system. These efforts center largely in fact on expanding family production from the present garden plots out into the communal lands of the collective and state farms. A family under contract may keep all its product after a fee for the use of land, equipment, and livestock.

Gorbachev has praised family-contract farming and its brilliant results in no uncertain terms and remains its staunch patron.[63] This form of farming received a boost in September 1987, through a resolution of the CPSU Central Committee. One part of that resolution on increasing food production paid attention to aiding private farming by family contract and on garden plots. It ordered local officials to remedy "incorrect, prejudiced attitudes toward contract farming by families and individuals, and not to underestimate their great potential."[64] Apparently, local officials disregarded the resolution. The campaign for peasant-family enterprise in the USSR limped along after 1987 Party resolutions, prompting the Party under Gorbachev's prodding to reiterate its support of contract farming in 1989.[65]

The Chinese could depend on the vigor of peasant families so much more than could the Soviets because peasants made up 80 percent of the population in China, whereas they constituted only 20 percent of the Soviet population. Soviet peasants had lived through a much longer and more destructive saga of socialization when Gorbachev pushed the contract system in 1987–1989 than the Chinese had when Deng Xiaoping launched the family-responsibility system in 1978. "In principle," said Stanislav Shatalin about the Soviet peasants, "the deideologization of economic relations is occurring now and that will of course help. Unfortunately the process of destroying the peasantry took place much earlier, and finding peasants able to work the land, loving the land is becoming more difficult."[66]

Moreover, the urgency and legitimacy of private enterprise remained unclear to many in the nearly full-employment economy of the USSR. Many peasants in northern China may still thresh their wheat by letting vehicles drive over the stalks lying on the highway. Peasants in China perform backbreaking manual labor, but they work largely for themselves. The results in Chinese peasant prosperity contrast sharply with the depressed Soviet rural scene, especially in the Russian Republic. As the Soviet family's economic rights and roles grow, so will spouses' independence change to mutual dependence, strengthening the ties that bind and stabilize the family.

Epilogue

Perestroika brings such rapid and unpredictable changes (and setbacks) that "epilogue" serves better than "conclusion" as an end to these thoughts on the family and its problems. The initial Soviet conflict between distrusting and needing the family faded with Stalin's legitimation of the family, shaken by violence, conflict, and famine, as the basic unit of Soviet society. In the mid-1930s the government under Stalin moved to honor and "strengthen" the family, though in a suffocating embrace particularly deleterious to women's equality and rights. For Stalin's successors, this policy raised the issues of how much to move from a stance of coercion toward one of accommodation and how much to restore women's equality and men's obligations as parents. What the government views as problems of family size and stability appear to family members as results of role conflicts, as gaps between wishes and actual possibilities, and as tensions between spouses engendered by strains and attachments originating outside the family as well as in it.

The Soviet representative from Belorussia to the UN Committee on the Elimination of Discrimination Against Women (the USSR, unlike the

United States, ratified the 1979 covenant setting up this committee) stated in March 1989 that women had made "revolutionary progress" under Mikhail Gorbachev's *perestroika*.[67] That is a dubious claim. Women's problems in the family overall seemed little closer to solution during the first years of *perestroika* than they had been before Gorbachev. Outside of scant coverage in legal publications, near-silence persists about child and wife abuse. Perhaps tradition plays a role here, a tradition so strong that it appears to inhibit the emergence of a strong, independent organization for women. Serious defects prevent the authorities from meeting elementary needs of everyday life and health care. This only adds more family burdens on top of strains on women associated with what Gorbachev described as their special "destiny as keepers of the hearth."[68]

Perestroika brought further attention to problems of birthrates, health, and private enterprise. Measures affecting maternity rights began to emerge under Gorbachev, such as extending the permissible period for abortions, a greater openness on the health crisis, and the toleration of public activism of the environmental organizations and of new forms of public participation in health and family issues. Together these make up a wide-ranging but as yet mainly untested beginning of a new approach to securing maternity rights.

Demographic policy bears watching. Once again the issue is open of how much to adhere to literal equality in birth incentives, how much to differentiate so as to eliminate regional "disproportions" in birthrates. Experts float proposals for more differentiation in family allowances on the basis of family size (favoring small families to stimulate the birth of a second and third child), region, children's developed talent, and what a mother loses for staying home to have a child. Special birth-incentive measures have begun to appear within the Baltic republics. A policy of differentiation, if carried further, will jolt old notions of "social justice" in family rights and may add irritants to already-troubled relations with, and among, national minorities.

Soviet people are experiencing unprecedented contradictions in their lives. On one side, they see more openness of knowledge and choice in resolving their family problems. On the other, they feel constraints of traditional inequality in gender roles and of economic decline and prejudices against private enterprise. Once again, family problems reflect changes in leadership and policies. By their sheer numbers, Soviet families, some 73 million of them, have made their problems in transmuted form the problems of the demographically concerned Soviet government.[69] But women's demands as yet do not enjoy the independent organized advocacy now become typical of Soviet society.

A new and dramatic source of family unity in the border republics has been the open, ubiquitous surge of nationality activism through "popular fronts," churches, and human rights and cultural groups. Nobody attending a national front meeting of the young, mature, and elderly together, as this writer did in Tallinn, would underestimate the role of the family in transmitting ethnic pride and values or the potential of a common ethnic cause in uniting families within the group even while it begins to pit them against families in other groups. Russian-Balt tensions and violence in the Caucasus exemplify this. Under *perestroika,* the interplay of "the social and the personal" keeps taking on new and surprising forms alongside the enduring compromises.

Notes

1. "In the first postrevolutionary years, when the country was entering a period of socioeconomic transformation, a thorough restructuring of the family institution took hold, which many took to be the beginning of the end. The idea of eliminating everyday family ties, of the complete communalization of everyday life, of children's upbringing, circulated widely." See A. Vyshnevskii, "Led tronulsia? O demograficheskikh protsessakh i sotsial'noi politike," *Kommunist,* no. 6 (1988), p. 68. But Lenin's government did not seek to destroy the family, only its religious and patriarchal features. See H. Kent Geiger, *The Family in Soviet Russia* (Cambridge, Mass.: Harvard University Press, 1968); Rudolph Schlesinger (ed.), *Changing Attitudes in Soviet Russia: The Family in the U.S.S.R.* (London: Routledge & Kegan Paul, 1949). On the impact of revolution, civil war, and famine, including 7 million homeless waifs, see Peter H. Juviler, "Contradictions of Revolution: Juvenile Crime and Rehabilitation," in *Bolshevik Culture: Experiment and Order in the Russian Revolution,* ed. Abbot Gleason, Peter Kenez, and Richard Stites (Bloomington: Indiana University Press, 1985), pp. 261-78.

2. *Pravda,* June 28, 1987; February 19, 1988.

3. Yuri I. Luryi, *Soviet Family Law* (Buffalo, N.Y.: William S. Hein & Co., 1980), including Peter Juviler, "Foreword," pp. i-vi.

4. Peter H. Juviler, "Family Reforms on the Road to Communism," in *Soviet Policy-Making: Studies of Communism in Transition,* ed. Peter H. Juviler and Henry W. Morton (New York: Frederick A. Praeger, 1967), pp. 29-60, and "Whom the State Has Joined: Conjugal Ties in Soviet Law," in *Soviet Law after Stalin: The Citizen and the State in Contemporary Soviet Law,* ed. Donald D. Barry, George Ginsburgs, and Peter B. Maggs, Law in Eastern Europe, pt. 1, no. 20 (Leiden: Sijthoff, 1977), pp. 119-157.

5. Vyshnevskii, op. cit., p. 69. Some Westerners giving Soviet policies a superficial glance overreacted to extremist proposals of the early 1960s for "living and working communes" and mass boarding schools. The communes remained on the drafting table. The boarding schools remained in fact what they had been, repositories for orphans, extramarital children, problem children, and the children of negligent or absent parents. Khrushchev specifically rejected all projects for replacing the family and set sociologists to studying it. Peter Juviler, "Marriage and Divorce," *Survey,* no. 48 (1963), pp. 104-117; "Soviet Families," *Survey,* no. 60 (1966), pp. 51-61.

6. Covenant, Article 10, USSR Constitution (1977), Article 53.

7. The 1986 version of the program of the CPSU (Communist Party of the Soviet Union) reiterates this long-standing concern: "The CPSU holds that improving how we *care for the family* is of great importance. The family plays an ever more significant role in building up the health of the younger generation and in their upbringing, thus ensuring the economic and social progress of society and improving demographic processes." *Pravda,* October 26, 1986.

8. "Postanovlenie No. 9 Plenuma Verkhovnogo Suda SSSR ot 28 noiabria 1980g. o praktike primeneniia sudami zakonodatel'stva pri rassmotrenii del o rastorzhenii braka," *Biulleten' Verkhovnogo Suda SSSR* [*Biulleten'* hereafter], no. 1 (1981), p. 12.

9. Vyshnevskii, op. cit., p. 65.

10. Peter H. Juviler, "The Family in the Soviet System," Carl Beck Papers in Russian and East European Studies (Pittsburgh: University of Pittsburgh, 1984), pp. 18–27. The incentives to women to have more children and stay home with them a while showed up in the main measures on grants, allowances, and leaves especially. For the first time, mothers received lump-sum grants for the first and second child (50 and 100 rubles). Grants increased from 20 to 100 rubles for the third child. The measures of 1981 left in effect the rest of the previous grant schedule, rising to 250 rubles for the eleventh child and following. Monthly allowances remained in effect beginning with fourth child (only 4 rubles a month, to maximum 12.5 beginning with ninth child). Monthly extra allowances for unwed mothers increased from 5 rubles to 20 per child, up to the age of 16, not 12, and 18 if child was still in school.

The main incentive emphasized women's mothering role by introducing, in addition to the 112-day paid maternity leave, an optional maternity leave with partial pay for up to a year after birth at 35 rubles a month (50 rubles in hardship areas like Murmansk and Archangel and gravely depleted areas like Novgorod and Pskov provinces), plus an optional six-month unpaid leave without loss of seniority. Several other lesser measures accompanied these, including increased leave to care for a sick child and waiving of the tax on childless couples for a year after their marriage. *Pravda,* February 24, March 5, and 11, and September 6, 1981. The tax on single persons, bachelors, and persons with small families (passed in 1941) is a tax on men aged 21–49, women 21–44 (except those exempted: single women and widows, payers of the agricultural tax, students under 25, members of the armed forces and their wives, disabled persons, et al.) who earn 70 or more rubles a month, at a progressive rate up to 6 percent of salary at 90 rubles or more a month. E. H. de Jong in *Encyclopedia of Soviet Law,* 2d rev. ed., ed. J. M. Feldbrugge, G. P. Van den Berg, and William B. Simons (Dordrecht/Boston/Lancaster: Martinus Nijhoff, 1985), p. 757.

11. Bill Keller, "Mother Russia Makes a Comeback on Births," *New York Times,* December 26, 1987.

12. A precensus sample of 13,000,000 people surveyed in 1985. "Osnovnye itogi vyborochnogo sotsial'no-demograficheskogo obsledovaniia naseleniia SSSR 1985 goda," *Vestnik statistiki,* no 6 (1986), p. 53. Only 699 babies were born to every 10,000 women in the USSR aged 15–49 in 1978–1979, but 760 in 1982–1983, and 797 in 1986–1987. See *Narodnoe khoziaistvo SSSR v 1987 g.* (Moscow: Finansy i statistika, 1988), p. 405. Birthrates dropped from 24.9 per 1,000 in 1960 to 17.4 in 1970 and 18.3 in 1980. That year marked a low point also for natural increase, 8.0 down from 17.8 in 1960. Births increased from 4,851,000 in 1980 to 5,599,000 in 1987. See p. 352.

13. The results of a survey show the increased popularity of a one-and-a-half-year's maternity leave, adding a year's partially paid leave (minimum 35 rubles a month, introduced in all but the Caucasus and Central Asia by November 1, 1982, and there a year later) to the possible unpaid maternity leave. In both urban and rural areas, per thousand women giving birth, women took the full year and a half (with first year partially paid) at a rate 9 times higher in 1983 than in 1979. Women giving birth now are more likely to take more than the standard 112-day paid

maternity leave in effect before the 1981 measure than they were before the new partially paid leave came in. *Vestnik statistiki,* no. 9 (1986), p. 78.

14. Permanent preschool facilities serve about 17 million children. Since 1985 the share of children served by them has leveled off at 57–58 percent. *Narodnoe khoziaistvo SSSR v 1987 g.,* op. cit., pp. 492–493.

15. Proponents of differentiation argue that only women having one or two children need the raised grants and allowances for a second or third child, not women whose expectations and traditions are geared to large families anyway. They insist that differentiation is not discrimination, simply a recognition of differences in motivation and need and the way to increase family size in low-fertility groups from one or two children to an ideal "model" of a family with two or three children, the minimum for net population reproduction. They argue not only for favoring small families in distributing allowances but also for pegging those allowances to salary levels, to compensate for loss of pay during maternity leave. Ibid., pp. 71–72.

16. Juviler, "The Family in the Soviet System," op. cit., p. 32.

17. Married women aged 18 to 44 surveyed in 1985 had these expectations of children by nationality: Russian—1.961, Uzbek—5.568, Kirgiz—5.562, Tadzhik—5.937, and Turkmen—6.310. *Vestnik statistiki,* no. 9 (1986), pp. 76–77.

18. The six republics with lowest birthrates are RSFSR, Ukraine, Belorussia, Latvia, Lithuania, and Estonia. Increases of fertility there have not returned any of them to net population reproduction. Vyshnevskii, op. cit., 67–68. See also Timothy Appel, " 'Birth Dearth' Begins to Show in Some Developed Nations: Population Dip Most Noticeable in West Europe," *Christian Science Monitor,* March 2, 1988; Viktor Perevedentsev, "Growing Proportion of Aged Persons," *Moscow News,* no. 4 (1988), p. 12.

19. Vyshnevskii, op. cit., p. 68.

20. A. Ganelin, "Under the Yashmak—Cruel and Abnormal Customs Have Long Been Concealed," *Komsomol'skaia pravda,* August 8, 1987, p. 4, transl. in *Current Digest of the Soviet Press* [*CDSP* hereafter] 39, no. 32, p. 20.

21. Yurii Riurikov, "The Kind of Family We Need—Invitation to Discussion," *Nedelia,* November 23–29, 1987, in *CDSP* 39, no. 47 (1987), pp. 25–27.

22. Latvia is under orders of the USSR Supreme Soviet to enhance many forms of family assistance, from children's food and clothing to family and marriage counseling, housing, and closer scrutiny in court cases dealing with family relations. Estonia adopted a comprehensive program to help young families with housing, medical care, food, and other needs in January 1987 and a graduated income tax inversely proportional to family per capita income, for families with four or five children, covered out of republic resources. "V Prezidiume Verkhovnogo Soveta SSSR," *Pravda,* May 29, 1988, p. 2; L. Levitsky, "In Republic Governments: Family Benefits," *Izvestiia,* March 2, 1988, in *CDSP* 40, no. 9, p. 25; and Party-Government-Trade Union Decree, "On Additional Measures to Improve the Demographic Situation in the Republic," *Vedomosti Verkhovnogo Soveta Estonskoi SSR,* no. 5 (1988), item 64, January 20, 1988.

23. "Sem'ia," *Molodezh' Estonii,* March 7, 1989.

24. Yevgeniya Albats, "Reporter's Assignment: Have a Baby," *Moscow News,* no. 9 (1988), p. 16.

25. A Soviet survey found that women in urban blue- and white-collar families of various sizes, from single-person to families with several children, spent on the average 2.6 times more hours a week on homemaking than men do, in fact more

than a regular work shift. For mothers, the figures would be higher than these. *Narodnoe khoziaistvo SSSR v 1987 g.,* op. cit., p. 384.

26. Paid leaves to tend sick children rose as of November 11, 1987, from seven to fourteen days, at 50 percent pay for the second week, but at full pay for ten days for single mothers, widows (and widowers), divorced women (and men), and draftees' wives. *Pravda,* October 22, 1987. Low-income, single-parent families with three or more children received extra subsidies for their children in a range of benefits ranging from free school and athletic uniforms and breakfasts, to free holiday passes. Alimony (and child support) to the spouse with custody (usually the wife) may not drop below the required one-quarter of a payer's salary for one child, one-third for two, one-half for three, unless excessive obligation make this impossible. In this case under the new rule, a minimum of 20 rubles a month per child is required, regardless of supporter's other obligations. If the alimony payer is missing, then the local soviet must pay the 20 rubles until he is found and made to pay. Prices of children's goods must be held down. See joint government-trade union decree, *Izvestiia,* October 31, 1987, trans. in *CDSP* 38, no. 42, p. 26.

27. In the long run, family allowances count for less in family policy than do "other aspects of family life" such as "employment, wages, prices, housing construction, public health, education, etc." Vyshnevskii, op. cit., p. 70.

28. Albats, op. cit. Another found no convenient "kangaroo" infant carriers like the ones Western women have, which leave the mother's hands free, though some private entrepreneurs are supplying a tiny part of the need. N. Volkova, "O 'kangaru,'" *Sem'ia,* no. 21 (May 25, 1988), p. 4.

29. M. Tol'ts, "Razvod," *Vestnik statistiki,* no. 1 (1988), p. 76; Gail W. Lapidus (ed.), *Women, Work, and Family in the Soviet Union* (Armonk, N.Y.: M. E. Sharpe, 1982).

30. Women make up 51 percent of the labor force in the USSR, 55 percent in Latvia, 52 in the Russian Republic, and the lowest percentage, 38, in the Tadzhik Republic. *Narodnoe khoziaistvo SSR v 1987 g.,* op. cit., p. 368.

31. Annette Bohr, "Resolving the Question of Equality for Soviet Women—Again," *Radio Liberty Report on the USSR* 1, no. 14 (April 7, 1988), p. 13.

32. "We have discovered that many of our problems—in children's and young people's behavior, in our morals, culture and in production—are partially caused by the weakening of family ties and slack attitudes to family responsibilities. This is a paradoxical result of our sincere and politically justified desire to make women equal with men in everything. Now, in the course of *perestroika,* we have begun to overcome this shortcoming. That is why we are now holding heated debates in the press, in public organizations, at work and at home, about the question of what we should do to make it possible for women to return to their purely womanly mission." Mikhail Gorbachev, *Perestroika: New Thinking for Our Country and the World* (New York: Harper and Row, 1987), p. 117.

33. Stanislav Shatalin, "Kak pereprygnut' propast'?" *Ogonek,* no. 17 (April 1989), p. 22; interview of April 15, 1989.

34. Albats, op. cit.

35. N. Boyarkina, "Every Day in This Spot: AIDS and Kids," *Komsomol'skaia pravda,* January 28, 1989, condensed in *CDSP,* 41, no. 5, p. 26, citing twenty-six deaths and a later report by TASS, February 24, 1989, giving the higher figures, cited in Aaron Trehub, "Growing Alarm About AIDS in the Soviet Union," *Radio Liberty Report on the USSR,* 1, no. 14 (1989), p. 4.

36. Stated by a Communist party official from Volgograd during a panel discussion in which I participated, May 13, 1989.

37. David Kugultinov, "Emergency Situation: Be People!" *Izvestiia*, February 23, 1989, excerpted in *CDSP* 41, no. 8, p. 23.

38. Peter H. Juviler, "The Urban Family and the Soviet State: Emerging Contours of a Demographic Policy," *The Contemporary Soviet City*, ed. Henry W. Morton and Robert G. Stuart (Armonk, N.Y.: M. E. Sharpe, 1984), pp. 84–112.

39. Infant-mortality statistics became secret after 1974, adult-mortality statistics after 1975–1976. Ibid., p. 89.

40. "Following a Cry of the Heart: Constituent Conference of the V. I. Lenin Soviet Children's Fund," *Izvestiia*, October 18, 1987, excerpted in *CDSP* 39, no. 41 (1987), pp. 27–28. Recorded infant-mortality figures showed a death rate of 25.4 per 1,000 live births up to one year old in 1986. V. I. Kulakov, head of the All-Union Research Center for the Protection of the Health of Mother and Child, "Rebenok bez prismotr?" *Pravda*, August 10, 1987. Rates were down a bit from the 1985 figure of 26, but up overall since 1970, *Vestnik statistiki*, no. 12 (1986), p. 71. Better reporting from Central Asia explains only part of the rise.

41. The comparisons are actually worse since Soviet figures understate infant mortality by at least 15 percent. The Soviet definition of infant mortality departs from the usual one by excluding from the count of dead infants under one year old those underweight or who die within a week of their birth; those cases are dubbed "spontaneous abortion." Mark G. Field, "Soviet Infant Mortality," November 9, 1987, Kennan Institute for Advanced Russian Studies, *Meeting Report*.

42. *Narodnoe khoziaistvo SSSR v. 1987 g.*, op. cit., p. 357.

43. "Following a Cry of the Heart," op. cit.

44. Murray Feshbach on "*Glasnost'* and Health Issues in the USSR," October 5, 1987, Kennan Institute for Advanced Russian Studies, *Meeting Report*.

45. *From Below: Independent Peace and Environmental Movements in Eastern Europe & the USSR* (New York: Helsinki Watch Committee, October 1987) traced the beginning of what is now a vast series of mass green movements in the USSR and Eastern Europe, many tied in with movements of national or regional self-assertion. Field, "Soviet Infant Mortality," op. cit.; Annette Bohr, "Infant Mortality in Central Asia," *Radio Liberty Report*, RL 352/88, August 4, 1988.

46. V. Kirillov, "Ostorozhno—narkotik!" *Sem'ia*, no. 20 (May 15, 1988), pp. 14–15; L. Sal'nikova, "Allo, vas slushat!" *Sem'ia*, no. 20 (May 18, 1988), p. 16.

47. "Following a Cry of the Heart," op. cit., and CPSU resolution on improving orphans' life, *Pravda*, August 8, 1987; G. Polozhevets, "Dva oblika detstva riadom: vysokaia atmosfera nravstvennosti i . . . glubina zabveniia," *Sem'ia*, no. 20 (May 18, 1988), p. 5.

48. A demographer gave these figures for abortion rates in 1978–1979 per 1,000 women of reproductive ages 15–49: West Germany—5.9, England—11.4, United States—27.5, Czechoslovakia—28.9, Hungary—36.9, Bulgaria—68.3, Soviet Union—102.4, RSFSR (1985)—123.2. See Larissa Remennik, "A Sensitive Subject: The Life That Has Been Killed Inside You," *Nedelia*, September 21-27, 1988, *CDSP* 39, no. 44, p. 15. The rates for the USSR reflected by far the world's highest recorded ratio of abortions to live births, 2.04 in 1984 (probably about 2.5 or more in European parts of the USSR), compared with 0.93 in Bulgaria, 0.42 in the United States, 0.23 in France (figures of Christopher Tietze and Stanley K. Henshaw of the Alan Guttmacher Institute, cited by Jodi L. Jacobson in "Choice At Any Cost," *World Watch*, March-April 1988, p. 33).

49. The callous, traumatizing, and painful treatment at the hands of a gynecologist in a state abortion clinic was related, for example, in Yekaterina Nikolaeva, "I Don't Want to Be Sorry I'm a Woman," *Moscow News*, no. 4 (1989).

50. *Sem'ia*, no. 21 (May 25, 1988), p. 11.
51. "Behind the Order," *Meditsinskaia gazeta*, February 12, 1988, *CDSP* 40, no. 7, p. 24.
52. Since Gorbachev's first year, national divorce rates have remained at a level of 3.4, down a bit from their 1984 high of 3.6 per 1,000. Divorce rates in the largest Soviet cities appear to be at more or less the level of the U.S. big cities. *Vestnik statistiki*, no. 12 (1981), p. 62, and no. 12 (1987), p. 65. Divorces, marriages (per 1,000 population), and ratios of divorces to marriages in the USSR, 1979 to 1987, were reported as follows:

	Divorces	Marriages	Divorces/Marriages
1979	3.6	10.9	0.330
1980	3.5	10.3	0.340
1982	3.3	10.3	0.320
1984	3.4	9.6	0.354
1985	3.4	9.8	0.347
1986	3.4	9.8	0.347
1987	3.4	9.8	0.347

Source: *Narodnoe khoziaistvo SSSR za 70 let* (Moscow: Finansy i Statistika, 1987), p. 404; *Narodnoe khoziaistvo SSSR v 1979 godu* (Moscow: Finansy i Statistika, 1980), p. 35; *Narodnoe khoziaistvo SSSR v 1987 g.*, op. cit., p. 352.

53. M. Tol'ts, "Razvod," *Pravda*, December 22, 1987, p. 6; M. Talalai, "'Zhenatykh ne propisyvaet': Vzgliad sotsiologa na problemu molodezhnykh obshchezhitii," *Pravda*, September 29, 1986, p. 7.
54. Peter H. Juviler, "Cell Mutation in Soviet Society: The Family," in *Soviet Society and Culture: Essays in Honor of Vera S. Dunham*, ed. Terry I. Thompson and Richard Sheldon (Boulder, Colo.: Westview Press, 1988), pp. 39–57.
55. RSFSR Family Code, *Kommentarii k kodeksu o brake i sem'e RSFSR* (Moscow: Iuridicheskaia Literatura, 1982).
56. "Postanovlenie No. 5 Plenuma Verkhovnogo Suda SSSR ot 18 iunia 1987 'O vypolnenii Verkhovnym Sudom Latviiskoi SSR postanovlenii Plenuma Verkhovnogo Suda SSSR o primenenii zakonodatel'stva, reguliruiushchego brachno-semeinye otnosheniia,'" *Biulleten'*, no. 4 (1987), pp. 8–11.
57. Vyshnevskii, op. cit., pp. 74–75.
58. "Napravlenie glavnogo udara," *Sem'ia*, no. 20 (May 18, 1988), pp. 1–2; "Spasti rebenka!" ibid., pp. 1–2.
59. "Dvadtsat' otvetov na tri voprosa," *Sem'ia*, no. 21 (May 25, 1988), pp. 2–3; letters in ibid., p. 11; E. Kheifits, "'Uspet'' vy eshche i polechit,' gor'ko zametil odin iz vrachei, kotorogo ia zastala za pochinkoi tualetnogo bachka . . . ," ibid., pp. 11–12, 14.
60. Interview with Ol'ga Lipovskaia for Radio Liberty, March 23, 1989, cited in Bohr, "Resolving the Question of Equality for Soviet Women—Again," op. cit., p. 14. The contributors to *Reading for Women* carry on the tradition of a Leningrad group, Women and Russia, disbanded by the KGB after a brief spell of activity in 1979–1980. Tatyana Mamonova (ed.), *Women and Russia: Feminist Writings from the Soviet Union* (Boston: Beacon Press, 1984).
61. Bohr, "Resolving the Question of Equality for Soviet Women—Again," op. cit., pp. 14–16.
62. "Among Us Women: While the Men Talk. Report by Feuilleton Writer Marina Lebedeva from the Plenary Session of the Soviet Women's Committee," *Izvestiia*, October 23, 1988, condensed in *CDSP* 40, no. 43, p. 23.

63. *Pravda,* June 26, 1987.
64. "V Tsentral'nom Komitete KPSS. Tsentral'nyi Komitet prinial postanovlenie 'O neotlozhnikh merakh po uskoreniiu resheniia prodovol'stvennogo voprosa v sootvetstvii s ustanovkami iun'skogo (1987g) Plenuma TsK KPSS,'" *Pravda,* September 25, 1987, pp. 1–2.
65. Gorbachev's address to the Party Central Committee and its resolution on agriculture, *Pravda,* March 16 and 17, 1989; an edict of the USSR Supreme Soviet authorizing the private leasing of land, farm inventory, and nonfarm buildings and equipment, "Ob arende i arendnykh otnosheniiakh v SSSR," *Pravda,* April 9, 1989.
66. Shatalin, op. cit., p. 23.
67. Mihalisko, "Women Workers and *Perestroika* in Ukraine and Belorussia," *Radio Liberty Report on the USSR* 1, no. 15 (April 14, 1989), p. 30.
68. Interview with Tom Brokaw, NBC-TV, November 30, 1987.
69. Calculated from average size, 3.5 members living together, 91 percent in those family units (*Vestnik statistiki,* no. 6 [1986], p. 53), in a population for January 1, 1987, of 281.3 million (ibid., no. 12 [1987], p. 44).

CHAPTER 12

Problems in the Schools

Anthony Jones

In all industrial nations, education seems to be a magnet for the social problems of the entire society. It is in the school that the values of individuals, families, communities, professional and business organizations, political groups and parties, and the organs of the state and government meet. It is in the schools that the goals of a variety of social, ethnic, and racial groups come into contact. It is the schools that are called upon to provide the kinds of people the economy needs; to instill civic awareness; to pass on the culture of the society to each new generation of children; to deal with conflicting views about "acceptable" behavior; and to instill in their young charges all of the desires and motivations expected of them by diverse groups and organizations. All of this, of course, is in addition to the expectation that schools will actually teach a curriculum of academic subjects—yet another topic for argument and conflict.

The school, then, can become a battleground on which is fought a series of wars. Social problems do not stop at the school gate, but intrude into the lives of pupils and teachers alike, causing difficulties for both groups. In a sense, then, almost everything that goes on in schools can be seen as a social problem of one kind or another—it is only the precise nature of the problems, and the intensity of concern shown about them, that change.

Finally, societies often experience a crisis of confidence in which there are fears for the nation's economic, political, or social future; at such times, the school may be designated as a contributor to the problem or as a part of the solution. At such times, the school is seen as being out of step with the goals of the nation and in need of reform to bring it into line.

What makes education so vulnerable to these pressures are its crucial functions of socialization and training, as well as the fact that in industrial societies it is the main channel through which people are assigned to positions in the economy and the society. In the Soviet Union, this situation exists just as much as it does in other societies. In the 1980s there was growing concern in the USSR as well as in the United States, Europe, and even Japan that the educational system was failing in some way. At the official level, the driving force in all these cases was concern about the economy and the ways in which education could contribute to an improvement in economic performance. At the grass-roots level, concern seemed to be more about having access to quality education for one's children and the consequences of this for upward mobility.

Given the range and complexity of "the problems in the schools," it will be possible in this chapter to touch on only a fraction of the problems facing education in the Soviet Union. In what follows, therefore, I will only indicate some of the major issues. I shall explain why they have become defined as problems, look at the public responses to (and debate on) these problems, and broadly outline the basic trends in school issues. It is hoped that this will provide the reader with an understanding of why many people in the USSR see their educational system as being in a state of crisis, and of the enormous difficulties faced by those who are trying to bring about changes in the Soviet schools.

Educational Trends

One of the proudest claims of the Soviet regime has always been its success in raising the level of literacy and education of the population. Although levels of literacy were improving before the Revolution (from 21 percent of the population in 1897 to 40 percent in 1913), in 1917 Russia was still predominantly a nation of illiterates.[1] Following a series of crash programs in the 1920s, and a steady expansion of the educational system in the 1930s, the Soviet Union had become a relatively educated society by the 1980s. By 1987, about three-quarters of the labor force had received at least some secondary education, and a further 12 percent had had at least some higher education.[2] As of 1989, there were about 105 million pupils and students (full and part-time, including adults) enrolled in the educational system, studying in more than 130,000 schools and about 900 universities and institutes. Personnel for this system included more than 3 million teachers.[3] The difficulties involved in managing a system of 108 million people (many times the size of the population of most countries), let alone trying to reform it, would clearly be a major challenge for any society. Trying to change this giant to keep it in step with a continually evolving industrial society is a daunting prospect, and yet this is exactly what the Soviet authorities have been doing for the past five decades or more. The innately conservative nature of educational systems in most societies almost guarantees that education will lag behind the needs of the society at large. The Soviet case, as we shall see, is no different, in spite of virtually constant efforts to reform the schools.

Educational reform has been on the Soviet agenda since the Revolution itself. Looking back over the past seventy years, it is difficult to see a period of more than a few years when Soviet education was not undergoing some reform or other. In the decade following the Revolution, radical changes were introduced in the curriculum and in the organization of the classroom. Pupils were encouraged to challenge teachers, the grading system was either nonexistent or based on group evaluations, and in many ways Soviet education was among the most experimental and "progressive" in the world. Under Stalin in the 1930s, however, there was a return to the earlier traditional system and a restoration of authority in the classroom. Pupils were seen as the recipients of already-organized and tightly controlled information, interaction and discovery being kept to a minimum. This emphasis on control and on the passivity of pupils remained a cornerstone of Soviet education until recent years.

The changes introduced by Khrushchev in the late 1950s marked a move toward greater emphasis on labor training in the schools as well as the beginning of a constant struggle to provide equal access to education (especially to higher education) for all, while maintaining standards. The reform set up a quota system in higher education for children from working-class and peasant families and increased the emphasis on polytechnical education in the secondary schools. Until the reform was reversed in 1964 following Khrushchev's ouster, all except a very few students in special categories had to have two years of work experience before they could be admitted to a university or institute, and preference was given to applicants from working-class and peasant backgrounds. The consequences for educational performance were, as one might predict, harmful. In the secondary schools, pupils were expected to spend a considerable amount of time preparing for their future work life.[4]

From the mid-1960s to the early 1980s, the school system was subject to constant tinkering, and enormous pressure was put upon teachers and administrators to achieve universal secondary education. (This did not mean that all pupils would be in full-time education, but that all young people would complete a high school education in some way or another.) During this period, there was a growing disjuncture between the needs of the economy, the kind of education being provided in the secondary schools, and the desires of the pupils. Aspirations for higher education had always been strong among those who remained in the system until high-school graduation, and the increasing number staying in school during the 1970s encouraged many more to aspire to this goal. As a result, apparently, young people entered the labor force reluctantly, performed their work in a less than satisfactory way, and moved constantly from job to job. In the reforms of 1984, drastic measures were introduced to deal with this situation.

These reforms were bound to fail not only because they were unpopular,[5] but also because they were overambitious, contradictory, and not well thought-out. The authorities were essentially attempting to solve too many problems at once. The reasons given for the changes were that new technologies required pupils to be prepared for a more complex workplace; that labor education needed somehow to fit the personality of the pupil to the needs of the economy; that more effective socialization in the schools was necessary to curb undesirable behavior and make pupils more ideologically committed; that parents and pupils were to be held responsible for performance in the classroom; that the material conditions of teachers were to be improved; and that there should be closer ties between the school, the family, and the wider society in order to make education and upbringing more effective. Concretely, these "needs" were to be met by having children start school at age six instead of at seven, by doubling the percentage of pupils who would attend vocational-technical schools (PTUs), by having pupils spend more of their time engaged in "productive" (i.e., industrial) labor, and by introducing courses on "family" matters (a relatively sanitized sex-education course plus lectures on personal responsibility in sexual relationships and in family life). In addition, there was to be added emphasis on maintaining discipline in the school.[6]

All these changes were controversial to some degree, but the most contentious was that in the area of vocational education. Although in principle the decision to attend a PTU was to be made voluntarily, the goal was set of having approximately 60 percent or more of fifteen-year-olds (at the end of the new ninth grade) go to a PTU. Since about 10 percent of pupils go on to the specialized secondary schools, this would leave only 30 percent or less of pupils in the general schools (the traditional path to higher education). In spite of official assertions that the PTUs would provide a general as well as a vocational education and that there would be no barriers in the way of these children going on to higher education, it was clear that the consequence of this reform would be to stratify schools even more along social-class lines and to reduce the chances of those from lower socioeconomic backgrounds continuing their education beyond the secondary level.[7]

The reform was based on a misconception of the relationship between the career and work orientation of young people and their experience in school.[8] Sociological studies have consistently shown that parents and peers and the life-style a particular occupation promises have far more influence on attitudes of pupils toward work than does the school—so, herding two out of three pupils into vocational schools would be unlikely to influence them in a positive way. Indeed, their resentment and that of their parents would in all probability be increased.[9] Moreover, research also shows that most young people do not end up working in occupations for which they have been trained in secondary schools: Therefore, expanding vocational training does not make much sense.[10]

Schools in Crisis

In spite of much talk, and constant exhortations to make the reforms a reality, the resistance of the educational establishment (backed by a public opinion that was unenthusiastic about the provisions of the reform) managed essentially to sabotage them. As it became clear in the years following 1984 that the reforms were not being implemented, the press began a campaign in which it sought to blame various parts of the educational system for the lack of progress. This culminated in an attack focused on the Ministry of Education and on the Academy of Pedagogy. In a scathing indictment of the ministry in *Pravda* in 1987, N. Anisin wrote that ever since the mid-1960s the ministry had done everything it could to prevent change and to cover up the true extent of the problems: "As a result, the educational system was preserved under glass for many years."[11]

Acknowledgment that the reforms were a big mistake came in 1988 in a major speech by Egor Ligachev at a plenum of the Central Committee of the CPSU.[12] During the previous two years he had complained many times that the reforms were not going well and that they were being virtually ignored by the educational establishment. In this speech, however, he condemned the reforms not only for their lack of progress but also for their being fundamentally ill conceived. The reform, he said, reflected the old thinking and was therefore out of step with *perestroika*. The attempt to divert pupils to the PTUs was damaging general education and had even led to a fall in the proportion of those going to specialized secondary schools. What was needed was not job training but rather an increase in the quality of general education. The reform failed to allow for democratization of education, and bureaucratism and conservatism still held sway over the system. Control still came from above, and teachers were given no room for innovation and creativity in the classroom. As a result, education in the USSR was lagging behind the changes occurring in the rest of the society and behind the standards achieved in the rest of the industrialized world. The consequences of this, he noted, would be serious and might take decades to overcome.

In addition to this sweeping attack on the 1984 reforms, Ligachev painted a dismal picture of the state that the schools themselves were in. For example, 21 percent of pupils were in schools with no central heating, 30 percent of the schools had no running water, 40 percent had no indoor toilets, and 40 percent had no indoor gymnasiums. In large part this was the result of a failure to invest in education—although in 1988 the education budget was 40 billion rubles, this was a lower percentage of the state budget (8 percent) than it had been in 1970 (11 percent). To deal with these deficiencies, the school building program would need to be doubled, an enormous task even if the economy were healthy and growing, which it was not.[13]

A few weeks after the Ligachev speech, the campaign that had been waged against the Ministry of Education since mid-1987 bore fruit. The ministry was abolished, together with the Ministry of Higher and Secondary Specialized Education and the state committee responsible for vocational-technical education, and in their place was created the State Committee for Education, under the direct control of the Central Committee of the CPSU. The stated goal of this change was to make it easier to integrate the entire educational system, a task not possible as long as there was a large number of separate bodies responsible for various parts of the nation's schooling.[14] As is the case in so many bureaucratic reshuffles, however, the same people continued to run the educational system, the old inertia began to reassert itself, and the state committee has failed so far to be any more successful in bringing about change in the schools than were its predecessors.

It is not surprising that many people think that the schools are in deep trouble and desperately in need of improvement. In a large public-opinion survey conducted in major urban centers in November 1988, 72.6 percent of the teachers polled said that they thought the school was in "deep crisis" and in need of "fundamental restructuring"; only 1 percent thought that the schools were fine as they were! About one-third of the parents were not satisfied with the schools that their children attended, and about one in five said they would like to transfer their children to another school. A quarter of the teachers were either actively seeking a change of career or would change their occupation if a chance presented itself. On a large number of employment issues, the vast majority (80–90 percent) of teachers were dissatisfied, including more than four out of five who thought that their own level of education was inadequate. There was also general dissatisfaction with the performance and interest of pupils and with the overall conditions found in the schools.[15]

Since Ligachev's speech, another wave of reforms has been proposed and a wide array of new tasks assigned to the school system. Unlike earlier reforms, however, these have been very vague and have lacked the detailed provisions that earlier decrees have set out. In part this is because the new goals are themselves vague and ill defined, as is the course being followed in the general society during the period of *perestroika*.

In addition to the effort to harness the schools to *perestroika*, there has developed a greater candor about the state of the educational system. This has exposed the hardships endured by the schools and the enormous amount of resources that will be needed to bring them up to a reasonable level. Although the figures given by Ligachev and others paint a bleak picture of conditions in Soviet schools, the situation is especially bad in rural schools. They account for three-quarters of all the schools in the nation, and 54 percent of all teachers and 42 percent of all pupils are in village schools.[16] In the mid-1980s, a census of rural schools reported on by V. Ermolaev found that 75.5 percent of them had no running water, "almost the same percentage lack a sewer system, and 57.4 percent have no central heating. Thousands of rural school buildings have no installed utilities whatever; most such schools are located in Azerbaidzhan, Uzbekistan, and Turkmenia."[17] Rural schools have fared so badly, Ermolaev went on to note, because of the "spinelessness and timidity" of the educational leaders, and because the nation had no "precise, well-thought-out strategy that would take account of all of the diversity of ethnic, socioeconomic, and natural conditions in which our rural schools operate."[18]

The cost of eliminating these shortcomings will be considerable, and it is clearly beyond the resources currently available for the task. However, these and other educational institutions are being asked to be more economically accountable and to take on the task of self-management, a phrase much discussed in the Soviet Union but little understood in concrete terms. In the recent discussions on the kinds of changes needed in the schools, there were challenges to the basic nature of the educational system that had not been heard since the experimental views of the 1920s. As one commentator put it, "In the forty years since the war, the schools have undergone only 'cosmetic' changes . . . but for some reason no one has examined the roots of their incorrect structure."[19] Many people are very wary of reforms being put forward by the educational establishment, since in the past changes have been introduced that did more harm than good. For example, according to one press report, the Academy of Pedagogical Sciences "wasted millions of rubles on an unsuitable, harmful, stupid program and then decided: 'Yes, we agree that the program is no good, but since we have spent so much money on it we ought to adopt it someplace.' "[20]

Perestroika for the Schools?

As in the rest of society, there is a call for the radical restructuring of Soviet education, but so far there is little understanding of, or agreement on, what exactly this should entail. As one observer put it, "It is amazing to note that not a single worker in our education system is able to give a clear explanation of what radical restructuring of the school system consists of."[21]

At the forefront of the movement to restructure the schools there has been a relatively small group of people who have come to be known as "the teacher innovators." In 1986-1987, the *Teachers' Gazette* launched a campaign to publicize the work of a number of teachers who for years had been quietly developing their own more effective teaching methods. Whereas they use a variety of techniques, what they have in common is a rejection of the official approach to teaching that has been in effect since the 1930s. The official view places the curriculum and the mechanics of teaching at the center of classroom activities, rather than the individual characteristics and needs of the child.[22] The innovators, therefore, represent a return to a child-centered form of education, in which the pupil and the teacher cooperate in the learning process. This is a dramatic departure from the prevailing emphasis on the teacher as the expert and the child as a receptacle for predigested information. The innovators try to get the pupils to participate in their education, to contribute to it in an active way. Participation, though, requires that some of the control in the classroom be shifted from the teacher to the pupil. Thus, "for children to feel that they are the educator's colleagues in learning, they must, wherever possible, be presented with freedom of choice."[23] The task of the teacher in this approach is to help shape and direct this process, not to dominate it totally. The basic goal of the innovators is to give both teachers and pupils "as much freedom as possible in the organization of the learning process, in the choice of methods and textbooks, and in their relations with higher school bodies. They believe that this is the only way to rescue schools from the present crisis and to combat the growing aversion of pupils to school and to the learning process."[24]

This movement is in harmony with the political leadership's call for a democratization of education to parallel that occurring in the wider society and to prepare children to participate in the new structures as they enter adulthood. It has met with some resistance, though, just as has democratization in the society. For teachers used to exercising unchallenged authority in the classroom (unchallenged from pupils, that is—administrators are a different matter altogether), the new methods can be very threatening. There is also considerable jealousy of the publicity and fame that some of the innovators have achieved. For the most conservative teachers, the answer to the education problems is not more freedom in the classroom but more effective control and discipline.

Those in support of the new methods lobbied for them vigorously through 1988, hoping to get the All-Union Congress of Educational Workers that took place in late December of that year (after a number of postponements as the conflict heated up) to endorse and work for the introduction of innovations. However, at the congress those against a radical change in the educational system and the adoption of new methods of teaching prevailed, and the innovation movement has (at least for the present) stalled.[25] The movement will not go away, however, for it is part of a broader attempt to take into account "the human factor" in creating a new basis for Soviet society. What this means concretely is that new institutions and organizations have to be based on people's diverse and often contradictory interests and capabilities and not on an illusionary search for a single, standardized approach for everyone. The motto of those advocating this flexible approach might well be "One size does not fit all!" In education, the failure to recognize differences, say some observers, has restricted the development of talents, and those in charge of the system have "attempted to educate the individual by binding his behavior and thinking with a multitude of prohibitions."[26]

Just as democratization is presenting challenges to the schools, so is *glasnost'*. The reconsideration of the past, and the rewriting of history that this has led to, have created something of a crisis in the classroom, and teachers are not prepared to deal with it. They can no longer present the materials and interpretations that they have used for decades, since every day children can read in the newspapers and see on television things that contradict what they have heard in the schools for years. Thus the curriculum in social, political, and historical studies has become obsolete.

The speed with which history is being addressed in a more honest manner presents a special problem, for the textbooks and the examinations on which they are based are ludicrously wrong. As a result, the school examinations in history were canceled in 1988. Later that year a new textbook for the tenth grade was introduced, but it was criticized as inadequate virtually as soon as it appeared.[27] This followed on the heels of a debate that had been going on throughout 1988, in which it was suggested by some that a variety of history textbooks were needed, not just one for the entire system. There were also complaints that pupils were not prepared for the changes, that they were "unaccustomed to debate or to a critical and analytical approach to their studies. They had become completely indifferent to history lessons; they simply asked teachers to tell them what they were supposed to write when taking entry examinations to higher educational institutions and not to bother with discussing complicated issues."[28] In 1989, another history textbook appeared; this one dealt more realistically with the Stalin period and included estimates of the number of people who died or were repressed. This book, however, is already out of date and is scheduled to be replaced at the end of 1990.

There is a debate under way on the extent to which there should be a greater variety of schools available to pupils. Soviet education is already differentiated along "functional" lines; that is, there are different types of schools to prepare children for different career tracks. There are also schools for those with special gifts in mathematics, music, languages, and so on. But now there is a recognition that schools need to be more responsive to the special needs of individuals, groups, and geographic areas. As the first-deputy chairman of the State Committee for Public Education expressed it:

> A great deal of work on developing diversity in schools will still have to be done. Until now we have never talked and even now we try to keep silent about the obvious truth: Different social strata and groups in our society have different needs for education. In other words, the question of what school a given region or a settlement needs, the question of the content of the curriculum of this school, whether it needs specialization, and what kind, should be solved individually each time,

not by the regional education authorities but by local people according to their expressed needs.[29] Moves have already been made in this direction, with the creation of school councils, boards, and associations run by members of a variety of local interests and groups. What this means in practice is that schools will become more closely tied to the goals and values of the various nationalities and ethnic groups, since localism almost inevitably means the greater influence of national cultures. And this, as Shadrikov acknowledged, is "one of the most delicate problems" facing the Soviet Union.[30] This view was echoed in an article in the *Teachers' Gazette,* which expressed "considerable concern about the penetration of nationalistic and chauvinistic ideas into the educational establishment."[31] For those who are involved in gaining greater independence for their republic, the school is an important vehicle for regenerating local culture and local languages in particular. Recent years have seen increasing concern about the decline in the use of native languages in the schools.[32]

In addition to all the other changes being urged on the schools, there is now a call for an increased emphasis on continuing education. The constant need to adapt to a changing economy and technological base and to develop individual skills as much as possible means that adult education should be both more available and of higher quality than it is at present.

The problems found in the elementary and secondary schools, however, are present to an even greater extent in adult education. The poor physical conditions and teaching staff, the lack of adequate equipment and books, poorly developed (and undifferentiated) courses, and inadequate administrators call for enormous investment and creative restructuring if the system is to be really effective. Given the other problems faced by the educational system, though, it is unlikely that the necessary resources will be forthcoming. As a result, the schools cannot count on their shortcomings being compensated for after their pupils leave the school system and enter the workforce.

Problems and Solutions

The schools are being asked to assist in the struggle to overcome the social problems that are overwhelming the society, the scope and consequences of which are the subject of enormous publicity and of great activity on the part of unofficial citizen groups. Courses on ecology are being introduced, and ways are being sought to integrate ecological education into existing courses, such as biology and geography. Likewise, there is a great deal of talk about the necessity for pupils to be taught about the hazards of drug and alcohol abuse. Given the still rather rigid structure of the curriculum, and the lack of knowledge and experience on the part of teachers, very little is being accomplished along these lines. It is not surprising that teachers are not rushing forward to add new burdens to an already-overloaded and poorly integrated curriculum. Nevertheless, the demands by various constituencies to add yet another social problem to the existing list of topics dealt with in the classroom continue to escalate.

The school, as well as being seen as a source of aid in the struggle against social problems, is seen by some as a contributor to them. Many children, it is clear, find Soviet schools a source of unnecessary stress. Thus, according to Iurii Azarov:

> Mental disorders, nervous breakdowns, and even children's suicides are largely due to useless overburdening with school studies, belittling their human dignity at school and at home, and alienation in the children's environment, which frequently imposes severe and unjustified demands on the personality. I have received many letters, including ones like this: "My child is afraid to go to school. He finds it hateful. A month ago someone smeared his coat with paint. When he told the teacher, she said abusively, 'Just what you deserve!' Then yesterday, in labor training class, someone poured acetone on his shoelaces and set them afire. My son cried out and the children laughed. But the worst thing was what happened at home: seeing his ruined shoes, his father beat him."[33]

For this child, as for many others, problems in the schools are compounded by the problems they face at home. As more and more children come from single-parent homes, and as the family comes under increasing pressure, children can arrive in the school with less support than their peers, bring the stresses of home with them, and are often less prepared than other children. As a result, they fall behind in their studies and may turn to alcohol and gangs as a way of dealing with their problems. The schools are not equipped to deal with this, since attention has always been on grades rather than the specific needs of pupils. If this situation is to be changed, special training for teachers will be needed, as well as the development of special services on which teachers can draw.[34]

As we have seen, the school in the Soviet Union is facing great difficulties and a wide array of new demands. The material, technical, pedagogical, and moral problems the schools face are unlikely to be solved in the near future, and probably cannot be solved unless the economic, social, and political problems in the wider society are also successfully addressed. The material resources that the schools so desperately need are unlikely to be forthcoming from an economy that worsens year by year.

In addition to material resources, there will have to be psychological changes on the part of educators. In their study of the alcohol problem in schools, Levin and Levin found that about half of the teachers in their survey were either against teaching children about the dangers of alcohol abuse or were unenthusiastic about having to do so.[35] If this resistance is found in other areas, such as sex education, environmental problems, or drug abuse, then it is going to be very difficult for the schools to meet the new demands being made of them. The fate of the attempt to introduce even a mild form of sex education in 1984 may be a guide to the fate of these other new programs. Due to a lack of books and materials, and what one observer has referred to as the "unteachability" of teachers, courses are found in only a few schools. As a result, such organizations as the Children's Fund, together with a number of informal groups, are offering sex-education programs outside of the schools. This may prove to be the model for educating children about social problems in general, given the difficulty of getting schools to change quickly enough. Because teachers in the USSR have always been trained to teach a particular subject, rather than to help children develop broad interests and skills, a reorientation of teacher training may be necessary to adapt to the complexities arising out of *perestroika*. And this, of course, will take time.

During 1989, there was a tentative move toward the introduction of religious education in what was clearly an attempt to influence the moral upbringing of pupils. In October 1989, *Izvestiia* published a story about an Orthodox priest teaching a course on the history of religion in a Leningrad school. The tone of the article was clearly very supportive of the project. Courses on the Bible and on religion are also now found in a number of universities, and children can put together their own Bible by cutting out of *Veselye kartinki* the special versions of Bible stories that this children's magazine now publishes. They can also attend one of the growing number of Sunday schools now being formed in the Soviet Union.[36]

There are also tentative movements in the direction of private education. For many years, parents have been able to hire special tutors for their children privately, and despite attacks on this practice, it has continued to flourish.[37] With the legalization of private enterprise in 1987, the way was cleared for the development of tutoring services on a more open and organized basis, and these services seem to have grown. One of them, the Stankevich School in Moscow, was opened in October 1987 and has been very successful; in fact, enrollment has been capped at 600, since the school does not have the facilities necessary for a larger student body. This school is not an alternative to the state schools, however, for its pupils attend only twice a week. The fees for this are 40–55 rubles per week, and pupils may enroll for any or all of the curriculum's twelve years of study.[38] In addition to private "cooperative" schools, there are also a number of different kinds of semiprivate, selective schools operated as branches of the state system or by organizations of one kind or another. Clearly, a number of experiments in alternative education are under way, and although they have not affected the situation of very many children as yet, it seems likely that this trend will continue.

The development of private and of selective education is, as one might imagine, highly controversial, although there have been a number of newspaper items in recent years calling for the introduction of private schools as an alternative to the state system.[39] At the same time, there has been increasing criticism of those schools that cater to the children of the elite, in which facilities are much better than in others, where tutoring is widely resorted to, and from which most graduates go on to the best universities and institutes.[40] Opening schools for people who can afford to pay the special fees will further anger those who are already upset at the amount of inequality and privilege in Soviet society. It is too early to predict how much privatization there will be in the future, but now that the ice has been broken this kind of school may develop fairly rapidly in spite of opposition.

As political and educational reformers search for solutions to current problems, there is an increasing willingness to learn from the experiences of other societies and to borrow from them those institutions that hold the promise of success. As one recent article pointed out:

> We cannot fail to see that a number of problems in education are universal problems that are not linked solely to the experience of a specific country. All over the world, teachers complain about declining interest in studies on the part of the masses of youth, it is proving difficult everywhere to harmonize centralization with decentralization in the administration of education, and so on. It is essential here to take account of both the positive and negative experiences of foreign countries.[41]

As Soviet schools are pulled further into the process of social, political, and economic reconstruction, we can expect a great deal of dislocation of, and conflict in, the educational system. Because education is one of the more conservative institutions in Soviet society, it is unlikely that change will be either rapid or smooth. At the same time, Soviet schools will probably come to resemble more and more the schools in other industrial societies, in which a large number of groups and organizations try to use the school to achieve their own special agendas. If comparative history is any guide, it is unlikely that the Soviet schools will be any more successful in meeting the contradictory demands made of them than have been the schools of Western Europe or North America. For the foreseeable future, then, schools in the USSR may be expected to be both the beneficiaries and the victims of changes occurring in the wider society.

Notes

1. J. Brooks, *When Russia Learned to Read* (Princeton, N.J.: Princeton University Press, 1985).
2. *SSSR v tsifrakh v 1987 godu* (Moscow: Finansy i Statistika, 1988), p. 251.
3. *Narodnoe khoziaistvo SSSR v 1988 godu* (Moscow: Finansy i Statistika, 1989), pp. 183–196.
4. M. Matthews, *Education in the Soviet Union: Policies and Institutions Since Stalin* (Boston: Allen and Unwin, 1982); D. Shurman, *The Soviet Secondary School* (Boston: Routledge, 1988).
5. V. D. Voinova and V. S. Korobeinikov, "Obshchestvennoe mnenie o reforme shkoly—edinstvo i mnogoobrazie," *Sotsiologicheskie issledovaniia,* no. 4 (1984), pp. 97–101.
6. For the details of the law on education see *Current Digest of the Soviet Press* [*CDSP* hereafter] 36, no. 18 (1984). Discussions of the reform may be found in J. Dunstan, "Soviet Schools and the Road to Reform," *Journal of Russian Studies,* no. 49 (1985), and B. Szekely, "The New Soviet Educational Reform," *Comparative Education Review* 30, no. 3 (1986).
7. For a discussion of this see "We Discuss the CPSU Central Committee's Draft," *CDSP* 36, no. 9 (1984), p. 14.
8. For a discussion of the problem of fitting the desires of young people to available jobs, see S. Marne, "Transition from School to Work: Satisfying Pupils' Aspirations and the Needs of the Economy," in D. Lane, ed., *Labor and Employment in the USSR* (New York: New York University Press, 1986), pp. 209–222.
9. For recent data on this, see V. K. Demidenko, "Motivy vybora professii shkol'nikami," *Sovetskaia pedagogika,* no. 7 (1989), pp. 26–30.
10. F. R. Filippov and V. A. Malova, "O nekotorykh napravleniiakh povysheniia effektivnost' obrazovaniia," *Sotsiologicheskie issledovaniia,* no. 2 (1984), pp. 62–71; V. G. Nemirovskii, "Obraz zhelaemogo budushchego kak faktor formirovaniia sotsial'no-professional'noi orientatsii podrostkov," *Sotsiologicheskie issledovaniia,* no. 2 (1984), pp. 85–89.
11. N. Anisin, *CDSP* 39, no. 34 (1987), p. 11.
12. E. Ligachev, "O khode perestroike srednei i vysshei shkoly i zadachakh Partii po ee osushchestvleniiu," *Uchitel'skaia gazeta,* February 18, 1988, pp. 1–4.
13. Ibid.
14. "V Prezidiume Verkhovnogo Soveta SSSR," *Uchitel'skaia gazeta,* March 15, 1988, p. 1.
15. V. Sobkin, "Otsenki i samootsenki," *Uchitel'skaia gazeta,* December 17, 1988, p. 2.
16. *Dinamika naseleniia SSSR 1960–1980 gg.* (Moscow: Finansy i Statistika, 1985), p. 163.

17. V. Ermolaev, "The Rural School: A Dramatic Change Needed," *Soviet Education*, February 1990, pp. 3–22.
18. Ibid., p. 11.
19. M. Postnikov, "Schools with a Bent for the Future," *Soviet Education*, May 1989, p. 4.
20. Iu. Azarov, "Learn in Order to Teach," *Soviet Education*, May 1989, p. 17.
21. Ibid., p. 20.
22. J. Muckle, *A Guide to the Soviet Curriculum* (New York: Croom Helm, 1988).
23. "The Pedagogy of Cooperation," *Soviet Education*, February 1988, p. 89. For materials on the innovation movement in education, see the February and March 1988 issues of *Soviet Education*.
24. Sergei Voronitsyn, "After the Unsuccessful 'Teaching Revolution,'" *Report on the USSR*, Radio Liberty, March 24, 1989, p. 9.
25. See ibid. for an account of this congress.
26. A. Tsipko, "Chelovek ne mozhet izmenit' svoei prirode," *Politicheskoe obrazovanie*, no. 4 (1989), pp. 68–78.
27. *Ogonek*, no. 44 (1988), p. 4.
28. Vera Tolz, "New History Textbook for Soviet Schools," *Report on the USSR*, Radio Liberty, September 1989, p. 6.
29. *Komsomol'skaia pravda*, November 25, 1988.
30. Ibid.
31. *Uchitel'skaia gazeta*, December 29, 1988, p. 1.
32. For example, see "Keruyuchys' chuttyam yedinoi rodyny," *Literaturna Ukraina*, April 9, 1987.
33. Azarov, op. cit., pp. 12–13.
34. B. Levin and M. Levin, "Watch Your Step . . . ," *Soviet Education*, January 1990, pp. 1–92.
35. Ibid.
36. Oxana Antic, "Sunday Schools in the Soviet Union," *Report on the USSR*, Radio Liberty, March 30, 1990, pp. 11–13.
37. "The Tutor from Bolshaya Polyanka Street," *CDSP* 36, no. 33 (1984), pp. 7, 20.
38. D. Marchenko and R. Papikyan, "Teaching English the Cooperative Way," *Soviet Life*, May 1990, p. 45.
39. For an example of the argument for the development of private schools for gifted children, see the article by G. Kreidlin in *CDSP* 39, no. 38 (1987), pp. 20–21, 32.
40. Sh. Muladzhanov, in *CDSP* 39, no. 8 (1987), pp. 1–5.
41. Z. Mal'kova et al., "Pedagogical Science at a New Stage," *Soviet Education*, March 1990.

CHAPTER 13

Youth Problems in the Soviet Union

Richard B. Dobson

Youth problems have become a subject of mounting public concern in the USSR. Soviet television shows angry teenagers challenging their parents' values and questioning the worth of socialism. Newspapers run countless stories about drug addiction and black marketeering. And in their public pronouncements, Communist officials deplore young people's seemingly insatiable appetite for Western fashions and rock music.

Literature and films also present a picture of the younger generation that differs strikingly from the happy, confident young men and women depicted on Communist propaganda posters. For example, Yuris Podnieks' film *Is It Easy to Be Young?* provides a jarring view of indigenous youth subcultures—among them, punks, "heavy metal" fans, drug addicts, Hare Krishna devotees, and disillusioned veterans home from Afghanistan. The film, which won first prize at the 1987 Tbilisi film festival, sparked heated debate over young people's values and life-styles. Other popular films, such as *Dear Elena Sergeevna* and *Little Vera,* have also created a stir, with their dark portrayals of ruthless, troubled, and disoriented young Soviets.

Meanwhile, the official organizations charged with molding the younger generation have fallen on hard times. As its leaders frankly acknowledge, the Young Communist League (Komsomol) is confronting a crisis of confidence. Its membership has been declining, while unofficial youth groups have been gaining strength. Officials recognize that many young people are fed up with the Komsomol's regimented structure and are abandoning Marxism-Leninism, the ideological bedrock of the regime. Facing this challenge, the Komsomol has begun to restructure itself, hoping to regain young people's allegiance.

The Nature of Soviet Youth Problems

The term *youth problems* generally refers to problems of cultural discontinuity, nonconformity, deviance, and rebelliousness associated with adolescents and young adults.[1] In the Soviet Union, such problems are commonly thought to include:

- The proliferation of informal youth groups (punks, soccer "fanatics," gangs of street toughs, hippies, and so on) whose life-styles depart from official or commonly accepted standards
- Various types of deviant behavior, including juvenile delinquency and alcohol and drug abuse
- An obsession with the acquisition of consumer goods (*potrebitel'stvo*) and material possessions (*veshchizm*)
- Widespread involvement in the black market, often to obtain artifacts of the youth subcultures or drugs
- Attraction to various religions and cults, contrary to the official stress on atheism and materialism
- Unacceptable political attitudes and behavior, ranging from cynicism and withdrawal to political activism that challenges official norms and institutions

In the mid-1980s, the Komsomol conducted a survey to find out what "negative traits" young people found in their age-mates. The results provided a revealing view of problems common to the younger generation. The most often cited negative traits were passivity in civic affairs (mentioned by 54 percent of the respondents), breaches of labor discipline and shoddy work (47 percent), drunkenness (40 percent), indifference (39 percent), and narcotics and substance abuse (34 percent). About a quarter of the young people polled said that some of their peers were vulgar and self-centered, caused public disturbances, and desired to work as little as possible for as much pay as possible. A fifth of them cited income from speculation and black-market trading, adulation of the Western way of life, and lack of interest in political affairs. One out of ten named young people's observance of religious rites as a negative trait.[2]

Of course, some segments of the USSR's youth population are more susceptible to such "negative phenomena" than others. As in other societies, the incidence of crime and deviance is higher than average among children from disadvantaged and "problem" families (e.g., families in which the parents are alcoholics, criminals, or child abusers). It also tends to be quite high among secondary-school dropouts and trade-school students.[3] Yet, boys and girls from stable, advantaged, "middle-class" families are no strangers to deviance and crime. As the writer Vasilii Rosliakov pointed out, "Drunkenness, drug abuse, licentiousness, and foreign currency speculation—all these vices have even infiltrated the secondary schools, particularly the so-called 'special schools' for children of the 'elite,' with their in-depth study of foreign languages."[4]

Sources of Youth Problems in the USSR

It is not surprising that some of the problems described above resemble those found among youth in the West. Young people in modern societies face similar challenges in maturing, gaining independence, forging their identities, finding a suitable job, and establishing a family. As in other societies, Soviet society's differentiated social and occupational structure gives rise to marked disparities in income, wealth, and opportunity—and hence to a sense of deprivation and frustrated ambition among some. Furthermore, modern communications permit the rapid diffusion of ideas, fashions, and life-styles from one society to another.

In other respects, however, Soviet young people's problems differ from those in the West. First, political controls have been much stronger and more pervasive in the USSR. More so than in the West, deviations from official standards have been viewed by the authorities as smacking of political opposition. Rock music, for instance, was treated as decadent and subversive for three decades. Second, the centrally administered Soviet economy has been geared to meeting the needs of heavy industry and the military, rather than to satisfying consumer demands. Goods have often been in short supply; therefore, more than their counterparts in the West, young Soviets have depended on the illegal black or semilegal gray market to acquire what they need. Third, despite its failings, the Soviet economy has generally managed to provide young people with jobs, although not necessarily creative or satisfying ones. Unemployment, one of the factors linked with crime, withdrawal, and rebellion among young people in the West, has not figured as prominently in the picture in the Soviet Union. However, unemployment may rise sharply if the USSR embarks on radical market-oriented reforms.

In the next section, we will examine more closely the factors that have exacerbated youth problems. As in other countries, long-term social trends linked with modernization have played an important role. Urbanization, rising educational levels, increasing affluence and leisure time, the spread of the mass media, and a weakening of traditional social controls have created the soil for the growth of youth subcultures and the problems associated with them.

Other changes that have contributed to the emergence of youth problems are more specific to the USSR and other Communist countries. They include an erosion of the authority of official institutions, the Komsomol's unresponsiveness to young people's interests, and a recent relaxation of the Party's controls.

Social Change: Youth in the Urban Milieu

Within a few decades, the Soviet Union has changed from a predominantly rural society to one in which the bulk of the population lives in urban areas. At the end of the 1980s, two-thirds of the 78 million young Soviets between the ages of fourteen and twenty-nine were urban dwellers. Most of them (particularly in the European part of the USSR) have grown up in small nuclear families in which both parents work. In an urban environment, young people are not subject to the pervasive community control of a traditional village-based society. Towns afford young people an opportunity to congregate, communicate with one another, learn about the latest styles, and gain access to goods through the black market. As Soviet social scientists have discovered, a distinctive "youth economy" involving trade in Western rock-music records, stylish imported clothing, electronic gear, and videotapes has developed in the cities.[5]

In recent years, educational requirements have risen. Today boys and girls are expected to complete a secondary education, usually lasting ten or eleven years. As a result, they are older when they start working than their counterparts were thirty or forty years ago. While increasing the time young people remain dependent on their parents, rising educational requirements have raised expectations. Young people's demand for interesting jobs, satisfactory housing, cars, and consumer goods has outpaced the Soviet economy's ability to satisfy it, leading to a sense of frustration and deprivation.[6]

Less firmly established in families and jobs than older people, young people experience more acutely the tensions and contradictions in Soviet society. As Valerii I. Tsybukh, the chairman of the Supreme Soviet's Committee on Youth Affairs, pointed out in 1989:

> Youth in our country comprise 43 percent of the able-bodied population. And if today we say that social tension is increasing in the country, it is increasing mainly in this environment. Low wages, the impossibility of obtaining housing or placing children in day schools, and along with this, the lack of confidence in youth and their lack of an opportunity to really influence their destiny—all these are facts of our life. Not to notice them will lead the country into the most critical social conflicts.[7]

Meanwhile, the rapid pace of change has contributed to a split between the generations. Igor Kon, a leading Soviet sociologist, stated, "Generally speaking, we can say that the faster historical development becomes, and the more significant the changes which occur within a period of time, the more noticeable the differences between generations will be, the more complicated the transmission mechanisms and the transmission of culture from the old to the young will be, and the more selective the attitude of the young toward their social and cultural heritage will be."[8] Kon noted that differences between the young and the old are generally more evident in consumer preferences, use of leisure time, artistic taste, and accepted norms governing relations between the sexes than they are in basic values. Fashions change more rapidly than values do, and young people often use style and jargon to distinguish themselves and their group from other groups and from adults.[9] These observations appear to be borne out by Komsomol surveys. The polls show that most young people feel they share general values, such as "love of the Motherland," with their parents. When it comes to music, style, and other aspects of culture, the story is quite different: Three-quarters say they disagree with their parents' tastes.[10]

The Appeal of the West

Many young urban Soviets, especially the trendsetters of their generation, associate the West with an abundance of consumer goods, innovation, dynamism, and greater personal freedom. Increased travel and modern means of communication made what was once the Iron Curtain permeable. The policy by which for decades the Soviet government restricted the flow of information from the West (from 1980 to 1987, and in prior years, it jammed most Western radio broadcasts to the USSR) has been reversed. Young Soviets learn more about the outside world and have more contact with foreigners than their parents did. Soviet sociological studies have found that young people, especially those who obtain information from foreign sources (e.g., shortwave radio broadcasts, magazines, and films), "evaluate certain elements of life in capitalist countries more highly" than other Soviets do.[11]

Especially in major Soviet cities, signs of the spread of Western styles abound. Trendy Soviet teenagers show their "sophistication" by wearing conspicuously non-Soviet clothing, playing Western pop music on shortwave radios, and spicing their speech with foreign words. With evident dismay, one journalist described the sight of young people on the street:

> The words "Free Love" are written in English on a girl's blouse. . . . The owner of a jersey urging people to vote for one of the candidates in an overseas presidential election acknowledges that he bought it secondhand in Odessa for 25 rubles. . . . One finds T-shirts emblazoned with the stars and stripes, portraits of rock-music idols, dollar bills, and inscriptions in English that the owners don't even attempt to translate before putting on.[12]

Another journalist described the slang of students, "mainly those from large cities," who sounded like "strangers from the hinterlands of some sort of Michigan, Texas or California with their endless strings of distorted English words like *leibl* (label) and *batton* (button), *voch* (watch) and *beg* (bag)."[13]

An Erosion of Authority in Official Institutions

Through its control of education and the mass media, the Communist party has long tried to bend truth to meet its needs. Today, in an era of *glasnost'* and *perestroika,* Soviet commentators openly admit that falsehood, hypocrisy, and efforts to conceal problems have eroded the authority of the political leaders and of parents and teachers as well. As one man explained in a letter to the youth newspaper *Komsomol'skaia pravda* in 1987:

> Many parents didn't tell [their children] what they thought, but what they "had to"—so that their children would live safely in this world; so that their way of looking at the world, their state of mind, would be protected from contradictions that even adults can't always handle. Children see through such a lie quickly, and the results are catastrophic. Anyone who watched Leningrad

Television's recent series called "Test for Adults" could see for himself that not one of the 15-year-olds who were shown on camera could think of a single adult whose opinion would be authoritative for them.[14]

The pervasive mendacity about Soviet history and society led many young people to develop a "dual morality" (one for public display, another for their private lives).[15]

The gradual erosion of authority and credibility has taken its toll on the Komsomol, undercutting its ability to instill Marxist-Leninist values and to foster loyalty to the Communist party. Surveys conducted in the mid-1980s by the Komsomol's research center revealed widespread disaffection. A third of all Komsomol members polled admitted that the Komsomol had no effect on their lives. The responses showed that "regardless of the indicator selected—whether it is the attitude toward restructuring of the Komsomol, personal participation in it, level of political awareness, or the evaluation of the results of the 20th All-Union Komsomol Congress [in 1987]—one finds a yawning chasm of pessimism, non-participation, and skepticism."[16] In 1988, the second plenum of the All-Union Komsomol Central Committee devoted principal attention to "winning back young people's lost trust."[17]

According to Igor Il'inskii, who headed the Komsomol's research center, young people's disaffection stemmed largely from "the reluctance and inability of many Komsomol workers and activists to concern themselves with the real problems of young people, of inquisitive, restless, rebellious, defiant, and 'difficult' youth. . . . I am certain," he added, "that the growth of young people's informal associations is largely a reaction to formalism in Komsomol activity and to the failure of the methods of this activity to correspond to the spirit of the times and to young people's intellectual and cultural level."[18] As another commentator observed, Komsomol workers dealing with informal youth groups found themselves "looking into an unmerciful mirror that reflected the shortcomings of our work with young people."[19]

In 1989, the Komsomol surveyed nearly 10,000 young people between the ages of fourteen and twenty-nine to learn what they consider the underlying causes of "negative phenomena" among them. The young people felt that poor organization of leisure time (cited by 46 percent), the bureaucratic nature of the Soviet system (44 percent), and disenchantment with socialism as an ideal (40 percent) were the basic causes. About a third felt that youth problems were caused by social injustice, family troubles, or formalism and bureaucracy in the Komsomol.[20]

Glasnost' and an Easing of Restrictions

Without a change in official information policy, youth problems would surely not have gained the widespread public attention that they have. Owing to *glasnost'*, Soviet journalists have gained more latitude to investigate and discuss controversial issues. I. I. Karpets, a leading Soviet criminologist, noted in 1987:

Frankly, I'm amazed that many ideological workers have suddenly "discovered" negative behavior among young people, as if it came into being only yesterday. This applies, for example, to drug addiction. As a former chief of criminal investigations, I can testify that we were already making a colossal effort to combat this evil a quarter of a century ago. But our press, one of the main social institutions with an educational function, pretended for all those years that drug addiction did not exist.[21]

Glasnost' has allowed scholars greater freedom, too. In the past, the Party authorities expected social scientists to follow its guidelines, to show Soviet society in a positive light, and to emphasize socialism's superiority to capitalism. Soviet scholars for the most part complied: They treated social problems as "survivals of the past" (customs that had survived from pre-Communist times), as the result of corrupting influences emanating from capitalist countries, or as problems arising in a particular "microenvironment" (*mikro-sreda*). A Soviet editor pointed out, "This approach imposed a kind of 'taboo' on attempts to look for the causes of negative behavior on the level of the macro-environment [the larger society] or to find reasons in the fundamental socioeconomic relations of our society."[22]

Thus, until recently Soviet scholars generally denied that young people in the USSR experienced problems comparable to those found in the West. Writing in the Party journal *Kommunist,* Igor Kon noted that "if comparisons were made, they invariably followed the formula that nothing of the sort exists in our country, nor can it exist!" As Kon emphasized, however, "many of the features and trends of contemporary youth subculture are international."[23]

Types of Youth Groups and Subcultures

Since the late 1970s, there has been a proliferation of unofficial "informal" (*neformal'nye*) youth groups in the USSR. The groups are diverse and fluid. For the most part, they lack official sponsorship and have been either ignored or opposed by official organizations such as the Komsomol. The groups have varying orientations, life-styles, symbols, and slang. They vary, too, in their size and degree of organization. Some are little more than groups of neighborhood friends who congregate after school to play rock-music tapes. Others, such as the preservationist, environmental, and political-action groups in Moscow, Leningrad, and other towns, have explicit goals and can mobilize hundreds or thousands of people in demonstrations.[24]

Iurii Shchekochikhin, the youth editor for *Literaturnaia gazeta,* has played a leading role in publicizing these various youth groups—and in giving them a sympathetic hearing. In the early 1980s, struck by the appearance of sports "fanatics" (*fanaty*) and other informal groups in Moscow, he began to investigate why young people joined groups with unconventional life-styles. He met with young people and even set aside

Thursday afternoons to talk with those who called a special phone number published in the paper.

Shchekochikhin recognized that teenagers have always formed groups based on common interests. He discovered, however, that today's youth groups differ from those seen earlier in Soviet society. In his view, "never before has membership in a group or gang caused the teenager to submit so completely to the group's rules and standards, ranging from ways of dressing and musical tastes to particular ways of expressing themselves that are often unfamiliar and incomprehensible to adults."[25]

The reasons that young people have for joining groups are complex. Many adolescents seek a sense of community with friends outside the regimented routine they find in the schools and the Komsomol. They are often motivated by a quest for self-expression, the desire to make a statement. For example, one self-declared "punk," an eighteen-year-old named Sergei, came to Shchekochikhin's office at *Literaturnaia gazeta* in an outfit that seemed to say it all. Sergei had fifteen large safety pins stuck through his clothes, a bell dangling from his leg, and various insignias on his jeans. As he explained, he began dressing in an unconventional way when he was about fifteen because he wanted to protest against banality, to gain attention, to offend:

> My thing at that time [in the eighth grade] consisted of wearing a pair of pants, a black shirt, and a black tie. . . . I shaved my temples, convinced some of my friends to do the same, and we walked along the street, putting ourselves on display. . . . We want people to turn around and look at us, to notice us. It's fun to walk along the street and see the confused expressions of the people we pass. Some sedate man walks by, gives you a supercilious look, and you feel that your very appearance has somehow offended him. . . . It warms the soul.[26]

A Soviet journalist provided further illustrations of youthful rebellion with the following thumbnail sketches:

> Georgii Z., born in 1970, a secondary-school student: "I consider myself a heavy-metal fan (*metallist*). I enjoy the music tremendously. In my opinion, heavy-metal fans don't have any particular world view; they just love music."
>
> Sergei P., born in 1965, a student at a technicum: "I believe in Russian Orthodox religion. I listen to Western radio stations. I'm registered at the narcotics clinic. I love hard rock. I wanted to create a rock group with my friend Andrei K., but they didn't let us."
>
> Dmitrii D., born in 1968, a test mechanic: "I consider myself a hippie. I became a hippie to protest against the 'New Wave' [in rock music] and breakdancing. I didn't join the Komsomol, because I didn't see anything to gain from it and thought it was pointless just to pay dues. I took music lessons, and my friends and I asked the factory committee for musical equipment and a place to play, but they turned us down. My friends call me 'Monk.' "[27]

The writer pointed out that these young people had something in common aside from their age and unconventional life-styles: They all had been detained by Komsomol volunteers for allegedly violating public order. It is clear that many of them had been badgered and persecuted by Komsomol activists seeking to combat such "unhealthy" phenomena.

In the next sections, we will survey a few of the more notable youth subcultures and groups that have appeared on the Soviet scene. Many of them are centered on shared interests, such as rock music, devotion to a soccer team, belief in a particular philosophy or religion, or control of a territory (the group's "turf"). Others seek to achieve political or cultural goals.

Rock-Music Fans

For many years, the Communist authorities opposed *rok* (rock music), seeing it as an example of bourgeois decadence and a subversive influence on Soviet culture. Although Soviet television and the official musicians' unions shunned rock groups, the appeal of *rok* continued to spread in a counterculural underground. Rock-music fans came to number in the tens of millions (often overlapping with other youth subcultures). Those at the heart of the "movement" are the musicians themselves and their closest followers. Although there is a good deal of cultural rebelliousness in Soviet rock music, the fans are largely apolitical and cynical about the regime.[28]

In the late 1980s, official policy toward rock music eased dramatically. In 1985, the Leningrad youth newspaper *Smena* acknowledged the existence of hundreds of thousands of rock associations (*rokob"edinenii*) throughout the country. That same year, Moscow opened its first rock recording studio. Leading rock groups such as Boris Grebenshchikov's "Aquarium" began to receive favorable treatment in the press, to have records issued under the Soviet "Melodia" label, and to receive permission to perform abroad.

"Heavy metal" rock has considerable appeal, especially among teenage boys, who use chains, spikes, and riveted bracelets to identify themselves as *metallisty*. Other types of rock-music followers are known as *serki* (members of "family rock communes," *semeinye rokkomuny*), *roksi* (followers of rock groups, *roksistemy*), and *rokery* (this term is applied to rock fans generally but also to members of motorcycle gangs associated with a particular rock group or genre).

Although Soviet rock music has been heavily influenced by Western musicians, some Soviet rock groups represent a bizarre amalgam of influences. For example, one member of a "family rock commune" wrote about his group's desire to revive Russian culture:

> It's the only salvation from all troubles.... The goal of our movement is to build communes, revive ancient Russian customs, holidays, tools, costumes, food, etc., etc., to try to convince hippies, punks and nostalgists (*nostalgisti*) to give up their trends and come over to ours, to develop Soviet rock and fight for its freedom, and to combat currency speculators and young people who conspicuously dress in Western fashions (*mazhory*) as well as suburban

toughs (*liubery*) and the Leningrad association OAD. . . . We revere the ideas of October, we admire the genius of Lenin, and we hope to revive the spirit of bygone times of battle and to drive out Western trends, fashions and symbols, replacing them with our own.[29]

Hippies and "God-Seeking" Cults

In the 1960s, the Soviet version of the hippie (*khippi* or *khipparei*) began appearing. Like their Western counterparts, the *khippi* usually have long hair, wear jeans, headbands, and beads, and express contempt for the production- and consumption-oriented society by "dropping out." Some identify themselves collectively as being members of the "System" (*sistema*) and call themselves "the people" (*piplz*). They value peace, close personal relationships, love, and equality. Many have jobs that do not force them to conform to the demands of society, such as seasonal or part-time work, and some panhandle to eat. Many of them are rock-music fans, too.[30]

In addition, there are religious groups (for example, Orthodox, Baptist, or Buddhist) as well as groups of a "god-seeking" (*bogoiskatel'nyi*) or occult nature, including Hare Krishna devotees and practitioners of Satanism.[31] One journalist, for instance, described "Bulgakov idolizers." These young people engage in "Satanic" rites in the house where, according to the novel *Master and Margarita*, the Evil Spirit once resided.[32]

The proliferation of religious groups and cults has elicited much commentary. A. Bondarenko argued:

> The reemergence and growth of interest in religion among young people is in large measure a negative reaction to the indiscriminate rejection of religion by vulgar atheism [in the schools and Komsomol] and senseless attacks on the subject, [ranging] from the physical destruction of temples to the wholesale condemnation of religious philosophers and writers as ignoramuses and obscurantists.[33]

Bondarenko believed that young people were attracted not so much by the philosophical and spiritual content as by "the cult aspect of religion"—the sense of belonging to a group with a distinctive world view. He observed:

> This is the origin of various quasi-religious movements: home churches with their own preachers, various unions such as the Christian Patriotic Union which held its first congress in Moscow in January 1988, the Union of Religious Socialists, neo-Christian youth groups like the born-again, and the burgeoning pseudo-Christian movements such as "Lord's Children," the Unification Church, and so on.
>
> Eastern and European mysticism have also become widespread. In Moscow alone, more than 10 religious mystics' groups are known to exist. . . . Typically, groups with a quasi-religious orientation spring up in the ambience of the so-called unofficial youth movement, including such groups as "Cosmos," "Peace Watch," the "Common Cause Federation," and the like.[34]

Youth Toughs, *Fanaty,* and *Afgantsy*

Youth gangs, long associated with troublemaking and "hooliganism," have become more common in Soviet cities. As K. G. Vaino, who was then head of the Estonian Communist party, noted some years ago:

> How often one sees on the streets of our cities in the evenings groups of young people idly lounging about, behaving defiantly and literally looking for a fight. They have their leaders—the older boys—and their own twisted ideas about honor and decency. . . . It is very easy for this idle, herdlike way of passing time to lay the groundwork for misdeeds that young people then spend years paying for.[35]

Vaino expressed consternation that Komsomol activists had lost their former militancy, no longer rallying to the cry, "Let the ground burn under the hooligans' feet!" as they had in the 1960s.[36]

In the 1970s and 1980s, groups known as *fanaty* appeared. The *fanaty* are supporters of popular soccer teams, such as Spartacus and Dynamo, who wear hats and scarves with their team's color and congregate at stadiums. The authorities have viewed the *fanaty* with alarm because they can be uncontrolled and unruly. Many of the *fanaty* are teenagers from working-class neighborhoods.

In January 1987, the popular magazine *Ogonek* publicized another distinctive group—the *liubery,* toughs from Moscow's working-class suburb of Liubertsy. The *liubery* engage in bodybuilding, cultivate physical prowess, and are intolerant of Western styles. Hoping to rid Moscow of hippies, rock-music enthusiasts, and punks, they come to Moscow to beat up such "undesirables."[37]

In many towns, adolescents have formed self-styled vigilante groups to fight against what they perceive to be corruption and injustice. In 1986, for instance, a newspaper published a letter from a teenager in Novosibirsk who said he belonged to an unofficial group called Law and Order.[38] Another group, made up of young men who had served in the army, sent the following letter to *Komsomol'skaia pravda:*

> "The Communists" are writing to you. Our group came into being January 1, 1987. There's nothing worth buying around here, and we've come together in a group to rectify matters. We've already drawn up a plan of action. We're going to monitor all the city's bosses (unofficially, of course). And if they do anything wrong (not in the spirit of restructuring), we'll beat them up. But first, of course, we'll warn them what must be done, using our common sense. In short, we're declaring war on those who are holding up restructuring.[39]

Some of these groups attract *Afgantsy* (veterans of the war in Afghanistan) who have had difficulty readjusting to civilian life. Some *Afgantsy* are so disgusted with the laxity and corruption in Soviet society that they are tempted to take the law into their own hands.[40]

To the shock and horror of older citizens, even neo-Nazi youth bands have arisen. On the evening of April 20, 1982, the ninety-fourth anniversary of Hitler's birth, so-called fascists (*fashisty,* also called *fashiki*) gathered in Pushkin Square in the heart of Moscow. Some wore black shirts and caps with swastikas and had shaven heads; others wore ropes around their necks with a knot over the Adam's apple, as a sort of necktie.[41] Since then, similar groups have been reported in Leningrad, Murmansk, and many other towns. In 1987, for instance, *Leningradskaia pravda* carried an article about the so-called Russian National Socialist Workers' Party and other Nazi groups in Leningrad. Members of the party reportedly painted swastikas on walls and distributed leaflets with chauvinist appeals for a revival of nazism.[42]

Subsequent reports suggested that neo-Nazism may be gaining strength. As one writer noted in 1989:

> There are dozens of places in Leningrad where the "*fashiki*" meet. And everywhere younger boys hang around them and listen spellbound. That is, they freely spread their views among those who can be enticed by the performance to the fair-haired rogues, Nordic character, supreme race, and "Black International." We have quite a few adolescent boys without their own world view, yet craving something to believe in, something to live for.[43]

Grass-Roots Activists

In recent years, young people have also played a growing role in grassroots associations seeking political and social change. Under Gorbachev, many groups have arisen that seek to protect the natural environment, preserve cultural monuments, and promote national languages and culture.

In March 1987, for example, members of several informal organizations, including Salvation, Peace, the Council of Cultural Ecology, and the literary group Club 81, staged demonstrations in Leningrad to protest the local authorities' decision to demolish the Angleterre Hotel, where the Russian poet Sergei Esenin committed suicide in 1925.

The growth of these informal organizations has been one of the most notable developments of the 1980s. As the journalist Miroslav Buzhkevich observed:

> Such organizations are now functioning in practically all province, territory, and republic centers as well as in the country's major industrial cities. Some of them support positions alien to our ideology. But the range of interests . . . is extremely wide: discussion of the progress of restructuring, the fight against bureaucracy, corruption, and a coercive and bureaucratic work style, as well as ecology, urban planning, the preservation of architectural monuments, art, culture, folklore, and many, many other subjects.[44]

Buzhkevich was told at the Moscow Communist Party City Committee that there were about 2,000 such independent action groups and clubs in the capital.

Unlike the subcultures described above, these associations tend to attract young adults, especially those with a higher education. According to Buzhkevich, "the public independent action movement is to a certain degree an elitist movement, especially in Moscow, Leningrad, and a number of other of the largest centers." It is supported "chiefly by young scientists and scholars (25–35 years old)," who are drawn from the humanities and, to a lesser degree, technical fields.[45]

In recent years, these diverse groups have made some efforts to coordinate their activities. In August 1987, the first officially sanctioned conference of unofficial groups was held in Moscow, and 300 representatives (mainly young people) from forty-seven informal groups attended. Among the groups present at the meeting were the *Perestroika* Club, the Community Club, the Fund for Combatting Bureaucratism, the Extramural Social and Political Club, and the Club of Social Initiatives. The activists discussed a range of proposals, including a plan to build a monument to victims of Stalin's purges, steps to democratize the USSR's electoral system, measures to aid persons who were subjected to errors by judicial and investigative bodies, and ways to aid the needy.[46]

Nationalist Extremists

The potentially most explosive groups draw on nationalism, both among Russians and the other peoples of the USSR. Russian chauvinist groups such as *Pamiat'* (Memory) and proponents of fascism seek youthful adherents who will help them achieve their goals. Young people drawn into these movements sometimes adopt extremist views. A twenty-two-year-old university student in Vladivostok wrote:

> The Communists are now disavowing Stalin. But the values that they impose on us are not changing. Take, for example, the thesis of the so-called equality of all peoples. Its ludicrousness is apparent to everyone.
>
> I assert: Fascism alone is the real alternative to the degeneration of the nation. We demand an end to assimilation, the destruction of handicapped individuals who are disgracing the nation with their existence, the sterilization of inferior peoples, and resolution of the housing problem by the resettlement of inferior people from well-appointed apartments.
>
> I am confident that very many will support us. At the university where I am studying, the majority of students view my arguments favorably, and the rest are inferior people who do not have the right to exist.[47]

Nationalist views find expression among non-Russian peoples as well. In recent years, especially since the December 1986 anti-Russian riots in Alma-Ata, there has been a growing awareness that ethnic-based informal youth groups can provide a fertile ground for nationalist extremism.[48] In the Baltic republics, the Caucasus, Central Asia, and other regions, young people have taken an active role in both peaceful demonstrations and bloody inter-ethnic conflicts. For example, during the 1989 pogrom in

Uzbekistan, in which thousands of Uzbeks attacked Meskhetians, "it was mainly youth 20–25 years of age who participated in the disorders."[49]

Crime, Drugs, and the Black Market

As Soviet criminologists are aware, youth groups can provide the basis for criminal activity, including hooliganism, currency speculation, drug trafficking, extortion, and theft. Studies conducted by the All-Union Institute for the Study of the Causes of Crime and Development of Crime-Prevention Measures indicated that most teenagers' crimes are committed in groups.[50] In recent years, Soviet criminologists have found that young people are responsible for a growing number of robberies, thefts, and violent crimes and that they show more "criminal professionalism" than they used to.[51]

Spontaneous disorders have also become more common. In the fall of 1988, for example, a Soviet journalist described a riot in Volgograd:

> I looked at the photo, and it seemed that I had seen it all before in the newspapers and magazines—the defaced railroad cars and trolley-buses, the smashed windows of stores and apartment buildings, the overturned kiosks, and the wrecked State Motor Vehicle Inspectorate post. . . . No, this is not a train wreck. A "typhoon" struck the streets of Volgograd. How else can you describe the wild rampage by the throng of thousands of young people who spilled out of the central stadium the other day after being "turned on" for about two hours by visiting rock groups?[52]

Even more disturbing than such disorders, however, are the growing number of bloody fights between rival gangs. In an unusually frank account, Iurii Shchekochikhin described the increase in gang violence in the country. Kazan, which had gained notoriety for its frequent gang battles, was (he noted) only an "extreme case"—gangs have been clashing in many other towns. In Ulyanovsk, for example, a mob of teenagers armed with sticks, chains, and brass knuckles swept through the city, beating up everyone in their path. In Moscow, police tried to break up a fight between two gangs on the Arbat, but the gangs turned on the police and besieged the police station. It took all night to restore order.[53]

Some gangs are linked with professional criminal rings, which use them to extort money, train criminals, and distract attention from their own illegal operations. A specialist at the Ministry of Internal Affairs viewed young people's adoption of criminal traditions as "an unprecedented phenomenon" in Soviet society. Another crime specialist noted that such gangs (said to be composed largely of school dropouts, trade-school students, and young workers) are most likely to arise in new working-class districts bereft of more enduring types of organizations.[54]

The Drug Problem

Although alcohol use by minors has been recognized as a serious problem for decades, only since the mid-1980s has there been public discussion of drug use by young Soviets. Soviet authorities now recognize that drug abuse is a dangerous and widespread problem. Aleksandr Vlasov, the USSR Minister of Internal Affairs from 1986 to 1988, pointed out that four out of five drug addicts were under the age of thirty and that drug abuse was much more closely linked with crime than alcoholism was.[55] Studies conducted in Georgia found that 80 percent of the addicts had started using drugs before they were twenty-five years old and that most used a range of drugs. The most common were hashish (used by 84 percent), morphine (47 percent), and opium (44 percent). Drugs were often used in company, particularly "at gatherings of hedonistic youth, where the use of drugs, especially the smoking of hashish, is prestigious and fashionable."[56]

To combat the problem, Interior Minister Vlasov called for further steps to educate young people, parents, teachers, and medical personnel about the consequences of drug addiction, to rehabilitate addicts, and to cut back on the supply of narcotics. Principal attention was given to closing the channels through which narcotics were distributed. At the beginning of 1987, compulsory treatment began to be organized for juvenile drug addicts at therapy and labor-rehabilitation centers, and some schools started distributing antidrug literature.[57] In Moscow, Leningrad, and other cities, "hot lines" and drug-abuse centers were established.

Fighting drugs has been an uphill battle. In a 1987 interview, the RSFSR minister of public health, A. I. Potapov, noted: "On the whole, the level of preventive work with teenage drug addicts is depressingly low. In some provinces, only one (!) teenager diagnosed as a drug addict is registered. In others, only one or two teenagers have taken a course of inpatient examination and treatment. To believe these figures would be naive at the very least, if one bears in mind the group nature of drug addiction."[58]

A year later, V. Pankin, chief of the Main Administration for Criminal Investigations of the USSR Ministry of Internal Affairs, reported:

> The two-year effort to destroy the crop base has altered the situation. . . . [But] the evil has begun to emerge in a new form. In certain regions 30 to 40 percent of those addicted now use medicinal types of drugs. This kind of drug addiction is more serious from the standpoint of treatment and prevention. . . . It is characteristic of the Baltic region, Central Russia, Leningrad, and Moscow. We have [also] had cases of clandestine laboratories for the manufacture of synthetic drugs.[59]

Meanwhile, the press has carried a seemingly inexhaustible stream of articles about the problem. One account published in Moscow's evening newspaper told about how a young woman had joined the hippies in the 1970s and began experimenting with drugs. "At 15, you understand, you're curious about everything," she wrote. "In the entrance way of one of the apartment houses on Pushkin Street, [a friend] injected three cc's of morphine into one of my veins." After that, her life began to revolve around drugs. The woman confessed that she had sold hundreds of rare books from her family's library to buy drugs on the black market.[60]

In some localities, drug use has been spreading through the schools, at times (if one is to believe the press accounts) reaching epidemic proportions. In a letter to a newspaper, a tenth-grade girl described her plight: "There are more than 30 people in my class. Only three of them haven't tried drugs. All the others are either regular or occasional users. You have to have money for all this. So we have a kind of 'commune.' Today you have money, tomorrow I have some. Everyone owes someone something, so it's simply impossible to escape from this circle!"[61]

Another girl, from Moscow, explained: "In our class everyone knows how to 'extract' the narcotic from a regular medication. Two years ago— I was in the seventh grade then—that's all anyone talked about. A fellow offered to let me try it—he had already injected himself before. . . . Later, after I had been sucked in, he sold me 'raw materials'—first for 2 rubles, then for 10 and even 15 rubles for an apothecary vial."[62]

Under these circumstances, it is hardly surprising that black-market trades have increasingly involved drugs. The magazine *Sobesednik* described how drugs were being bought and sold in a movie theater: "Here, people who are driven by their 'habit' but have no money pay for a bag of opium 'weed' with a gold wedding ring stolen from their mother or a pair of foreign jeans. . . . For dope you can buy a *Zhiguli* [automobile], for instance. Dope has become a kind of currency."[63]

The Challenge to the Komsomol

The Komsomol was created after the Bolshevik Revolution as an official youth organization that would mobilize young people to carry out the Party's directives, provide ideological indoctrination, and train future Party members and officials. Before World War II, the youth league enrolled a minority of the young people. After the war it expanded greatly. By the 1960s, it claimed most young people between the ages of fourteen and twenty-eight as members.[64]

Today Party officials, Komsomol organizers, and sociologists agree that millions of young people are alienated from the Komsomol. Many boys and girls had joined the organization because its recommendations were important for admission to higher education, promotion at work, and permission to travel abroad. Since the early 1980s, however, a growing number of young people have been leaving the Komsomol, and fewer have been enrolling. Komsomol membership declined from 42 million in 1982 to 36 million in 1988 and 31 million in 1990.[65] Discussions in the Komsomol press suggested that a large share of those who remained on the books were members in name only. By 1990, the Komsomol was rent by serious political and ethnic divisions.

Party and Komsomol officials acknowledge serious problems in the youth league's work. When CPSU General Secretary Gorbachev addressed the 20th All-Union Komsomol Congress in April 1987, he criticized the Komsomol for being enmeshed in bureaucracy and detached from young people's concerns. Gorbachev complained that "an elite" of privileged leaders had formed within the youth organization and that the activists had lost touch with the rank and file. As he put it, "It's as if the young people are walking on one side of the street while the Komsomol activists are walking on the other side, and, what's more, in the opposite direction."[66] Others have noted that rampant careerism and Komsomol officials' willingness to use their positions for personal gain have helped to undermine the youth league's authority.[67]

The Decline in Ideological Commitment

Viktor Mironenko, who headed the Komsomol from 1986 to 1990, echoed Gorbachev's criticism on many occasions. Mironenko noted that efforts at political indoctrination often had little effect: "Unfortunately, dialogue between party and Komsomol workers, teachers, and veterans, on the one hand, and young people, on the other, has often resembled a conversation between the deaf and the mute. The world outlook shaped in this way is very fragile and disintegrates at its first encounter with real life or the complexity of the historical path covered by our country."[68]

Mironenko's somber assessment is backed up by considerable evidence showing that many young people are disenchanted with routinized Komsomol study groups, Marxism-Leninism, and loud claims about socialism's superiority to capitalism. Komsomol studies have found that young Soviets want to obtain more political information but have "very little interest in joining Komsomol political education groups."[69]

Other studies conducted by the Komsomol revealed that many young people rejected key tenets of the official worldview. In one poll, half (48 percent) of the young people surveyed saw no need to evaluate works of literature, art, and music from a class position (i.e., to judge them according to whether they serve the interests of the "working class" or "reactionary" classes). Komsomol sociologists also noted that young people's "critical feelings about the negative features of our life sometimes turn into excessive fault-finding and the denial of socialism's material and spiritual achievements."[70]

Results of a poll of 1,657 full-time students in higher education likewise gave little comfort to Party and Komsomol officials. The students were asked the loaded question, "How important is it for a highly skilled professional to have a good knowledge of Marxist-Leninist theory?" A quarter of the students (23 percent) answered simply, "It's not important [*nevazhno*]." The proportion giving this response was lowest among students attending agricultural and teacher-training institutes (10 percent in each case). The proportion increased among students at universities in scientific and technical fields (16 percent), at medical institutes (27 percent), at engineering and technical institutes (33 percent), and at art institutes (44 percent).[71]

In 1987, when the Komsomol weekly *Sobesednik* opened a discussion about communism as an ideal, some readers openly ridiculed communism.

For example, a reader named Valerii, from a provincial town, dismissed "fairy tales about communism," saying "me and my friends need well-paying work, money, automobiles, nice stylish clothes, and the ability freely to travel abroad as tourists."[72] Of about 300 letters on this topic, 52 percent of the letter writers said they believed in communism. Another 15 percent said they believed but had doubts; 10 percent said they tended not to believe (*skoree ne veriat*); and 21 percent said they did not believe at all.[73] It should be noted that these responses came from readers of the Komsomol press, among whom the proportion of "believers" would be expected to be higher than among young people as a whole.

Can the Komsomol Regain Young People's Devotion?

Komsomol officials recognized that the youth league must take steps to rekindle young people's interest and devotion to the Communist cause. Leading spokespersons argued that young people must be given more independence and allowed to assume more responsibility. As Igor Il'inskii put it, there must be "greater tolerance for their way of life—their thinking, language, manners, clothes, music, and other interests."[74] Another Komsomol spokesperson argued that "the time has come for administrative and forceful pressure on informal youth associations, didactic exhortations, and excessive surveillance to be decisively eliminated from the Komsomol arsenal."[75]

Some steps are being taken to restructure the Komsomol. Local Komsomol units are reportedly being granted greater discretion for structuring their programs and spending Komsomol funds. A degree of democracy has been introduced into some local Komsomol organizations, where several candidates compete for election to leadership posts. Political-education classes are supposed to be revamped to allow more open debate on controversial issues.

In addition, the Komsomol Central Committee has taken some tentative steps to accommodate Komsomol members who are attracted to independent clubs and groups. Special departments have been established in some local Komsomol committees to oversee the activities of informal groups and to work with them. In some localities, the Komsomol organizations have begun to show initiative. For example, the Moscow Komsomol sanctioned the formation of a "Rock Laboratory" under its auspices, and in 1988, the Komsomol in Nizhnii Tagil organized a mass protest against environmental pollution in the city.

Yet it is ever more doubtful that the Komsomol will be able to win back disaffected young people. Many Komsomol staff workers still rely on old "passive-dependent relations" and are unwilling to relinquish their strict control over young people's activities.[76] One journalist noted, "If we are to be honest, we have to admit that the Komsomol has lost the initiative in influencing a significant segment of boys and girls."[77] Even if it improves its work, he observed, the informal groups will probably live on. "Over 60 percent of the members of the informal associations declared that they would stay in the associations even if clubs with corresponding interests were organized within state and public organizations."[78]

So far, the Komsomol's restructuring has had little impact on its members. According to a 1989 survey of 10,000 young people, only a fifth of the Komsomol members polled had noticed any effect of restructuring in their Komsomol organizations. What is more, two-fifths reported that their opinion of the Komsomol had gotten worse since they joined; only 5 percent said it had improved.[79]

Conclusion

Youth problems in the Soviet Union result from many of the same forces that are transforming societies throughout the world: among them, urbanization, rising levels of education, affluence, leisure time, and the spread of Western popular culture. They are also produced by social tensions in Soviet society and features of Communist rule. The leaders' attempts to restrict, regiment, and indoctrinate young people have caused a backlash and contributed to undermining the authority of official institutions.

Regarding what should be done to address the problems, a clear clash of values and perspectives has emerged. The principal division is between "liberals" and "conservatives" in society and within the Party. Liberals have favored a more tolerant approach to young people, one that shows respect for individual differences and values creativity and freer expression. Conservatives, in contrast, have stressed the primacy of society's need for "law and order" over young people's quest for self-discovery and self-assertion.

Espousing a "liberal" point of view, Igor Kon took issue with those who have "narrow and doctrinaire" ideas about upbringing. Such people, he maintained, dream of creating a flawless socialization system that will negate all possibilities for deviation from a single standard of conduct. In Kon's view, this idea is not only utopian but also harmful because it represses individuality. "In education, as in economics," he noted, "total planning means in practical terms bureaucratic formalism, [from] which any more or less creative individual will try, successfully, to escape." Kon believed that there should be multiple, possibly conflicting, socializing influences because they "increase the level of autonomy of the developing individual." The diverse influences were likely to promote "creative initiative and autonomy," though they might alsc give rise to "antisocial deviant behavior." A degree of deviance, Kon implied, is the price that society must pay for fostering individual creativity.[80]

"Conservatives" have disagreed with this tolerant, individual-centered approach. Some officials apparently saw a threat to Soviet rule (and presumably to their own privileged status) in every manifestation of youthful independence. After listening to a proposal from a cultural preservation group, for instance, one Belorussian official thundered, "We aren't going to allow a Solidarity in Vitebsk!"[81]

Some Party leaders, including then–Politburo member Egor Ligachev and former candidate-member Iurii Solov'ev, stressed the importance of the more traditional conceptions of Party-directed socialization and indoctrination. They felt the Party should suppress, if necessary, youth groups that challenge Communist values and norms. In a March 1988 interview, Solov'ev, who headed the Leningrad Province Party Organization, noted:

> Leningraders have a natural aversion to the various groups which accompany their gatherings with ballyhoo and antisocial behavior. We must all stop and think: Why does the irrepressible energy of some young people not find an outlet in useful activity? Why do dual morality, adventurism, an obsession with consumer goods, materialistic attitudes, cupidity, and drug addiction exist among young people? . . . It is time, and the sooner the better, for the Komsomol to overcome its timidity in the struggle against abnormal phenomena and against the scum of demagoguery that has appeared on the wave of *glasnost'*. It is necessary to learn to be militant and assertive as well as tactful in work with various youth groups and associations.[82]

Conservatives are also much harsher than liberals in their evaluation of rock music and other Western influences. As Solov'ev put it in the same interview: "Aping Western 'mass culture' is not exactly innocuous. It is a kind of time bomb planted under our ideology and morals. Underestimation of such phenomena sometimes leads to the most serious consequences."[83]

Such views are also voiced by conservatives among the intelligentsia. Believers in the "old virtues"—hard work, deference and obedience, a shared belief in community values—lash out against what they perceive as too much permissiveness and self-indulgence among the young. They are prepared to consign rock music and other modern "fads" to the ash heap of history. A good example of this point of view is the letter from Iurii Bondarev, Vasilii Belov, and Valentin Rasputin, written in response to Podnieks's film *Is It Easy to Be Young?* The three writers approvingly cited a letter by the composer A. S. Lobzov, who considered rock music "the real scourge and poison of our life." They contended that "verbiage and smooth talk about a special so-called youth culture are imbued with demagoguery." Young people, they asserted, need to learn to work hard; they need lofty moral ideals and true heroes to emulate.[84]

Thus, problems connected with youth's desire for self-expression and independence are intertwined with the debate over the future of Soviet society. On the Komsomol's seventieth anniversary, in 1988, Mikhail Gorbachev exhorted young people to support *perestroika*. "Both today and especially tomorrow," he declared, "the success of restructuring depends to a decisive degree on the contribution of young people."[85] In 1989 he returned to this theme, criticizing Party and Komsomol officials for lagging behind the changes occurring in society. "Restructuring is a revolution," he said, "and young people must be an active and enterprising force in it."[86]

Notes

The author wishes to express his gratitude to the John M. Olin Foundation and the Kennan Institute for Advanced Russian Studies of the Woodrow Wilson Center for their support and to Thomas Hammack for research assistance. The views expressed herein are those of the author only—not of the U.S. government or any of its organizations.

1. See also Jim Riordan (ed.), *Soviet Youth Culture* (Bloomington: Indiana University Press, 1989); Bill Keller, "Russia's Restless Youth," *New York Times Magazine,* July 26, 1987, pp. 14–20ff.; Virginie Coulloudon, *Génération Gorbatchev* (Paris: Jean-Claude Lâttes, 1988); and John Bushnell, *Moscow Graffiti: Language and Subculture* (Winchester, Mass.: Unwin Hyman, 1990). Soviet studies of youth include S. N. Ikonnikova, *Molodezh': Sotsiologicheskii i sotsial'no-psikhologicheskii analiz* (Leningrad: Leningrad State University Press, 1974); V. T. Lisovskii and A. V. Dmitriev, *Lichnost' studenta* (Leningrad: Leningrad State University Press, 1974); A. A. Kozlov and A. V. Lisovskii, *Molodoi chelovek: Stanovlenie obraza zhizni* (Moscow: Politizdat, 1986); S. I. Plaksii, *Otkloneniia ot norm sotsialisticheskogo obraza zhizni v molodezhnoi srede: Sushchnost' i puti preodoleniia* (Moscow: Molodaia gvardiia, 1986); and V. V. Bovkun, *Obraz zhizni sovetskoi molodezhi: Tendentsii, problemy, perspektivy* (Moscow: Vysshaia shkola, 1988).

2. Bovkun, op. cit., p. 112.

3. Studies by Soviet criminologists showed that three-quarters of all juvenile delinquents and 90 percent of all teenagers who committed violent crimes came from troubled families. See "Derzkie, neponiatnye mal'chishki," interview with I. I. Karpets by Vitalii Smirnov, *Nedelia,* no. 7 (February 11, 1985), p. 9; and G. M. Minkovskii, "Neblagopoluchnaia sem'ia i protivopravnoe povedenie podrostov," *Sotsiologicheskie issledovaniia,* no. 2 (April-June 1985), pp. 105–112.

4. Interview with Vasilii Rosliakov, *Sotsialisticheskaia industriia,* April 4, 1987, p. 4.

5. "Pered zerkalom," *Literaturnaia gazeta,* no. 37 (September 2, 1987), p. 13; and E. Valentinova, "'Chernyi rynok' video," *Pravda,* August 10, 1988, p. 6.

6. The housing shortage is felt keenly by the millions of young people who have to wait for years before acquiring their own apartments. Young workers and married couples often have to stay in their parents' cramped apartments, rent a room in someone else's apartment, or live in dormitories. Bovkun, op. cit., pp. 73, 119.

7. Interview with V. I. Tsybukh by I. Korokov, *Izvestiia,* June 17, 1989, p. 3.

8. I. Kon, "Estafeta pokolenii," *Kommunist,* no. 4 (April 1987), p. 94.

9. Ibid., p. 95.

10. Bovkun, op. cit., p. 105.

11. A. A. Voz'mitel', "Nekotorye voprosy differentsirovannogo podkhoda," in A. S. Loginova, comp., *Obshchestvennoe mnenie i lektsionnaia propaganda: Teoriia, metodika, opyt* (Moscow: Znanie, 1986), p. 88.

12. A. Golovkov, "What We Think About: Fashion or Vulgarity?" *Izvestiia,* October 2, 1981, p. 6; trans. in *Current Digest of the Soviet Press* [*CDSP* hereafter] 33, no. 40 (November 4, 1981), p. 21.

13. M. Gorbanevsky, "Is Slang Really So Innocuous?" *Komsomol'skaia pravda,* November 26, 1981, p. 4; trans. in *CDSP* 33, no. 47 (December 23, 1981), p. 24.

14. A. Shcherbakov, "Ne budem krivit' dushoi," *Komsomol'skaia pravda,* May 16, 1987, p. 2.

15. See I. M. Il'inskii, "Nash molodoi sovremennik (voprosy mirovozzrencheskogo vospitaniia)," *Sotsiologicheskie issledovaniia,* no. 2 (March-April 1987), pp. 16-22.

16. V. Lukov and G. Inozemtseva, "Kuda vedet krivaia rosta?" *Komsomol'skaia pravda,* February 13, 1988, p. 2.

17. Ibid.

18. I. Il'inskii, in "Kommentarii spetsialista," *Sotsiologicheskie issledovaniia,* no. 1 (January-February 1987), p. 94.

19. Vladimir Kulikov, " 'Gomo NOMO' zhdet vnimaniia," *Molodoi kommunist,* no. 12 (December 1986), p. 25.

20. A. Aret'ev, "Molodezh' i perestroika," *Argumenty i fakty,* no. 20 (May 20, 1989), p. 5.

21. Cited in the roundtable discussion, "Ideino-politicheskoe stanovlenie molodezhi: opyt, problemy," *Sotsiologicheskie issledovaniia,* no. 2 (March-April 1987), p. 24.

22. V. A. Pechenev, cited in ibid., p. 25.

23. Kon, op. cit., p. 102.

24. On types of youth groups, see Kulikov, op. cit., pp. 23-29; Iu. P. Shchekochikhin, "Po kom zvonit kolokol'chik?" *Sotsiologicheskie issledovaniia,* no. 1 (January-February 1987), pp. 81-93; Iurii Bluvshtein and Viktor Iustitskii, "Neformal'naia gruppa: Chto eto takoe?" *Molodoi kommunist,* no. 6 (June 1987), pp. 61-68; D. I. Fel'dshtein, "Psikhologo-pedagogicheskie aspekty izucheniia neformal'nykh molodezhnykh ob'edinenii," *Sovetskaia pedagogika,* no. 6 (June 1987), pp. 42-47; V. Ovchinskii, "Netraditsionnal'nye gruppy molodezhi," *Sovetskaia iustitsiia,* no. 17 (September 1987), pp. 13-14; I. Iu. Sundiev, "Neformal'nye molodezhnye ob'edineniia: Opyt ekspozitsii," *Sotsiologicheskie issledovaniia,* no. 5 (September-October 1987), pp. 56-62; A. Afanas'ev, "Uchenyi idet k 'neformalam,' " *Komsomol'skaia pravda,* December 11, 1987, p. 4; S. I. Plaksii, " 'Neformaly'—synov'ia ili pasynki?" *Politicheskoe obrazovanie,* July 1988, pp. 83-89; M. Topalov, "Molodye neformaly: kto oni?" *Argumenty i fakty,* no. 31 (1988), pp. 6-7; and V. Lisovskii, " 'Neformaly': za i protiv," *Agitator,* no. 9 (May 1989), pp. 26-29.

25. Shchekochikhin, op. cit., p. 89.

26. Cited in ibid., p. 92.

27. V. Evseev, "Kuda zhe nam det'sia?," *Pravda,* February 9, 1987, p. 3.

28. For further details, see S. F. Starr, *Red and Hot: The Fate of Jazz in the USSR, 1917-1980* (New York and Oxford: Oxford University Press, 1983); Pedro Ramet and Sergei Zamascikov, "The Soviet Rock Scene," Occasional Paper No. 223, Kennan Institute for Advanced Russian Studies, The Wilson Center, Washington, D.C., 1987; Artemy Troitsky, *Back in the USSR: The True Story of Rock in Russia* (Boston: Faber & Faber, 1988); and Paul Easton, "The Rock Music Community," in Riordan, op. cit., pp. 45-82. Recently, Soviet social scientists have begun studying rock music and its relation to youth life-styles. See, for instance, N. P. Meinert, "Po vole roka," *Sotsiologicheskie issledovaniia,* no. 4 (July-August 1987), pp. 88-93; N. D. Sarkitov, "Ot 'khard-roka' k 'khevi-metallu,' " *Sotsiologicheskie issledovaniia,* no. 4 (July-August 1987), pp. 93-94; and "Rok: muzyka? subkul'tura? stil' zhizni? (obsuzhdenie za 'kruglym stolom' redaktsii)," *Sotsiologicheskie issledovaniia,* no. 6 (November-December 1987), pp. 29-51.

29. Cited in S. Kushnerev, "Are You Serious, or Are You Just Playing Around?" *Komsomol'skaia pravda,* July 28, 1987, p. 2; trans. in CDSP 39, no. 39, p. 7.

30. See Linda Feldmann, "Lenin Meets Lennon," *Christian Science Monitor,* December 8, 1987, p. 16; and A. P. Fain, "Liudi 'sistemy' (mirooshchushchenie

sovetskikh khippi)," *Sotsiologicheskie issledovaniia,* no. 1 (January-February 1989), pp. 85-92.

31. On Hare Krishna followers, see Mariem Salganik, "Karma-kola ili okhota na nosorogov," *Ogonek,* no. 9 (February 27, 1988), pp. 20-21; A. Frolov, "We Are Vaishnavas," *Molodezh' Estonii,* March 31, 1989; and Anna Tkacheva, "Krishna, khare!" *Molodoi kommunist,* no. 6 (June 1989), pp. 77-83.

32. Kulikov, op. cit., p. 23.

33. A. Bondarenko, "Rebirth of Faith, or Change of Idols?" *Molodezh' Estonii,* March 31, 1989, p. 3.

34. Ibid.

35. "Republic Meeting of the Party Aktiv: Speech by K. G. Vaino," *Sovetskaia Estoniia,* August 5, 1984, p. 1; trans. in *CDSP* 36, no. 31 (September 29, 1984), p. 24.

36. Ibid.

37. Vladimir Iakovlev, "Kontora 'Liuberov,'" *Ogonek,* no. 5 (January 31 1987), pp. 20-21. See also Jim Riordan, "Teenage Gangs, 'Afgantsy' and Neofascists," in Riordan, op. cit., pp. 122-42.

38. Vera Tolz, "'Informal Groups' in the USSR," *Radio Liberty Research,* RL 220/87 (June 11, 1987).

39. Cited in S. Kushnerev, "Prishel'tsy?" *Komsomol'skaia pravda,* May 22, 1988, p. 4.

40. Tolz, op. cit., p. 2.

41. Richard Tempest, "Youth Soviet Style," *Problems of Communism* 33, no. 3 (May-June 1984), pp. 63-64.

42. See Julia Wishnevsky, "More About Neo-Nazis in Leningrad," *Radio Liberty Research,* RL 312/87 (July 29, 1987).

43. Vitalii Eremin, "Fashiki," *Nedelia,* April 10-16, 1989, p. 14. See also Valerii Konovalov, "Neo-Nazis in the USSR: From 'Mindless Childish Games' to Program of Action," in *Radio Liberty Report on the USSR* 1, no. 24 (June 16, 1989), pp. 10-13.

44. Miroslav Buzhkevich, "Demokraticheskoe polovod'e," *Pravda,* November 11, 1988, p. 3.

45. Ibid. On students' political activity, see Richard B. Dobson, "Soviet Union," in Philip G. Altbach (ed.), *Student Political Activism* (Greenwich, Conn.: Greenwood Press, 1989), pp. 263-78.

46. See Vladimir Iakovlev, "Proshchanie s Bazarovym," *Ogonyok,* no. 36 (September 5, 1987), pp. 4-5. See also Vera Tolz, "'Informal Groups' Hold First Officially Sanctioned Conference," *Radio Liberty Research,* RL 380/87 (September 23, 1987).

47. Cited in Eremin, op. cit., p. 15.

48. For example, a sociologist who worked for the Ministry of Internal Affairs called for a serious examination of "national tendencies in informal youth organizations." He maintained that "many students who took part in the disorders [in Alma-Ata] were former upper-grade secondary school students who a few years earlier were united in informal national groups." V. S. Ovchinskii, "Kriminogennye proiavleniia v moldezhnoi srede," *Sotsiologicheskie issledovaniia,* no. 4 (July-August 1987), p. 86.

49. "Molodezhnaia politika: Nachalo puti," interview with V. I. Tsybukh by I. Korokov, *Izvestiia,* Moscow evening ed., June 15, 1989, p. 3.

50. "Derzkie, neponiatnye mal'chishki," op. cit., p. 9. In 1987, 67 percent of the criminal acts by minors were reportedly committed in groups. See the interview

with A. Pankratov by A. Petrov, *Argumenty i fakty,* no. 44 (October 29, 1988), pp. 6–7.

51. Ovchinskii, "Kriminogennye proiavleniia," op. cit., p. 85.

52. Iu. Shcherbinin, "Posle rok-kontserta," *Pravda,* October 23, 1988, p. 6.

53. Iurii Shchekochikhin, "Ekstremal'naia model'," *Literaturnaia gazeta,* no. 41 (October 12, 1988), p. 13.

54. Ibid.

55. "Kovarnye grammy durmana" (Answers to readers' questions from the USSR Minister of Internal Affairs), *Pravda,* January 6, 1987, p. 3.

56. A. A. Gabiani, "Narkomaniia: Gor'kie plody sladkoi zhizni," *Sotsiologicheskie issledovaniia,* no. 1 (January-February 1987), pp. 48–53.

57. "Kovarnye grammy durmana," op. cit., p. 6. In January 1987, for example, 3 million copies of a leaflet entitled "Beware of the White Cloud!" were sent by the newspaper *Uchitel'skaia gazeta* for distribution in the schools. (See *Uchitel'skaia gazeta,* January 15, 1987, p. 4.) The authorities believed that hashish and opiates had been derived from the large plantings of wild hemp (*anasha*) and opium poppies in Central Asia. Through one large-scale operation, "Poppy-86," the police claimed to have destroyed more than 3,000 illegal plantings of opium poppies and 100,000 hectares of wild hemp and to have arrested 300 narcotics carriers and over 4,000 procurers of raw drugs. The following year, "Operation Poppy-87" reportedly led to the discovery of about 4,000 illegal fields of opium poppies and marijuana and to the destruction of more than 140,000 hectares of such plants growing wild. See the interview with V. Pankin, chief of the Main Administration for Criminal Investigations of the Ministry of Internal Affairs, by A. Illesh and E. Shestinskii, *Izvestiia,* February 29, 1988, p. 4.

58. "Opasnoe pristrastia," *Literaturnaia gazeta,* August 20, 1986, p. 11.

59. Interview with V. Pankin, *Izvestiia,* February 29, 1988, p. 4. See also G. Ovcharenko, "Narkoman po prinuzhdeniiu," *Pravda,* February 3, 1988, p. 6.

60. Cited in D. Gai and A. Russovskii, "It's Real Suicide," *Vecherniaia Moskva,* September 5, 1987, p. 2; trans. in *CDSP* 38, no. 34, p. 6.

61. Cited in Igor Korol'kov, "A kogda oglianesh'sia . . . ," *Sobesednik,* no. 40 (September 1986), p. 12.

62. Cited in V. Iudanov, "The 'Pushers' of Tusinsk," *Sovetskaia Rossiia,* August 12, 1987, p. 2, trans. in *Joint Publications Research Service,* JPRS-UPA-87-041 (December 29, 1987), p. 37.

63. Korol'kov, op. cit., p. 12.

64. See Jim Riordan, "The Komsomol," in Riordan, *Soviet Youth Culture,* op. cit., pp. 16–44.

65. V. Mironenko, "O dal'neishei demokratizatsii zhizni Komsomola," speech to the Fourth Plenum of the Komsomol Central Committee, *Komsomol'skaia pravda,* November 19, 1988, pp. 3–4; and TASS dispatch, March 23, 1990.

66. "Molodezh'—tvorcheskaia sila revoliutsionnogo obnovleniia. Vystuplenie M. S. Gorbacheva," *Pravda,* April 17, 1987, pp. 1–2.

67. Among such critics was the sociologist N. M. Blinov: "The people who volunteered for Komsomol work and then for party work were . . . those who wanted to get closer to goods in short supply and to foreign travel." Cited in "Ideino-politicheskoe stanovlenie molodezhi," op. cit., p. 27.

68. "Dela ne uspevaiut za slovami," interview with Viktor Mironenko by Y. Evseev and A. Cherniak, *Pravda,* April 25, 1988, p. 4.

69. Il'inskii, "Nash molodoi sovremennik," op. cit., p. 17.

70. Ibid., pp. 17–18.

71. E. P. Vasil'eva et al., "Otnoshenie studentov k obshchestvennym naukam," *Sotsiologicheskie issledovaniia,* no. 4 (July-August 1987), pp. 20–24.
72. Cited in Vladimir Misiuchenko, "Kommunizm i ideal," *Sobesednik,* no. 4 (January 1987), p. 5.
73. Vladimir Misiuchenko, "Ubezhdenie i techenie," *Sobesednik,* no. 39 (September 1987), p. 6.
74. Il'inskii, in "Kommentarii spetsialista," op. cit., p. 94.
75. Kulikov, op. cit., p. 29.
76. Leonora Bagriantseva and Margarita Fedorova, "Eksperiment: pervye itogi," *Komsomol'skaia zhizn',* no. 10 (May 1987), pp. 11–12.
77. Kulikov, op. cit., p. 25.
78. Ibid., p. 26.
79. Aret'ev, "Molodezh' i perestroika," p. 5.
80. Kon, op. cit., p. 100.
81. Anatolii Misenia, "Kto oni, 'neformaly'? [cont.]," *Sovetskaia Belorussia,* October 2, 1987, p. 3.
82. "Idushchim vosled," interview with Iu. F. Solov'ev by V. Gerasimov and V. Kozhemiako, *Pravda,* March 10, 1988, p. 2.
83. Ibid. It is indicative of the changing times, and the precarious position even of well-placed conservatives, that Solov'ev was defeated when he ran unopposed for a seat in the Congress of People's Deputies in March 1989. Most Leningrad voters crossed his name off the ballot. Solov'ev was removed from his Leningrad leadership post in July of that year.
84. "Legko li byt' molodym?" (Letter from Iurii Bondarev, Vasilii Belov, and Valentin Rasputin), *Pravda,* November 9, 1987, p. 6.
85. "Vystuplenie M. S. Gorbacheva," *Pravda,* November 1, 1988, p. 2.
86. "Perestroika raboty partii—vazhneishaia kliuchevaia zadacha dnia. Doklad M. S. Gorbacheva," *Pravda,* July 19, 1989, p. 2.

CHAPTER 14

Crime in the Soviet Union

Louise I. Shelley

Glasnost' has removed the shackles from many areas of discussion, including the issue of Soviet crime. Moreover, crime has figured as prominently as it has in the revelations in the press and on television because a frank appraisal of the growing crime problem is now considered essential to its control.

The extent and nature of crime were removed for so long from public inquiry because the Soviets had adopted the Marxist ideological tenet that crime would wither away with socialism and would disappear under communism. Unable to reconcile ideology with the actual situation, they refrained from discussing crime.

The Soviet leadership has promised its population a greater degree of order than in Western society. Although crime has grown noticeably in the past twenty years, the crime rate remains significantly below that of U.S. society. The USSR has thus been able to deliver on one of its fundamental promises to its citizenry. But this goal has been achieved at the cost of the personal freedom of the citizenry. Internal movement is controlled by a passport system, more individuals are incarcerated on a per capita basis than in most other industrialized societies,[1] and the criminal justice system is heavily weighted on the side of the state rather than the criminal defendant.

Gorbachev has yet to move against the passport system, but significant steps have already been taken to humanize the treatment of criminals. The pressure on the *militsiia* to solve crimes has been reduced, more alternatives to incarceration are used, and labor-camp sentences have been shortened, as judges are no longer pressured by the Party to impose heavy penalties.[2] As a result a significant number of labor camps have been closed. The newly drafted criminal code eliminates the death penalty for economic offenses and makes all women exempt from execution. As the reins are loosened in society, the possibilities for committing crimes increase, since much of the Soviet success in limiting crime and deviance in the past was attributable to control rather than to panaceas.

As Gorbachev has relaxed the controls on society, crime rates have increased, and this challenges him to deliver on his promise to pursue democratization while maintaining discipline. Conservatives, already disturbed by many of Gorbachev's reforms, closely monitor crime rates and protests in the streets, as they fear the social chaos liberalization may bring. Armenia has even been under military rule in an attempt to limit further disturbances. Crime and social order in the contemporary period are not only social problems but also central issues in the political debates raging within Soviet society.

Glasnost' and Crime

Glasnost' has already eliminated many of the illusions Soviet citizens had about crime and criminal justice in their country. Even those who do not read newspapers cannot escape the revelations of widespread crime and corruption within Soviet society, for television and radio also vividly document these problems. The alarming revelations of criminality are equalled, if not surpassed, by the exposés of abuses by justice system personnel. These exposés portray a system in which many personnel are as criminalized as those they are supposed to control, a fact supported by the announced dismissal of 161,000 militia personnel following Brezhnev's death.[3]

Criminal statistics (once a state secret) have now been declassified. The MVD (Ministry of Internal Affairs), which assembles crime statistics, has since July 1987 provided weekly briefings to foreign journalists on the state of criminality in Moscow. The data also are summarized in the evening newspaper *Vecherniaia moskva* for domestic consumption.

The information imparted in these briefings would make headlines in U.S. newspapers, but they are hidden on the back page of the Moscow daily. For example, in September 1987, *militsiia* officials seized two separate shipments of eight and nine kilos of narcotics from different dealers.[4] In the first nine months of 1987, 240,000 individuals were placed in sobering-up stations, suggesting a very high level of citizen involvement with the law-enforcement apparatus. Yet all this is calmly reported with no sense of drama. The reasons such police coups are published without sensationalism is that in the USSR, crime stories are printed in the state-controlled newspapers for didactic, rather than commercial, purposes.

The facade has been removed from Soviet life, and Soviet scholars and journalists now graphically acknowledge problems that in the past were said to have been eliminated by socialism. Narcotics, once seen solely as a Western curse, is now recognized as a major source of crime commission. Between 1979 and 1985 the amount of drug addiction tripled. Although more recent growth has not been so rapid, it remains substantial: MVD statistics indicated in 1988 that it had grown 10 percent since 1985.[5] Prostitutes, who were supposed to have disappeared with the creation of the "new Soviet man," now not only ply their trade but also are accused of perpetrating serious offenses against their clients.[6] Yet these deviants are not the only ones to be blamed for the growth of crime. Soviet sources acknowledge the existence of an underclass that produces a disproportionate share of ordinary criminals. Frank discussions illuminate the dynamics of the significant problem of street crime. Alarming reports surface on the massive and pervasive theft from state enterprises, yet the most problematic reports are those of the reemergence of organized crime.

MVD researchers now contend that organized crime in the Soviet Union is "rooted in the bureaucratization of society, in the administrative-command system whose methods invariably breed an alternative economy."[7] Members of crime organizations are involved in protection rackets, and they launder money through cooperative restaurants. Drug trafficking, as in the West, is linked with organized crime.[8]

Gangsters and hit men are supervised not only by a crime syndicate but also by high-ranking Party officials and members of the law-enforcement apparatus. The head of the Ministry of Internal Affairs admitted, "Organized crime also exists in our country, and what is more, it has been established that in the past internal affairs officials occupying senior posts were involved in it."[9] Officials not only admit to such abuses but also describe them in graphic detail.

The sensationalism of such crime surpasses almost anything one can read in the West. The helplessness of the citizenry at the hands of an irresponsive and frequently brutal law-enforcement apparatus subjugated to the demands of high-ranking officials is in some ways more disturbing to the population than the gruesome revelations of the Stalinist period. Whereas the abuses associated with Stalin are clearly a phenomenon of the past, the abuses of individual rights that have been recently documented are associated with many leaders who still retain power.

Illustrative of such lurid crime revelations is the case of Akhmadzhan Adylov, director of the "Lenin" State Farm in the fertile Fergana Valley of Uzbekistan. Individuals such as Adylov have been accused of embezzling half a billion rubles (the equivalent of nearly $850 million at the official exchange rate) from the state during Sharaf Rashidov's rule as Party first-secretary of Uzbekistan. This embezzlement was facilitated by an organized crime ring uniting Party, law-enforcement officials, and ordinary criminals who terrorized and intimidated the local population.

On Adylov's farm, an underground prison, like the subterranean facilities of the oriental khans who preceded him, was maintained. There, he held individuals who refused to do his bidding. People who dared to challenge his authority—even pregnant women—were viciously tortured with whips and branding irons. He removed part of a man's scalp when he thought the man needed a haircut. This despot also had local girls kidnapped. After he had organized gang rapes of his youthful victims, he would marry them off to the "village idiots." Whistleblowers who ventured to the republic capital for help disappeared, as if in a Latin American dictatorship.

The story of this nightmare kingdom, where the rule of law was ignored and the law enforcers became the servants of a local tyrant who was engaged in massive corruption and embezzlement, did not surface in a dissident document. This account was given a full page in one of the most prominent and respected Soviet weeklies.[10]

Why would Soviet leadership admit to such large-scale criminality in the very recent past? The desire to discredit Brezhnev and his ally, the former Uzbek leader Rashidov, was certainly central to its appearance. By accusing Brezhnev associates of criminality, Gorbachev could justify their removal, a step necessary for the attainment of the reform program. But as the author of this exposé reported, Adylov's successor had to be removed only eighteen months after Adylov's ouster. His malfeasance resembled Adylov's—false reporting and physical abuse.

This exposé is just one of the more colorful accounts of violations by high-ranking personnel. Recently Iurii Churbanov, Brezhnev's son-in-law and former deputy minister of the MVD, was sentenced to twelve years' deprivation of freedom for corruption, following a lengthy trial.[11] A public outcry protesting the mildness of the sentence ensued.

The barrage of articles on official corruption indicated that the problems were systemic and not the consequences of merely sadistic or corrupt individuals. They were the result of a system in which the law had been subordinated to the desires of the Party and its high-ranking officials. These articles mobilized opinion for change. With such newspaper reports as groundwork, Gorbachev rallied support for his program to grant greater autonomy to the legal apparatus, an agenda item incorporated in his Party theses adopted at the 19th Party Conference in June 1988. The realization of these changes over the objections of many in the entrenched bureaucracy represented a major victory for Gorbachev.

Glasnost' has reversed a long-term policy of keeping the populace ignorant as to the nature of crime. Prior to the mass campaign of revelations, many citizens felt safe to walk the streets. Although many knew there was corruption in the bureaucracy, they were not aware of the extent of its existence or the close ties between the Party leadership and the criminals.

Soviet reformers now face a dilemma. *Glasnost'* about crime has more far-reaching implications for Soviet society. The revelations have clearly undermined citizens' confidence in their safety and in the integrity of the system and its officials. Soviet authorities have difficulty justifying a law-enforcement apparatus that is so encompassing if it has not limited crime and if it has become so corrupted. If Soviet citizens believe that they no longer can rely on the state to maintain order, will they support reforms that will deliver change without any guarantees of improvement? Does *glasnost'* about crime and corruption undermine the confidence in the system that is necessary for its reform?

Explaining Crime

Prior to *glasnost'*, Soviet scholars were restricted in their discussions of the causes of crime. For three decades the only acceptable explanations for its endurance under socialism were the legacy of the bourgeois past and the capitalist influences from abroad. But with the new frankness, scholars have moved away from explanations that blame others for the problems of Soviet crime and instead look to conditions within their society.

This has given rise to a much more sophisticated analysis of crime, in which the causes are seen to lie very much in the developmental process,[12] in the anomie that characterizes contemporary urban life,[13] and in the psychological and sociological problems of socialization.[14] Difficult living conditions and problems of morale lead to alcoholism and family conflicts, producing crime and deviance. The increasing problem of youth crime results from the influence of a poor home environment, of peers, and of schools that fail to provide adequate education and supervision.[15] In the homes of many delinquents, drunkenness and abuse are the norm.[16] Yet the preconditions for criminality exist even in homes where both parents are hardworking Soviet citizens. Soviet authorities, echoing U.S. research, comment on the problems of youth raised in homes where both parents work and do not properly supervise their children.[17] In discussing causation, Soviet theorizing seems to be converging with Western thought on the origins of crime.

Soviet conditions, however, influence crime in ways not common in Western societies with higher standards of living. Soviet sources acknowledge that the tensions of daily life help contribute to the emergence of violent crime, particularly those centered in the domestic environment. For example, the housing shortage, which forces even divorced individuals to live together; the tense life in communal apartments; and the absence of sufficient places to go for recreation all help to explain the large number of cases of hooliganism in homes and apartments.[18] Violence also erupts as a consequence of overcrowded buses and of rudeness in ill-stocked stores.[19]

Such admissions about the causes of crime shatter the Soviet claim to having created a superior society. Soviet analysts now reveal that the USSR has not been able to escape the unfortunate side effects of development, including rising crime rates and the collapse of the family that have been observed in most industrialized societies.

The Nature of Crime

The crime situation in the USSR for many years remained less severe than in most Western societies. This fortunate situation could not be ascribed to ideology but rather to Stalin's domestic policies. Stalin inherited a serious crime problem, the result of years of internal struggle and of the dislocation of millions of individuals. But like his fellow dictators, Hitler and Franco, he was able to return order to the streets. Stalin repressed not only political offenders. Large numbers of professional criminals were incarcerated and sentenced to lengthy periods of confinement. Although conditions were harsher in the Gulag (the system of Stalinist labor camps) for political offenders, many members of the criminal underworld perished without training successors.

Stalin's death released both politicals and ordinary offenders from labor camps, making it possible for criminals to train a new generation. The cost of crime commission was reduced when the criminal-justice reforms of the Khrushchev period put limits on the sentences that could be imposed. Within fifteen years of Stalin's demise, the USSR again faced a serious crime problem. Crime rates grew steadily throughout the Brezhnev years, their rise continuing even after his death in 1982. Party leaders prior to the 1986 Party congress admitted that the Soviet Union was facing a serious problem of social order, representing a threat to daily life.[20]

Crime Rates

The crime rate peaked at 1.98 million crimes in 1986, experiencing a slight decline of approximately 200,000 offenses the following year, probably due to the strict anti-alcohol campaign in force at the time, and the rate rose only slightly in 1988.[21] The official figure of nearly 2 million offenses, though, severely underestimated the crime figure. The Party's pressure on the *militsiia* to leave no more than 5 percent of all recorded crimes unsolved meant that many offenses would simply go unrecorded, particularly cases of petty theft, economic crime, and violations of safety rules.[22] Furthermore, many serious offenses committed by Party members were never recorded as crimes because they were disciplined within the Party apparatus.[23] Despite the high figure of latent crime, the reported level of crime (especially of the most violent offenses and property crimes) is significantly below that of the United States, which recorded 12 million offenses during the same time period.[24]

The Soviet Union has certain crimes that are a consequence of its socialist system. For example, speculation (the purchase and sale of goods at a profit, which is the essence of capitalism) is an offense only in a socialist economy. Crimes against central planning and the issuance of substandard goods are also offenses unique to a centrally planned economy. But these distinctive offenses represent a small share of total crime (see Table 14.1). The majority of offenses are universally acknowledged as crimes, such as property crime, crimes against persons, and vehicular offenses.

According to the data in Table 14.1, property crime is the most frequent of offenses, constituting almost half of total crime commission in 1987. These statistics do not indicate what percentage of theft covers state and what percentage covers personal property, but other sources suggest that the two categories are affected about equally.[25] Theft of state property is considered more severe, as the individual's offense is harming the general welfare of society rather than that of a single individual. But there is more differentiation between the two categories of property crime than the nature of the victim. Those who steal from the state are usually older than the thief of personal property, who is frequently youthful. Many women are accused of stealing from stores where they are employed, but more males than females take personal property.

Most citizens steal small amounts from their workplace, but they are able to elude detection or avoid criminal sanctions. In 1986–1987, 1.6

TABLE 14.1
Fundamental Changes in the Structure of Crime

	Percent of General Structure of Crime		
	1967	1977	1987
Major crimes against persons	4.9	6.3	3.3
Intentional homicide	1.5	1.6	0.8
Serious bodily assault	2.0	3.3	1.6
Property crime	37.0	42.1	44.5
Theft	21.9	25.2	29.7
Embezzlement	5.7	5.0	5.4
Armed robbery and open stealing	3.3	4.3	3.1
Speculation	1.9	1.9	2.4
Other forms of crime	58.1	51.6	52.2
Hooliganism	28.5	12.1	7.4
Home brewing	3.7	1.3	6.5
Vehicular crimes	5.1	7.8	6.5

Source: A. Vlasov, "Na strazhe pravoporiadka," *Kommunist*, no. 5 (1988), p. 58.

million individuals were detained for removing items from their enterprise. Many of these were multiple offenders. For example, at a meat factory in Vladimir where 600 individuals were employed, 500 of them were detained in 1986, 16 percent of them repeatedly.[26] With such institutionalization of petty theft, particularly in the consumer sector, it would be impossible for the state to prosecute and incarcerate all the thieves without clogging the justice system and removing needed employees from the work force.

There have been certain important changes in crime-commission patterns in the past two decades (Table 14.1). Property crime has increased significantly as a share of overall crime commission, whereas hooliganism has dropped dramatically. Petty hooliganism is defined as "intentional actions violating public order in a coarse manner and expressing a clear disrespect toward society"; malicious hooliganism can involve the use of a weapon and can carry up to seven years' institutional confinement. The decline in hooliganism's share of criminal offenses may be explained by its more frequent treatment as an administrative rather than a criminal offense, because hooliganism still remains a common phenomenon. Some activity formerly prosecuted as hooliganism is now defined as vandalism, which in 1988 represented 8 percent of total crime commission.[27]

A significant decline may be noted in the proportional contribution of the most serious violent offenses between 1977 and 1987. The drop in the frequency is a direct consequence of the reduction in alcohol consumption following the anti-alcohol campaign initiated in 1985. Restrictions on alcohol consumption did not affect only these offenses, however, for alcohol-related crime had dropped by 40 percent since the start of the campaign.[28] This drop has not been retained because the will to enforce the unpopular limitations on alcohol production and sales has weakened.

Even with the decline, though, the Soviet Union was still recording approximately 5 offenses per 100,000 (a total of 16,710 in 1988).[29] Although this figure was almost half the rate recorded in the United States, it was significantly above that of most other industrialized nations.[30] Such a high homicide rate is surprising in a country in which guns are strictly controlled. But the high rate of alcoholism and the poor quality of emergency medical care help explain this fact. Less-serious forms of violent crime against the person contribute approximately another 5 percent of total crime commission.[31]

Significant fluctuations in the percentage of cases ascribable to home brewing and speculation may be explained more by changes in enforcement patterns than by changes in crime patterns. Soviet law enforcement operates by Party-initiated campaigns against particular forms of crime commission. Numerous arrests of home brewers followed the initiation of the anti-alcohol campaign in 1985. For example, in 1987 more than half a million individuals were punished for this activity, many of them under the administrative law.[32] At the same time, efforts to apprehend speculators and other economic offenders were also intensified.[33] These campaigns indicate that many crime statistics are artifacts of Party policy.

Not ascertainable from these statistics are other important changes in the dynamics of crime commission. Economic-crime prosecutions rose 39 percent between 1978 and 1988, partly as a consequence of the decision to weed out corruption in the Central Asian republics. In 1987, 97,000 cases of embezzlement, 7,800 cases of bribery, and 43,000 incidents of speculation were investigated.[34] Despite the significant increase in crimes in this category, prosecutions represent the tip of the iceberg. As previously mentioned, millions of petty offenses are handled administratively. But many serious economic crimes go undetected, and many are perpetrated by Party members who escape criminal sanctions.

The growth of the narcotics trade has affected crime commission in significant ways. Not only were 131,000 individuals on drug registries administered by the MVD throughout the country, but also criminal proceedings were initiated against 80,000 individuals for drug-related crimes between 1986 and 1988.[35] A significant share of the growing problem of apartment burglaries in Moscow is attributable to drug offenders.

Soviet authorities do not manage to prosecute many of the reported crimes. In 1987, 44 percent of all reported crimes were property offenses, indicating that they numbered approximately 790,000. That year there were 238,000 convictions for property offenses (Table 14.2). This shows that less than a third of reported crimes resulted in convictions (although some cases may have been diverted to the comrades' courts). This is better than the U.S. rate but far from the certainty of punishment promised by the Party. The relationship of convictions to recorded offenses is closer for homicide: There were approximately 14,000 recorded homicides in 1987, and 9,900 individuals were convicted of the offense.

One very noticeable aspect of these statistics is that the number of convictions declined dramatically between 1985 and 1987 in all categories except home-brew- and narcotics-related crime. The decline in convictions

TABLE 14.2
Court Figures (by Type of Crime, in 1,000s)

	1985	1986	1987
Theft of state or public property	192.1	166.7	115.1
Theft of personal property	178.2	161.3	123.4
Premeditated murder	12.6	9.8	9.9
Hooliganism	161.1	133.9	94.5
Home brewing for sale	2.0	5.4	6.1
Traffic offenses with serious consequences	29.4	26.5	21.9
Narcotics-related crimes	25.6	33.6	26.8

Source: "Tsifry dlia razmyshleniia: Sudebnaia arifmetika," *Literaturnaia gazeta*, November 2, 1988, p. 2.

for most offenses is much greater than the 10 percent reduction in the overall crime rate would suggest. The advent of the anti-alcohol campaign and the increased growth in narcotics usage explain the divergent trend for these two crime categories. The sharp reductions in the other categories may be attributed to the reduction in Party pressure to produce convictions. The *militsiia* was no longer under such pressure to produce arrests, and prosecutors were no longer so afraid to drop cases.

The character of crime also changed in a more subtle way. Situational crime increased, the consequence of increased alcohol consumption.[36] The decline in premeditated crimes also contributed to an increase in crimes in which the victim and the offender were unknown to each other.

A significant increase in crime was recorded by the police in 1988 (see Table 14.3). According to reports, it has continued to escalate rapidly, particularly in the area of violent crime. There is every indication that this growth is real and has not been manufactured by the police to challenge Gorbachev's efforts to democratize.[37] Rather, it has occurred in serious offenses that would not be ignored at any time. Very significant growth has been observed in violent offenses and in property crimes using violence. Interviews with Soviet criminologists indicated that this growth might be the result of a lessening of social control and of the increasing economic differentiation in society, both of which have contributed to anomie.

No statistics are provided on political or on antistate crimes, but Soviet authorities have reduced the number of individuals held for anti-Soviet slander and activities (Articles 70 and 190-1). This has been achieved by releasing several hundred individuals incarcerated on these charges, as well as by limiting arrests. The escalating protests in the Nagorno-Karabakh region and in other parts of the country in 1989–1990, however, provided a challenge to Gorbachev's efforts to expand the limits of personal political expression. Three thousand Armenian activists were reportedly detained at the time of the Armenian earthquake as public attention was focused on the disaster victims and away from the political protesters.

Despite these changes, unique features of Soviet crime endure. Particularly distinctive are the patterns of interpersonal violence, including such

TABLE 14.3
Growth of Crime Rates (by Type of Crime)

	Number of Crimes		
	1987	1988	Growth Rates
Premeditated murder (including attempts)	14,651	16,710	+14.1
Premeditated serious bodily injury	28,250	37,191	+31.6
Rape (including attempts)	16,765	17,658	+5.3
Banditry (state and private property)	9,047	12,916	+42.8
Robbery (state and private property)	46,485	67,114	+44.4
Theft of state or private property	132,377	165,283	+24.9
Theft of private property	401,599	548,524	+36.8
Swindling (state or private property)	23,897	21,543	-9.8
Pilferage of state or public property through appropriation, embezzlement, or abuse of official position	96,986	87,450	-9.8
Speculation	43,372	45,235	+4.3
Violation of traffic rules and fatal accidents	18,469	22,492	+21.8
Violation of traffic rules and nonfatal accidents	97,947	106,531	+8.8

Source: "MVD Releases 1987-88 Crime Rate Statistics," *FBIS Daily Reports*, March 1, 1989, p. 77.

offenses as homicide, grave injury (aggravated assault), and rape. Soviet violent crime is often committed in groups, and a greater proportion of offenders either are intoxicated or are individuals with serious drinking problems. Furthermore, violent offenses are more often committed in newly developed cities than in established urban areas or rural communities, which are the locations for most violent crime in other societies.

The Russian tendency to act in groups, reinforced by Soviet educational and socialization practices that emphasize collective activity, helps account for this distinctive pattern of violence. Over one-third of rapes,[38] at least three-quarters of armed robberies, and 18 to 30 percent of homicides have been committed in groups.[39] This group activity, while characteristic of youthful offenders,[40] is not confined to gangs with members under eighteen.

Soviet perpetrators of violent crime are more likely to commit their crime while intoxicated. Data indicated that two-thirds of all intentional homicides and three-fourths of grave bodily injuries were committed by offenders who were intoxicated,[41] and in some parts of the country the figure was even higher.[42] These figures exceeded the correlation between alcohol use and crime in most countries for which data are available.[43]

The rural location of many violent offenses is explained by the distinct geography of crime. Population controls in force in the USSR for more than the past half-century have produced crime-commission patterns unknown in societies where the processes of industrialization and urbanization were not controlled.

The Geography of Crime

Crime patterns are far from uniform throughout the Soviet Union. Significant variations are noted—a consequence of cultural differences, levels of urbanization, and patterns of migration. Fourfold differences in crime rates are observable in different parts of the country. Stable, more traditional communities usually have lower rates of crime than do areas recently populated by migrants. For example, in the Far East and Siberia more than 1,000 crimes are recorded per 100,000 population, whereas in the Caucasus the rate is only 250.[44] Especially high levels of crime are found in the most Westernized regions of the USSR, e.g., in Latvia, the RSFSR, Estonia, and Moldavia. Crime rates noticeably increased in thirty parts of the RSFSR.[45]

The geography of Soviet crime differs in certain important respects from that observed in other societies. In most societies, the greater the degree of urbanization is, the higher the crime rate. In the USSR, though, the largest cities do not have the highest crime rates. Even within individual republics it is not always the largest cities, but often the secondary and tertiary cities, that have the highest rates of crime.[46] This anomaly occurs because the administration of the internal-passport system permits Soviet authorities to exile serious offenders from major cities and to deny entrance to crime-prone youth. The highest crime rates are found in the newly established cities of Siberia and the Far East, where the planning process creates communities with disproportionate numbers of young men and insufficient numbers of women.

The largest cities are not entirely spared crime problems, however, for commuters from surrounding communities and transients contribute significantly to urban crime rates. Unlike in the United States or Western Europe, suburbs are not the privileged retreat of the prosperous but are homes to those who could not obtain residence permits within major cities. The toughs from the suburban community of Liubertsy known as the *liubery* received much publicity in 1987 for their habit of beating up punks within Moscow.[47] Yet this is just one example of commuter youth creating problems for urban residents.

The Soviet Union defies the general laws of the geography of crime in another important respect. In most countries of the world, rural crime rates are significantly below those of urban areas. In these areas the social controls exercised by family and neighbors suppress the level of crime. Soviet studies in 1985 suggested that only a slight majority of all crimes were committed in urban areas, and that certain rural areas had crime rates that exceeded those of urban areas.[48]

One explanation for this pattern is that many former offenders are forced to settle in rural communities, where they return to their life of crime. The crimes perpetrated by these no-goods who prey on the single women in the countryside was graphically portrayed in the distinguished novella *Pozhar* (Arson) by the recently selected member of the presidential council, Valentin Rasputin.[49] This novel portrays the poverty of village life, yet in some regions (particularly in the Caucasus) agriculture has brought prosperity to the village. In these rural communities there has been an urbanization of rural life.[50] The prosperity of agricultural life in Georgia has brought many more urban workers into the countryside than in other parts of the Soviet Union, thereby increasing levels of rural criminality.[51] Research has also indicated that in certain agricultural areas where some of the population have a higher education, the level of crime is higher than in urban areas.[52] Rural areas have acquired some of the problems of urban life without acquiring its amenities.[53]

The Offender Population

The criminal population, as elsewhere in the world, consists of both youthful and adult criminals as well as of recidivists. The Soviet archetypical offender is similar to his foreign counterpart, a male of between eighteen and twenty-five years of age. But in the USSR there is a greater range in the age of offenders than in most other industrialized societies. The explanation for this lies in Soviet conditions. Soviet authorities have criminalized many activities that would be legal elsewhere, but conduct that is deemed illegal is necessary for survival. Consequently, many middle-aged offenders (particularly women) are prosecuted for speculation, feeding bread to their livestock, or stealing meat from factories for family members. Many elderly women produce home brew to supplement their small retirement pensions.

Considering these circumstances, it is hardly surprising that significant growth has been noted in the contribution of female offenders. In 1977, women contributed 12 percent of all crime, but presently their share equals 22 percent. This figure is approximately double the share attributable to women in other industrialized nations. It supports the thesis that women's share of crime commission increases with greater participation in the labor force. Consistent with this hypothesis is women's crime being most pronounced in the work arena.[54] In the categories of official and economic crimes, women contribute approximately half, and in home brewing prosecutions their share is an even higher 60 percent.[55] Home brewing, once almost entirely the domain of women, became professionalized with the initiation of the anti-alcohol campaign. In 1987 the profile of the remaining home brewers was that of the typical offender, a youthful male.[56]

Adult male offenders have lost ground not only to female offenders but also to youths. In the past two decades youth crime has grown one-and-one-half times, and that of adolescents has doubled. In 1987, minors committed 165,000 offenses, and in 1988 the number of their recorded offenses increased to 183,953.[57] In both years their criminality contributed approximately 10 percent of total crime commission. One-third of these youthful offenders were students at technical schools, 28 percent were grade-school students, and one-fifth were working adolescents.[58] More alarming than just their numbers and youth was the brutality of their crimes.[59] In one case reported in the Soviet press, three drunken youths between fourteen and seventeen years old killed a ten-year-old boy. Before drowning him in a ditch, they cut off his ear, hit his head on a stone, and cut him with broken glass. This case was not unique, but rather part of a series of accounts of gruesome murders perpetrated by very young offenders.[60] Although all youthful crimes are not so horrible, juveniles are responsible for 21 percent of all recorded crimes of violence.[61]

Delinquents have traditionally come from the least-privileged strata of Soviet society. Research conducted two decades ago suggested that the income levels of the families of delinquents were below the established minimum standard.[62] Furthermore, many offenders reported that they felt materially deprived.[63] Soviet sources have acknowledged that it is the lowest social and economic class that is perpetuating the criminal subculture. There is a willingness to admit that there are disadvantaged children who need more social assistance.[64] Soviet authorities also recognized that children raised in children's homes, often the offspring of criminals, alcoholics, and drug users, are at greater risk of becoming criminals themselves.

Criminals are by no means confined to the less educated and affluent. Although the standard of living of the families of many offenders remains low, more recent research indicated that many come from affluent homes. Rather like the rationale of the affluent delinquents studied by U.S. researchers, the cause of their criminality lies in their peer relations and their feelings of social inadequacy.[65]

The labeling and incarceration of large numbers of offenders have not helped deter many from renewed crime commission. Soviet authorities acknowledged that their penal institutions were often schools for crime, their inmates so institutionalized that they had trouble living again in the community.[66] It is hardly surprising, then, that one-fifth of all crimes are committed by recidivists. Yet it is among the more serious offenses that recidivism is more pronounced: "Thirty to forty-five percent of all murders, robberies, and burglaries are committed by people with previous convictions."[67] Indicative of the poor readaptation of released offenders to society was the fact that one-third of the recidivists committed new offenses within the first year after their release.[68] The rapid return to crime is explained, in part, by militia methods. Police personnel closely scrutinize returning criminals, who are placed on registries at their local militia precincts.

Parasites, those who refused to work despite militia warnings, contributed disproportionately to crime commission. In some urban areas parasites contributed almost 30 percent of all crimes.[69] Nationwide, parasites "are responsible for one-fourth to one-third of all crimes committed for monetary gain."[70] Because approximately 80 percent of all parasites were alcoholics or heavy drinkers, it was hardly surprising that they also contributed significantly to hooliganism cases.[71]

Offenders can be differentiated by the crimes they commit. The characteristics of those convicted of homicide, rape, and assault differ significantly from those who commit nonviolent offenses. Unlike those convicted of economic and official crimes, who are often of middle to high social status,[72] those convicted of the most serious violent offenses come from the lowest strata of society. On the average, they have a lower level of educational attainment and have poorer job qualifications than the general population. Most were raised in working-class homes where abuse of alcohol, children, and spouses were the norm.[73] The backgrounds of property offenders are similar, but the majority have more education than the most serious violent offenders.

The perseverence of recidivists, the existence of professional and organized criminals, and the growth of youth crime indicate that crime will remain a festering problem within Soviet society in coming decades. Soviet conditions have not eliminated criminals. Poor domestic situations have produced offenders similar to their foreign counterparts, while specific Soviet conditions have created a wider range of offenders than are found in most industrialized capitalist nations.

Conclusion

The Soviet Union, despite its ideological commitment to the elimination of crime, has acknowledged that crime is a disturbing and widespread fact of life. Crime affects the way individuals live, reducing their ability to walk the streets and feel comfortable in their environment. Yet its impact is on the societal as well as on the personal level. Pervasive economic crime has far-reaching consequences for the economy. The embezzlement of hundreds of millions of rubles and the corruption of the law-enforcement apparatus and members of the ruling elite are problems affecting not only the man in the street but also the very nature of Soviet society.

The present leadership realizes the implications of the current crime problem, and both conservatives and liberals are united in their desire to reduce corruption and instill greater discipline within Soviet society. Gorbachev's expressed desire for order in his opening remarks at the Party conference in 1988 were among his most appreciated statements. Yet the expression of this objective does not ensure its realization. Many conservatives fear that further liberalization will also increase crime and social disorder, undermining the discipline that is so valued by many Soviet citizens. We should remember that the post-Stalin liberalization also contributed to higher crime rates. With reduced repression, professional and organized crime have reemerged since Stalin's death. Increasing affluence has made more private property available to steal. Persistent shortages of needed and desired commodities have made many ready to embezzle and shortchange the state. Increased opportunities to commit crime and reduced repression have facilitated the growth of criminality.

Although criminal justice in the post-Stalin period is no longer draconian, the Soviet system still has many more resources available to prevent and control crime than is the case in Western democratic societies. The Soviet Union has always had a very large police force, unhampered by legal protections for the citizenry. Also, the Soviet law-enforcement apparatus has been more intrusive into the lives of its citizenry, with the internal-passport system to monitor individual movement, with militia records to identify and label deviants, and with large numbers of citizens being required to cooperate with police as informants and auxiliary patrol personnel. A criminal-justice system that has permitted few acquittals has provided a certainty of punishment unmatched by other societies.

Currently, legal reformers in the Soviet Union are seeking to provide more guarantees for the defendant in relation to the state. They are seeking to enhance efficiency and to reduce corruption while simultaneously augmenting procedural safeguards. Their objectives, sometimes at odds with each other, cannot all be achieved at once.

The number of potential offenders may rise as more sentenced individuals serve their terms in the community, as procedural rules are more closely observed, and as efforts are made to convict only the guilty. But rising crime rates may be the litmus test of Gorbachev's program. If social order appears to be diminishing, Gorbachev may lose the support he needs for his economic and political reforms. In the Soviet Union, crime is not just a social ill—it is also a major social indicator.

Notes

1. "Reform of Prisons, Penal Colonies Urged," *Foreign Broadcast Information Service Daily Reports* [*FBIS Daily Reports* hereafter], no. 096 (1988), p. 63.

2. "V Tsentral'nom komitete KPSS," *Pravda,* April 13, 1988, pp. 1-2.
3. A. Vlasov, "Na strazhe pravoporiadka," *Kommunist,* no. 5 (1988), p. 47.
4. "Vstrecha v GUVD," *Vecherniaia moskva,* September 9 and 30, 1987, p. 3.
5. L. Sharov, "Narkomaniia: Bolezn', prestuplenie, moda," *Literaturnaia Rossiia,* no. 34 (1988), p. 20.
6. "A Hard Look at Prostitution in the USSR," *Current Digest of the Soviet Press* 39, no. 11 (1987), p. 2.
7. Gennady Khohkryakov, "The Shadow Economy and the Administrative-Command System," *Moscow News,* no. 46 (1988), p. 12.
8. Natalia Gevorkyan, "A Meeting That Did Not Take Place," *Moscow News,* no. 46 (1988), p. 4; and Viktor Turshatov, "Organized Crime," *Moscow News,* no. 39 (1988), p. 14.
9. "Vlasov Holds Talk with Writers, Journalists," *FBIS Daily Reports,* no. 081 (1988), p. 42.
10. Vladimir Sokolov, "Zona molchaniia," *Literaturnaia gazeta,* April 20, 1988, p. 13.
11. Dmitrii Likhanov, "Koma," *Ogonek,* no. 1 (1989), pp. 26-30; no. 2 (1989), pp. 25-29; no. 3 (1989), pp. 28-30; no. 4 (1989), pp. 18-22.
12. S. B. Alimov, "Aktual'nye voprosy preduprezhdeniia nasil'stvennykh prestuplenii," *Voprosy bor'by s prestupnost'iu,* no. 38 (1983), p. 33.
13. G. M. Reznik, "Protivorechiia sovremennoi urbanizatsii i prestupnost'," *Sovetskoe gosudarstvo i pravo,* no. 9 (1985), p. 52.
14. A. M. Iakovlev, *Teorii kriminologii i sotsial'naia praktika* (Moscow: Nauka, 1985), pp. 84-198.
15. B. S. Volkov and M. D. Lysov, *Pravonarusheniia nesovershennoletnykh i ikh preduprezhdenie* (Kazan: Izd. Kazanskogo universiteta, 1983).
16. L. L. Soldatov, "Vliianie rannei kriminalizatsii na prestupnoe povedenie lits molodogo vozrasta," in *Opyt kriminologicheskogo izucheniia lichnosti prestupnika* (Moscow: Vsesoiuznyi institut po izucheniiu prichin i razrabotke mer preduprezhdeniia prestupnosti, 1981), p. 81.
17. T. M. Kafarov and Ch. T. Musaev, *Bor'ba s posiagatel'stvom na obshchestvennyi poriadok* (Baku: Elm, 1983), p. 186.
18. Ibid., pp. 46, 154.
19. Alimov, op. cit.; Reznik, op. cit., p. 15; G. V. Antonov-Romanovskii, "Problemy kriminologicheskogo izucheniia iznasilovaniia," *Voprosy bor'by s prestupnost'iu,* no. 34 (1981), pp. 46-48.
20. D. I. Patiashvili, "For a Model City—Exemplary Order in Everything," *FBIS Daily Reports,* no. 010 (1986), pp. R13-15.
21. The figures for 1986 and 1987 were calculated by extrapolating percentages from actual numbers given in Vlasov, op. cit., pp. 50-51. For 1988, see *Statisticheskie dannye o prestupnosti i pravonarusheniiakh po SSSR* (Moscow: MVD USSR, 1989), p. 18.
22. Ger P. Van den Berg, *The Soviet System of Justice: Figures and Policy* (Dordrecht: Martinus Nijhoff, 1985), p. 14.
23. A. Shtromas, "Crime Law and Penal Practice in the USSR," *Review of Socialist Law* 3, no. 3 (1977), p. 307, first discussed the fact that Party members could not stand trial unless they were expelled from the Party. This is now freely admitted and criticized in the Soviet press.
24. *Sourcebook of Criminal Justice Statistics—1986* (Washington, D.C.: U.S. Department of Justice, 1987), p. 249.

25. *Kurs sovetskoi kriminologii* (Moscow: Iuridicheskaia Literatura, 1985), p. 194; A. A. Gabiani and R. G. Gachechiladze, *Nekotorye voprosy geografii prestupnosti* (Tbilisi: Izd. Tbiliskogo universiteta, 1982), pp. 86-108; "RSFSR Prosecutor Views Law Enforcement Tasks," *FBIS Daily Reports,* no. 049 (1988), p. 60.

26. Vlasov, op. cit., p. 52.

27. "RSFSR Prosecutor Views Law Enforcement Tasks," op. cit., p. 60.

28. "Militia Chief on Statistics, Responsibility," *FBIS Daily Reports,* no. 081 (1988), p. 43.

29. "MVD Releases 1987-88 Crime Rate Statistics," *FBIS Daily Reports,* March 1, 1989, p. 77.

30. See Louise I. Shelley, "American Crime: An International Anomaly?" *Comparative Social Research* 8 (1985), pp. 81-95; Report of the Secretary General, *Crime Prevention and Control* (New York: United Nations, 1977), gave the average homicide figure in the industrialized nations as 2.7 per 100,000 in the 1970s.

31. *Kurs sovetskoi kriminologii,* op. cit., p. 194.

32. Vlasov, op. cit., p. 54.

33. Ibid., p. 51.

34. Ibid.

35. "Official Describes Efforts Against Drug Use," *FBIS Daily Reports,* no. 036 (1988), p. 54.

36. Ibid., p. 50.

37. It is a more common police practice in many societies to arrest more individuals when the police disapprove of a leader's policies. The opposition can then suggest that existing policies undermine order.

38. V. N. Kudriavtsev et al. (eds.), *Lichnost' prestupnika* (Moscow: Iuridicheskaia Literatura, 1971), p. 121.

39. Ibid., p. 83.

40. V. Smirnov, "Juvenile Crime—Some Statistics and Explanations," *Current Digest of the Soviet Press* 36, no. 14 (1985), p. 14.

41. Ilya Zeldes, *The Problem of Crime in the USSR* (Springfield, Ill.: Charles C. Thomas, 1981), p. 44.

42. Walter Connor, *Deviance in Soviet Society* (New York: Columbia University Press, 1972), pp. 47-48.

43. Ibid., p. 47.

44. Vlasov, op. cit., p. 50.

45. "MVD Releases 1987-88 Crime Rate Statistics," op. cit., p. 77.

46. Volkov and Lysov, op. cit.; Gabiani and Gachechiladze, op. cit.; A. Leps, "Izuchenie prestupnoi aktivnosti v razlichnykh regionakh respubliki," *Sovetskoe gosudarstvo i pravo,* no. 2 (1981), p. 126.

47. Bill Keller, "Moscow's East Side Story: Teen-Age Toughs," *New York Times,* March 7, 1987, pp. 1, 5.

48. Reznik, op. cit., pp. 54-55.

49. Valentin Rasputin, "Pozhar," *Nash sovremennik,* no. 7 (1985), pp. 3-38.

50. Gabiani and Gachechiladze, op. cit.; Iu. M. Antonian, "Osobennosti prestupnosti v sel'skoi mestnosti i ee preduprezhdenie," *Sovetskoe gosudarstvo i pravo,* no. 8 (1978), p. 81.

51. A. A. Gabiani and M. Didebulidze, "O nekotorykh printsipakh sravnitel'nogo analiza prestupnosti v gorodakh i sel'skoi mestnosti," in *Aktual'nye voprosy preduprezhdeniia pravonarushenii,* ed. A. Alapishvili (Tbilisi: Izd. Tbiliskogo universiteta, 1981), pp. 106-108.

52. *Kurs sovetskoi kriminologii,* op. cit., p. 196.

53. Reznik, op. cit., pp. 53-54.
54. See Freda Adler, "The Interaction Between Women's Emancipation and Female Criminality: A Cross Cultural Perspective," *International Journal of Criminology and Penology,* no. 5 (1977), pp. 101-112.
55. Vlasov, op. cit., p. 50.
56. Interview with a leading Soviet criminological researcher in October 1987.
57. "MVD Releases 1987-88 Crime Rate Statistics," op. cit., p. 77.
58. Vlasov, op. cit., p. 57.
59. "RSFSR Prosecutor Views Law Enforcement Tasks," op. cit., p. 60.
60. Valerii Konovalov, "Juvenile Murderers," *Radio Liberty Research,* no. 292/86 (1986).
61. Kudriavtsev et al., op. cit., p. 111. See also V. Smirnov, "Juvenile Crime—Some Statistics and Explanations," *Current Digest of the Soviet Press* 37, no. 6, p. 14.
62. Ibid., p. 256.
63. A. A. Gabiani, M. Shonia, O. Mylnikova, and M. Didebulidze, "O resultatakh konkretno-sotsiologicheskogo issledovaniia uslovii formirovaniia lichnosti podrostkov-pravonarushitelei," in Alapishvili, op. cit., p. 125.
64. "Growing Crime Problem Among Young People in Moldavia," British Broadcasting Corporation, *Survey of World Reports,* SU/0009, November 25, 1987, pp. B/6-8.
65. Terry McNeil, "Battling the Problems of Today with the Weapons of Yesterday," *Radio Liberty Research,* no. 288/80 (1980), p. 4.
66. Viktor Loshak, "Lichnost' za provolokoi," *Moskovskie novosti,* no. 38 (1988).
67. "RSFSR Prosecutor Views Law Enforcement Tasks," op. cit., p. 59.
68. Vlasov, op. cit., p. 58.
69. Gabiani and Gachechiladze, op. cit., p. 182.
70. "Legal Dialogues: The Parasite in Profile and Full Face," *Current Digest of the Soviet Press* 37, no. 14 (1985), p. 8.
71. V. T. Kalmykov, *Khuliganstvo i mery bor'by s nim* (Minsk: Belarus, 1979), p. 87.
72. Kudriavtsev et al., op. cit., p. 89.
73. Gabiani and Gachechiladze, op. cit., p. 133; Kudriavtsev et al., op. cit., p. 100; Kalmykov, op. cit., p. 87.

CHAPTER 15

Prostitution, the Press, and Agenda-Building in the Soviet Policy Process

Andrea Stevenson Sanjian

> Prostitution. *Type of socially-deviant behavior. Prostitution is a historically conditioned social phenomenon, originating in the class antagonisms of society and an organic characteristic of it.* . . . *With the victory of the Great October Socialist Revolution in the USSR, the root causes of prostitution were wiped out. In the first year of the Soviet state's existence a purposeful program of educational, medical, and legal measures was implemented, rendering social assistance to women formerly engaged in prostitution, but equally eliminating the circumstances contributing to prostitution.* . . . *In the 1930s, prostitution was eradicated as a widespread social phenomenon. Individual manifestations of prostitution bear a strictly local character and are considered a form of parasitic existence.*
> —Bol'shaia sovetskaia entsiklopediia

Until very recently, official Soviet policy on the social problem of prostitution could be readily inferred from the brief entry on the issue in the *Bol'shaia sovetskaia entsiklopediia:* As a by-product of presocialist conditions whose objective causes have thus disappeared, prostitution does not—cannot—exist as a significant social problem in the USSR. In other words, policymaking on prostitution had become obsolete, and if the phenomenon did surface sporadically, its appearance was as unusual and unexpected as that of some rare disease long-thought eradicated.

As any number of tourists and other foreign visitors can testify that prostitution has not in fact vanished, this position would seem to have represented a classic case of policymakers playing ostrich and refusing to see what they would prefer to believe does not exist. At the same time, however, the encyclopedia entry also offered some more-useful insights into official attitudes. For example, prostitution was termed "socially deviant behavior," rather than "sexually deviant behavior," which reinforced the sense that it was the result of social forces and not of character or psychological flaws on the part of the prostitute; in addition, this suggested that such behavior was not only a negative consequence of various social forces but that it also had negative consequences of its own. It was, moreover, a "parasitic existence," indicating that prostitutes were not thought to perform any valued labor or service for which they were rewarded, but instead were simply taking advantage of the labor of others. Finally, the entry was marked by internal contradiction: On the one hand, the notion that prostitution was "organic" to certain social conditions implied that both its presence and its eradication were essentially inevitable by-products of historical developments; on the other hand, the implied success of "purposeful" programs to eliminate prostitution injected a more voluntaristic note. Similarly, if prostitution was itself the product of negative social forces, presumably beyond the control of any individual, then was not the prostitute a victim rather than a parasite?

In the 1980s this official position on the nature and causes of prostitution became important again and relevant to the making of social policy, for the first time since the 1930s. One of the targets of *glasnost'*, prostitution was the subject of media scrutiny throughout the USSR, and the press coverage culminated in 1987 in legislation outlawing the act of prostitution for the first time in Soviet history. This chapter will explore some of the reasons why prostitution emerged as a policy issue when it did, how it was presented to the Soviet people, the perceived nature of the problem itself, and the ultimate official response.[1]

Prostitutes and Prostitution in the Soviet Context

When the Bolsheviks came to power in 1917, they inherited all the social problems that had afflicted czarist Russia, including widespread and flagrant prostitution. Because they considered prostitution a problem, for ideological reasons as well as its threat to public health and public order, they had three basic policy options: They could regulate it, they could criminalize it, or they could put their faith in their theory and assume that it would disappear along with the social forces that had bred it.

Czarist policy had combined regulation with criminalization, with the former intended to contain the spread of venereal disease by restricting entry into the trade and requiring routine medical inspections by those practicing it. An official apparatus for inspecting and licensing prostitutes was established in 1843, and the "yellow passport" entitled women to earn a relatively handsome income—albeit one that often had to be shared with pimps and/or extortionists among the police. For many female newcomers to the cities—often peasants without any skills—the prospect of earning fifteen to twenty rubles a month in a factory or as a domestic servant soon paled once they realized that they could earn at least twice that, and often much more, through prostitution. Eventually, their ranks were swelled by women from all social classes and age-groups who were eager to pursue one of the more lucrative "professions" open to women.

Although official regulation was intended to stem the growth of what was piously considered a social evil, in practice it did little to protect either the public or the prostitutes from degradation and disease. State control had no effect on the growth of the number of prostitutes, and their share of the total population of St. Petersburg, for example, was roughly the same as that of most major cities in Western Europe; between 1853 and 1867, the number of licensed prostitutes in St. Petersburg grew by 20 percent, while the total population of the city grew by just 6 percent. Worse, its semilegalization created an environment in which white slavery and child prostitution not only persisted but also flourished. The Moscow police, for instance, had pubescent girls as young as eleven on their official registry rolls, and even younger children worked among the unlicensed prostitutes.

All this regulation might have been acceptable to the many groups opposed to state-sanctioned prostitution if it had actually accomplished its original goal of controlling the spread of disease, but in this it failed abysmally. Despite the routine medical inspections to which registered women (but not their male clients) were subjected, some three-quarters of the prostitutes were infected; one might assume figures at least as high for the unregistered women, who were thought to be approximately equal in number to the licensed ones. It is a measure of how ineffectual regulation was that syphilis was the most prevalent diagnosis in St. Petersburg hospitals, and as Stites commented, "It would be difficult to find a better example of institutionalized impotence of the Imperial bureaucracy" than its handling of institutionalized prostitution.[2]

The circumstances surrounding prostitution were therefore such that by the turn of the century it had become a significant social issue. Its abolition or at least its regulation by a state ostensibly opposed to all manner of promiscuity became popular rallying points for feminists, moralists, public-health advocates, aristocratic charity organizations, and reformers and radicals of every stripe. The Bolsheviks, however, were—at least from the perspective of hindsight—conspicuously absent from this and other campaigns devoted to various aspects of the "woman question." Their commitment to the class struggle translated into hostility toward specifically women's movements or issues as detrimental to proletarian solidarity. This being the case, the Bolshevik leaders, male and female, had little familiarity with the prostitution issue, and to the extent that they had a policy, it was one of somewhat simplistic opposition to this manifestation of bourgeois exploitation. Lenin, for example, had nothing more to offer on the subject than the recommendation that prostitutes be found honest work to occupy them, a singularly unhelpful prescription given that so many women had turned to prostitution to escape "honest" drudgery in the first place.[3]

Though the Bolsheviks were not noticeably exercised by the increasingly negative consequences of prostitution, they were nonetheless unambiguously opposed to it, and once they came to power there was never any question of their pursuing the czarist approach of regulation. (It was, in any case, the Provisional Government that finally abolished the licensing and inspection system.[4]) Neither, apparently, was there much consideration of the most common alternative, which was simple criminalization, though throughout the civil war period it did seem that any official action had become unnecessary, and that prostitution really had vanished in the wake of revolution: When the conditions permitting its practice disappeared, then so too did prostitution, at least for the most part. The combination of female labor requisitions, the emigration of the wealthy, the unavailability of hotel rooms and the like, and the shortage of money in general all rendered the buying and selling of sex simply impractical. In addition, the near-total breakdown of traditional values (especially in the cities), including the radicalization of sexual attitudes among many sectors of society, meant that recourse to prostitutes became both unnecessary as a sexual outlet and unacceptable as a political act.[5] Thus, while the civil war years witnessed extensive rewriting of legal codes, including new definitions of the legal status of women under socialism, the subject of prostitution went unaddressed and its practice was neither legalized nor criminalized.

As war communism gave way to the New Economic Policy (NEP), however, and as the day-to-day life of the average citizen began to approach the prewar norm, the Soviet leadership was disturbed to discover the resurgence of prostitution. Legal instruments were brought into play for the first time, including outlawing brothels, procuring, and white slavery, but this did little to stem the upsurge in the numbers of women walking the streets, and by 1922 their numbers in Petrograd had reached prerevolutionary levels.[6]

Once again, as good Marxists should have been able to predict, the creation of socioeconomic conditions conducive to the flourishing of prostitution did in fact lead to its growth. The NEP, with its return to limited private enterprise, permitted the reopening of hotels and cafes and similar meeting spots, while generating enough prosperity for some to make such luxuries as the purchase of sex possible again. At the same time, however, it created great hardship for large numbers of women. The end of labor conscription exacted a far heavier toll on women than on men—some 70 percent of the unemployment it created was among women[7]—while the cuts in rations, in maternity and child-care benefits, and in access to maternity homes and child-care facilities exacerbated women's financial difficulties. In addition, the disruption of traditional mores in the wake of civil war had contributed to the rapid increase in illegitimacy, and the new divorce legislation had made the dissolution of relationships a simple process but proved incapable of enforcing alimony awards. In short, the number of women without the traditional source of support (a spouse) and thus in need of work was multiplying at the same time that opportunities for employment were shrinking.

Given the lack of skills on the part of most women and the sharply reduced demand for domestic help (which had absorbed much unskilled female labor in the past), large numbers of women again turned to the streets. The portrait of this life that emerged from disparate sources, however, suggested an even greater sense of desperation than that characterizing prerevolutionary prostitution. Whereas in the earlier period prostitution was undeniably degrading, dangerous, and debilitating, it was also the case that for at least some of its practitioners a short-term rational choice was involved: For the most successful prostitutes, there were at least a few years of prosperity and glamour, and even the common streetwalker sometimes saw advantages to this life compared with the drudgery and low wages of factory or domestic work.[8] For the women who turned to prostitution after the Revolution, though, there were no alternatives and not even the illusion of the "good life"; there was only material need.

Although the resurgence of such need was welcomed by the NEPmen, students, and other traditional patrons, it was a stunning blow to the revolutionaries. This was, of course, far from the only problem confronting them in the 1920s, and certainly not the most serious, but it was still an impressive indicator of how far they had to go in transforming society. A still more appalling measure was the fact that child prostitution was a worse problem than it had been before the Revolution, due largely to the huge numbers of orphaned and abandoned children created by war and social chaos.[9]

That the NEP could generate adult and child prostitution and other forms of "dissoluteness" eventually contributed to the disillusionment with the economic policy, but in the meantime the Soviet state felt compelled for the first time to take action against prostitution. The result was remarkably similar to czarist-era practice. As the extralegal harassment by the police continued unabated in some areas, the state turned to the earlier methods of the ladies' aid societies and imperial philanthropy, even though the Bolsheviks had denigrated and ridiculed them only a short while before. The official response thus included heavy doses of propaganda, training programs, placement services, and committees patrolling urban railroad stations to warn newly arrived peasant girls of the dangers of the streets. Such measures were no doubt satisfying to those implementing them, embodying as they did the Leninist credo that the solution to the problem was full employment and class consciousness, but they were no more effective than they had been a generation earlier; if nothing else, there was still the fact that there was no full employment. (It should be noted, however, that although Leninist pragmatism might have been callous, it was still an improvement over the contempt for women inherent in czarist-era approaches, and the perception of prostitutes as sinners and victims of their own lusts.)

Of somewhat more practical value was the institution of *profilaktorii,* or medical clinics, which not only provided most of the above services, but also treated women for venereal disease and provided them with shelter.[10] Such clinics were far too few in number to be effective, however, and the training and related programs were defeated by continuing high unemployment. More legalistic methods, such as the closing of brothels, merely forced women onto the streets rather than put them out of business.

By the end of the first decade of Soviet rule, then, public policy on prostitution had proved no more effective at eliminating or controlling it than had czarist policies. True, there was less exploitation of prostitutes by postrevolutionary police authorities, and fewer obstacles to their exit from the trade, than in the past. Nonetheless, it was still the case that Soviet policies indirectly encouraged prostitution by recreating the conditions that made it both possible and, for some women, even necessary.

What finally eliminated prostitution as a social problem—at least as a common and widespread phenomenon—was not directed social policy but the creation of a new socioeconomic environment, with the introduction of the First Five Year Plan. As crash industrialization got under way, urban unemployment disappeared and did so at an even faster rate than the plan had anticipated; by 1932, in fact, labor shortages had become pervasive. This not only opened opportunities for women beyond any available to them in the past, but it was also accompanied by intense official pressure on women to take advantage of them. There was thus no longer a need for women to turn to prostitution once alternatives were again available, and perhaps as important, it was no longer really practical to do so. For although wages were rising rapidly, a parallel rise in the inflation rate limited discretionary spending. Also, overcrowding in the cities was becoming so acute that even the practice of licit sex was problematic.[11]

Moreover, any remnants of postrevolutionary libertinism were suppressed by Stalinist social and family policies, which reemphasized selected traditional values, such as monogamy and procreative sex, while impressing upon women the radical notion that society valued and was dependent upon them. It is difficult to determine the impact of the Stalinist treatment of women—it failed in many of its goals, such as raising birthrates and stabilizing marriage, for example—but it may have contributed to women's awareness that they had more to offer society than their bodies alone.[12]

Despite the Stalinist assault on many other traditional values and the intensified social dislocations of the 1930s, all of which might have favored prostitution's survival, it ceased to be a visible phenomenon on the urban landscape during the 1930s. It was in this period that propagandists felt confident enough to declare, "By the victory of socialism, the economic roots of prostitution in our country have been eliminated."[13] The coming of World War II, and the further mobilization of all available labor resources as the economy was put on a war footing, reinforced these trends: The employment prospects for women, and the pressure to fill them, were greater than ever, while conditions on the home front in general provided little opportunity for prostitution to reassert itself.[14] The labor shortages and other conditions lasted well into the postwar reconstruction period.

Prostitution Today

Stalinism thus set the stage for the contemporary situation regarding prostitution. It is still not as visible a social problem in the USSR as it is in many other industrialized societies and not simply because of the greater degree of control exercised by the system over the individual. More significant factors include the following.

Until recently, there was no significant unemployment, and female participation in the labor force still remains high. The roughly 90 percent of all working-age women who are employed outside the home make up over half of the total paid labor force, so economic necessity does not appear to be a major factor encouraging prostitution. In addition, the Stalinist system of social programs, designed primarily to help women combine their dual assigned roles of mothers and workers, have been expanded in the post-Stalin era and provide additional support for participants in the legitimate work force. Also, women are more likely to be skilled workers (or professionals) than in the past, as employment opportunities not only expand but also grow more attractive. Moreover, even though women remain concentrated in the lower-paying, less-skilled segments of the labor pool, there are evidently enough women in positions of responsibility to undermine the image of women as sex objects utterly dependent on men. This is reinforced by the vigorously expressed official image of womanhood that emphasizes maternity at home and dedication at the workplace and by the absence of sexually suggestive images of women in the arts or advertising. Thus, although Soviet men—and women—still tend to hold very traditional perceptions of femininity, they generally stress such supposedly innate traits as "softness," "weakness," and a predisposition toward nurturing rather than sexuality.[15]

At the same time, however, the very success of the Stalinist model in creating the foundations for a modern industrial society has prevented prostitution from dying out completely (assuming that this would ever be possible under any conditions). There is, for instance, the continued negative impact of urbanization and secularization on traditional values, including erosion of traditional inhibitions against extramarital sex; this change is reflected both in survey research and in escalating illegitimacy rates.[16] On the one hand, the new attitude creates less demand for prostitutes as women in general become more amenable to sexual relations outside of marriage, but on the other, it may make it easier for some women to take a less personal, and more instrumental, view of sex.

Add to this the fact that increasing prosperity has generated rampant materialism within Soviet society, as the media never tire of complaining. The concern with basic subsistence, so prominent in the past, has given way to a near-obsession with the accumulation of consumer goods, especially those with desirable foreign labels. It is also the case that the opening of Soviet society to the West over the past twenty years or so has not only increased awareness of those goods, but has permitted ever-larger numbers of Western businessmen, tourists, and others to enter the country, bringing with them the various objects of desire that they themselves take for granted.

Together, these two forces—permissiveness and materialism—plus, no doubt, some limited relief from the still-chronic housing shortage, may help explain the persistence of prostitution. It is important to recognize, however, that the fundamental nature of prostitution has undergone great change in the years since the NEP. To judge from available evidence, the Soviet leadership is justified in taking pride in the fact that Soviet women are no longer driven to sell sexual favors in the absence of any other means of survival; neither does their society generally treat women in such a way that their self-esteem suggests few alternatives.

At the same time, however, policymakers' reluctance to satisfy the craving for more consumer goods, a craving that they themselves helped to create, has led to the phenomenon of the part-time prostitute. These are women who hold full-time jobs in the regular economy but who moonlight, as it were, purely to earn money for luxuries. (Regular jobs in public catering, retailing, and similar services are especially popular with these women, since they permit steady contact with potential clients.) Then, too, there are many Soviet prostitutes for whom the practice provides their livelihood: For such women, the material rewards of prostitution and, in some cases, the relatively easy work involved compared to many unskilled legitimate jobs clearly outweigh the official pressure to conform to assigned female roles. These women have no objective need to engage in prostitution. Neither abject economic necessity nor systematic police exploitation can account for their actions; the desire for a shortcut to material well-being can. (This generalization, of course, does not apply to women who are unable to maintain legitimate employment.) Finally, there is the infrastructure of third parties that facilitates the buying and selling of sex: the pimps and madams, the taxi drivers who supply mobile bordellos, and the barmen and doormen and the like who direct potential clients to available women. They, too, are driven by material desire rather than by material need.

Of particular importance is the absence of many scarce and desirable goods from Soviet stores when such goods are readily available through foreign contacts. Not only has this created a flourishing trade among illicit entrepreneurs who buy foreigners' goods and resell them on the black market, it has created another kind of trade as well: women who exchange sex with foreigners for jeans, perfume, electronic goods, and other commonplace items—even bars of soap.[17] The persistence of this behavior suggests that, contrary to ideological explanations, prostitution is not the simple by-product of economic need and the class-based repression of women. It would be far more accurate to say that as long as there are women who want more material goods than they have, and as long as there are men both with access to these and who want what women have to offer, then some of these men and women are going to get together and satisfy each others' needs and/or wants.

Beyond stating that such exchanges do take place, however, it is difficult to generalize about the practice of prostitution in the Soviet Union today. At present, little reliable data exist, except for the results of small-scale local studies. Most information is anecdotal or comes from incomplete police statistics. Virtually no scholarly work has been carried out on this issue, not only because the topic had been considered illegitimate, but also perhaps because until recently it was thought to be too insignificant a problem to warrant much attention. The recent surge of publicity has awakened scholars' interest in prostitution as a social problem, but the initial efforts to grapple with it are still clearly exploratory.[18] The picture should improve with more research, especially once the division created in 1988 within Goskomstat (the State Statistical Committee) begins publishing vice and crime statistics (*moral'naia statistika*).[19] In the meantime, the most valuable source of data is an empirical study based on a sample of 532 prostitutes in Georgia. Its findings are especially useful because the sample is not only large but also diverse: Georgia's resorts attract visitors from throughout the country, who in turn attract prostitutes, and thus 42.5 percent of the respondents come from other regions of the Soviet Union.[20]

Beyond the Georgian findings, however, meaningful statistics are scarce. In their absence, no one seems willing to hazard any estimates on the size of the prostitute population or to generalize about any of its characteristics. One is left trying to form a picture of the situation from fragmentary information. Moscow police, for example, claimed in 1987 to have a list of more than 3,500 prostitutes working there, though what portion of the total that list represented is unknown.[21] The number of prostitutes is thought to be larger in resort areas and in any cities frequented by foreigners—tourists or sailors or both—since foreigners can pay in ways that local males usually cannot. (There is rarely any suggestion from Soviet sources, however, that foreigners are to blame for prostitution, or that they are callously taking advantage of Soviet womanhood; if anything, the dominant popular image is of materialistic women with no respect for themselves or their country, assaulting innocent guests.) Because prostitutes can also be found in regions foreigners rarely visit, it is assumed that relatively small-scale local black markets can usually support some strictly native trade. Frunze police, for example, reported dealings with about 100 "immoral, anti-social women" in 1987, and prostitutes are not uncommon even in remote rural areas.[22]

The Moscow police list also showed an age range extending from seventy years old down to fourteen; Frunze police reported that 20 percent of the women in their files were underage, though only 3.3 percent of the Georgian sample were under the age of eighteen. The nature of adolescent prostitution in the Soviet Union is not well defined, however, and is probably little better understood. Soviet commentators, for instance, tend not to draw clear distinctions between simple promiscuity and actual prostitution, though the prevalence of commodity-based prostitution, or sex in exhange for consumer goods, does make it difficult to discriminate between the two. It cannot, of course, be assumed that the women who talk to reporters constitute a representative sample of Soviet young people (or of prostitutes, for that matter), but it does seem that for many there is no significant difference between engaging in sexual acts with someone who has taken them out for a night on the town and doing the same things with someone who gives them perfume or a silk scarf or something else; such quid pro quos come to be expected, to the point where sex is eventually exchanged for the gift. Many young women describe just such exchanges and then claim that they are not, of course, prostitutes. There are, doubtless, many young women across the country who operate in this gray area, just at or just over the brink into prostitution.

What this suggests most strikingly is a very dramatic breakdown in traditional sexual mores. Soviet sociologists, like those in the West, have come to attribute such change at least partly to modernization and urbanization, and thus one expects to find (and does find) increased permissiveness in the European cities of the USSR.[23] What the reports on prostitution around the country show, however, is the extent to which sexual attitudes have changed in the less-developed areas as well, where traditional values have remained relatively strong. Even the less-permissive environments of Georgia, Armenia, and Central Asia have changed enough that syphilis and gonorrhea among secondary-school students are becoming a significant public-health problem. There is some evidence, too, that adolescents are increasingly likely to experiment with homosexual acts.[24]

In the absence of studies highlighting other factors, the best explanation available for prostitution among young girls is the fusion of promiscuity and materialism; the promiscuity itself is often blamed on the combined effects of boredom and thrill seeking, the lack of parental supervision, and the dismal quality of Soviet sex education, which typically avoids frank discussion of the health and other risks of indiscriminate sexual relations. Then, too, social controls over adolescent behavior in general are weakening, so that permissiveness and even prostitution are part of a larger pattern of rising juvenile delinquency, gang formation, adolescent alcoholism, and so on. As with prostitution itself, such behavior has only recently been subject to serious study. On the basis of available information, however, there is no reason to believe that there are large numbers of runaways or drug addicts among the young prostitutes. Thus, in the Soviet case, this class of prostitution may be the result of social trends but not the direct consequence of other deviant behavior, as it so often is in the West.

This is not to suggest, though, that prostitutes of any age are not involved in other forms of socially deviant behavior; they are, which is one reason why they are typically considered undesirables. Some 15 percent of the women on file in Frunze had prior convictions for parasitism, vagrancy, or drug charges, though since many engage in various black-market transactions, the drug convictions are at least as likely to be for dealing or smuggling as for actual use. Alcoholism is more commonly associated with prostitutes, especially older ones, than drug abuse, but it is not clear whether this is because prostitutes are more likely to become alcoholics or because alcoholic women turn to prostitution to support themselves. (However, the widely cited relationship between prostitution and alcoholism may be exaggerated: In the Georgian study, only 7.8 percent of the women claimed to drink alone habitually.) Worse, from the public's perspective, is the association of prostitutes with venereal disease, though few statistics are yet available on the extent of these infections. Treatment appears to be largely haphazard, with many women preferring to treat themselves rather than turn to state-run clinics; in consequence, jobs in hospitals and clinics are attractive because they offer access to drugs and testing facilities for self-treatment.

The women are generally not married and are often raising one or more children. Of the Georgian sample, 51.7 percent of the women were divorced, 33.8 percent had never married, only 4.9 percent were married and living with their husbands, and the rest were separated or widowed; about half had children. Police in Kiev claimed that the majority of prostitutes there were single mothers, and in Frunze one in seven had had a child whose father was unknown. Police also claimed, however, that the rising divorce rate was to blame for any increase in prostitution; if so, then the number of illegitimate children involved there might actually be fairly small, given the easy access to abortion. (One assumes that the average prostitute has undergone multiple abortions, considering the lack of birth-control alternatives, but there are no figures on this.) If divorce is in fact a contributing factor in the rise of prostitution, then prostitution is not merely a symptom of rapid social change and deficient upbringing, the two explanations most commonly offered by Soviet analysts. Instead, financial hardship may be a more significant factor than is commonly supposed. This would also indicate that the financial impact of divorce is less neutral than intended, and that the wife suffers greater economic hardship than her husband when a marriage dissolves, especially when there are children involved. It is impossible to draw firm conclusions on this, given the nature of the data, but the Georgian study showed that not all earnings from prostitution go for luxury goods, and that some cover basic needs: Asked what they spend the money on, 72.6 percent mentioned clothes and cosmetics (though given their business, even these could be considered necessities), but 64.7 percent mentioned food, 28.2 percent spent part of their earnings on their children's upkeep, and 21.6 percent put money toward housing.

Once one goes beyond the imported luxuries and fine clothes, the reality of prostitution in the Soviet Union is, as elsewhere, quite unattractive and fraught with risk and hardship. The situation is made worse by the practical, if not legal, constraints on trade. Hotel rooms, for example, are not only in very short supply, but also the heavily bureaucratized booking procedure makes it virtually impossible for anyone to get a room on short notice. Indeed, hotels housing the highly desirable foreign clients (among whose very attractions are their own rooms) have been essentially off-limits to Soviet citizens, and thus it is usually necessary to bribe—or otherwise satisfy—doormen, clerks, and others before the women can even enter the lobby. It has been easier to mix with tourists at resort hotels, but there, too, profits must be split several ways in order to reserve several "vacation" stays in a year. Massage parlors and other establishments that serve as camouflaged bordellos elsewhere are unavailable in the Soviet Union or else fail to provide necessary privacy.

Private homes are thus the only viable venue for many women, but difficulties are commonplace there as well. The principal problem is the chronic, nationwide shortage of housing. Statistics published in 1988 for thirty major cities, for example, showed that from 12 percent to 36 percent of families were eligible for better housing because their current housing was considered substandard.[25] One effect of the shortage is that single women (and some with families) are usually ineligible for housing except for dormitory-style accommodations available through employers. Even women with families have great difficulty getting apartments both large enough to afford some privacy and close to urban centers. Privacy and proximity are, of course, desirable to anyone seeking housing, but they are essential to the prostitute. Only 40.6 percent of the respondents in the Georgian study could claim comfortable (*blagoustroennyi*) housing, while 19.9 percent lived in communal apartments, 3.7 percent in dormitories, and 27.5 percent in otherwise unsatisfactory quarters; 8.3 percent had no housing of their own at all.

The privacy issue is perhaps the most troublesome because it is so pervasive a problem. Even if one has an apartment of one's own, and even if there is no serious overcrowding within it, there is still the likelihood that it will be part of a communal arrangement whereby a group of households share kitchen and bath facilities and a common hall. Under such conditions, one's affairs quickly become everyone's, and the woman suspected by neighbors of "indecent trade" is usually denounced to the police.[26] The problems involved in trying to service clients under such conditions are often severe enough to make working for a pimp or madam, who will take care of such logistical issues, appear attractive, even though this cuts deeply into profits. Through bribery and other means, however, such individuals are able to gain control of several flats and then provide the requisite privacy for a number of women and their clients. Cars, taxis, and train compartments sometimes serve as alternative places of business, but besides the discomfort and inconvenience, there are payoffs required there as well. Therefore, one way or another, the housing problem has a great impact on income: The prostitute must either pay someone a great deal for reliable and private quarters or forgo earnings because she cannot provide a comfortable place in which to do business.

The practice of prostitution, then, requires significant trade-offs. The earnings can be attractive, it not being uncommon for an urban prostitute to make at least 100 rubles—roughly half the average monthly wage—in an evening, while items received in place of cash may be even more valuable. However, profits can be quickly depleted by payments to procurers and bribes to others, and earnings decline sharply with age. For example, in Georgia, the younger, though otherwise average, prostitutes typically receive 50 rubles for their services; as they grow older, the price drops to 10, even 5 rubles. In fact, everything about the trade grows worse with time, to judge from the apparent "life cycle" of prostitutes working in Georgia. The women begin on a part-time basis, supplementing their official incomes to buy luxuries and simply for the excitement. Since they have full-time jobs, they can afford to be selective and usually go off with only one man in an evening. However, the financial rewards of prostitution, plus the stress of working at two jobs, generally persuades the women to quit their regular jobs, though this means that they must seek out more men to make up for lost wages. This grows more difficult as age and the strains of their life-style make them less attractive to clients, until they find themselves working the streets and train stations instead of restaurants and parties, and for less money each year.

Also, public opinion against prostitution has risen dramatically due to recent publicity, and this has been accompanied by demands to deny the women various rights and benefits, including those intended to aid their children. Although it is unlikely that basic social benefits will be denied them, it is still the case that prostitutes have suddenly found themselves operating in a far more hostile environment than in the past, both socially and legally.

The Legal Context of Prostitution

The persistence of prostitution in the Soviet Union is more than simply an ideological problem. Its every appearance is a reminder that either Soviet socialism has far to go yet in its efforts to create the optimal society or that the optimal society is not in fact likely on this earth. For the policymaker concerned with the problems of the here and now, however, there are more practical issues generated by the presence of commercialized sex. Prostitution contributes greatly to the spread of venereal diseases; it diverts not only women but also their male hangers-on from more productive pursuits; it engenders a general disrespect for official norms and values; it is associated with crime (as when prostitutes steal from their clients and when pimps and prostitutes use violence against each other or against rivals) and with other types of antisocial behavior (such as drunkenness and drug abuse).

The basic official response, as noted, has been to hope for the eventual "withering away" of the phenomenon, as with other forms of social deviance. However, the traditional government approach of instituting legal prohibitions against undesirable behavior had not, until recently, been applied against prostitutes per se, most probably because of the general Marxist perception of them as victims of forces beyond their control (despite the actual common perception of them as parasites). There may also have been a preference for refusing to acknowledge the perseverance of a phenomenon that should be impossible under socialism, especially since it survived on such a small scale that it was easily overlooked without too much risk to society. Other "bourgeois holdovers" such as alcoholism or theft or acts of violence might equally present doctrinal problems to the purist, but are far more difficult and dangerous to ignore.

If Soviet lawmakers have been reluctant in the past to ban prostitution outright, however, they have been far less reticent in using legal methods to fight its externalities. It should be noted that the Soviets are not unique in pursuing this strategy: In the modern world, prostitutes are commonly pitied for one reason or another rather than simply condemned, whereas pimps and other secondary manifestations of prostitution are uniformly loathed. Thus, Great Britain has no statutes against prostitution itself, although most of the practices associated with it, from soliciting to procuring, are subject to penalties.[27]

In the Soviet case, there are a variety of ways in which the legal system and police authorities may be brought to bear on the practice of prostitution. Procuring, running a brothel, and coercing women to engage in prostitution have been illegal since 1922, when the first Soviet criminal codes were introduced.[28] There are specific provisions, too, against inducing juveniles to enter into prostitution. The criminal penalties for "the keeping of dens of debauchery" and "pandering" are up to five years' deprivation of freedom or exile, with or without confiscation of property; for enticing minors into deviant behavior, the punishment is not more than five years' deprivation of freedom.[29]

The prostitute herself has always been vulnerable to prosecution on a variety of other charges as well. The public-health aspects of prostitution have been prominent in all countries' attempts to combat it, and Soviet prostitutes (like all Soviet citizens) have faced criminal charges for the spread of venereal disease since 1922. Engaging in sexual intercourse while knowing that one has a venereal disease, whether one's partner becomes infected or not, can lead to up to two years' imprisonment and a fine of up to 100 rubles; if one's partner actually becomes infected, then the punishment can increase to up to three years in prison or "correctional tasks" for up to a year. For second offenses, for infecting two or more partners, or for infecting a minor, the prison term increases to five years.[30] Family codes can also be used to punish the prostitute, since if she has children, her "immoral, anti-social conduct" and consequent "harmful influence" on them can be grounds for deprivation of parental rights; the parent so charged can face the additional punishment of eviction from the children's residence without authorization for new housing.[31]

The harshest penalties accrue to prostitutes and their associates who run afoul of currency regulations, making the specialty of servicing foreigners not only the most lucrative branch of the trade but also the riskiest. (Note, however, that many of these foreign clients are not wealthy businessmen or tourists or diplomats but sailors on leave in port cities. Some of these "*valiuta* girls" constitute an elite within the trade, but many others work with rougher customers and for lower compensation.) Depending on the scale of one's involvement in illegal currency exchanges, the penalties can range from three to eight years plus possible exile, five to fifteen years plus possible exile, and, in extreme cases, can extend to capital punishment.[32] Currency violations on the scale that the individual prostitute is likely to engage in would bring the lesser penalties, but these are still more severe than any other to which she might be vulnerable.

By far the most useful legislation, though, from the perspective of law-enforcement authorities, is that against parasitism. "Systematically engaging in vagrancy or begging, or leading any other parasitic way of life" can result in a year spent in prison or performing correctional tasks, and a second offense raises that to two years.[33] (This is a violation not only of union-republic law but, since 1970, of all-union law as well.) The extremely broad scope of these statutes has made them ideal weapons against prostitutes and others engaged in undesirable behavior that is not otherwise illegal. Regulations involving residency permits have also been useful to the police. Laws such as these seem to have helped Moscow police exile some seventy prostitutes from the city prior to the Olympic Games held there in 1980.[34]

Despite this loose network of laws that can be, and sometimes are, used against prostitutes, in practice the violations are all very difficult to prove. The police complain of the near impossibility of winning convictions in most cases and of their impotence in the face of behavior they would prefer to help control. Given the essentially private nature of prostitution's consumation, for instance, it is hard to witness any exchange of money that might lead to currency violation charges; sex in exchange for "gifts" of clothing or cosmetics or the like could bring no charges whatsoever. It is also very difficult to convict someone of knowingly infecting another with venereal disease. Even the enforcement of antiparasite laws has been hampered by the fact that many prostitutes could claim to have legitimate employment in the regular economy, thus exempting them from prosecution.[35]

Although it is unlikely that the police were quite as helpless as they insisted, it is no doubt the case that the problems involved in applying existing sanctions helped make the introduction of new ones more attractive. This situation should also serve as a useful lesson to those who believe that Soviet police officials are bound by no legal niceties to speak of: They have been constrained by legal realities to some degree in their efforts to combat prostitution.

Once it was decided that the existing legal environment was an inadequate deterrent to prostitution, new legislation was introduced. The Presidium of the RSFSR Supreme Soviet issued a decree in June 1987, and similar legislation was introduced in other union republics.[36] Engaging in prostitution (which the decree itself does not define) can now result in a warning or a fine of up to 100 rubles; the maximum fine is 200 rubles for a second offense committed within a year. (According to officials of the Ministry of Internal Affairs, however, it is only after the third incident of suspected prostitution that a woman is usually even charged with violating the decree.) In the course of arrest for suspected prostitution, the accused can have "objects" confiscated, presumably any items that might have been received as payment in lieu of cash; she is also subject to a medical examination for the purpose of detecting and controlling venereal diseases. The problem of prostitutes' dealings with foreigners has been explicitly addressed by the legislation as well, and the same fines for cash prostitution now apply to sexual relations in exchange for material goods. (Actually, this last regulation is not restricted to prostitution and instead outlaws all cases of "harassing foreign citizens for the purpose of purchasing, trading or acquiring objects in any fashion.")[37]

There are three important features of the decree. First, there are still no penalties involved for the male clients of prostitutes, nor is there any suggestion that they, too, should be examined by medical officers for signs of disease. Second, the decree makes prostitution only an administrative offense, not a criminal one, though many in law enforcement and in the public continue to demand that the sale, and perhaps even the purchase, of sex be made a crime. Third, the penalties for prostitution really are quite modest, especially compared to some roughly similar offenses. Recall that the pimp can get up to five years in prison, and the penalty for the spread of venereal disease is up to two years. Similarly, engaging in homosexual relations can lead to deprivation of freedom for up to five years, and sexual relations with a minor up to six years.[38] Compared to these penalties, the fine of 100 rubles (or less) does not constitute especially onerous punishment, particularly since the going rate for servicing even truck drivers—not one of the more high-status practices—is 10 rubles.[39]

There are several possible explanations for such leniency. One is a possible preference for easing slowly into the criminalization of prostitution. This would allow the police, the courts, the prostitutes, and society in general a period in which all can acclimate themselves to the new situation, implying, as it does, a shift in attitude toward those women who use their bodies for financial gain. If so, it is likely that the existing legislation will be supplemented, or replaced, by stricter and perhaps more extensive laws in the future. Second, this could be indicative of the traditional reluctance to draw attention to social problems. Though the recent heavy press coverage certainly has publicized the existence of prostitution, it may still be the case that the relatively minor sanctions subsequently introduced are intended to downplay the scale of the problem; they do, in any case, suggest the absence of deep official concern. Third, it is possible that the legislation is the result of the persistent image, created by Marxism, of the prostitute as victim, and of the sense that her family and the education system and society as a whole must have failed her if prostitution seems to her to be a viable life-style. Thus, whereas it is appropriate to punish severely those exploiting such women through procuring and related activities (though not through paying for their services), these women themselves should be treated with more compassion. These explanations are not mutually exclusive, and thus it may be that the new law represents the combined effects of all three, or rather, a compromise between them and the evident desire to crack down on a troubling manifestation of social deviance.

The Media and Agenda-Building

The promulgation of the antiprostitution decree should have come as a surprise to no one: The public was carefully prepared for its introduction, though the degree to which this was planned from the outset is unclear. It appears as though prostitution was slowly permitted to become a publicly discussed phenomenon, after nearly a half-century of official silence on the subject, as part of the general trend toward more openness in the media. At some point, however, the coverage took on a more purposeful character and was oriented toward the announcement of penalties for engaging in prostitution.

Press reports of prostitution first surfaced in 1985, though they were few enough to suggest that their appearance was essentially spontaneous. *Literaturnaia gazeta* broke the ice with a story of young women who frequented a particular bar waiting to be picked up—preferably and usually by a black marketeer. In December of that year, the Komsomol newspaper in Kirghizia took advantage of *Literaturnaia gazeta*'s opening and ran a similar story on "restaurant girls," many of whom, the paper noted, were listed in police files as being Komsomol members. The pace began to pick up in early 1986, with stories appearing in other regional newspapers and in several central ones as well.[40]

The first wave of press reports was notable for the great delicacy with which the articles approached their long-taboo subject. The word "prostitute" was never mentioned, nor was there any explicit description of the exchanges that take place. It was left to the reader to conclude that these young women (as young as sixteen) were trading sexual relations for money and/or gifts. These early reports also shared a characteristic tone of sadness, that these girls were paying for "illusory pleasures . . . with their ruined youth, with their health."[41] The girls were treated with more pity than contempt, and because of the evident reluctance to discuss the more sordid aspects of prostitution, the ultimate impression created was that the principal cost to society and to the girls themselves was their materialism, their cynicism, and loss of faith in the concept of romantic love. The stories were so low-key, in fact, and so likely to describe their subjects as attractive young girls who had lost their way but received material rewards in return, that they came unwittingly close to glamorizing the trade. Indeed, since the stories began appearing, many teachers have voiced concern over their students' tendency to view prostitution in a positive light and even to consider it a viable—and attractively lucrative—way to make a living.

Each of these stories was somewhat more frank than the one preceding it, however, so that the last few expressed greater shock and disgust than the first few and portrayed the prostitute's milieu as being more squalid. Nonetheless, it would be a mistake to see too distinct a pattern in the early coverage. Most of the stories appeared in the regional press, so readers in one republic would be unlikely to read more than one or two stories because the others were published in different republics and sometimes in different languages. There could thus be no cumulative effect intended, and if each story grew successively more explicit, this can be explained by the ever more open media environment. Still, it is no doubt important that as the stories continued, they were more likely to mention the prostitute's role in spreading venereal disease and to mention the fact (disapprovingly) that efforts to control this were hampered by the absence of legislation prohibiting prostitution.

In other words, the press's gradual reintroduction of the issue of prostitution to the Soviet public became a critical element of the agenda-building process, in which public-policy issues emerged and were brought to the attention of policymakers. The essentially haphazard way in which the problem was initially presented to readers suggests that the issue came just as gradually to the attention of policymakers as it did to the public at large, and very possibly from the same source, the press. This is in contrast to the more traditional Soviet approach, whereby decisionmakers first determine that a problem exists, then present the problem to the public, and only at that point invite discussion, which may or may not influence the ultimate official response. In the case of prostitution, however, the press introduced the issue, rather than simply serving as a passive mechanism through which to address it.

However, once the press placed the problem on the policymakers' agenda, more standard methods reasserted themselves. At that point, the press was no longer the instigator, initiating debate, but became an instrument for mobilizing the public and preparing the ground for the new penalties that the regional press itself had first suggested. One sign of this was the fact that the central press organs took on a more important role: The process of publicizing the social costs of prostitution was no longer entrusted exclusively to union-republic newspapers but was supplemented by Russian-language newspapers and magazines published in Moscow. In this way, a greater degree of uniformity could be imposed on the process of shaping public opinion.

Why, however, would policymakers have been so easily persuaded that there was an issue requiring their attention? There is no evidence that prostitution had suddenly become more widespread, making it more visible and intensifying its negative consequences. Nor were the stories initially met with the same degree of public indignation and concern that has been the response to other issues, thereby almost forcing an official response. For example, stories on new labor policies or on changes in the price system routinely generate impassioned expression of public opinion. Indeed, the initial treatment of prostitutes as pitiable misfits, rather than social deviants, may have helped keep public opinion subdued and forestalled any need for an official response.

The catalyst that transformed prostitution from a relatively low-level social ill into a major social pathology requiring the full force and vigilance of the Soviet state appears to be AIDS. The initial official response to the AIDS epidemic was denial: Early press coverage insisted that it was a foreign disease, rooted in the depraved practices and moral turpitude of contemporary Western society, and was thus irrelevant to the Soviet environment.[42] Once the disease surfaced within the Soviet Union, however, it was more difficult to dismiss, and *glasnost'* made it feasible to use the press as one medium through which the epidemic could be confronted.

Existing public policy could be mobilized against the two most common means of AIDS transmission: intravenous drug use and homosexual relations. Drug abuse was one of the earliest victims of *glasnost'*, and legal, medical, and other instruments were already in place (if not always very effective) in the effort to combat it.[43] Homosexuality, too, has long been illegal, and although it has not been eliminated, the legal sanctions against it have inhibited development of the type of gay subculture that facilitated the rapid spread of AIDS in the West. Another important source of infection is in the blood supply, through inadvertent use of contaminated blood for transfusions. This means of transmission has been the cause of great anxiety in the West but has received scant publicity in the Soviet Union, and there appears to be little public pressure for extraordinary measures to protect the blood supply. This has meant that medical authorities have been able to deal with the problem at their own pace, and that there has been no need for political authorities to announce any specific policies that might have the additional effect of alarming the public. Finally, discretionary testing of foreigners began in 1987 in an attempt to restrict the disease's entry into the Soviet population. Given Soviet testing procedures, and especially the shortage of disposable syringes and autoclaves for sterilizing reusable ones, the medical value of this may prove limited. The political value is no doubt considerable, however, given the repeated official insistence that AIDS is fundamentally alien to Soviet society.

In October 1985, officials still insisted that no cases had been reported within the USSR; by December they had admitted to a number of cases "fewer than the number of fingers on one's hands"; by February 1987 the number had grown to 13, including 1 Soviet citizen, and by November of 1988 there were 96 Soviet citizens infected with the virus (the foreign nationals carrying it having since been expelled from the country); a month earlier, the first AIDS death in the Soviet Union was reported.[44] AIDS was thus a growing phenomenon in the Soviet Union, both in terms of the number of cases and in terms of public awareness. Uncertainty about the magnitude of the epidemic persisted, however, as indicated in a 1989 television report in which an AIDS specialist estimated that there were "1,000 to 10,000" Soviet HIV carriers.

One policy response to the problem has been educational and includes not only increasingly frequent and candid press coverage but also the distribution of informational pamphlets, a poster campaign, and cassette "minilectures" for various types of group meetings. Since the minilectures are very "mini" indeed—two to three minutes in length—one suspects that the amount of information being disseminated is extremely limited and avoids blunt discussion of the types of behaviors that cause the disease and that can help protect people from it.[45] Prophylactic measures are described only with great reticence: Analysts complain of both official and public reluctance to discuss frankly anything related to sex, and one of them noted that people "throw a fit" at the mention of the word "condom." Others admitted that condoms were in notoriously short supply anyway and available only in pharmacies.[46]

Other policy responses include intensifying the battle against drug abuse, continued repression of homosexuality, quiet testing of the blood supply, and developing AIDS testing, treatment, and research facilities. That left unaddressed the single remaining channel through which the disease might be spread: prostitution. Thus, as public discussion of AIDS was stepped up in 1987, so too was discussion of prostitution, even though there had been no reported cases of prostitutes becoming infected with the virus. (The suspected AIDS fatality mentioned above, however, was subsequently reported to involve a prostitute who—it was noted pointedly—often met with foreign clients.[47])

In contrast to the earlier coverage, which seemed aimed primarily at shedding light on a little-known underside of Soviet life, the second stage of coverage expressed far greater hostility to prostitution. The negative, especially the antisocial, aspects of prostitution became much more pronounced, and the undercurrent of compassion was replaced by righteous indignation. There was, too, a new note of offended patriotism: Many professed shock and humiliation at the thought of Soviet womanhood debasing itself before strangers, while others denounced the treasonous "fifth columnists" jeopardizing the motherland with a lethal plague.

There was also a new emphasis on the squalor of prostitution, especially among older women, and reports of how such women were reduced to selling themselves at train stations for a single glass of liquor. Stories suggested, too, that alcoholism was not only rampant among prostitutes but, when combined with many hours spent outdoors even in winter, also resulted in frostbite and frequent amputations. Others stressed the violence and the scarring and maiming from street fighting. The message was clear: There is no glamour, no material comfort, to be found in this life. Other reports warned young women against the idea that they could work as prostitutes for a few years and prosper while still young and attractive: The weapon there was publicity about pimps and madams who took half their girls' pay, controlled their hours and client lists, and beat them to maintain discipline. In this way, the media were utilized to have a deterrent effect, to warn young women of the dangers and degradation and lack of rewards that are the reality of prostitution.

For the public at large, there are still other messages being communicated on the social costs of prostitution. One is the common practice of stealing from clients, confident that they will be too embarrassed or frightened to report it to the police. Another is the violence surrounding prostitution on the part of pimps, customers, and female rivals. Then, too, prostitution has been associated with various types of criminal activity, from currency speculation to smuggling to the drug trade.

Two features of the coverage have been especially notable, however. One is the role of prostitution in the spread of venereal disease, which the stories suggested is endemic and poses a significant threat to public health. (A report from Riga provided rare statistics on this, noting that 180 prostitutes were examined over a period of several months, and 38 of them were found to be infected.[48]) The second is the difficulty the police have confronted in trying to control prostitution and the consequent aggressive expressions of the need for specific penalties for engaging in prostitution. Complaints initially demanded specific penalties for engaging in prostitution; since the 1987 decree, complaints are less numerous but still often insist that more extensive provisions—from harsher penalties to the creation of vice squads—are needed. (Riga, a port city with a particularly high incidence of prostitution, has responded to this pressure by establishing a special militia unit for dealing with prostitutes and by registering them with the police.[49])

Thus, the two press topics gradually converged, with reports on prostitution stressing the threat of sexually transmitted disease, reports on AIDS highlighting the role of prostitutes in infecting the public, and both identifying sexual relations with foreigners as a dangerous activity. The president of the USSR Academy of Medicine, for example, stated explicitly that anyone engaging in sex with a foreigner was running a grave risk of contracting AIDS.[50]

The continued heavy emphasis on the role of foreigners in transmitting AIDS has generated yet another epidemic, of xenophobia, similar to the intensified homophobia that the disease has bred in the West. For example, young women in one small city who have had sexual relations, commercial or otherwise, with visiting Italian workers have had their hair shorn by gangs of young men claiming to be protecting the rest of the population from AIDS; they went about this with the tacit approval of police and citizens. Similarly, African students and others reported growing prejudice against them and an increasing incidence of harassment, due to the identification of AIDS with Africa. The obvious fear of any contact with Africans indicates that the message that the virus cannot be spread through casual contact is still poorly understood.[51]

Hostility against others in high-risk categories has grown as well. In one highly publicized letter, for example, sixteen physicians proclaimed their "categorical opposition" to treating and researching AIDS, since that "noble epidemic" has the potential to "destroy" all prostitutes, homosexuals, and drug addicts.[52] Many responding to the letter were clearly appalled, but others strongly supported the doctors' perspective. An even more striking example of how opening the press to such topics can backfire came from the effort to reform the criminal codes. It has been reported that attempts to modernize the codes have been hampered by the development of strong public opinion against liberalization in three areas: abolishing capital punishment, decriminalizing homosexuality, and retaining the (noncriminal) status quo regarding prostitution.

The climax of this phase of the effort to contain AIDS thus consisted of two stages in 1987: The first, in June, introduced penalties against prostitution; the second, in August, introduced specific penalties against transmitting AIDS. The measures include obligatory (and, if necessary, forcible) AIDS testing of Soviet and foreign citizens, when the minister of public health so orders; expulsion of foreigners who refuse examination; up to five years' deprivation of freedom for knowingly putting another at risk of AIDS infection, with the term rising to eight years in case of actual infection; and an extension of other, existing, public-health codes to permit public-health officials to apply various provisions in the fight against AIDS and any other diseases that might surface in the Soviet environment.[53]

The anti-AIDS legislation, unlike that outlawing prostitution, is in the form of an all-union decree rather than a union-republic one. This illustrates the primacy of AIDS on policymakers' agendas and further suggests that the campaign against prostitution was instrumental in nature. In other words, it was not so much that prostitution presented a grave social problem that had to be tackled for its own sake, as it was that prostitution is one possible (and in practice relatively minor) source of AIDS and thus must be confronted as part of the larger drive against AIDS. (The first AIDS fatality notwithstanding, prostitution should be a lesser factor in the spread of AIDS in the USSR than in the West because of the lesser relationship between prostitution and drug use there.)[54] As a result of the two sets of decrees, however, public-health officials and policymakers can reassure an increasingly anxious public that what were presented as the primary sources of infection—drug use, homosexuality, and prostitution—"are punishable crimes."[55]

Conclusions

The serial exposé of prostitution within the Soviet Union was not a random event. The initial stories on this issue were probably motivated by little more than the press's desire to expand the boundaries of the acceptable in terms of what might be legitimately covered. The gradual introduction of *glasnost'* made it possible to shed some light on the seamier side of Soviet life; in the meantime, state and Party officials were probably delighted with the sensationalistic aspects of the stories since they distracted public attention away from the more usual targets of *glasnost'*—bureaucratic corruption, ineptitude, and stagnation.

Once policymakers accepted the fact that they were confronting the beginnings of a major public-health crisis, however, in the form of the slow but inexorable spread of the AIDS virus, then the stories took on a new meaning. They could be used to educate and warn the public, initially in nonalarming terms, by associating the disease with "promiscuity and perversion" and with foreigners. As the public became more familiar with the problem, more candid treatments of the risk became possible. At the same time, the stories could incorporate demands for the imposition of penalties—penalties against those spreading AIDS and, as a secondary tactic, penalties against those who might be spreading AIDS through their contact with possible carriers. In this fashion, public opinion could be mobilized sufficiently to accept and even welcome restrictive new legislation rather than perceive it as another set of limitations on individual behavior.

However, the longer-term effects of this policymaking strategy are perhaps even more important than any impact that it might have on AIDS itself. Story after story, especially those involving public-health experts, bemoaned the traditional Soviet practice of ignoring anything unpleasant and minimizing the scope and impact of various social problems. Time and again, Soviet readers—and officials—are warned that their puritanism, and their desire for insulation from harsh reality, is endangering, not protecting, them.

The entire prostitution/AIDS episode thus becomes a case study, and object lesson, in the utility of *glasnost'*, for both the public and for still-unconvinced policymakers. The message has been made abundantly clear: Refusal to confront social problems can suppress but not eradicate their effects and, far from enhancing political control, may undermine it by permitting antisocial behavior to flourish under cover of secrecy. And worse, as the AIDS case illustrated, such an approach could conceivably lead quite literally to the fatal weakening of the society that the secrecy was intended to protect.

Notes

1. For the purposes of this chapter, "prostitution" will be limited to female commercial prostitution. Although it is unlikely that the male variety has been eradicated any more completely than the female type, there exist no data whatsoever on male prostitution. Moreover, since male prostitution usually implies homosexuality, and since there is little indication that policymakers will reverse long-standing policy by decriminalizing homosexual acts between males, it is not relevant to this analysis. Also excluded here is the use of women and sex as instruments for espionage purposes.

2. Richard Stites, *The Women's Liberation Movement in Russia. Feminism, Nihilism, and Bolshevism, 1860–1930* (Princeton: Princeton University Press, 1978), pp. 60–63, 182–185; Linda Harriet Edmondson, *Feminism in Russia, 1900–1917* (Stanford, Calif.: Stanford University Press, 1984), pp. 143–146. This section on the historical background to the issue owes much to Stites's comprehensive treatment of women under late imperial and early Soviet rule.

3. The Russian Marxists' lack of interest in this particular expression of class antagonism is especially noteworthy in light of Engels's evident sympathy for women in general and prostitutes in particular. See especially Friedrich Engels, *The Origin of the Family, Private Property and the State, in the Light of the Researches of Lewis H. Morgan* (Moscow: Foreign Languages Publishing House, 1959) and *The Conditions of the Working Class in England in 1844* (London: George Allen and Unwin, 1952). For more on Engels's and Marx's thoughts on women, see H. Kent Geiger, *The Family in Soviet Russia* (Cambridge, Mass.: Harvard University Press, 1968), pp. 11–24; Alfred G. Meyer, "Marxism and the Women's Movement," in *Women in Russia*, ed. Dorothy Atkinson, Alexander Dallin, and Gail Warshofsky Lapidus (Stanford, Calif.: Stanford University Press, 1977), pp. 85–112. Another important influence on Marxist attitudes toward the "women's question" was August Bebel's *Woman and Socialism* (New York: Socialist Literature Co., 1910).

4. Stites, op. cit., p. 341.

5. For a review of sexual attitudes in the immediate postrevolutionary years, see Geiger, op. cit., pp. 60-71.

6. Peter H. Juviler, "Women and Sex in Soviet Law," in Atkinson, Dallin, and Lapidus, op. cit., p. 250; Stites, op. cit., p. 372.

7. A. M. Kollontai, "Novaia ugroza," *Kommunistka* (1922), cited in Beatrice Brodsky Farnsworth, "Bolshevik Alternatives and the Soviet Family: The 1926 Marriage Law Debate," in Atkinson, Dallin, and Lapidus, op. cit., p. 141.

8. Laurie Bernstein, "Saving the Fallen Woman: The Rehabilitation of Prostitutes in Late Imperial Russia," paper delivered to the American Association for the Advancement of Slavic Studies, November 1987, Boston, Mass.

9. Stites, op. cit., p. 373.

10. Fanina Halle, *Woman in Soviet Russia* (London: Routledge, 1933).

11. See Alec Nove, *An Economic History of the U.S.S.R.* (New York: Penguin Books, 1984), pp. 196-209.

12. For more on Stalinist policy on women and the family, see Gail Warshofsky Lapidus, *Women in Soviet Society: Equality, Development, and Social Change* (Berkeley and Los Angeles: University of California Press, 1978), pp. 95-122; Geiger, op. cit., pp. 76-116.

13. V. Svetlov, "Socialist Society and the Family," in *The Family in the U.S.S.R.,* ed. Rudolf Schlesinger (London: Routledge and Kegan Paul, 1949), p. 345.

14. Nove, op. cit., pp. 267-288; Mark Harrison, *Soviet Planning in Peace and War: 1938-1945* (Cambridge: Cambridge University Press, 1985), passim.

15. For more on Soviet attitudes, see Lapidus, op. cit., pp. 322-334; Lynne Attwood, "The New Soviet Man and Woman—Soviet Views on Psychological Sex Differences," in *Soviet Sisterhood,* ed. Barbara Holland (Bloomington: Indiana University Press, 1985), pp. 54-77; and the interviews conducted by Carola Hansson and Karin Liden in *Moscow Women* (New York: Pantheon, 1983).

16. Between 1980 and 1987, the number of illegitimate births increased by 28 percent, from 8.8 percent of all births to 9.8 percent. See V. I. Perevedentsev, "Bezotsovshina," *Sem'ia,* no. 34 (August 25, 1988), p. 12. For studies of sexual attitudes, see I. S. Kon, "O sotsiologicheskoi interpretatsii seksual'nogo povedeniia," *Sotsiolkogicheskie issledovaniia,* no. 2 (1982), pp. 113-121; Chingiz Adil ogly Mansimov and E. V. Foteeva, "Osobennosti predstavlenii molodezhi Azerbaidzhanskoi SSR o semeinoi zhizni," *Sotsiolkogicheskie issledovaniia,* no. 3 (1982), pp. 128-132.

17. There is considerable anecdotal evidence that foreigners are attractive for another reason as well: Many prostitutes apparently hope to marry one of their Western clients and thus get permission to leave the USSR for the West. This strategy is actually successful in some cases.

18. See, for example, S. I. Golod, "Prostitutsiia v kontekste izmeneniia polovoi morali," *Sotsiolkogicheskie issledovaniia,* no. 2 (1988), pp. 65-70, which is largely historical in nature.

19. *Izvestiia,* September 10, 1988, p. 2. It appears that "moral" issues include the practice of religion as well, and that the new division will therefore be responsible for data on believers, clergy, services, and so on.

20. A. A. Gabiani, M. A. Manuil'skii, "Tsena 'liubvi.' (Ovslevdovanie prostitutok v Gruzii)," *Sotsiolkogicheskie issledovaniia,* no. 6 (1987), pp. 61-68.

21. *Sovetskaia Rossiia,* March 11, 1987.

22. *Sovetskaia Kirgiziia,* May 16, 1987, p. 3; trans. in *Current Digest of the Soviet Press* [CDSP hereafter] 39 (November 18, 1987), p. 13.

23. See, for example, Golod, op. cit.; Kon, op. cit.; G. A. Navaitis, "Otnoshenie molodezhi k dobrachnym polovym sviaziam," *Sotsiolkogicheskie issledovaniia,* no. 2 (1988), pp. 79-80.

24. Iu. I. Bytko and A. S. Ladno, "Deviantnoe povedenie podrostkov," *Sotsiolkogicheskie issledovaniia*, no. 4 (1988), pp. 77-79.

25. *Argumenty i fakty*, no. 32 (1988), p. 5.

26. Mark Popovskii, *Tretii lishnii: On, ona i sovetskii rezhim* (London: Overseas Publications Interchange Ltd., 1985), pp. 289-290.

27. Kingsley Davis, "Sexual Behavior," in *Contemporary Social Problems*, 3rd ed., ed. Robert K. Merton and Robert Nesbit (New York: Harcourt, Brace, Jovanovich, 1971), p. 350.

28. Juviler, op. cit., p. 270.

29. Articles 226 and 210, Criminal Code of the RSFSR, October 27, 1960 [hereafter RSFSR Crim. Code], as amended July 15, 1974, in *The Soviet Codes of Law*, ed. William B. Simons (The Hague: Martinus Nijhoff, 1984). These references are all to RSFSR codes rather than to all-union ones. Just as in the United States, the details of criminal and other law in the USSR tend to be written separately within each unit of the federal system. The RSFSR codes do often serve as the models for other union-republic codes, however, even though local conditions (especially in Central Asia) and other factors create some disparities.

30. Art. 115, RSFSR Crim. Code, as amended October 20, 1971.

31. Arts. 60 and 61, The RSFSR Code on Marriage and the Family, July 30, 1969, in *The Soviet Codes of Law*, op. cit.

32. Art. 88, RSFSR Crim. Code, as amended July 25, 1967.

33. Arts. 209 and 209-1, RSFSR Crim. Code, as amended August 7, 1975, and February 25, 1970, respectively.

34. *Izvestiia*, August 14, 1987.

35. See, for example, *Sovetskaia molodezh'*, August 30, 1986; *Sovetskaia torgovlia*, June 4. 1987; *Komsomol'skaia pravda*, October 9, 1986.

36. Valerii Konovalov, "Prostitution Made an Administrative Offense," *Radio Liberty Research*, RL 311/87 (August 12, 1987), p. 1.

37. *Vedomosti verkhovnogo soveta RSFSR*, sect. 1, no. 23 [1493], June 4, 1987, pp. 479-480; *Sovetskaia Rossiia*, October 25, 1988, p. 4.

38. Arts. 121 and 119, RSFSR Crim. Code.

39. It appears that young women in rural areas often start their "careers" in this fashion, making enough money along the highways to finance a move to the big city, and to pay for the clothing and so on needed to attract foreigners. Konovalov, op. cit., p. 3.

40. For a chronological review of the reports, see Konovalov, "Does Prostitution Exist in the Soviet Union?" *Radio Liberty Research*, RL 374/86 (October 1, 1986), pp. 1-5.

41. *Komsomolets Kirgizii*, December 24, 1985, p. 4, quoted in ibid., p. 3.

42. See, for example, *Trud*, October 6, 1985, p. 4, and *Sovetskaia kul'tura*, December 7, 1985, p. 8. This period also saw efforts to blame the epidemic on biological warfare experiments in the United States, as reported in *Literaturnaia gazeta*, October 30, 1985, p. 14.

43. For media coverage of the Soviet drug problem, see, for example, *Izvestiia*, August 12, 1986, p. 3; *Pravda*, January 6, 1987, p. 3; for a sampler of articles on drug abuse from around the USSR, plus citations to others, see *CDSP*, 39 (February 11, 1987), pp. 1-7, 14. See also John M. Kramer, "Drug Abuse in the USSR," *Problems of Communism*, March-April 1988, pp. 28-40.

44. *Trud*, October 6. 1985, p. 4; *Sovetskaia kul'tura*, December 7, 1987, p. 8; October 6, 1988; and November 29, 1988, p. 8; *Literaturnaia gazeta*, February 25,

1987, p. 12; *Izvestiia,* May 31, 1987, p. 6; *Komsomol'skaia pravda,* October 7, 1988; *Sovetskaia Rossiia,* October 25, 1988, p. 4.

45. *Izvestiia,* September 15, 1987, p. 6.
46. *Komsomol'skaia pravda,* August 1, 1987, p. 4, and October 28, 1987, p. 3.
47. *Izvestiia,* October 12, 1988, p. 6.
48. *Trud,* May 4, 1988, p. 4.
49. Ibid.
50. V. Pokrovskii, in *Leninskoe znamia,* March 7, 1987.
51. *Sobesednik,* no. 50 (December 1987), p. 10; *Komsomol'skaia pravda,* October 28, 1987, p. 3.
52. *Komsomol'skaia pravda,* August 1, 1987, pp. 3–4.
53. *Izvestiia,* August 26, 1987, p. 2.
54. To date, and keeping in mind the still-inadequate data available on the spread of AIDS in the USSR, it appears that the most significant source of transmission there is essentially negligent medical practice. Testing procedures are careless and additionally hampered by supply shortages, and despite all warnings health-care professionals continue to use nonsterile syringes and catheters. One consequence of such gross carelessness was the highly publicized situation in the Kalmyk Autonomous Republic, reported in early 1989, where forty-one children and eight mothers in a single children's hospital were infected with AIDS through use of unsterilized instruments.
55. *Izvestiia,* June 16, 1987, p. 3.

CHAPTER 16

Adapting to New Technologies

Loren Graham

How well is the Soviet Union adapting to new technologies? How receptive are Soviet citizens and Soviet institutions to new means of manufacturing and communicating if those means bring with them disruptive social consequences? Most attempts to answer these questions are based on evaluations of economic performance. In this chapter I wish to approach the questions more broadly; I will examine them on two different levels, the first of which I call the "cultural," the second the "organizational-managerial." On each level I will discuss characteristics of Soviet society that are affecting Mikhail Gorbachev's effort to transform the Soviet Union into a modern state making full use of high technology.

Technology and Soviet Culture

If the Soviet Union is to become an equal competitor in technology with countries like the United States and Japan, enthusiasm for technological culture must spread through the whole society and not be confined to the armed forces and heavy industry. The importance of broad social support for technological change becomes clear when one notices that in Japan and in the West in recent years the major forces for technological advancement in crucial areas like computers and biotechnology are not primarily coming from the military or the political leadership; instead, those forces are pulling from below, from the consumer and business economies. The relative lack of such pull from below is a major Soviet weakness.

In fact, the enthusiasm of Soviet citizens for technological progress and industrial expansion is probably declining rather than increasing. Reading current Soviet newspapers and journals in this age of *glasnost'*, one gets the impression that what the Soviet reading public is most excited about is not economic acceleration on the basis of the latest technology but a reexamination of their nation's history, protection of the environment against pollution, preservation of prerevolutionary architecture, investigation of the significance of religious and spiritual factors in the human personality, and exploration of the psyche of their fellow citizens. These are reflective and introspective concerns much more than they are modernizing ones.[1] Indeed, in the conservation, historical preservation, and religious discussions there are latent elements of an antitechnology worldview, a reaction of Soviet citizens against decades of having modernization and acceleration rammed down their throats.

Every nation that has undergone extremely rapid industrialization has experienced a counterreaction at one point or another. Unfortunately, most of the literature describing these revolts against modernization is not very illuminating when explored for insights that might help us to understand the ability of Soviet citizens to adjust to technological change. The classic works, written by scholars like Eric Hobsbawm and Maxine Berg, are about England and Western Europe in the industrial revolution of the eighteenth and nineteenth centuries.[2] The assumptions of these authors have been that the major causes of resistance to technology are class conflict, the threat of unemployment, and the destruction of craft skills. Leo Marx's exploration of early American ambiguity toward the railroad, as expressed in literature and painting,[3] and Fritz Stern's description of the cultural pessimism caused in late-nineteenth-century Germany by the trauma of rapid industrialization[4] are closer to the Soviet experience, but even in these works few helpful comparisons can be found. The new questioning by the Soviet populace of the official doctrine espousing technology and modernization is a special case and needs to be examined in its own terms. Unemployment and the destruction of craft skills have not been major issues; the neglect of aesthetic and spiritual values in the mad drive to modernize has been.

If we compare attitudes toward science and technology in early Soviet history to those emerging in recent years, we will notice some striking changes. These changes might be summarized as a shift from the celebration of machine culture to ambiguity or even hostility to it.

Bolshevik Celebration of the Machine

In early Bolshevik culture the metallic world of the machine was one of the main motifs of literature and poetry. One group of proletarian poets after the revolution was known as the *Kuznitsa,* or smithy; its members wrote odes to the machine as a "friend and a deliverer."[5] Aleksei Gastev, a promoter of industrial acceleration with his time-and-motion studies of work habits, was also a poet who wrote verses celebrating machines and technology.[6] Architects, artists, and even musicians followed the same path, including Vladimir Tatlin, who promoted "machine art," Vladimir Maiakovskii, who called his study a "word workshop," and the constructivist artist Vladimir Krinskii, who produced drawings approvingly showing the conversion of churches into factories (see Figure 16.1).[7] In parades in the 1920s workers pushed floats on which rested enormous reproductions of gears and machine tools, fitting symbols of their trades and of the future of communism. Probably no other culture in history has gone so far in producing an apotheosis of the machine as did Soviet Russia in the 1920s.

To be sure, this adulation of machines in the 1920s was officially promoted and was not received with enthusiasm by all Soviet citizens. The majority of the Soviet population were still peasants far removed from

Figure 16.1 The mechanized individual is reduced to a mere component part in the mass that has become the machine (constructivistic-symbolical drawing by Krinskii).

rhapsodic eulogies to the machine and even farther removed from the machines themselves. It would be a mistake, however, to think that the promotion of technology was only an official program, without popular roots. The support of Party organizations for the campaign for a machine culture was accompanied by genuine enthusiasm for the effort among many urban intellectuals, artists, and workers. This support was illustrated by the fact that in a few cases the adoration of machines in the 1920s went to such extremes that even the Party criticized it, as was the case when a few wayward Marxist intellectuals suggested the actual worship of the machine in semireligious ceremonies.[8]

The praise of technology in early Soviet culture was based on a turning away from the past history of peasant Russia and a greeting of the technological future. In a passage that today would seem as remarkable to a contemporary Soviet intellectual as it does to us, Leon Trotsky wrote:

> Faith merely promises to move mountains; but technology, which takes nothing "on faith," is actually able to cut down mountains and move them. . . . Man will occupy himself with re-arranging mountains and rivers, and will earnestly and repeatedly make improvements in nature. In the end, he will have rebuilt the earth, if not in his own image, at least according to his own taste. We have not the slightest fear that this taste will be bad. . . .
>
> Through the machine, man in Socialist society will command nature in its entirety, with the grouse and its sturgeons. He will point to places for mountains and passes. He will change the course of the rivers, and he will lay down rules for the oceans. . . .
>
> The present village is entirely of the past. That is why its aesthetics seem archaic, as if they were taken from a museum of folk art. . . . The passive enjoyment of nature will disappear from art. Technology will become a more powerful inspiration for artistic work.[9]

The Emergence of Pastoralism

If we move from the 1920s to the recent period, what attitudes toward technology do we find in Soviet literature and culture? We see some major shifts. One of the most powerful trends in recent Soviet literature has been the rise to prominence of the *derevenshchiki* (rural writers), the authors who celebrate not the machine but the virtues of pretechnological rural life. In many of their writings an antitechnological theme is clearly visible. One of the best known of the *derevenshchiki* is Valentin Rasputin, whose novel *Farewell to Matyora* tells the story of the ancient Russian village on an island that is submerged when the river is dammed in order to construct a hydroelectric-power station. The flooding of the village with its old Orthodox church is used as a metaphor for the general destruction of rural values in the Soviet Union by onrushing technology.

In art, a corollary to the rural writers can be found in the paintings of Ilya Glazunov, who portrays old villages in a nostalgic style somewhat reminiscent of Andrew Wyeth in the United States. In architecture, one of the most popular movements in the Soviet Union in recent years has been the restoration of prerevolutionary churches and village huts. The power of such themes in contemporary Soviet culture needs to be viewed against the background of Trotsky's statement of decades ago that "the peasant village is entirely of the past," a place of "archaic" aesthetics. The artists and writers of the Soviet Union today are praising old rural Russia, a dramatic shift from the early Soviet period when writers ridiculed "humpbacked peasant Russia" and constructivist artists made drawings and posters of Orthodox churches converted to machine shops, with figures of Communist agitators in the spandrels of the Byzantine domes instead of angels (see Figure 16.2).

The current interest in the Soviet past goes far beyond the restoration of churches and village huts; it is a powerful yearning for an older, more variegated culture than the machine age permits. It is worth recalling that the great poet Maiakovskii, in his period of revolutionary enthusiasm in the 1920s, believed that even classical literature and poetry would be replaced. In his poem "Radovat'sya rano" (Too early to rejoice) he wrote, "And why not attack Pushkin and other generals of the classics?" Compare that question for a moment to the popular song of the late 1960s of the "guitar-poet" Bulat Okudzhava, which contained the lines:

> You can never bring back the past, it's pointless to rue it.
> Every age has its own forest growing up.
> But it's a pity all the same that one can't have dinner with Pushkin.
> Even drop into the Yar Cafe for fifteen minutes.
>
> I bow down before the unbounded sea of knowledge.
> I'm fond of my rational, highly experienced age.
> But it's a pity all the same that we still dream of idols as we did before,
> And we still sometimes count ourselves slaves.
>
> You never can bring back the past. I go out onto the street—
> And suddenly notice that right by Nikitsky Gate
> Stands a hansom. And there's Pushkin taking a walk.
> Ah, tomorrow, probably, something will come to pass.[10]

A Conflict of Two Styles of Life

In the name of industrial strength and the scientific-technological revolution, Soviet citizens in the past two generations have been so harangued and coerced that many of them have become immune to, if not alienated from, further calls for technological modernization or, for that matter, acceleration. A conflict between two styles of life is occurring in the Soviet Union, between a pastoral tradition and a campaign for a technological future.[11] Whereas similar conflicts have occurred in other countries experiencing rapid modernization, including the United States, the division is particularly deep in the Soviet Union. The split is exacerbated by the unrelenting demand of the Soviet government for modernization and acceleration, by nostalgia and romantic recall of ancient Russia's 1,000-year-old history, and by the denigration of much of this history by the Soviet government. In

Figure 16.2 A temple of the machine-worshippers: a Byzantine dome. Instead of angels, figures of Communist agitators have been placed in the spandrels (drawing by Krinskii).

this environment, the unsuccessful struggle to preserve the old Angleterre Hotel in Leningrad, or the continuing effort to stop the dike across the Bay of Finland, or the battle to save ancient villages from the bulldozers of the regime, quickly takes on political overtones. One of the leaders of a Soviet environmental group was quoted as saying that he felt closer to the West German Greens than to the Communist party.[12] Gorbachev's policy of *glasnost'* is releasing popular energy, but little of this energy so far seems directed toward an embracing of modernity and technology. Indeed, much of it seems headed in the opposite direction.

An example of the emergence of criticism of science and technology in Soviet culture is Tengiz Abuladze's film *Repentance,* a work that has attracted wide attention in both the USSR and the West. Throughout much of the film a comparison is made of the scientific and religious approaches to human issues, with the advantage given to the religious. A protest is mounted against the destruction caused by scientific workers performing research in an institute housed in an ancient church. In discussing the film with a Western reporter, Abuladze remarked: "Be sure to notice the woman with a book on her head and a rat on top if it. She is the medieval symbol of overreaching science which is destroying us."[13]

If we wish to determine whether the new Soviet questioning of science and technology is broad enough to hinder Gorbachev's modernization effort, we need to know much more than we do currently about Soviet attitudes toward technology. Much of the literature criticizing technology appearing in Soviet publications is produced by intellectuals living in Moscow and Leningrad. They are people who have benefited from technology, but who now have turned against it emotionally. They no longer have to haul water from the village well, although some of their grandmothers are still doing it. No doubt some of the urban intellectuals now look upon the village well nostalgically, seeing it as serving a binding social function for the village, the place where conversations are held with the neighbors and rumors spread. The grandmothers probably worry about their sore backs and look hopefully to the day when they have running water in the kitchen.

If the current ambiguity toward technology that we see in Soviet publications is confined only to the urban intellectuals, then it may not be, in the final analysis, a very significant development. After all, urban U.S. intellectuals on the East Coast who can afford it love to flee modernity to their summer homes in Maine, Vermont, or on Cape Cod. What we need in order to assess the degree of a turn away from modernization in the Soviet Union is more knowledge about the attitudes of Soviet industrial workers. Has the din of propaganda for increased production and higher quality goods over the past sixty years deafened Soviet workers, so that they no longer hear Gorbachev's call for modernization or much care if they do? We do not know the answer to this question. Even if they have not been deafened by the traditional propaganda, it is a little difficult to imagine workers cheering the idea of working harder and producing goods of higher quality, since it only brings trouble to them. An external challenge, such as the threat of war, might rouse them, but international tensions are dramatically decreasing. Soviet workers are probably not as interested in economic challenge from abroad, such as that coming from Japan, as are U.S. workers, whose jobs are more vulnerable to international competition.

Some white-collar Soviet citizens are much more interested in technology than others. Physicians who are aware of how poorly equipped their hospitals are, computer engineers who are trying to catch up with Western and Japanese models, military officers who are concerned about weapons and Star Wars systems—all these people can be expected to be more interested in technology than the Moscow or Leningrad literati. However, because those technocrats do not produce very many writings for the educated public, their opinions are much less visible.

The Decline of Interest in Engineering

One way of judging Soviet interest in technology is by looking at the popularity of engineering as a career choice among young people. During the Stalinist period engineering education was considered one of the most promising avenues to success in the government or Party bureaucracies. By the late 1950s the top governmental and Party positions were dominated by men with technical training. In 1974 Kendall Bailes wrote, "What lawyers and businessmen are in the American political system—the major professional groups from which most politicians and policy makers are recruited—men with engineering backgrounds have become to a large extent in the Soviet Union."[14] The majority of the members of the Politburo had such backgrounds even in the late 1980s.[15] Attitudes among young people have changed so dramatically, however, that the top engineering institutions in Moscow and Leningrad were having trouble in 1988 filling their freshman classes with students of customary quality.[16] Children of educated parents preferred such fields as economics, law, or international relations; only among collective-farm families, for whom it continues to be an assured path of social mobility, did engineering still seem attractive.[17] The latest leader of the Soviet Union seems to symbolize the change, as Gorbachev the lawyer criticizes the social insensitivity of Brezhnev the metallurgical engineer. Gorbachev seems to favor top advisers who do not have engineering backgrounds (Aleksandr Iakovlev, Abel Aganbegyan, Eduard Shevardnadze, Nikolai Petrakov).

Several leading Soviet scientists and engineers have expressed fear that the Soviet public is not as interested in technology as is the U.S. public. The former president of the Soviet Academy of Sciences, A. P. Aleksandrov, lamented in a speech that people in the Soviet Union were not sufficiently interested in computers and expressed the fear that even if Soviet industry managed to produce computers in large numbers, people would not use them in ways that would be helpful to the economy. He noted that pocket calculators sometimes lay unpurchased on the shelves, with people ignoring them or preferring abacuses.[18]

A year or two ago I interviewed several dozen Soviet citizens on the streets of Moscow for the PBS television program "NOVA," asking them if they had any interest in acquiring personal computers. The overwhelming response was that they did not, that computers were something for scientists and technicians at their work. They expressed surprise that many private U.S. citizens not only wanted computers at home but already have them.

It should be added that the Soviet citizens with whom I talked displayed much more interest in technology that they believed could directly benefit them. Adults were interested in automobiles, the young wanted cassette players and stereos. It is possible that the Soviet desire for technology is merely less developed than the U.S. one and will constantly grow until it matches the U.S. level of attachment. However, the gap may be a result of long-lasting differences in the American and Soviet psyches.

Americans have traditionally had a strong interest in technology, perhaps even an exaggerated one. They often look for "technological fixes" to social problems. For two generations Soviet leaders have tried to transplant a U.S.-style fascination with technology to the Soviet population. It is still not clear that this effort has succeeded. If it has not, the long-range results could be significant.

Technology and Industrial Management

Behind Mikhail Gorbachev's efforts to reform the Soviet Union is the realization that his recent predecessors allowed the country to slip in areas of high technology that are essential to international power and status. The world is in a different technological and managerial phase than it was when the patterns of Soviet science, technology, and industry were formed, and principles of manufacturing that were once novel and exciting are now obsolete. The traditional principles of Soviet manufacture have been strong central management, production based on machine tending and assembly lines, and emphasis on quantitative output.

U.S. Influence on Early Soviet Industrial Management

The place of origin of the traditional Soviet principles of industrial management was primarily the United States. It is easy for us to forget as we approach the end of the twentieth century that at the time of the Russian Revolution in 1917 these principles were very new. It was Henry Ford who had pioneered the system of mass production, first introducing it at Highland Park, Michigan, in 1913, just four years before the Bolsheviks came to power. In the first decades of the twentieth century, Frederick Winslow Taylor, another American, introduced his system of time-and-motion studies that revolutionized machine-shop practice. The use of his system at the Watertown Arsenal in Watertown, Massachusetts, in the period 1909–1915 has become a part of the standard history of U.S. technology.[19]

Figure 16.3 "Let us take the storm of the Revolution in Soviet Russia, unite it to the pulse of American life, and do our work like a chronometer!" (Aleksei Gastev's appeal for Americanization).

The Bolsheviks who took over Russia in 1917 were eager to utilize the latest methods of industrial management, and they turned to the Americans for instruction. *Fordizm* and *Teilorizm* became standard terms in the lexicon of the Soviet industrializers.[20] Lenin himself sanctioned the new industrial-management methods when he asserted in 1918, "We must introduce the Taylor system and the scientific American system of increasing the productivity of labor throughout all of Russia."[21] Aleksei Gastev, director of the Institute of Labor in the 1920s, declaimed to the Soviet workers, "Let us take the storm of the Revolution in Soviet Russia, unite it to the pulse of American life, and do our work like a chronometer"[22] (see Figures 16.3 and 16.4).

Figure 16.4 Time and motion studies at Alexei Gastev's Institute of Labor.

Taylor's system was based on the assumption that there was one best way of performing a mechanical task or an industrial operation, and that this optimum way could be exactly specified in physical and temporal terms. Although Taylor himself believed that adoption of his method would mean that the individual effort of the worker would be simplified and eased, in fact, in both the United States and the Soviet Union, the pace of effort was intensified with the new management methods, increasing the levels of stress and fatigue. Bolshevik propaganda of the 1930s added a strongly volitional element to Taylor's allegedly scientific system by emphasizing the necessity of making herculean efforts to meet production quotas. This tendency received its point of extreme development in the Stakhanovite movement, launched on August 31, 1935, when the Donbas coal miner Aleksei Stakhanov was celebrated for exceeding his norm by a factor of almost fifteen.[23]

The Demotion of Quality

Western specialists on the Soviet Union often emphasize the damage that was done to Soviet agriculture in the collectivization drive of the late 1920s and early 1930s with the elimination of the creative and entrepreneurial peasants, the so-called kulaks. Much more rarely do they consider the damage that was done to the quality of Soviet manufacturing output during forced industrialization by the emphasis on quantity at the expense of quality at a time when the Soviet work force was being expanded rapidly by the addition of unskilled workers. Hiroaki Kuromiya, in his study of Soviet industrialization, has shown that one of the results of the frantic pace and transformations of those years in industry was the destruction of skills and the demotion of qualitative standards.[24] Master-machinists and experienced workers learned that rewards came not from attention to detail or time-consuming training of apprentices but from simple plan fulfillment. The problem was made worse by the fact that the skills and standards of most Russian workers had not been high even before the industrialization drive began, a result of undereducation and the losses of World War I and the civil war. Nonetheless, a small elite of skilled craftsmen existed in Soviet Russia in the 1920s. In the years that followed, these highly qualified workers lost much of their influence. The master-workers were not removed from their positions, as were the highly skilled kulaks in agriculture, but they were swamped by the influx of untrained new workers and demoralized by the management's emphasis on meeting production quotas at all costs. In such an environment, they were not able adequately to train a replacement generation that would take pride in technical proficiency and quality products.

Despite the weaknesses of the Soviet system of industrial organization, the system produced impressive quantitative results for many years, as is evidenced by the fact that in the beginning of the 1990s the Soviet Union is the world's largest producer of a number of basic industrial commodities, including steel, oil, lead, cement, and machine tools.

In the post-Stalin period the Soviet system of management was modified in several ways that softened the extreme Taylorist and Stakhanovite features of the 1930s. One of the most important of these changes in the management of Soviet labor was the wide-scale introduction of the "brigade system," an innovation aimed at giving workers greater control over their work.[25] Management makes the entire brigade, rather than the individual worker, responsible for the production quota.[26] The goal is not only higher productivity but also greater worker satisfaction. A result of the brigade form of organization is to reduce the arbitrary features of the system, to make the life of the factory worker more predictable and secure. Gradually a series of accommodations, assumptions, and implicit agreements has evolved between Soviet workers and management that alleviates pressure on workers at any given factory except during the final days of plan fulfillment and yet at the same time assures the management that the factory's record will be no worse than that of others in the region. On the shop floor, however, not very much has changed. The brigade system even increases controls in one respect, since it facilitates the policing of workers' activities by their colleagues. The workers do not have much incentive to promote product quality or to favor technological innovation. The brigade system may have been a social reform of some merit, but it did not involve a thorough reevaluation of the relationships between workers and their machines. The technical element, based on appreciation of the characteristics of new technology, was largely missing.

A New Era of Manufacturing

In the meantime, other leading industrialized nations were entering a new era, one based on careful research of human-machine interaction. The new approach suggested organizing work in dramatically different ways than the ones Taylor, Ford, or even the Soviet promoters of the brigade system had envisioned. The Japanese are often given the credit for initiating this new period, but it actually began after World War II in Europe. In the 1950s E. L. Trist and his colleagues in Britain advanced new ways of looking at "socio-technical systems."[27] This work was followed by similar research in Norway in the 1960s and in the United States, Western Europe, and Japan in subsequent years. Japan was particularly successful in applying the research to production, in part, perhaps, because of its social customs.

One of the assumptions of the new approach was that technology must be viewed in the context of social relations and organizations. New technology by itself will not result in marked gains in productivity unless its introduction is accompanied by a reevaluation of the human resources involved in its use. Furthermore, because human beings differ markedly in their habits and traditions, there is no "one best way" to organize a workplace. The characteristics of the employees, the technology, and the market must all be considered as one sets up an automated factory and trains its personnel.

At the same time that a new appreciation of the social dimensions of technology was beginning to emerge in the leading industrial nations outside the Soviet bloc, the demands placed upon industrial production were changing. No longer was the production of enormous quantities of basic commodities like coal, steel, and cement the major challenge facing advanced industrialized countries. In this environment, industrialists were beginning to consider quantity less important than quality, and basic industrial commodities less significant than a sophisticated array of specialized metallurgical, biochemical, pharmaceutical, electronic, plastic, and agricultural products. Flexible manufacture—the production at the same factory of one product, then another, then still another, with each change of product timed to fit with changes in the market—began to supplant standard assembly-line-production methods. Cost consciousness became so important that extensive inventories of parts to be assembled were too expensive to maintain; instead a "just in time" supply system was introduced in advanced factories, with supplies arriving only a day or even hours before they were needed. Once instituted, such a supply system turned out to have many beneficial side effects, since it quickly exposed to remedial action any weak points in the production process. Small inventories also made it possible to switch over to the production of a different product without financial losses because of unused inventories.

Several years ago Michael Piore and Charles Sabel analyzed some of these changes in a book entitled *The Second Industrial Divide*.[28] They divided the history of twentieth-century manufacturing into two phases, the first characterized by mass production of the type I have described, and a second phase, which they called "Flexible Specialization." In the second period the mass production of a relatively few industrial commodities is replaced by batch production of a staggering variety of different products, many of them so specialized that something approaching the old craft tradition needs to be restored.

Soviet Difficulties in Responding to the New Era

These novel requirements obviously present challenges to all industrialized nations. The United States, like the Soviet Union, recognized the seriousness of the challenge from Japan and other competitors only tardily.[29] Because of the nature of the Soviet system, however, finding an appropriate response in that country is a particularly difficult task. The new system of manufacture requires great sensitivity to market changes, an ability difficult to achieve in an economy where both prices and production quotas have traditionally been set by the state. Supply distribution in the Soviet Union has been such a perennial problem that "just in time" inventory controls would amount to a minor revolution. Soviet workers reveal just how far they are from an understanding of the "just in time" policy by defining a "supply problem" as a shortage in raw materials or assembly parts;[30] the new Japanese approach considers a large inventory as much a violation of sound management practices as an empty one. Traditionally, however, Soviet managers and workers have considered large inventories of parts and raw material to be guarantees of security. The concept of unproductive capital tied up in these inventories is weakly developed in Soviet economic thought.

Another problem in adapting to the demands of the new manufacturing system is the shortage in the Soviet Union of highly qualified workers with the necessary skills for responding to a variety of problems that may arise in an automated work situation. Traditionally, the Soviet government has placed far more emphasis on the education of scientists and engineers than it has on the training of skilled workers, an ironic feature of an alleged workers' state. By 1975 the Soviet Union had three times as many engineers as the United States but still suffered from severe shortages of highly skilled blue-collar workers. In the Soviet Interview Project supervised by James Millar in the 1980s, emigré workers reported that in their factories "there appear to be too many engineers and scientists and too few skilled white and blue collar workers. The scarce labor resource appears to be the worker with the industrial skills applied at the shop-floor level."[31] In order to overcome this situation the Soviet Union has forced many engineers to work in positions that would be occupied by workers in other societies, causing a diminishing of the prestige of Soviet engineers.[32] Few of these engineers, with advanced educations, aspire to be skilled workers or machine supervisors. At the same time, the ordinary workers have not been able to move into positions of responsibility because of the surplus of low-level engineers, causing a serious morale problem among workers.

The Age of the Smart Machines

The problems in industry have been exacerbated by the characteristics of new automated-production facilities, which are making surprising demands on both workers and management. Both in the United States and abroad, many inexperienced observers of the new computerized "smart machines" have assumed that one of the results of their introduction will be the further deskilling of workers. If the robots and computers are so "smart," why do we need intelligent, resourceful workers? Some analysts speak of "workerless" factories and question whether we will need any workers at all. Recent studies of industries where such equipment has been installed for a number of years reveal, however, a much more complicated picture.

In her book *In the Age of the Smart Machine,* Shoshana Zuboff of the Harvard Business School described the results of her studies of a series of computerized workplaces.[33] She emphasized that the new "intelligent technology" performs two functions, one well known and widely appreciated, the other much less so. The well-known function is "to automate," to increase productivity by performing work operations much more efficiently. The other important but little-known function is "to informate," which means to create a vast amount of information about the production process itself. Information technology in the workplace introduces reflexivity; it produces not only objects but also a description of the production process that is available for analysis. When irregularities develop in automated processes, as happens rather frequently, this information is crucial for corrective action, ideally taken by workers before breakdown occurs. The same information can also suggest another way of performing a particular task. In an automated paper mill studied by Zuboff, the machine operators could call up on their computer screens information on over 1,500 variables. These variables were not only physical, chemical, and temporal but also economic. Indeed, they included information on safety records, breakdowns, and variant methods of production required to meet different economic conditions and different qualities of paper. All this information was instantly available on-line for a period covering the past three months; after three months it was retained off-line. Thus, a complete historical record of almost every detail of production and performance was indefinitely retained in the data-base memory of the enterprise.

A crucially important question is, Who will have access to all this information, just the managers or the workers themselves? Zuboff found that different U.S. companies have tried different answers to this question. Some have believed that management should maintain tight controls over the information, giving the workers only enough to perform their assigned tasks. Others have opened up the enterprise data base to blue-collar operators as well as management. Both systems have resulted in productivity increases, showing that both approaches are feasible, but the "open" approach has been more productive. The open approach is particularly successful in overcoming worker alienation and achieving social integration in the plant.

Zuboff conducted interviews with U.S. workers in both types of plants. Workers in the "closed" plants reported stress and frustration in their jobs. They feared the new technology and they resisted further technological change. One such operator observed:

> With the change to the computer it's like driving down the highway with your lights out and someone else is pushing the accelerator. . . . It is like you are riding a big, powerful horse, but someone is sitting behind you on the saddle holding the reins, and you just have to be on that ride and hold on. . . . Well, I would rather be holding the reins than have someone behind me holding the reins.[34]

In contrast, Zuboff found quite different attitudes among workers at plants where they had full access to the production data base and had been trained in the meaning of this information. These workers had developed "intellective skills," the ability to understand and improve what they were doing. One worker in an open plant reported: "The more I learn theoretically, the more I can see in the information. Raw data turns into information with my knowledge. I find that you have to be able to know more in order to do more. It is your understanding of the process that guides you. . . . If you want to handle a problem, you have to want to know this."[35]

Another worker with full access to the computer data in his plant remarked: "To do the job well now you need to understand this part of the mill and how it relates to the rest of the plant. You need a concept of what you are doing. You have to check through the data on the computer to see your effects. And if you don't know what to look for in the data, you won't know what's happening."[36]

The Implications of "Open" Factories

Opening up the computer records of automated plants to the workers is very unsettling to traditional managers. It changes the relationships of power and authority in the plant. It destroys the myth that there is one best way of performing any task and that the management has already found that way. It suggests experiments and variations. It publicizes the technical and financial history of the plant, and it illuminates the responsibility of individuals. It displays the trail of past actions and results. It reveals slowdowns in production and tells exactly when they happened. If an accident occurs, such as the explosion of a boiler or the overflowing of a pulp vat, the record will show what was done and what was not done and who was responsible.

Many managers and even quite a few workers in all industrialized countries would prefer that this information not be known by everyone in the plant. And yet research has indicated that the best plants, both in terms of productivity and social relations, are those where such information has been widely available. The operation of these factories is "transparent," and therefore capable of improvement in a way that opaque operations are not. And the workers are less resistant to new technology because they feel that they are more in control of it.

The point here is not that the United States is uniquely favorable to the creation of open automated factories and the Soviet Union uniquely unfavorable. In the middle of the twentieth century both countries subscribed to "scientific management" methods that were based on a similar assumption about the need to have informed management and uninformed workers. In the United States this assumption exacerbated confrontational relations between management and unionized workers that still hinder movement into a new, more egalitarian, and less antagonistic stage. Japan, with its emphasis on consensus and cooperation (at least for males), may have a better social base for the new stage of automated production than either the United States or the Soviet Union, both of which face formidable obstacles as they adjust to the new era.

The difficulties in meeting the challenge of "smart machines" are particularly great in the Soviet Union because the ethos of factory production formed under Stalin still remains powerful in that country.[37] The traditional Soviet factory atmosphere is antithetical to the ethos suited for getting the best results from computer-based manufacture. Stalinist management was highly centralized, with the factory director possessing great power. Increases in output were achieved by command methods, often coercive under Stalin, usually hortatory in more recent decades. Both workers and low-level engineers functioned under highly specialized job descriptions and usually possessed little knowledge of the overall operation of the plant. The plant director and his immediate staff kept close control over the operating statistics of the plant and the distribution of funds. Managers often had to resort to unofficial or even illegal measures to ensure continuity of supplies, such as purchasing materials on the black market or making under-the-table payments. Economic criteria of efficiency were hard to identify or utilize because most costs and prices were unrealistic. Production quotas were manipulated by managers who at the beginning of each planning period strove to get them set falsely low and then fulfilled the quotas by *shturmovshchina,* or rush work, near the end of the period. Statistics on accidents, absenteeism, and alcoholism were often kept secret. Criteria of success, whether by weight, volume, or value of production, were manipulated to provide the appearance of good results. Throughout the plant the principle of inequality in wisdom and influence was strongly defended. In the final analysis, the most powerful influence was that of the Communist party, whose superior status was ensconced in its official description as the "vanguard of the proletariat."

It is a little difficult to imagine that the management of such an organization will greet hospitably the advent of the "transparency of operation" that information technology creates when its results are open to examination. Even today, in the age of *glasnost',* openness in the Soviet Union has affected the intelligentsia much more than it has the workers. A director of a Soviet factory today may accept new automation technology as long as its impact can be confined to the mechanical process of production, but he will almost surely resist suggestions that it transform relations of authority and power in his enterprise. As Anthony Jones noted, new technology has not yet changed power relations in Soviet factories.[38] The Soviet factory director will surely use smart machines "to automate," not "to informate." The computer records that are created will be kept under the control of the management. The workers will be told what to do with the new machines, but they will not understand why they are supposed to do it.

If Zuboff was correct in her analysis of the new smart machines, the result of their introduction in the Soviet Union will probably be a failure to take advantage of the best aspect of the technology. She wrote, "When information and control technology is used to turn the worker into 'just another mechanical variable,' one immediate result is the withdrawal of the worker's commitment to and accountability for the work."[39] The workers will then "search for avenues of escape through drugs, apathy, or adversarial conflict."[40]

Worker Alienation

Even before the advent of the smart machines the sort of alienation described by Zuboff had been growing among Soviet workers. Soviet factories tend to be very large, and for the most part, their workers are involved in mass production and machine tending rather than in crafts or continuous processing. These are the sorts of factories in which social alienation is usually the highest, and the discontent often centers more on the conditions of work than on wages.[41]

Alex Pravda, in a 1979 article, analyzed "spontaneous workers' activities" (protest actions) in the Soviet Union; he found that in the period from the late 1950s to the early 1970s the nature of the most common grievances among Soviet workers changed.[42] In the early 1960s the issues that caused workers to take unofficial action were salaries and basic living conditions. By the middle of the 1960s, however, work conditions became an increasingly common stimulus to action, and by the late 1960s and early 1970s a major cause of protest was "dissatisfaction with the way in which labor is organized."[43]

Before one concludes that the problem of worker alienation stemming from their treatment as cogs in a machine is a uniquely Soviet phenomenon, one should remember that one of the most famous cases of labor unrest in the United States—which occurred in the 1970s in the Lordstown, Ohio, plant of General Motors—was also an episode in which younger, better-educated, sophisticated workers were no longer willing to put up with the repetitive, mind-numbing conditions of assembly-line production.[44] They were working in a highly automated plant that was pleasant and clean compared to many other factories. Yet they were unwilling to act as unthinking automatons almost entirely shorn of control over themselves or their work. The reason the Lordstown strike became so famous was that

General Motors and other automakers eventually recognized it as a watershed in labor relations, the beginning of a painful rethinking of the problem of how to make the jobs of educated workers in modern factories more meaningful. This process is still going on.

Somewhat belatedly, Soviet economists and managers have begun to consider the same issues, especially since the ascent of Gorbachev.[45] Soviet industrial enterprises are seeking to add sociologists to their staffs in order to alleviate these problems; in 1988 the Ordzhonikidze Institute of Management in Moscow announced that when it advertised a new course of study for industrial sociologists it received 550 applications for 50 vacancies.[46] The influential Soviet economic sociologist Tatiana Zaslavskaia has been a leader in arguing that the basic problem facing Soviet managers is not so much acquiring new technology as reconstructing the social relations of production. Writing in September 1986 in the main theoretical journal of the Communist party, she said that the most important change that had occurred in Soviet factories was that in recent years there was a "weakening of the extent to which a person can be forced, by either administrative or economic means, to work hard."[47] A new kind of worker has arisen in the Soviet Union, she noted. "As workers' education grows and their range of interests broadens, they strive to become more autonomous in their work, to participate actively in decision-making and to realize their full creative potential."[48] She observed that these goals were frustrated in many Soviet factories where the management continued to order the workers around, and that as a result the workers "often become alienated from labor and turn their interests elsewhere."[49]

Conclusions

Both the United States and the Soviet Union face the same challenge in adjusting to the new era of manufacturing, but the United States has a better chance of reforming its management methods than the Soviet Union. With its open economy and convertible currency the United States faces international competition much more intimately than the Soviet Union. If the Japanese with their quality circles and family-like relationships between supervisors and employees manage to produce better quality automobiles than the United States, the U.S. auto manufacturers must move to meet the challenge by reorganizing their manufacturing methods. There is considerable evidence that they have begun to do this.[50] Every one of the failures of the United States to meet the competition is quickly apparent in the worsening of trade deficits. The Soviet Union has been largely shielded from this competition, and it often does not even realize how far it has fallen behind in a certain area until the gap is very wide.

Furthermore, although the United States imbibed deeply the principles of low-quality mass production, just as the Soviet Union has done, the United States did not combine these principles with the wholesale nationalization of industry in the Soviet fashion. Therefore, the United States, with its heterogeneous and decentralized economic system, is better suited for the current period of experiment and reform, a time of searching for ways to adapt to new technologies.[51]

The Soviet Union, with its relatively closed economy and (as of 1990) nonconvertible currency, is shielded from international competition and thus can conceal its failures for a long time. The rigidity of the Soviet economic and political system has enormously encumbered Gorbachev's brave attempts at reform. The combination of Soviet socialism and U.S. mass-production methods was exactly what excited Lenin seventy years ago, but this mixture today appears increasingly to be a drag on innovation and reform. What Lenin saw as an innovative combination of "revolutionary fervor and American efficiency" has become a sluggish combination of "bureaucratic socialism and sloppy mass production." It is an irony of history that escaping from the trap of old-fashioned U.S. management methods is probably more difficult in the Soviet Union than in the United States because of the innate conservatism of the Soviet bureaucracy.

Notes

1. For a pessimistic account of the Soviet Union's ability to catch up with the "Scientific-Technical Revolution" in the West, especially with regard to computerization, see "Zavtra budet pozdno," *Literaturnaia gazeta,* January 27, 1988, p. 10. There is an enormous recent Soviet literature on the reexamination of the past. Two examples will have to serve: Igor' Kliamkin, "Kakaia ulitsa vedet k khramu?" *Novyi mir,* no. 11 (1987), pp. 150-188; and V. P. Danilov, "Diskussiia v zapadnoi presse o golode 1932-1933 gg. i demograficheskoi katastrofe 30-40 kh godov v SSSR," *Voprosy istorii,* no. 3 (1988), pp. 116-121. The latter article reassessed the violence of collectivization and its aftermath, one of the most painful episodes in Soviet history. Also see R. W. Davis, "Changing Official Views of Soviet History," *Détente,* no. 11 (1988), pp. 12-13; and Mark von Hagen, "History and Politics Under Gorbachev: Professional Autonomy and Democratization," *Harriman Institute Forum* 1, no. 11 (November 1988).

2. Eric Hobsbawm, *Industry and Empire: An Economic History of Britain Since 1750* (London: Weidenfeld and Nicholson, 1968); Eric Hobsbawm and George Rude, *Captain Swing* (London: Lawrence and Wishart, 1969); Maxine Berg, *The Machine Question and the Making of Political Economy, 1815-1848* (Cambridge: Cambridge University Press, 1980). Also see Peter Mathias, *The Brewing Industry in England, 1700-1830* (Cambridge: Cambridge University Press, 1959), and his *The First Industrial Nation: An Economic History of Britain, 1700-1914* (London: Methuen, 1969).

3. Leo Marx, *The Machine in the Garden: Technology and the Pastoral Ideal in America* (New York: Oxford University Press, 1964).

4. Fritz Stern, *The Politics of Cultural Despair: A Study in the Rise of the German Ideology* (Berkeley: University of California, 1974).

5. Herman Ermolaev, *Soviet Literary Theories, 1917-1934: The Genesis of Socialist Realism* (New York: Octagon Books, 1977), pp. 19-26.

6. Kurt Johansson, *Aleksei Gastev, Proletarian Bard of the Machine Age* (Stockholm: Almquist and Wiksell International, 1983).

7. Ermolaev, op. cit.; and René Fulop-Miller, *The Mind and Face of Bolshevism: An Examination of Cultural Life in Soviet Russia,* trans. F. S. Flint and D. F. Tait (New York: A. A. Knopf, 1929; New York: Harper & Row, 1965).

8. A drawing of a "Communist Mass" devoted to the "visible God," the machine, is in the German edition of René Fulop-Miller, *Geist und Gesicht des Bolschewismus: Darstellung und Kritik des kulturellen Lebens in Sowjet-Russland* (Vienna: Amalthea-Verlag, 1926).

9. Leon Trotsky, *Literature and Revolution* (Ann Arbor: University of Michigan, 1960), pp. 251–253.

10. Gerald Stanton Smith, trans., *Songs to Seven Strings: Russian Guitar Poetry and Soviet "Mass Song"* (Bloomington: Indiana University Press, 1984), p. 125.

11. A Soviet debate in the late 1950s and early 1960s, often called "physicists versus lyricists," was a premonition of continuing reevaluation of science and technology in the 1970s and 1980s. See B. Slutskii, "Fiziki i liriki," *Komsomol'skaia pravda,* October 13, 1959, and other articles on the theme appearing in *Komsomol'skaia pravda* and *Literaturnaia gazeta* in late 1959 and early 1960.

12. For discussions of Soviet environmental groups see Bill Keller, "No Longer Merely Voices in the Russian Wilderness," and his "Soviet Scraps a New Atomic Plant," *New York Times,* December 27, 1987, p. 14, and January 28, 1988, p. 1.

13. Olga Carlisle, "From Russia with Scorn," *New York Times,* November 29, 1987, pp. H23, H34. My thanks to Catherine Reed of the Russian Research Center, Harvard University, for a copy of the Russian-language script of *Pokaianie* (Repentance). Neither my research assistant, Lisa Halustick, nor I has been able to locate the woman with the book and the rat in the film; perhaps it was subsequently deleted.

14. Kendall Bailes, "The Politics of Technology: Stalin and Technocratic Thinking Among Soviet Engineers," *American Historical Review,* April 1974, p. 469.

15. Thomas P. Barnett, "The Concept of Technocracy and the Soviet Politburo," Russian Research Center, Harvard University, unpublished paper.

16. Harley Balzer, "Engineers in Russian and Soviet Society: The Rise and Decline of a Social Myth," paper presented to Seminar on Humanistic Dimensions of Soviet Science and Technology, MIT, April 29, 1988.

17. Ibid.

18. E. P. Velikhov, vice-president of the academy, has also expressed concern at the lack of interest among Soviet citizens in computers. E. P. Velikhov, "Personal'nye EVM—Segodiashniaia praktika i perspektivy," *Vestnik akademii nauk,* no. 8 (1984), p. 6, and his "Fantastika budnei," *Literaturnaia gazeta,* July 10, 1985, p. 10.

19. Hugh Aitken, *Taylorism at the Watertown Arsenal: Scientific Management in Action, 1908–1915* (Cambridge, Mass.: Harvard University Press, 1960).

20. Kendall Bailes, "Aleksei Gastev and the Soviet Controversy over Taylorism," *Soviet Studies,* no. 3 (July 1977), pp. 373–394; Zenovia Sochor, "Soviet Taylorism Revisited," *Soviet Studies,* no. 2 (April 1981), pp. 246–264; Yuri Gastev, "The 'Social-Engineering Machine' of Alexei Gastev," *Journal of Social and Biological Structures,* forthcoming.

21. V. I. Lenin, "Variant stat'i 'Ocherednye zadachi sovetskoi vlasti,' " *Polnoe sobranie sochinenii,* 5th ed. (Moscow: Izdatel'stvo politicheskoi literatury, 1969), p. 141.

22. Fulop-Miller, *Geist und Gesicht des Bolschewismus,* op. cit., p. 29.

23. The Stakhanov model remained valid in official ideology throughout the Stalin period and even beyond. G. N. Estaf'ev, *Sotsialisticheskoe sorevnovanie— zakonomernost' i dvizhushchaia sila ekonomicheskogo razvitiia sovetskogo obshchestva*

(Moscow: Izdatel'stvo Politicheskoi Literatury, 1952). For a study of Stakhanovism and the evolution of its meaning, see Lewis H. Siegelbaum, *Stakhanovism and the Politics of Productivity in the USSR, 1935-1941* (Cambridge: Cambridge University Press, 1988).

24. Hiroaki Kuromiya, *Stalin's Industrial Revolution: Politics and Workers, 1928-1932* (Cambridge: Cambridge University Press, 1988).

25. David Lane, *Soviet Labor and the Ethic of Communism: Full Employment and the Labor Process in the USSR* (Boulder, Colo.: Westview Press, 1987), passim, esp. pp. 200–205.

26. L. N. Kogan and A. V. Merenkov, "Kompleksnye brigady: mneniia, otsenki, opyt, vnedreniia," *Sotsialisticheskie issledovaniia*, no. 1 (1983), pp. 86–91; A. Dovba and A. Andrianov, "Brigada—osnovnaia forma organizatsii truda," *Sotsialisticheskii trud*, no. 5 (1981), pp. 91–98; V. N. Zadorozhnyi and I. M. Vlasenko, "Brigadnoe dvizhenie: opyt, problemy, resheniia," *EKO (Ekonomika i organizatsiia promyshlennogo proizvodstvsa)*, no. 12 (1987), pp. 21–39.

27. "Socio-Technical Systems: Innovation in Designing High-Performance Systems," special issue of *Journal of Applied Behavioral Science* 22, no. 3 (1986). See especially the "Introductory Statement," by William Barko and William Pasmore, and "Sociotechnical Analysis of the Integrated Factory," by Gerald I. Susman and Richard B. Chase.

28. Michael J. Piore and Charles F. Sabel (eds.), *The Second Industrial Divide: Possibilities for Prosperity* (New York: Basic Books, 1984).

29. For a discussion of the new methods of manufacturing sweeping the Western industrialized world and a call for the United States to catch up, see *Toward a New Era in U.S. Manufacturing: The Need for a National Vision* (Washington, D.C.: Manufacturing Studies Board, National Research Council, National Academy Press, 1986).

30. Paul R. Gregory, "Productivity, Slack, and Time Theft in the Soviet Economy," in James R. Millar (ed.), *Politics, Work and Daily Life in the USSR: A Survey of Former Soviet Citizens* (Cambridge: Cambridge University Press, 1987), pp. 263–266.

31. Ibid., p. 273.

32. Balzer, op. cit.

33. Shoshana Zuboff, *In the Age of the Smart Machine: The Future of Work and Power* (New York: Basic Books, 1988).

34. Ibid., p. 64.

35. Ibid., p. 94.

36. Ibid.

37. A. Ershov, who has led the drive for computer literacy in the USSR and has called for an "information society," continued to lament the "vestiges of the administrative-command system of management in our society." Ershov, "Informatizatsiia: ot komp'iuternoi gramotnosti uchashchikhsia k informatsionnoi kul'ture obshchestva," *Kommunist*, no. 2 (1988), p. 91.

38. T. Anthony Jones, "Changing Course: Social Organization and the New Technology in the Soviet Union," in Richard Simpson and Ida Simpson (eds.), *Research in the Sociology of Work*, vol. 4 (Greenwich, Conn.: Jai Press, 1988), p. 229.

39. Zuboff, op. cit., p. 69.

40. Ibid., p. 5.

41. Robert Blauner, *Alienation and Freedom* (Chicago: University of Chicago Press, 1964).

42. Alex Pravda, "Spontaneous Workers' Activities in the Soviet Union," in A. Kahan and B. Ruble (eds.), *Industrial Labor in the USSR* (New York: Pergamon Press, 1979), p. 356.

43. The protests against state inspection, or *gospriemka*, introduced under Gorbachev, can also be seen as objections to the methods of organizing labor rather than disputes over pay, although we need better information to understand these actions. See Elizabeth Teague, "Stormy Protests at Soviet Truck Plant," *Radio Liberty Report*, RL 461/86 (December 4, 1986).

44. See Emma Rothschild, *Paradise Lost: The Decline of the Auto-Industrial Age* (New York: Random House, 1973), pp. 97–119. Also see U.S. Department of Health, Education and Welfare, *Work in America* (Cambridge, Mass.: MIT Press, 1973).

45. The journal *EKO*, published in Novosibirsk, has been a leader in viewing modernization of industry as a sociotechnical problem and not just a technological one. Authors in this journal call for "informational independence" for workers at automated work stations. See Iu. I. Tychkov, "Vozmozhnosti vychislitel'noi tekhniki i sovershenstvovanie upravleniia predpriiatiem," *EKO*, no. 7 (1987), pp. 58–80.

46. "Khronika nauchnoi zhizni," *Sotsiologicheskie issledovaniia*, no. 4 (1988), p. 119.

47. T. Zaslavskaia, "The Human Factor in Economic Development and Social Justice," *Kommunist*, no. 13 (September 1986), pp. 61–73.

48. Ibid.

49. Ibid.

50. *Toward a New Era in U.S. Manufacturing*, op. cit.

51. A Soviet analysis of reforms in U.S. industry is Iu. A. Ushanov, "Reorganizatsii v amerikanskikh kompaniiakh," *EKO*, no. 9 (1987), pp. 167–179.

About the Contributors

Walter D. Connor is professor of political science and sociology at Boston University and a fellow at the Russian Research Center at Harvard University. He served for eight years (1976–1984) in the U.S. Department of State before joining Boston University. He has held visiting appointments at Columbia and Georgetown universities and the Universities of Pennsylvania and Virginia. Connor is the author of *Socialism's Dilemmas: State and Society in the Soviet Bloc* (1988), and of three other books and many articles in journals in the United States and abroad. He has just completed *The Accidental Proletariat: Workers, Politics and Crisis in Gorbachev's Russia* (forthcoming).

Richard B. Dobson is a Soviet analyst at the United States Information Agency's (USIA) Office of Research. Before joining the USIA, Dobson taught sociology at the University of Colorado at Colorado Springs, was a national fellow at the Hoover Institution, and was visiting scholar in sociology and education at Stanford University. On IREX (International Research and Exchanges Board) exchanges to the Soviet Union, he spent eight months at Moscow State University and three months at the Institute of Sociological Research. Dobson has published numerous articles on Soviet society.

Mark G. Field is professor of sociology emeritus at Boston University, an adjunct professor at Harvard's School of Public Health, and a fellow at Harvard's Russian Research Center. He has been associated with the Russian Research Center since its foundation in 1948. His main interest is the Soviet social system and its welfare organization, more specifically, Soviet socialized medicine. He is the author, coauthor, or editor of 8 books and over 100 publications in the professional literature. He regularly teaches a course on Soviet society at the Harvard Summer School.

Marshall I. Goldman is the Kathryn W. Davis Professor of Soviet Economics at Wellesley College and the associate director of the Russian Research Center at Harvard University. A frequent visitor to the Soviet Union, he enjoys international recognition as an authority on its economy, environmental concerns, and foreign relations. His more recent publications include *Gorbachev's Challenge: Economic Reform in the Age of High Technology* (1987), *The USSR in Crisis: The Failure of an Economic Model* (1983), and *The Enigma of Soviet Petroleum: Half Empty or Half Full?* (1980).

Loren Graham teaches at MIT and Harvard and is a member of the Executive Committee of the Russian Research Center. His books include *The Soviet Academy of Sciences and the Communist Party; Between Science and Values; Science and the Soviet Social Order* (he was editor of the last-named); and *Science, Philosophy, and Human Behavior in the Soviet Union,* which is being published in a Soviet edition in 1990. His recently completed survey history of Russian and Soviet science is forthcoming.

Paul Hollander is professor of sociology at the University of Massachusetts at Amherst and a fellow at the Russian Research Center at Harvard University. He is the author of *Soviet and American Society: A Comparison, Political Pilgrims, The Many Faces of Socialism,* and *The Survival of the Adversary Culture.*

Anthony Jones teaches sociology at Northeastern University and is a fellow at the Russian Research Center at Harvard University. He has written numerous articles on various aspects of Soviet society. Together with E. Moskoff he edited *Perestroika and the Economy: New Thinking in Soviet Economics* and wrote *Ko-ops: The Rebirth of Entrepreneurship in the Soviet Union.* He also edited *Professions and the State* and is editor of the journal *Soviet Education.*

Paul R. Josephson teaches science policy and the history of science at Sarah Lawrence College and is an adjunct assistant professor of political science at Columbia University. He is the author of *Physics and Politics in Revolutionary Russia* (forthcoming) and of many articles on Soviet science.

Peter H. Juviler is professor of political science at Barnard College, Columbia University. He has written widely on crime and delinquency, Soviet law, and family structure and social policy. He is also the author of *Revolutionary Law and Order: Politics and Social Change in the USSR.*

John M. Kramer is distinguished professor of political science, Mary Washington College, Fredericksburg, Virginia. He has served as a research fellow, Russian Research Center, Harvard University, and as a senior fellow, National Defense University. He has written *The Energy Gap in Eastern Europe* (1990) and articles published in numerous professional journals.

Mervyn Matthews is reader in Russian studies at the University of Surrey in England. He is the author of many books and articles on Soviet society, including *Class and Society in Soviet Russia* (1972), *Privilege in the Soviet Union* (1978), *Education in the Soviet Union* (1982), *Poverty in the USSR* (1986), and *Patterns of Deprivation in the Soviet Union Under Brezhnev and Gorbachev* (1989).

Ellen Mickiewicz is Alben W. Barkley Professor of Political Science at Emory University and director of the Soviet media and international communications program at the Carter Center of Emory University. Her most recent book is *Split Signals: Television and Politics in the Soviet Union* (1988). She is the author of *Soviet Political Schools* (1967) and *Media and the Russian Public* (1981) and has edited and contributed to several other books. She has served as president of the American Association for the Advancement of Slavic Studies, the first woman to do so in the fifty-year history of the organization.

David E. Powell is a fellow at the Russian Research Center, Harvard University. He is the author of *Antireligious Propaganda in the Soviet Union* (1975) and numerous articles on political, economic, and social problems in the USSR.

Andrea Stevenson Sanjian is assistant professor of political science at Bucknell University. She has published a number of articles and book chapters on various aspects of social policy and economic policy in the USSR.

Louise I. Shelley is a professor and chair of the Department of Justice, Law and Society and a professor at the School of International Service, the American University in Washington, D.C. She has written numerous articles as well as two books, *Crime and Modernization* and *Lawyers in Soviet Work Life.* Shelley was part of the juridical committee of the Helsinki Watch and has been a guest of the Institute of State and Law, Academy of Sciences, in Moscow.

Vladimir G. Treml is professor of economics at Duke University. His research interests range from input-output analysis to Soviet foreign trade. He is the author of *Alcohol in the USSR: A Statistical Study* (1982) and a large number of papers on drinking and alcohol abuse in the Soviet Union.

About the Book

As a result of *glasnost'*, attention has been focused on social problems in the USSR to an extent unprecedented since the 1920s. Mikhail Gorbachev's regime now finds itself faced with issues that are remarkably similar to those that other societies must grapple with. This book describes and analyzes the Soviet Union's social problems, focusing on those it shares with Western industrial societies. Although the contributors emphasize the current period, they also provide a historical perspective on the development of long-standing problems and on the evolution of official attitudes toward them.

This is the first comprehensive text to assess the broad range of social concerns now confronting Gorbachev, including drug and alcohol abuse; nuclear and environmental calamities; poverty; prostitution; health, education, and family issues; crime and juvenile delinquency; and the difficulty of adapting to technological change. An important resource for historians, political scientists, and sociologists, this book is also a valuable text for courses dealing with Soviet society or with problems in contemporary industrial societies in general.

Index

Abalkin, Leonid, 140
Abortions, 20, 195, 200–201, 205, 210(n48), 280
Abuladze, Tengiz, 302
Academy of Medical Sciences, 162, 290
Academy of Pedagogy, 216, 219
Academy of Sciences, 43, 51, 63, 68, 161
Accidents, 126, 132, 312
Activist groups, 238–239
Adylov, Akhmadzhan, 254
AES. *See* Atomic-energy stations
Afgantsy, 237. *See also* Veterans
Afghanistan, 102, 113(n45)
Africa, 290
Agenda-building process, 287
Agitation, 35
Agriculture, 60, 63, 145, 157, 177, 203–204, 306
AIDS, 6–7, 87, 199, 287–289, 290–292, 295(n54)
Albats, Yevgeniya, 198, 199
Alcohol abuse, 4, 11, 18, 20, 87, 96, 98, 105, 119–134, 162, 175, 222, 223, 282
  alcoholics, 123(table), 125, 132, 265, 279, 289
  alcohol surrogates, 133
  causes, 126–128
  civilized drinking proponents, 125, 130, 133
  consumption, 120–121, 121–122(tables), 122–125, 126, 127, 129, 133, 173, 258, 260
  and crime. *See* Crime, alcohol-related
  data availability, 119–120, 126, 132, 134(n2), 312

  drinking patterns, 121, 122–125
  home brewing. *See* Home brewing; *Samogon*
  measuring effects, 125–126
  mortality, 123, 124(table), 125–126, 132, 134(n10), 136(n29)
  and national groups, 122–125, 122–123(tables), 128
  prices of beverages, 130–131
  production/supply of beverages, 127, 129, 135(n14), 258
  and prostitution, 279, 289
  and revenues from alcohol, 130, 131
  traffic accidents, 126
  of women, 127, 128, 279
  of youth, 127, 128, 228, 240, 241, 279
  See also Gorbachev, Mikhail, antidrinking campaign
Aleksandrov, A. P., 303
Alekseyev, B., 52
Alexandrov, Anatoly, 52
Alienation, 15, 313–314
Alimony, 209(n26), 273
All-Union Central Council of Trade Unions, 185
All-Union Central Executive Committee, 95
All-Union Congress of Educational Workers, 220
All-Union Council of Evangelical Christians, 166
All-Union Institute for the Study of the Causes of Crime and Development of Crime-Prevention, 240
All-Union Organization for Veterans of War and Labor, 158, 162, 170(n11)

INDEX

All-Union Volunteer Temperance Society, 130, 133, 135(n17)
Alma-Ata, 33, 239, 249(n48)
AMA. *See* American Medical Association
Amalrik, Andrei, 139–140
Amelkin, Anatoliy, 51
American Medical Association (AMA), 84
Amu Darya River, 46, 47
Anabolic steroids, 102
Andropov, Yuri, 126, 162
Anisin, N., 216–217
Aquarium rock group, 236
Aral Sea, 46, 47
Architecture, 299–300
Arctic mines, 137
Arctic Ocean, 45, 46
Armenia, 28, 30, 31–33, 36, 54, 99, 125, 128, 131, 156, 162, 253, 260, 279
Artists, 297, 299, 300
Arutiunian, V., 26
Ashkhabad, 147
Aspirations, 142
Athletic competitions, 102
Atomic culture, 57–62, 66, 68–69, 72, 73. *See also* Nuclear energy
Atomic-energy stations (AES), 65, 70, 76(n43). *See also* Reactors
Atommash reactor plant, 50, 73
Atomnaia energiia, 71
Authority erosion, 231–232, 245
Automation, 310. *See also* Technology, smart machines
Azarov, Iurii, 222
Azerbaidzhan, 28, 30, 31–33, 36, 125, 131, 156, 218

Babaian, E. A., 97, 130
Baikal, Lake, 41–45, 49, 55
Baikal-Amur Mainline (BAM) Railroad, 44, 45, 62
Bailes, Kendall, 303
Balakovo nuclear facility, 53
Baltic republics, 19, 34, 36, 54, 103, 123–124, 146, 197, 205, 206, 239
BAM. *See* Baikal-Amur Mainline Railroad
Barry, Donald, 71
Beauty pageants, 199

Beer, 128
Begging, 9, 188
Begovaya, Lyubov', 163–164
Belorussia, 26, 99, 122, 204, 208(n18)
Belov, Vasilii, 246
Berg, Maxine, 297
Berger, Peter, 15
"Beware of the White Cloud" (leaflet), 250(n57)
Bialer, Seweryn, 20
Bible, 223
Birthrates, 18, 19, 20, 174, 194, 195–196, 197, 201, 205, 207(n12), 208(n18), 275
Black market, 83–84, 87, 103, 229, 242, 277, 278, 279, 286, 312
Blinov, N. M., 250(n67)
Blood supply, 288, 289
Boarding schools, 206(n5)
Bolsheviks, 154–155, 271, 272–273, 274, 297, 299, 305, 306
Bondarenko, A., 236
Bondarev, Iurii, 246
Boredom, 129. *See also* Leisure
Borovik, Genrikh, 32–33
Boyer, Paul, 59
Brezhnev, Leonid, 79, 126, 138, 141, 149, 157, 195–196, 255, 257, 303
Brigade system, 307
Bromlei, Iu. V., 26
Bulgaria, 162, 210(n48)
Bureaucracy, 84, 85, 145, 155, 168, 232, 245, 255, 315
Burenkov, S. P., 78
Bush, K., 130
Buzhkevich, Miroslav, 238–239

Calculators (pocket), 303
Cancer, 162
Capitalism, 12, 14, 15, 39, 58, 94, 110, 140, 255, 257
Capital punishment. *See* Death penalty
Cardiovascular disease, 126, 173
Caspian Sea, 46
Caucasus, 29, 196, 206, 239, 262, 263
Census (1970), 174, 190
Central Asia, 26, 29, 36, 45, 46, 47, 66, 80, 102, 105, 124–125, 128, 162, 174, 178, 183, 196, 197, 202, 239, 259, 279

Central planning, 178–179, 257. *See also* Gosplan
Central Statistical Administration, 173. *See also* Goskomstat; State Committee on Statistics
Charity, 154–169, 185
Chazov, Evgenii Ivanovich, 78, 80, 83, 85, 89, 178, 179, 200
Chernobyl, 31, 33, 49–54, 68–72, 131, 156
Chief Social Security Administration, 188
Child abuse, 205
Children, 175, 196, 198, 200, 202, 205, 206(n5), 207(n10), 208(nn 15, 17), 209(n26), 222–223, 256, 264, 271, 274. *See also* Children's homes; Minors; Orphans; Youth
Children's Fund. *See* Lenin Soviet Children's Fund
Children's homes, 160–161, 162, 170(n16), 264
Chistiakov, N., 43–44
Churbanov, Iurii, 255
Churches, 165–167, 168. *See also* Religion
Church of Vsekh Skorbyashchikh Radost' (Moscow), 166–167
Civil war period, 273. *See also* Bolsheviks
Class issues, 59. *See also* Elites/nonelites
Climate, 174
Clinics, 274
Coal, 60
Collective farms/farmers, 157, 186. *See also* Agriculture; Collectivism/collectivization
Collectivism/collectivization, 11, 12, 195, 203, 306. *See also* Collective farms/farmers
Committee on Science and Technology, 43
Communes, 206(n5)
Communism, 57, 58, 59, 62, 94, 139, 243–244, 252. *See also* Leninism; Marxism; Socialism
Communist Party of the Soviet Union (CPSU)

Central Committee, 47, 133, 135(n23), 144, 161, 166, 185, 203, 217
Congresses, 16, 47, 48, 63, 64, 65, 66, 67, 132
and crime, 255, 257, 259, 267(n23)
and family care, 206(n7)
and industrial management, 312
19th Party Conference, 1, 255
Politburo, 132, 303
and television, 27–28
and youth, 246
Competition, 141, 148
Computers, 303–304. *See also* Industry/industrialization, open factories; Technology, smart machines
Condoms, 288
Congress of People's Deputies, 34, 36, 137
Constitution (USSR), 85, 86, 175, 183, 195
Consumerism, 12, 20
Consumer issues, 18, 139, 147–148, 150, 172, 229, 276, 277. *See also* Consumerism; Shortages; Waiting lines
Convergence hypothesis, 87–88
Cooperatives, 89, 145–148, 149, 156, 157, 161, 164, 203
Corruption, 11, 18, 84, 96, 114(n52), 133, 139, 155, 237, 255, 259, 266
Cotton, 45, 47
Council for Religious Affairs, 166
Council of Ministers, 44, 95, 179, 185
Council of People's Commissars, 95
CPSU. *See* Communist Party of the Soviet Union
Creativity, 245
Crime, 6, 11, 18, 19, 120, 124, 131, 147, 198, 228, 240, 247(n3), 252–266
alcohol-related, 126, 259, 260, 262
convictions, 259–260, 260(table)
criminal justice reforms, 257, 290
economic, 259, 265–266. *See also* Corruption; Embezzlement; Speculation
explaining, 255–256
geography of, 262–263
as group activity, 262

of justice system personnel, 253, 254, 266
offender population, 263–265
organized, 254, 266
patterns of, 258–259, 258(table)
political, 260
against property, 13, 18, 257, 258, 259
rates, 257–262, 261(table), 263
recidivism, 265
violent, 126, 258, 259, 260, 262, 264, 265, 282
See also Black market; Drug abuse, and crime; Internal Affairs, Ministry of; Russian Soviet Federated Socialist Republic, Criminal Code
CTV. *See* Television, Central Television
Cults, 236
Culture and Sobriety, 130
Currency violations, 283, 284, 289
Czarist period, 271–272, 274

Death penalty, 252, 283, 290
Democratization, 88, 244. *See also* Education, democratization in
Deng Xiaoping, 204
Derevenshchiki, 299
Deryugin, A. V., 170(n11)
De-Stalinization, 62
Determinism, 87. *See also* Technology, technological determinism
Deviance. *See* Social deviance
Diet, 17–18
Disabled, 163. *See also* Invalids
Diseases, 175. *See also* Heath issues
Dissidents, 84, 164
Divorce, 11, 21, 120, 126, 127, 160, 195, 201, 202, 211(n52), 273, 280
Dnepropetrovsk, 162
Doctors. *See* Health issues, doctor-patient relations; Physicians
Dollezhal', N., 71, 77(n59)
Dmitriuk, A. N., 28
Drug abuse, 4, 11, 18, 87, 94–111, 200, 222, 240–242, 282
causes, 101–103
conferences, 109, 118(n118)
and crime, 104–105, 106, 107, 114(n50), 253, 254, 259, 260, 289, 291
expenditures, 104
intravenous, 288
legal issues, 105–107, 115–116(nn 82, 86, 89)
and occupations, 101(table)
and prostitution, 291
response to, 105–111
smuggling into USSR, 104, 114(n62)
statistics, 98–99, 99(table), 101(table)
terminology, 96–97, 99–100, 112(nn 17, 21)
treatment, 107–109, 112(n23), 117(nn 106, 107), 241
of youth, 228, 233, 240–242
Durkheim, Emile, 17

Earthquakes, 131, 156, 162, 260
Economy, 14, 65, 66, 73, 74(n7), 137, 139, 179, 213, 229, 245
and antidrinking campaign, 131
and elderly, 186–190
and health issues, 79, 81, 82, 83
inflation. *See* Inflation
and material production, 150
stagnation, 138, 140, 166, 187, 195
youth economy, 230
See also Crime, economic; Enterprises; New Economic Policy; Second economy
Education, 5, 138, 174, 245, 314
adult, 221–222
and alcohol/drug abuse, 222, 223
child-centered form, 219–220
crisis in schools, 216–219
democratization in, 217
ecological, 222
engineering, 303, 309
general, 217
high-school graduates, 142–143, 215
institutions of higher education (VUZy), 142, 143
and opportunity, 142–145, 151, 215, 216
and *perestroika,* 218, 219–222
private, 223–224
problems in schools, 213–225
reforms, 144, 151, 214, 215–216, 217, 218
and religion, 223
sex education, 216, 223, 279
and socialization, 215

textbooks, 220-221
trade/academic schools (SPTU), 143, 144
trade schools (PTU), 143, 216, 217
trends, 214-216
Education, Ministry of, 216, 217
Egalitarianism, 139, 140, 149, 151
EKO (journal), 318(n45)
Ekonomicheskaia gazeta, 69-70
Elderly, 5, 11, 18, 87, 157-158, 159, 163, 165, 172-190
  medical care, 175-185
  See also Pensions/pensioners
Electricity, 50, 58, 59, 62, 63, 65, 66-67, 70, 73, 74(n8)
Elista, 199
Elites/nonelites, 79, 86, 87, 143, 224, 228, 266. *See also* Intellectuals/intelligentsia
Embezzlement, 254, 259, 266
Emergency First Aid Service, 182
Emergency Measures for the Improvement of Pension Security and Social Maintenance of the Population, 186
Emigration, 11-12
Employment, 138, 143-144
  grievances, 313-314
  part-time, 189-190
Energy consumption, 66
Engels, Friedrich, 292(n3)
Engineering, 303-304, 309
Enterprises, 156-157, 179, 203-304. *See also* Entrepreneurship
Entertainment. *See* Leisure
Entrepreneurship, 145, 146-147, 151-152, 156, 157, 203
Environmental issues, 3, 18, 222, 244, 296
  climatic effects, 46
  deception by government, 54, 55
  environmental movements, 73
  flooding of fields and villages, 46-47
  pollution. *See* Pollution
  and public debate, 51
  Western environmentalism, 49-50
  See also Nuclear energy
Equality of opportunity, 137-152
  and education, 142-145, 224. *See also* Education, and opportunity
  and employed citizens, 140-141

Erevan, 31, 32
Ermolaev, V., 218
Ershov, A., 317(n37)
Esenin, Sergei, 238
Estonia, 9, 123, 174, 197-198, 208(nn 18, 22), 262
Ethnic issues, 19, 24-37, 137
  conflicts, 239-240
  and education, 221
  and family allowances, 196-198, 208(n15)
  life-expectancies, 174
  populations, 196
Expectations, 12-13, 17-18, 21

Fairness, 147. *See also* Social justice
Fallout shelters, 61
Family-contract system, 203-204
Family issues, 5, 194-206, 209(n32), 216, 256, 275, 283
Famine, 154-155
Fanaty, 237
Far East (USSR), 262, 263
Farewell to Matyora (Rasputin), 299
Fascists, 238, 239
Fashions, 230
Fedorov, Svyatoslav, 89, 162
Feminism, 198, 202. *See also* Women
Feshbach, Murray, 196
Films, 102, 111(n11), 227
Finance Ministry, 146
Five Year Plans, 48, 49, 60, 63, 64, 67, 68, 76(n35)
  First, 139, 275
Ford, Henry, 304
Foreigners, 283, 284, 285, 288, 290-291, 293(n17), 294(n39)
Fossil fuels, 65, 66, 67. *See also* Petroleum
Freedoms, 21-22, 140
Friends of Children Society, 169(n3)
Frunze, 278, 279, 280
Fund for Health and Charity. *See* Soviet Fund for Health and Charity
Fusion. *See* Nuclear energy, fusion

Gabiani, A. A., 103, 106, 115(n82)
Gangs, 240, 279
Gastev, Aleksei, 297, 305
Gender imbalance, 201, 263

General Motors, 313–314
Generational conflict, 230
Georgia, 28, 30, 36, 95–96, 100, 101(table), 103, 104, 106, 113(n43), 115(n82), 125, 128, 131, 263, 279
  Institute of Public Opinion, 105
  Ministry of Internal Affairs, 95
  See also Prostitution, Georgian study
Ginzburg, Aleksandr, 164
GKUAE. See State Committee for the Utilization of Atomic Energy
Glasnost', 9, 25, 27, 32, 36, 40, 72, 73, 202, 291, 312
  and AIDS, 287, 292
  and alcohol abuse, 119–120, 129
  and crime, 253–255
  and drug abuse, 110
  and education, 220
  and media, 34, 96, 155, 287
  and prostitution, 271, 292
  and public welfare, 162
  and youth problems, 232–233
Glazunov, Ilya, 299
GNP. See Gross national product
Goldman, Marshall, 12
Gorbachev, Mikhail, 9, 10, 13–14, 15, 16, 25, 28, 44, 49, 79, 88, 89, 137, 139, 164, 255, 318(n43)
  advisers, 73, 303
  antidrinking campaign, 102, 113(n44), 125, 129–134, 176
  and cooperatives, 145
  and crime, 266
  and family-contract farming, 203
  and human factor, 51, 155
  and Komsomol, 242–243, 246
  and Patriarch Pimen, 166
  and women's roles, 199, 205, 209(n32)
  and youth, 242–243, 246
Gorky, 162
Goskomstat, 132, 135(n23), 278. See also Central Statistical Administration; State Committee on Statistics
Goskomtruda. See State Committee for Labor and Social Affairs
Gosplan, 42, 43, 44, 51. See also Central planning
Gospriemka, 318(n43)

Gosteleradio, 27, 32, 34. See also Television
Grain, 47
Granin, Danill, 164
Great Britain, 104, 109, 210(n48), 283
Great Soviet Encyclopedia, 155
Grebenshchikov, Boris, 235
Grigoryants, Sergei, 18–19
Gross national product (GNP), 82
Gulag. See Labor camps
Guznyakov, Father Boris, 167

Hashish, 100, 101, 102, 106, 107, 112(n17), 113(n45), 117(n115), 241, 250(n57). See also Marijuana
Health, Ministry of, 61, 73, 78, 89, 105, 106, 162, 166, 198, 201
  Chief Department of Medical Care and Hygiene for Children and Mothers, 199
  Standing Committee on the Control of Narcotics, 97
  See also Chazov, Evgenii Ivanovich
Health issues, 3, 18, 78–90, 162, 164, 174, 175
  and alcohol abuse, 126, 132, 136(n29). See also Alcohol abuse, mortality
  and child-care network, 196
  doctor-patient relations, 80, 84, 90, 179–180
  and elderly, 175–185. See also Elderly
  family care, 199–200
  financing, 83, 85, 88, 89, 177–178, 182
  health-care system failings, 177
  mental health, 105, 110, 222
  nuclear energy, 50, 51, 61
  personnel, 78, 84, 85, 104
  prenatal care, 199
  program assessment, 179–180
  public-health infrastructure, 174
  stratification of health care, 79, 86–87
  See also Hospitals; Shortages, medical drugs and equipment
Hemp, 103, 106, 107, 116(n90), 250(n57). See also Hashish; Marijuana

Higher and Secondary Specialized Education, Ministry of, 217
Hippies, 236
History, 220–221, 232, 296, 300
Hobsbawm, Eric, 297
Home brewing, 259, 264. *See also* Samogon
Homelessness, 1, 160
Homemaking, 208–209(n25)
Homicides, 126, 132, 259, 262, 264
Homophobia, 290. *See also* Homosexuality
Homosexuality, 279, 285, 288, 289, 290, 291, 292(n1)
Hooliganism, 237, 256, 258, 265
Hospital beds, 85, 175, 182. *See also* Hospitals
Hospitals, 80, 85–86, 88, 103, 164, 175, 178, 179, 180–182, 199, 202, 280, 295(n54)
Hotels, 280
Housing, 13, 18, 172, 184, 201, 247(n6), 256, 276, 281. *See also* Homelessness

Ideology, 14–15, 16, 59, 70, 73, 155, 204, 227
Il'in, Leonid, 52
Il'inskii, Igor, 232, 244
Illegitimacy, 276, 280, 293(n16)
Illness, 80–81, 157. *See also* Health issues
Incarcerations, 252
Income, 127, 141, 146, 188–190
  unearned, 141, 145, 148, 149, 150–151
See also Wages
Individualism, 20
Individual labor activity, 145. *See also* Entrepreneurship
Industry/industrialization, 8, 83, 87, 138, 150, 174, 177, 275, 297, 318(n45)
  basic commodities production, 307
  brigade system, 307
  management, 304–314, 317(n37)
  new era of manufacturing, 308–309, 314
  open factories, 311–313. *See also* Technology, smart machines
  quantity vs. quality, 306–307
  supply/inventory systems, 308, 309
See also Technology
Infant mortality, 78, 79, 80, 82, 86, 87, 126, 162, 200, 210(nn 40, 41)
Infants, 175, 203. *See also* Infant mortality
Inflation, 131, 187, 190, 275
Information, 9, 24, 30, 31–32, 35, 119–120. *See also* Industry/industrialization, open factories; Technology, smart machines
Institute of Atomic Energy, 50–51
Institute of Labor, 305, 306(fig.)
Institute of Sanitary Education, 61
Intellectuals/intelligentsia, 142, 246, 299, 302, 312. *See also* Elites/nonelites
Internal Affairs, Ministry of (MVD), 96, 106, 107, 114(n52), 197, 253, 254, 259, 284
  Main Administration for Criminal Investigation, 99, 103, 104, 109, 113(n44), 241
See also Georgia, Ministry of Internal Affairs
International Conference on the Peaceful Uses of Nuclear Energy (1956), 63
International Covenant on Social and Economic Rights (1966), 195
Internationalization, 26, 27
Interpol, 104, 109, 114(n63)
In the Age of the Smart Machine (Zuboff), 310–311
Invalids, 156, 157–158, 159, 165
Iron Curtain, 231
Irrigation, 46
"I Serve the Soviet Union" (television program), 36
Is It Easy to Be Young? (film), 227, 246
Islam, 124, 167. *See also* Muslims
Ivanov, G., 86
Ivanovo province, 184
Izvestiia, 43, 63, 86, 112(n24), 159, 162, 180, 223

Justice. *See* Social justice
Juvenile delinquency, 198, 247(n3), 256, 264, 279

Kalmyk Autonomous Republic, 199, 295(n54)
Kapitsa, P. L., 43
Karpets, I. I., 232-233
Kashchenko Psychiatric Hospital, 166
Kazakhstan, 28, 30, 33, 98, 134(n4), 197
Kazan, 240
Kaznacheev, V., 157
Kemerovo, 162
KGB, 6
Kholodnaia Lead and Zinc Refinery, 44
Khrushchev, Nikita, 63, 64, 110, 126, 138, 139, 159, 185, 206(n5), 215, 257
Kiev, 54, 280
Kirgizia, 98, 106, 124, 286
Kirillov, Igor, 29
Knaus, William A., 80, 179, 180
Kommunist, 150, 197, 233
Komsomol, 95, 105, 158, 165, 227, 228, 230, 237, 242-245, 250(n67), 286
  All-Union Komsomol Central Committee, 232, 244
  All-Union Komsomol Congress (1987), 242-243
Komsomol'skaia pravda, 43, 231-232, 237
Kon, Igor, 230, 233, 245
Korean War, 110
Koriakin, Iu., 71, 77(n59)
Kosygin, Aleksei, 126
Krasnovodsk, 85
Kravchenko, Maria, 157, 158
Krinskii, Vladimir, 297, 298(fig.), 301(fig.)
Kulaks, 306. *See also* Peasants
Kurchatov, I. V., 63-64
Kuromiya, Hiroaki, 307
Kuznitsa, 297

Labor. *See* Cooperatives; Employment; Individual labor activity; Labor conscription; Shortages, labor; Unemployment; Workers
Labor camps, 252, 256
Labor conscription, 273
Language issues, 26, 29, 30-31, 35, 155, 231

Latvia, 33, 123, 174, 197, 200, 208(nn 18, 22), 262
Law on Pensions and Benefits for Collective Farmers (1964), 186
Law on State Pensions (1956), 186
Legal issues, 71-72, 95, 201, 255, 266. *See also* Drug abuse, legal issues; Prostitution, legal context
Legitimacy issues, 14-15, 79
Leisure, 127, 172, 229, 232, 245
Lenin, V. I., 59, 173, 206(n1), 272, 274, 305, 315. *See also* Leninism
Lenin Fund for Aid to Children's Homes, 169(n3)
Leningrad, 103, 162, 163-164, 178, 202, 233, 238, 239, 241, 246, 251(n83), 302, 303
Leningradskaia pravda, 238
Leninism, 16, 227, 232, 243. *See also* Lenin, V. I.
Lenin Soviet Children's Fund, 160-162, 168, 200, 202, 223
Leukemia, 51
Levin, Boris and Mikhail, 130, 223
Life expectancy, 82, 125-126, 132, 173-175, 176, 179. *See also* Mortality rates
Ligachev, Egor, 14, 144, 217, 246
Likhanov, A. A., 161, 200
Lisitsyn, Yu., 130
Literature, 227, 243, 297, 302
Literaturnaia gazeta, 43, 164, 233, 286
Lithuania, 30, 34, 99, 123, 159, 174, 208(n18)
Little Vera (film), 227
Liubery,. 237, 263
Living standard. *See* Standard of living
Lobzov, A. S., 246
Lvov province, 184

McAuley, Alastair, 87, 187
Maiakovskii, Vladimir, 297, 300
Makukhin, Aleksei, 53
Maloobespechennye, 187. *See also* Poverty
Managers, 40. *See also* Industry/industrialization, management; Industry/industrialization, open factories
Manufacturing. *See* Industry/industrialization, new era of manufacturing

Marijuana, 106, 107, 112(n17), 250(n57). *See also* Hashish
Marriage, 10, 170(n16), 195, 197, 201, 211(n52), 275. *See also* Divorce; Family issues
Marx, Leo, 297
Marxism, 70, 71, 72, 73, 227, 232, 243, 252, 282, 285. *See also* Communism; Leninism; Socialism
Mass production, 69, 72, 315. *See also* Industry/industrialization; Reactors, prefabrication
Master and Margarita, 236
"Master" Social Services, 164
Materialism, 276, 279, 286
Maternity benefits/rights, 196, 205, 207–208(nn 10, 13), 273
Media, 2, 34, 72, 96, 127, 129, 130, 229, 271, 285–287, 289–291. *See also* Press; Television
Meskhetians, 240
Metallurgy, 60
Militsiia, 252, 253, 257, 260. *See also* Police
Millar, James, 309
Miloserdie groups, 163–165, 171(n25)
Mines/miners, 137, 150, 306
Minors, 127, 128, 156, 157, 160, 285. *See also* Children; Youth
Mironenko, Viktor, 243
Modernization, 11, 12–13, 14, 15, 21, 22, 73, 174, 229, 279, 297, 300
Moldavia, 99, 100, 124, 131, 262
Morphine, 241
Mortality rates, 82, 126, 176, 176–177(tables), 200. *See also* Alcohol abuse, mortality; Infant mortality; Life expectancy
Moscow, 29, 51, 80, 86, 103, 112(n24), 131, 147, 158, 161, 164, 166–167, 178, 183, 184, 188, 189, 198, 233, 236, 237, 238, 239, 240, 241, 253, 259, 272, 278, 284, 302, 303
City Council Main Health Administration, 166
Moskoff, William, 188
Moskvich car, 68
Mother Heroine awards, 196–197
Mother Teresa, 166
Mulina, Marina, 165
Murders. *See* Homicides

Music, 229, 230, 235–236, 243
Muslims, 102, 174, 196, 197. *See also* Islam
MVD. *See* Internal Affairs, Ministry of

Nagorno-Karabakh, 30, 33, 260
Narcomania, 97, 99(table). *See also* Drug abuse
Narcotics, 97, 112(n17). *See also* Drug abuse
National Center for Public Opinion Research (Moscow), 38(n35)
Nationalism, 47, 239–240. *See also* Ethnic issues
Nationalities, 19, 196. *See also* Ethnic issues; *individual republics*
Nationalization, 39
Nazism, 238
NEP. *See* New Economic Policy
New Economic Policy (NEP), 273, 274
New Soviet man, 57, 94, 101, 253
Newspapers. *See* Press
Nishanov, R. N., 47
Nizhnii Tagil, 244
Novosibirsk, 142
Novosti Press Agency, 162
Novyi mir, 60, 140
Nuclear energy, 49–54, 74(n1)
  capacity in USSR, 67–68
  fusion, 67, 73
  political issues, 62–68
  safety issues, 58, 61, 66, 67, 68, 69, 71, 72, 73, 77(n60)
  See also Atomic culture; Chernobyl; Pollution, and nuclear energy; Reactors
Nuclear Power, Ministry of, 73
Nursing homes, 184–185

Obninsk, 50
Ob River, 45
Ogonek, 1, 199, 237
Oil. *See* Petroleum
Okudzhava, Bulat, 300
Old people. *See* Elderly
Opiates, 102, 111(n11), 241, 250(n57). *See also* Drug abuse; Poppies
Opportunity. *See* Equality of opportunity
Ordzhonikidze Institute of Management (Moscow), 314

Orphans, 162, 165, 170(n16), 200, 274
Ovsiannikov, Nikolai, 40

Pamiat', 47, 239
Pankin, V., 241
Parasitism, 265, 270, 271, 279, 282, 283–284
Passport system, 252, 262, 266
Pastoralism, 299–300
Peaceful nuclear explosions (PNEs), 61. *See also* Atomic culture; Nuclear energy
Peasants, 204, 306. *See also* Rural issues
Pechora River, 45
Penal institutions, 265
Pensions/pensioners, 155, 156, 157, 158, 159–160, 182, 183, 185, 186–187, 188–190. *See also* Elderly
Perestroika, 6, 7, 37, 84, 131, 137, 138, 148
 and antidrinking campaign, 119, 129
 and charitable funds, 160
 and education. *See* Education, and *perestroika*
 and egalitarianism, 139, 140
 and enterprise, 146, 151–152
 and family issues, 194–206, 209(n32)
 and health care, 89, 178
 and pensions and benefits, 159
 and youth, 246
Petrograd, 273. *See also* Leningrad; St. Petersburg
Petroleum, 50, 52, 60, 65, 74(n8)
Petros'iants, A. M., 67
Petrovskii, B. N., 78
Pharmacies, 103–104, 114(n58), 160
Physicians, 84, 85, 89–90, 108, 150, 175, 303. *See also* Health issues, doctor-patient relations
Physics, 62–63
Pimen, Patriarch, 166
Piore, Michael, 308–309
Planning, 245, 263. *See also* Central planning
Pluralism, 20, 52, 54
Plutonium, 65, 67
PNEs. *See* Peaceful nuclear explosions
Podnieks, Yuris, 227
Poison gas, 34
Police, 284, 290. *See also* Militsiia

Political prisoners, 164
Pollution, 39–40, 87, 174
 air, 44
 and nuclear energy, 60, 61, 67, 68
 water, 41–45
Poppies, 103, 106, 107, 116(nn 90, 95), 250(n57). *See also* Drug abuse; Opiates
Popular Fronts, 34
Potanov, A. I., 241
Poverty, 4, 10, 15, 87, 139, 149, 155, 158, 159, 187–188, 198
Power and Electrification, Ministry of, 73
Pozhar (Rasputin), 263
"Pozitsiia" (television program), 32
Prager, Kenneth, 80
Pravda, 43, 52, 63, 66, 98, 216
Pravda, Alex, 313
 "Mutual Help Club" column, 163
Prefabrication. *See* Reactors, prefabrication
Preschools, 208(n14)
Press, 2, 163, 170(n22), 200, 202, 216, 233, 241, 271, 285, 287, 288, 289–290, 291. *See also* Media
Principles of Criminal Legislation of the USSR and the Union Republics, 95
Pripiat, 69
Private property, 39
Propaganda, 306
Prostitution, 6–7, 11, 96, 270–292, 294(n39)
 and AIDS, 6–7, 287–289, 290–292
 child, 272, 274, 283
 and crime, 253, 282
 criminalization of, 285, 290, 291
 data availability, 277–278
 and foreigners, 283, 284, 290
 Georgian study, 278, 280, 281
 health issues. *See* Prostitution, and AIDS; Syphilis; Venereal disease
 legal context, 282–285
 male, 292(n1)
 part-time, 277, 281
Psychiatry, 84
PTU. *See* Education, trade schools
Public Health, Ministry of. *See* Health, Ministry of
Public homes, 164

Public opinion, 218, 287, 291
Public property, 20
Pukhova, Zoya, 203
Pulp and Paper Industry, Ministry of, 42, 43
Puritanism, 292

Queues. *See* Waiting lines

Radio, 231. *See also* Radio Moscow
Radio Moscow, 111(n11)
R and D. *See* Research and development
Rapes, 126, 262
Rashidov, Sharaf, 47–48, 254
Rasputin, Valentin, 246, 263, 299
Reactors, 76(n35)
  Arbus, 70
  construction cancellations/slowdowns, 53, 71
  containment structures, 64, 71, 72
  "depth in defense" design, 71
  prefabrication, 65, 69, 70, 72
  RBMK, 69, 71, 72, 73
  VVER, 69, 73
  See also Chernobyl; Nuclear energy
Readings for Women, 202, 211(n60)
Red Crescent, 158, 162, 169(n3)
Red Cross, 157, 158, 162, 163, 169(n3)
Religion, 11, 47, 89, 154, 223, 228, 236, 296, 302. *See also* Churches
Repentance (film), 28, 302
Research and development (R and D), 59, 63
Residency permits, 284
Resource allocation, 18, 83, 177–178, 200
Riga, 289, 290
Rimashevskaia, N. M., 26
Riots, 33, 239, 240
Riurikov, Yurii, 197
River projects, 45–49, 54, 61
Rodionov, I. N., 34
Rosliakov, Vasilii, 228
RSFSR. *See* Russian Soviet Federated Socialist Republic
Running water, 80, 184, 217, 218, 302
Rural issues
  Chinese comparison, 204
  crime, 262, 263
  elderly housing, 184

  gender imbalance, 201
  hospitals, 80, 178, 180
  life expectancy, 174
  rural backwardness, 10, 11, 13, 18
  schools, 218
  writers, 299
Russian National Socialist Workers' Party, 238
Russian Orthodoxy millennium celebration, 166
Russians, 19
Russian Social Fund, 164
Russian Soviet Federated Socialist Republic (RSFSR), 26, 98, 108, 122, 160, 183, 197, 204, 206, 208(n18), 262
  abortions in, 210(n48)
  central pediatric hospital, 202
  Criminal Code, 94, 95, 105–106, 294(n29)
  drug abuse, 100
  immigrants from, 197–198
  Ministry of Land Reclamation and Water Management, 40
  Ministry of Social Security, 157
  nationalism, 47
  pensioners in, 189
  and prostitution, 284–285
  Red Cross, 163
Rybinski, E. M., 161, 170(n18)
Ryzhkov, Nikolai, 1, 49, 186

Sabel, Charles, 308–309
Safety issues. *See* Nuclear energy, safety issues
St. Petersburg, 272. *See also* Leningrad; Petrograd
Salaries. *See* Wages
Samogon, 113, 119, 121(table), 122, 123, 124, 125, 128, 131–132, 133, 136(n26). *See also* Alcohol abuse, home brewing
Satanism, 236
Science, 68, 70, 302
  cult of, 58, 62, 71
  See also Technology
Secession, 34
Second economy, 128, 141. *See also* Black market; Economy
Second Industrial Divide, The (Piore and Sabel), 308–309

Second Program. *See* Television, Second Program
Security, economic, 138, 141, 148, 149, 150
Sem'ia, 161, 170(n18), 202
Semipalatinsk, 21
Service industry, 150
Sewage disposal, 184, 218
Sexuality, 12, 273, 276, 279. *See also* Education, sex education; Prostitution
Shadrikov, 221
Shapiro, V. D., 183
Sharansky, Natan, 17
Shatalin, Stanislav, 14, 204
Shchekochikhin, Iurii, 233–234, 240
Shengelya, E. N., 34
Shevardnadze, Eduard, 29, 303
Shipler, David K., 88–89
Shkaratan, O. I., 35
Shmelev, Nikolai, 140
Shortages, 11, 18, 141, 147, 149
  condoms, 288
  consumer goods, 172, 199, 266
  food, 10, 172, 203
  housing, 13, 18, 247(n6), 256, 276, 281
  labor, 143–144, 275, 309
  medical drugs and equipment, 83–84, 178–179, 288, 295(n54)
  old-age homes, 184
  skilled workers, 309
  See also Sugar rationing; Waiting lines
Shubkin, Vladimir N., 142–143
Siberia, 45, 61, 65, 66, 70, 137, 262, 263
Sidorov, O. M., 158
Skoraia, 182
Slang, 231
Slavs, 29, 47, 122–123
Smena, 161, 235
Smuggling, 104, 114(n62), 289
Sobesednik, 164–165, 242, 243–244
Social assistance units, 183
Social benefits, 159–160
Social controls, 13
Social costs, 39
Social deviance, 228, 245, 270, 287
Socialism, 58–59, 61, 94, 138, 163, 232, 243, 252, 255, 257, 315. *See*
  also Communism; Leninism; Marxism; Social problems, socialist vs. capitalist
Socialization, 25, 27, 33, 35, 37, 215, 245, 246, 256
Social justice, 4, 139, 140, 145, 146, 148–151, 152, 182, 205, 232
Social problems
  and convergence between U.S. and Soviet Union, 21
  and political issues, 11, 14, 16–22
  socialist vs. capitalist, 12, 14–15
  sources of, 11–12
  Soviet view of, 13–16
  Western views of, 9–13
Societies for the Blind, Deaf and Dumb, 158, 169(n3)
Society for the Protection of Nature, 40
Sociologists, 314
Solov'ev, Iurii, 246, 251(n83)
Solzhenitsyn, Aleksandr, 164
Sotsial'noe obespechenie, 157, 158
Sovetskaia Kirghiziia, 48
Sovetskaia Rossiia, 48
Soviet Committee for the Defense of Peace, 166, 167
Soviet Fund for Health and Charity, 162–163, 165, 168
Soviet Health and Charity Foundation, 89
Soviet Interview Project, 309
Soviet Socialist Republics (SSRs), 99. *See also individual republics*
Soviet Women's Committee, 198, 202–203
Speculation, 257, 259
SPTU. *See* Education, trade/academic schools
SSRs. *See* Soviet Socialist Republics
Stagnation. *See* Economy, stagnation
Stakhanov, Aleksei, 306
Stalin, Joseph, 139, 155, 164, 172, 194–195, 204, 215, 221, 256, 275, 276, 303, 312
Standard of living, 81, 141, 147, 148, 155, 157, 172, 187
Stankevich School (Moscow), 224
State Committee for Education. *See* State Committee for Public Education

State Committee for Labor and Social Affairs (Goskomtruda), 157, 169(n7)
State Committee for Public Education, 144, 217, 221
State Committee for Television and Radio Broadcasting. *See* Gosteleradio
State Committee for the Supervision of Safe Working Practices in the Atomic Power Industry, 52, 73
State Committee for the Utilization of Atomic Energy (GKUAE), 68
State Committee on Labor and Social Questions, 188
State Committee on Statistics, 178, 278. *See also* Central Statistical Administration; Goskomstat
State Committee on Vocational-Technical Education, 144
State Hydrometeorological Committee, 73
State Institute for the Designs of the Pulp and Paper Industry Enterprises in Siberia and the Far East, 44
Stepanakert, 32
Stern, Fritz, 297
Stites, Richard, 272
Strikes, 137, 150, 313–314
Suburbs, 263
Success, 138–139, 148
Sugar rationing, 20, 132, 136(n26)
Suicide, 11, 12, 120, 126, 197, 223
Sumgait, 32, 33
Supreme Court (USSR), 95, 105, 107, 108, 195
Supreme Soviet, 95, 105, 137, 186, 208(n22)
  Presidium, 30, 100
Sverdlovsk, 184
Svetlova, Ekaterina, 164
Syphilis, 272, 279. *See also* Venereal disease
Syr Darya River, 46, 47
Syringes, 179, 199, 288, 295(n54)

Tadzhikistan, 99, 100, 124, 156, 174, 197
TASS news agency, 53
Tatlin, Vladimir, 297

Taxation, 130, 131, 145–146, 160, 207(n10)
Taylor, Frederick Winslow, 304, 305, 306
Tbilisi, 30, 34, 162
Teachers, 214, 218, 219–220
Teachers' Gazette, 219, 221
Technology, 7, 19, 58, 62, 68–69, 71, 296–315
  hostility toward, 297, 299–300, 302
  and industrial management, 304–314
  information. *See* Technology, smart machines
  large-scale, 72
  medical, 80, 88, 89–90
  smart machines, 310–311. *See also* Industry/industrialization, open factories
  social dimensions, 308, 314, 318(n45)
  and Soviet culture, 296–304
  technological determinism, 69, 70, 73
  See also Industry/industrialization
Television, 2–3, 24–37, 232
  Central Television (CTV), 28, 31, 36. *See also* Gosteleradio
  ethnic groups represented in newscasts, 29
  language issues, 29, 30–31
  reforms, 27
  republic-level vs. national, 28, 31, 34, 35, 36
  Second Program, 28, 36
  surveys concerning, 29, 36, 38(n35)
  television sets in republics, 25–26
  "Vremya," 32, 33, 34
Temperance Society. *See* All-Union Volunteer Temperance Society
"Test for Adults" (television series), 232
Tetriyakov, Vitalii, 155
Theft, 13, 254, 257–258, 259, 262, 266, 282, 289
Three Mile Island, 49, 53
Timber, Pulp and Paper and Wood Processing Industry, Ministry of, 44
Time-and-motion studies, 304. *See also* Taylor, Frederick Winslow
Togliatti automobile plant, 41
Tokamak fusion reactors, 62

Toxicomania, 97, 99(table). *See also* Drug abuse
Trade unions, 81, 157, 158
Trade Unions, 18th Congress of, 81
Transcaucasus, 125, 128, 183
Transportation, 60
Travel restrictions, 11, 12, 13
Trist, E. L., 308
Trotsky, Leon, 299
Trud, 50-51
Tsybukh, Valerii I., 230
Turchin, Valentin, 17
Turkmenia, 98, 100, 106, 114(n62), 124, 174, 197, 200, 218
Turkmenistan. *See* Turkmenia
Tutoring. *See* Education, private

Uchitel'skaia gazeta, 250(n57)
Ukraine, 50, 67, 98, 122, 137, 197, 208(n18)
Ulam, Adam, 15
Ulyanovsk, 240
Unemployment, 140, 229, 273, 274, 275, 276, 297
United Nations
  Committee on the Elimination of Discrimination Against Women, 204-205
  Convention on Psychotropic Substances (1971), 109
  Uniform Convention on Narcotics (1961), 109
United States, 21, 29, 110, 120, 162, 213, 308, 309
  abortions in, 210(n48)
  crime in, 257, 259
  Drug Enforcement Agency, 99, 109, 117(n115)
  Food and Drug Administration, 60
  health care, 83, 84, 90, 175, 180
  Institute of Drug Abuse, 96
  labor relations, 312, 313-314
  manufacturing, 314, 315
  Medicare Act, 84
  narcotics defined, 112(n17)
  National Commission on Marijuana and Drug Abuse, 97
  nuclear energy, 66, 72, 74(n8)
  and Soviet industry, 304-306
  Supreme Court, 201
  television in, 24-25, 29

Uralmash industrial complex, 142
Urban issues, 8, 87, 174, 229-231, 237, 245, 262-263, 275, 276, 279, 299-300
Uzbekistan, 30, 47, 48, 86, 100, 106, 124, 178, 218, 240, 254

Vaino, K. G., 237
Values, 24, 35, 230, 276, 297
Vandalism, 258. *See also* Hooliganism
Vasilev, Nikolai F., 48
Vecherniaia Moskva, 108, 253
Venereal disease, 279-280, 282, 283, 284, 285, 287, 289-290. *See also* AIDS; Syphilis
Veselye kartinki, 223
Veterans, 156, 163, 165, 184, 237
Vid, Leonard, 49
Vlasov, A. V., 98, 241
Vodka, 102, 123, 124, 128, 130, 131. *See also* Alcohol abuse
Volga River, 46, 47, 48
Volgograd, 199, 240
Voluntarism, 16
Voprosy narkologii, 105
"Vremya." *See* Television, "Vremya"
VUZ. *See* Education, institutions of higher education
Vychegda River, 45
Vyshnevskii, Anatoly, 197

Wages, 139, 141, 148-149, 150, 158, 160, 171(n34), 186, 190. *See also* Income
Waiting lines, 18, 135(n23), 141, 199. *See also* Shortages
Water. *See* Running water
Western influence, 255. *See also* Youth, Western influences
Wife abuse, 205
Wine, 122, 124, 125, 128, 129, 131
Women, 10, 29, 150, 157, 184, 188, 194, 195, 196-197, 198-203, 204, 208-209(nn 15, 17, 25), 209(n30)
  and alcohol abuse, 123, 125, 127, 128
  and Bolsheviks, 272
  and crime, 252, 257, 263-264
  and drug abuse, 100
  health issues, 80
  life expectancy/mortality, 173-174, 176

maternity benefits/rights, 196, 205, 207–208(nn 10, 13), 209(n26), 273
and *perestroika,* 205, 209(n32)
See also Abortions; Divorce; Family issues; Marriage; Prostitution
Workers, 98, 142, 144, 299, 302–303, 309, 310–312, 313, 318(n45)
Workmanship, 53
World Health Organization, 97, 112(n21)
World War II, 127, 155, 275

Xenophobia, 290

Yemelyanov, Ivan Y., 51, 53–54
Yenesei River, 45
Youth, 6, 100, 101–102, 103, 105, 142, 158, 164, 224
and crime, 228, 256, 264. *See also* Juvenile delinquency
groups/subcultures, 233–240, 244–245, 249(n48)
and liberals vs. conservatives, 245–246
Western influences, 231, 237, 245, 246. *See also* Music
youth problems, 227–246
See also Children; Minors
Youth Communist League. *See* Komsomol

Zaigrayev, G., 125, 130
Zaslavskaia, Tatiana, 14, 141, 314
Zastoi. See Economy, stagnation
Zuboff, Shoshana, 310–311, 313
Zvartnots Airport (Erevan), 32, 33

28 - Central/local tension — Diversity, ethnic or otherwise, also means local idiosyncrasies + tyrannies. (Reagan)